Hollywood and the O.K. Corral

Hollywood and the O.K. Corral

Portrayals of the Gunfight and Wyatt Earp

MICHAEL F. BLAKE

McFarland & Company, Inc., Publishers
Jefferson, North Carolina, and London

LIBRARY OF CONGRESS CATALOGUING-IN-PUBLICATION DATA

Blake, Michael F. (Michael Francis), 1957–
Hollywood and the O.K. Corral : portrayals of the
gunfight and Wyatt Earp / Michael F. Blake.
p.   cm.
Includes bibliographical references and index.

ISBN-13: 978-0-7864-2632-4
ISBN-10: 0-7864-2632-2
(softcover : 50# alkaline paper) ∞

1. Western films—United States—History and criticism.
2. Earp, Morgan, 1851–1882—In motion pictures.
3. Earp, Wyatt, 1848–1929—In motion pictures.
4. Holliday, John Henry, 1851–1887—In motion pictures.
I. Title.
PN1995.9.W4B583   2007   791.436'278—dc22   2006030940

British Library cataloguing data are available

On the cover: Poster art for the 1993 film *Tombstone* (Buena Vista Pictures/Photofest)

Manufactured in the United States of America

McFarland & Company, Inc., Publishers
Box 611, Jefferson, North Carolina 28640
www.mcfarlandpub.com

To

Cheryl Pappas

Thanks for always being there, Doc.

Jeff Morey

*I want you to know, I wouldn't
have made it without you.*

Beth Werling

You've been a good friend to me.

Kevin Kenney

I ain't got the words.

Acknowledgments

The following people deserve a big thank you for all their help in seeing this published.

Barbara Hall, at the Special Collections department of the Margaret Herrick Library of the Academy of Motion Pictures Arts and Sciences, is a patron saint for film historians. She went beyond being helpful and came up with suggestions of material to look at that I never thought of. My thanks also to Faye Thompson of the library's photograph collection for her help. As always, the entire staff at the library went above and beyond the call of duty. Saundra Taylor and the staff of the Lilly Library at Indiana University were very helpful in allowing me access to the material in the John Ford collection. John Cahoon of the Sever Center for Western History Research at the Natural History Museum allowed me to view the correspondence between William S. Hart and Wyatt Earp.

Paul Cool generously shared his information on the making of *Tombstone* and other history relating to Wyatt Earp's years in the Arizona mining town. His kindness and encouragement is most appreciated. Peter Brand, who has come up with groundbreaking information about some Tombstone characters, generously allowed me access to his articles. Bob Palmquist was always available to answer any of my questions about Wyatt Earp and Arizona Territorial Law and offered his memories of visiting the set of *Tombstone*. My thanks to a good friend. Pam Potter and Clay Parker were extremely helpful in sharing insights into the McLaury family history. My heartfelt thanks to all.

Jeff Morey is an amazing encyclopedia on Wyatt Earp and a devoted film buff. My deepest thanks to a fella who was never too busy to help and support me in this project. An equal debt of gratitude is due many people who share an interest in Wyatt Earp and events in Tombstone. Thank yous, in alphabetical order, to: Robin Andrews, Allen Barra, Sharon Cunningham, Bruce Dettman, Tim Fattig, Treesé Hellström, Bruce Olds, Nancy Pope, Jerry Prather, Max Roberts, Roller Doc, B. J. Smith, Linda at Tombstone Old West Books, Casey Terfiltiller, Kenneth Vail, and Clifford Neil Williams. Their encouragement and help was greatly appreciated.

Joseph Musso shared some amazing material on *Tombstone*. I cannot thank him enough for his help and friendship. Larry Zeug shared his experiences and photographs while working on *Tombstone*, as did Sal Cardile. A big thank you to two good friends. Peter Sherayko was equally generous with his time and memories.

Michael Mills and Gerald Quist, makeup artists on *Wyatt Earp*, shared their experiences working on the film, and their photographs. Thank you isn't enough to two good friends. Makeup artist David Atherton was very generous with his memories of working on *Tombstone* and graciously gave his time while working on a film location. Thanks are also in order for costume designer Joseph Porro who was equally generous in sharing his experiences on *Tombstone*.

David C. Smith, once again, came through with his expert eye in making this text better. As always, his opinions and friendship are highly valued. Kevin Kenney also lent his opinions and insights, helping me focus on what was and wasn't important in writing this book. Not only that, he's a good friend.

Big thank yous to friends who have always been there for me: Luisa Abel, Leith Adams, Sandi Berg, Kevin Brownlow, Connie Cardile, Ned Comstock, the late George Custen, Kim Dame, Brian, Jennifer, Nolan and Liam Dame, Mickey Fisher, Michael Germain, Steve Gustafson, Mike Hawks, Lisa Jacobs, Terry Lamfers, Clarke Lamkins, Philip Liebfried, Ross Melnick, Cheryl Pappas, Celeste Rush, Blanche Sands, Craig Smith, Patrick Stanbury, Jack Stewart, Steve Tanner, Nate Thomas, George Wagner, Tom Weaver and Beth Werling.

Before her passing, my mom, Teresa, read early drafts of this book and was very helpful with suggestions. Her support and faith kept this book, and me, going.

No list of acknowledgments could be complete without thanking my wife, Linda, who has been there from the beginning. She has endured countless conversations on the historical events and the numerous films, sat through marathon screenings (to the point of being able to recite the dialogue from the films), trudged around Tombstone in the broiling sun and read through numerous revisions. *I promise to love you the rest of your life.*

Michael F. Blake

Table of Contents

Preface

On a blustery Wednesday, October 26, 1881, a legend was born: Because of the gunfight at the O.K. Corral, Wyatt Earp over the next 125 years would be seen as the archetypal peace officer of the American West. (Ironically, the most famous gunfight in American Western history, which lasted only 30 seconds, didn't actually take place at the O.K. Corral but instead in an empty lot ninety feet to the northwest.) As the sounds of gunfire dissipated and the eighteen-foot-wide lot filled with black powder smoke, three men lay dead, two were wounded, and another was grazed by a bullet. Only Wyatt Earp emerged unscathed.

During his entire involvement with law enforcement, Wyatt Earp was never once scratched by a bullet. Even in the deadly gun battle at Iron Springs, where bullets flew like stones in a sandstorm, Wyatt Earp amazed members of his own posse: While his duster showed signs of bullets passing through it, he himself was not touched at all. That alone would anoint one for mythical status. Although other lawmen and gunfighters had been involved in gunfights and managed to emerge unhurt, Wyatt Earp's tale caught the public's fancy like no other.

The average American is most likely familiar with three major events in the history of the American West: the battle of the Alamo, Custer's defeat at the Little Big Horn, and the gunfight at the O.K. Corral. The battle of the Alamo and Custer's defeat, although still remembered, have lately lost some of their mythic status owing to new research by historians. Both events have their defenders and debunkers, which invites lively debates. Today, though, Davy Crockett is rarely seen as the heroic figure in buckskins, swinging his rifle at Mexican troops that surrounded him. The circumstances of his death are now open to question because of recent publicized material, which some say is factual, and others, fraudulent. Custer also was often painted in a heroic light, badly outnumbered yet standing bravely against an incredible force of Indian warriors. However, thanks to scholars and recent archaeological digs at the battle site, we have a much fuller picture of Custer's actions on that fateful day in June 1876. The same can be said of Wyatt Earp. He long has been regarded as a heroic figure, but facts are now being unearthed that give us a more detailed look at his life and at events in Tombstone, Arizona.

Yet the myth of Wyatt Earp and the famous gunfight remains strong. Unlike events at the Alamo and the Little Big Horn, Earp and the gunfight have continued to resonate with the public, both in and beyond America. In 1931, a reviewer of Earp's biography noted that both Chicago and New York, which were then experiencing lawlessness on the streets because of the effects of Prohibition and the Depression, needed a Wyatt Earp to bring law and order. Clashes between political and social groups have often conjured visions of a fateful showdown: "It's O.K. Corral time." The gunfight and Earp's involvement have become part of American slang, with any kind of armed conflict referred to as an O.K. Corral. In 1974, during the shootout between the Los Angeles Police Department and the revolutionary Symbionese Liberation Army, one reporter at the scene described it as a modern-day version of the gunfight at the O.K. Corral. As late as April 29, 2004, a *New York Post* op-ed piece suggested that the problems in Iraq did not need another brilliant diplomat but rather the actions of a Wyatt Earp. Why is it that Wyatt Earp and this gunfight still endure in our memory?

Is it the myth of a fearless law-and-order man standing up against a criminal element? Is it that, in all his years on the western frontier, Earp was *never once* touched by a bullet? Or is it the image of a man in a duster, guns blazing all around him, who stood tall and fearless, emerging unhurt? Could it be the sense of classic Greek or Shakespearean tragedy that surrounded the Earp family in Tombstone that strikes an emotional chord? Or is it simply that today, in a society bereft of heroes, we desire and need to embrace a symbol of heroic actions to make us feel safer?

The answer to all those questions is yes. The heroic stand against the "bad guys" is what draws some to the Earp saga. Others find that the personal misfortunes faced by Earp and his brothers in Tombstone catch their attention. Some cite the unexplainable bond of friendship between Wyatt Earp and Doc Holliday as the attraction. Then there are those who are fascinated with debunking the heroic image of Earp by proving he was hardly that knight in shining armor. There are probably a dozen other reasons why people are fascinated by this story—and why almost half a million visitors a year travel to the southeastern Arizona town where the legend was born. There they can stand on the spot where the gunfight happened and walk down the wooden boardwalk of Allen Street, their imaginations taking them back in time. The shootout and its main character have inspired dozens of professional and amateur historians to scour dusty files of historical societies and newspapers, searching for nuggets of information that will fill in the blanks about what happened in that mining town.

In recent years, many historians have unearthed an amazing amount of information relating to Earp, the other characters in Tombstone, and the gunfight, giving us a more accurate and detailed picture of what really happened. Those who believe that Wyatt Earp was the white knight denounce any facts that present a man of more ambiguous substance. Earp was hardly the unassailable figure presented in his 1931 biography, *Wyatt Earp: Frontier Marshal*, but he still remains fascinating—warts and all—as are the events in Tombstone. They have produced a cottage industry. From books about Wyatt Earp and the un-famed of Tombstone's past, to illuminating articles in historical journals and informal scholarly meetings held in the former mining town, the saga of the Earps and Tombstone hardly appears to be forgotten.

To help the reader have a better understanding of what really happened in Tombstone between 1877 to 1882, the first chapter serves as a compendium of relevant information. Due to the wealth of material relating to this period, I have chosen only to mention what is directly referenced in the eight movies. As space compelled me to delete some of the more minute details, I urge the reader to consult the endnotes as they go along, as they will provide a more comprehensive picture of historical events. The chapter is not intended to be a biography of Wyatt Earp or a history on Tombstone, as others have done a much better job. For those who wish to learn more about Wyatt Earp's life, I highly recommend Casey Tefertiller's *Wyatt Earp: The Life Behind the Legend* and Allen Barra's *Inventing Wyatt Earp: His Life and Many Legends*. For a detailed history of Tombstone, William B. Shillingberg's *Tombstone, A.T.* is extremely informative, as is Lynn R. Bailey's *Tombstone: The Town Too Tough to Die: The Rise, Fall and Resurrection of a Silver Camp; 1878 to 1990.* Other books which I found of interest are listed in the endnotes and bibliography.

Then there are the movies. Hollywood was quick to realize, once the movies began to talk, that the Earp story was the perfect vehicle for the Western genre. Some movie producers simply used the events to create their own world of silver-screen fantasy. Other filmmakers borrowed the basics, including Earp's name and the O.K. Corral, and fashioned their own rendering of what happened. History and Hollywood have never been synchronous when it comes to facts. At best, they are civilized adversaries and, at worst, churlish rivals. Historians bemoan the lack of historical accuracy in large numbers of movies, including many Westerns. Minor transgressions, and far more serious ones, allow unsympathetic historians to write off Hollywood's treatment of historical stories and events.

Filmmakers are quick to point out that they are making *movies*, adding the familiar cry, "If people want accuracy, let them go watch a documentary!" In many respects, they are right. First and foremost, movies are made to entertain. Education is a secondary consideration. A filmmaker can produce a historically accurate film that can be terribly dull; another can gloss over some facts, ignore others, combine several incidents into one scene for the sake of telling a story, and come up with a fascinating and entertaining film. Making a film based on a historical event or person is a precarious undertaking. One has to balance the facts with the necessity of keeping the audience's interest and sympathy with the main characters. It is a delicate job with few guidelines. Does a filmmaker forsake accuracy for the sake of a brisk, entertaining piece (which possibly can lead to box-office success)? Or does one make a film full of historical information that bogs down the flow of the story, making it uneven and turgid? Moviemaking is, after all, a business. And, as many producers note, it is an *entertainment* business.

Although several movies have used Wyatt Earp and the famous gunfight as their subject matter, numerous productions relied on fictional characters instead of the real people. (An example is Universal's 1932 *Law and Order* with Walter Huston playing Frame Johnson.) For this book, I have chosen to exclusively focus on the eight motion pictures that use Wyatt Earp, and other real-life characters, as their sources.

As the reader will see in the pages of this book, the filmmakers of the movies discussed had to face the debate about facts vs. fiction in telling their stories. Some of these films stretched the truth beyond the facts; others remained faithful to the events of and surrounding that fateful day in 1881. I have looked at each film individually, discussing how each one relates to the facts. Each movie must stand on its own merits. Another aspect I offer the reader is the way Wyatt Earp is presented in each film (hero or anti-hero, saint vs. sinner) and how the portrayal may reflect the times when the film was made. The Wyatt Earp of *Tombstone: Town Too Tough to Die* (1942) is much different from the one presented in *Hour of the Gun* (1967) and *Doc* (1971). In the fifty-five-year span of the films I am writing about (1939–1994), the reader will see the image of Wyatt Earp evolve from the saintly hero of *Frontier Marshal* to the revisionist portrayal in *Doc* to the more moderate yet accurate presentations of *Tombstone* (1993) and *Wyatt Earp* (1994).

Like most of my contemporaries, I became interested in Wyatt Earp and the gunfight through the movies. Although *The Life and Legend of Wyatt Earp* television series was popular when I was growing up, I was never a fan of the show. Instead, my hero of choice at the age of four was *Gunsmoke*'s Marshal Matt Dillon, a composite of Wyatt Earp and other lawmen.

My introduction to Wyatt Earp and the gunfight came at the age of twelve when I saw John Ford's *My Darling Clementine* (1946) and John Sturges's *Hour of the Gun* (1967). These two films, as different as day and night, gave me my first glimpse into the events of October 26, 1881. Earp and Tombstone were always subjects of interest for me—high points in my fascination with the American West—but it wasn't until the release of *Tombstone* (1993) and *Wyatt Earp* (1994) that things changed. These two films stimulated many historians to examine or reexamine the gunfight, and the people involved, with a new zeal. Since then, numerous bits of information about any and all aspects relating to the 1881 gunfight have surfaced.

My first trip to Tombstone in 2002 keenly reignited my interest. Watching all of the movies related to the gunfight, I was intrigued by how differently each related to the historical facts. That was the beginning of this book. As I started my own digging, I was fascinated to learn that many people's knowledge of Earp and the gunfight came entirely from the movies they had seen. Yet even though historical facts blur with Hollywood fiction, people all over the world are still mesmerized by this story. I grew up in the film and television industry and as a boy was able to play on the various Western streets of studio lots. Yet walking around Tombstone was an entirely different experience for me. Time went backward. This was where it really happened. History, as interesting as the movies I had watched, was right in front of me. In a moment, the events of October 26, 1881, became very real and gave the films I'd watched an added depth.

Was Wyatt Earp a hero or a villain? Did the gunfight happen as a cold, calculating plan of the Earps? Or was it a series of events that spun out of control and ended in gunfire? It is easy for an historian to sit back and second-guess the actions of those involved in the actual moment of any event. Theories have a place in history, but it is facts that the historian is left to deal with. Historians also have the luxury of seeing what is reaped by the actions of those involved, while the actual parties have only the moment at hand. The facts we do have about Tombstone allow us to see an event played out with tragic results for everyone involved.

The same can be said for those making the movies. Each one of these films has a story. The ups and downs of making a film are never easy, no matter how much spin the studio's publicity department puts on it. Making movies can be a frustrating effort. It is also a lot of hard work and long hours, sometimes spent far from home. Despite the hardships, it is the finished product that matters. Once a movie is done, very few care that the weather was harsh, the director was curt, or some scenes were left on the cutting room floor. The stories behind the movies discussed in this book are dramatic examples of what can happen—and did.

This book is about how the truth became mythic, Hollywood helped shape a legend.

1

October 26, 1881

The fight has commenced. Go to fighting or get away!
— Wyatt Earp

The town sat on a hill overlooking a valley filled with tall, coarse grass called grama, in the south-eastern part of what was called the San Pedro Valley in Arizona Territory. This portion of Arizona Territory was sparsely populated with cattle ranches, a few understaffed military forts (to handle the Apaches who occasionally raided the ranches), and the handful of hardy souls who were looking for that big mineral strike that would make them wealthy.

Still standing on that hill today, overlooking the plains that no longer have as much grama grass, is the town of Tombstone. To the northeast, at a distance of nine miles, are the Dragoon Mountains. Tall, silent, and virtually impenetrable, they provided Apache leader Cachise (commonly known as Cochise) with the perfect hideout for his people.[1] South and slightly east of the hill are the Mule Mountains, and across the Mexican border stands the San Jose range. Northwest of the hill are the Whetstone Mountains; to the southwest stand the Huachucas (pronounced *whaa-choo-kas*). Not far from the hill, and the town that would soon emerge on it, was a river named the San Pedro. Visitors to the area today see the river as little more than a trickle, but in the 1870s and 1880s, it was a constantly flowing body of water.[2] Several small towns and villages sprouted along the San Pedro as Tombstone came into being, using the water supply to run the mills that processed the newly mined silver.

It was to this desolate place that an inveterate miner named Ed Schieffelin made his way in 1877.[3] Schieffelin's solitary search for silver or gold proffered warnings that all he would find for his trouble would be his tombstone. When he made his first strike in August 1877, he named it Tombstone. In February 1878, Schieffelin found another silver vein so rich, one could press a coin into it and it would leave an exact imprint. Reports of these discoveries quickly generated dreams of striking it rich, and the influx began. Tombstone— the town—was born.[4]

Tombstone in 1878 and 1879 consisted primarily of canvas buildings and tents. As with many early boomtowns, originally nothing was built with an eye toward permanency. Most saloons were merely tents with a false front, and the bar might simply be two large barrels with a wooden plank across them. Mercantile was sold out of wagons, while prostitutes offered comfort and entertainment in tents. The town was laid out within a 320-acre rectangle. The east-west streets were named Toughnut, Allen and Fremont, while streets running north-south were numbered. The planners originally had hoped that Fremont Street (named for then governor John C. Fremont) would become the main street in the city, but that distinction quickly fell to Allen Street due to the large number of saloons populating the artery. The red light district was primarily located on the east side of Sixth Street between Fremont and Toughnut streets. Miners' cabins dotted the south end of Toughnut Street between Third and Sixth streets, while the local Chinese population was established in the area of Third and Allen streets, often referred to as "Hop Town."

Most new arrivals to Tombstone in 1878 and 1879 came by stagecoach, with two stage lines competing for business.[5] From Tucson to Tombstone, a stagecoach ride took an average of twelve hours, carrying twelve passengers, six of them riding on top of the coach.[6] Traveling conditions were hardly comfortable for the passengers. Most were seated in cramped spaces that allowed little room for movement over long periods of time. Men often smoked inside the coach, and pure chance dictated whether the person seated next to you had agreeable body odor. Sometimes passengers had to get out and walk up a steep hill to lighten the coach and make the climb easier on the horses. Depending on the weather, the ride to Tombstone could be hot and dusty or cold and soaking wet. Still another danger was the possibility of a stagecoach robbery.[7]

Arriving in this newly born town, passengers from more civilized cities found it hardly to be what they expected. Clara Spaulding Brown painted a descriptive picture of the town after her arrival in July 1880:

> We beheld an embryo city of canvass, frame and adobe.... The only attractive places visible are the liquor and gambling saloons, which are everywhere present, and are carpeted and comfortably furnished.... The soil loose upon the surface, and is whirled into the air everyday by a wind which almost amounts to a gale.... This is a place to *stay* in for a while; not a desirable spot for a permanent home.[8]

Into this blossoming mining town in the last month of 1879 arrived three wagons with members of a family that would forever be linked with Tombstone's notoriety. On December 1, along with his wife and two older brothers, James and Virgil, and *their* wives, Wyatt Earp rode into Tombstone.

Wyatt, third child of Nicholas and Virginia Earp, was born in Monmouth, Illinois, on March 19, 1849.[9] In 1864, at age 15, Wyatt made the westward trek to Southern California with his family. He eventually became a freight wagon driver before accepting the job of constable in Lamar, Missouri, in 1870. That same year he married Urilla Sutherland, but she died within a year, leaving Wyatt with emotional scars that many historians would say forever changed his outlook on life.[10] Wyatt found himself in trouble with the law in 1871, when he and two other men were accused of stealing two horses in the area called Indian Territory, now known as Oklahoma. Wyatt was indicted for horse theft in April, but never faced trial. (There is evidence Wyatt escaped from the local jail. Charges were later dropped against his cohorts.)

Returning from the Civil War, Texas ranchers found that their cattle stock had rapidly grown. Beef was needed to feed a hungry nation, and with the establishment of the transcontinental railroad in the Great Plains states, the cattle drive was born. Driving cattle up from Texas, through Indian country, and onto the plains of Kansas, cattlemen brought beef to meet the railheads that had sprung up literally overnight.[11] Like the mining boomtowns, cattle towns were filled with saloons, gamblers, and prostitutes. Wichita, Kansas, located along the Arkansas River, became the leading terminus for shipping cattle in 1874. For trailhands, the hamlet of Delano, just across the river, was the preferred stopping-off place where a cowboy could find whiskey, gambling, and physical comfort—all for a price, of course.

By 1874, Wyatt, along with his brother James and his family, settled in the cowtown of Wichita, Kansas, where he honed his gambling skills, becoming especially adept at the game of faro.[12] Because of Wyatt's imposing stature (he stood six feet and had an athletic build and a deep voice), he was offered a job as a deputy sheriff for the upcoming cattle season, which was generally from spring through summer. As a deputy, Earp had to straddle a fine line when it came to enforcing the law with rowdy and drunken cowboys in a boisterous cowtown. Merchants welcomed the cattle business, but they also wanted their property protected. Wyatt quickly became skillful at "buffaloing" a belligerent, drunken cowhand on the side of the head by using his gun.[13] By the end of May 1876, Wyatt left Wichita for a new cowtown and a new job enforcing the peace.

Dodge City became the newest railhead for the cattle trade, and boasted plenty of saloons, gambling, and female comfort for the Texas cowhands. Dodge City's ordinances included the prohibition of riding animals into a place of business, and the discharging of firearms, and all visitors were

Wyatt Earp, about five years after the gunfight (courtesy of Jeff Morey).

required to check their firearms upon arrival.[14] Wyatt served as an assistant marshal for the 1876 cattle season, before leaving Dodge City in October 1877. That fall, Wyatt was in Fort Griffin, Texas, where he met a dentist who spent more time in the saloons playing cards than fixing teeth. His name was John Holliday, although most people called him Doc. This was their first encounter and the beginning of a long friendship that to this day leaves historians and scholars puzzled. The son of a Confederate major, Holliday was born in Valdosta, Georgia, in 1851.[15] Doc graduated from the Pennsylvania College of Dental Surgery in Philadelphia in 1872, but shortly after graduation, he was diagnosed with tuberculosis. Doc traveled to Dallas, Texas, in 1873; four years later he headed to Fort Griffin, where he was living with his on-again, off-again paramour, Kate Elder.[16]

After the death of deputy marshal Ed Masterson (brother of Bat), Wyatt returned to Dodge City to serve as a deputy marshal.[17] A short time later, Doc Holliday and Kate arrived in Dodge City, where he advertised his dental services with the promise "[Where] satisfaction is not given money will be refunded." During this period, the friendship between Wyatt and Doc solidified. Their personalities were polar opposites (Earp tended to be more sedate, while Holliday was completely capricious), yet there was an unspoken bond between the two men. Earp once stated that Doc saved his life in Dodge City, forging their strong friendship, yet there is no record of any such incident.

By 1879, Dodge City, which garnered the reputation as a wild cowtown, was becoming more civilized. The rowdier elements, which catered to the visiting cowboys of the cattle drives, were quickly being forced out of business by the town's new moral leaders, leaving

Wyatt feeling that the town had lost its "snap." Receiving a letter from his brother Virgil (who was in Prescott, Arizona) about the monetary potential to be found in the new boom-town of Tombstone, Wyatt left Dodge City in early September and headed to Prescott with Mattie, his common-law wife, and his brother James and his wife.[18]

At the time of Earp's arrival in Tombstone, the community of tents had given way to buildings made of wood and adobe, and sporting fresh coats of paint; this gave the town a bright, vibrant look. Two hotels, the Cosmopolitan and the Grand, offered the latest in accommodations and luxury furnishing, while the culinary offerings ranged from steak and beans to a more exotic bill of fare (such as fresh oysters packed in ice) to appease the appetites of a more affluent clientele. The town boasted over 40 saloons, several banks, a Wells Fargo office, a newsstand, and even a few churches. Tombstone offered a dichotomy unlike any other mining town, having a population mixture (ranging in age from 20 to 40) of the rough crowd found in most mining camps and people from major metropolitan areas who were more refined, both educationally and socially.[19] The town's two major newspapers, *Tombstone Nugget* and *Tombstone Epitaph*, would play an important role in the events that would unfold during the next seventeen months.[20]

This area of the Arizona Territory was plagued by a criminal element, often referred to as the "Cowboy element" or "Cowboy faction." This group had free rein when it came to cattle rustling and stage robberies, and many of the cowboys—a loose-fitting term to describe a group of drifters, primarily from Texas and New Mexico—formed an unofficial band of thugs.[21] Although the cowboy element had no official leadership, it is widely suspected that Curly Bill Brocius and John Ringo were looked upon as the leaders.[22] Two other families that were involved in cattle rustling activities of the area were the Clantons and the McLaurys. It was believed that Newman Clanton, often called Old Man Clanton and the father of Ike, Phin, and Billy, was the ringleader in arranging and executing the cattle rustling. Although Frank and Tom McLaury maintained a fairly rep-

Doc Holliday, circa early 1880s (courtesy of Jeff Morey).

utable standing in the area as legitimate cattle ranchers, they had many dealings with the cowboys.

The Earp's first confrontation with the Cowboy element happened in July 1880 when the Earps were assisting in the recovery of some stolen military mules found on the McLaury ranch. The incident marked the beginnings of problems with the Cowboy faction for the Earps and set in motion a series of events. John Behan, a man with little law enforcement experience but an appetite for political power, was elected county sheriff in late 1880. Many believed he had close ties to the Cowboy faction and his actions further escalated an already volatile situation between the Earps and the Cowboys. In the fall of 1880, a young Jewish woman from San Francisco, Josephine Sarah Marcus—most family members called her Sadie*—came to the town with the intent of marrying Behan.[23] Meanwhile, Wyatt's relationship with Mattie was slowly deteriorating. It is unclear when Wyatt and Sadie started seeing each other, but it is likely it began in early 1881.[24]

Shootings in Tombstone, despite a ban on carrying concealed weapons, were common—especially when alcohol was involved. In most cases, these incidents happened when miners or cowboys had too much to drink and celebrated by discharging their pistols. Shortly after midnight on October 28, 1880, Marshal Fred White chased a rowdy shooter (who turned out to be Curly Bill Brocius) into a vacant lot. Wyatt, with a borrowed gun, ran to the lot in time to hear Fred White demand that Curly Bill hand over his gun.[25] White grabbed the barrel of the gunman's pistol and gave it a quick jerk, causing it to discharge. The shot hit White in the groin and his clothes were set on fire by the flame of the muzzle. Wyatt swiftly buffaloed Curly Bill to take charge of the situation. Although White's wound was serious, it was believed he would recover. But then White died two days later, on October 30, at the age of 32. After hearing testimony from Wyatt and others, including White's deathbed statement that the shooting was unintentional, the charges against Brocius were dropped.[26] Because of Fred White's death, the Tombstone town council revised the gun ordinance, prohibiting anyone from carrying a weapon on city streets.

Wyatt hoped to win the county sheriff's position over John Behan in the upcoming election. Wyatt lacked Behan's political skills at glad-handing and realized he needed an edge to win. Ike Clanton knew the men involved in the March 15, 1881, stage robbery and death of the driver, Bud Philpot. In June of 1881, Wyatt offered Ike a deal. He would allow Ike to take the $6,000 reward if he'd help lure the three robbers to a designated spot, where Wyatt could arrest them. Clanton would get the money and Earp would get the credit for the arrest, thereby giving him an advantage in the election. Ike was interested, though he expressed fear his involvement would mark him as a snitch. Wyatt assured him the deal would remain secret.[27]

As months went on, Ike Clanton's paranoia that his deal with Wyatt would be exposed continued to grow. Early in October, he accused Wyatt of mentioning their deal to Doc Holliday, and the former dentist was making it public. Wyatt's repeated denials did little to quell Ike's fears. To settle the matter, Wyatt sent Morgan to Tucson bring Doc back to the mining town. On Saturday, October 22, Wyatt questioned Doc about Ike's claims that he had publicly divulged Earp's deal. Doc said he knew nothing about it, which seemed to satisfy Wyatt. By bringing Doc back to Tombstone, Wyatt inadvertently had set up a confrontation between Doc and Ike. The maelstrom was approaching.

Tom McLaury and Ike Clanton rode into Tombstone the afternoon of October 25, 1881.

---

*For the sake of clarity, I will refer to her hereafter as Sadie.

Billy Clanton and Frank McLaury planned to meet them the following day, October 26, at the Grand Hotel, the favored gathering place for the Cowboys. After conducting business relating to their cattle enterprises, McLaury and Clanton visited some of the saloons. As darkness descended upon Tombstone on the evening of October 25, things were fairly calm. Ike Clanton and Tom McLaury had spent most of the late afternoon and early evening drinking and gambling. By 1 A.M., October 26, Ike was eating in the Alhambra saloon when Doc Holliday confronted him. A drunken Ike was insulted when Holliday yelled at him, in front of people, saying that he was a liar and not "heeled."[28] Sitting nearby were Wyatt and Morgan. Wyatt told his younger brother that since he was an officer, he should go do something. Morgan broke up the encounter, but Ike's continued drinking and growing paranoia fueled his belief that Wyatt had been telling others of their secret deal, making Ike a marked man. Being publicly insulted by Doc Holliday only inflamed the situation.

By 2 A.M., a poker game was well underway at the Occidental Saloon when Ike and Tom McLaury joined in. Seated with them were Virgil Earp, John Behan, and an unknown player. As the early morning hours of October 26 progressed, cards were dealt and drinks consumed, until the poker game ended around 7 A.M. Before leaving the saloon, Ike told Virgil to warn Doc Holliday he had a fight coming. Virgil admonished Ike that he did not want to hear him talking that way, and refused to give Holliday the message. Ike then ominously warned that Virgil also might have to fight before he knew it, a comment Virgil ignored. As the sun rose, a cold, blustery wind blew through Tombstone, a harbinger of what was to come that day.

Over the next five hours, Ike told anyone who would listen to his drunken ravings that when he saw the Earps on the street, "the ball will open." Two townspeople, concerned over the threats, awoke both Virgil and Wyatt to inform them of Ike's claims. The two brothers, believing Clanton's hangover would quiet him down, returned to bed. As the morning hours went by, anxiety increased about possible bloodshed on the streets. The bitingly cold wind continued to blow as the noon hour approached. Ike walked to Camillus S. Fly's Boarding House on Fremont Street in an attempt to find Holliday, but was told Doc was not there. (By now, Ike was sporting a Winchester rifle as well as a pistol.) Fly's wife quickly warned Kate of Clanton's inquiry, and she woke Doc with the news that Ike was looking for him. Doc sardonically replied, "If God will let me live long enough, I shall see him."

By noon, Virgil, Wyatt and Morgan went looking for Ike after several more people told them about his threats. Virgil, with Morgan following, turned the corner of Fourth Street, where they saw Ike aiming his rifle at Wyatt, who had just turned the corner at Allen and Fourth streets. Virgil quickly walked up behind Ike and buffaloed him on the back of the head. At a hearing in Judge Albert O. Wallace's courtroom, Ike was fined $27.50 for carrying weapons in the city limits and released.

Tom McLaury, hearing of Ike's altercation with Virgil, went to the courthouse and bumped into Wyatt coming out of the building. McLaury told Wyatt he would make a fight with him anywhere. Wyatt challenged him to make a fight right there, slapping Tom in the face with his left hand and buffaloing him on the side of the head.[29] Meanwhile, with the court action concluded, Virgil dropped off Ike's guns at the Grand Hotel and thought the matter had ended. But he was now told that Frank McLaury and Billy Clanton had arrived in town. It was now about 1 P.M.

At the corner of Fourth and Allen streets, Frank and Billy ran into Billy Claiborne, who told them Ike and Tom were at the doctor's office getting their heads bandaged. Within a few minutes, the McLaury brothers and Billy Clanton were walking down Allen Street, past Wyatt standing in front of Hafford's Corner saloon, to Spangenberg's Gun Shop on Fourth Street. Wyatt conferred with Virgil (who was now carrying a shotgun) outside the saloon, as a throng of citizens now began to grow, sensing an escalation of trouble. Morgan joined his two brothers just as the McLaurys and Clantons left the gunshop and headed back to the Dexter corral. Standing in front of the Dexter Corral, the McLaurys and Clantons discussed—some said argued—what to do next.

John Behan approached Virgil about the volatile situation. Virgil asked Behan if he would go with him to disarm the McLaurys and the Clantons, but the county sheriff declined. Behan offered to have a talk with the men and try to defuse the situation. Virgil agreed, adding that if they stayed off the streets he would leave them alone. The Clantons and the McLaurys now had crossed Allen Street and entered the O.K. Corral. H. F. Sills, a train engineer on layoff from the AT&SF railroad, was walking past the Clantons and McLaurys in front of the O.K. Corral when he overheard one of the group say he would kill Virgil Earp on sight. Learning Earp was the city marshal, Sills quickly sought out Virgil, and told him what he had overheard. The continued threats, combined with no communication from Behan, further escalated tension for the Earps. Doc Holliday, wearing a long gray coat and carrying a silver knobbed cane, now joined the Earps and offered assistance. Wyatt told him not to get mixed up in it, that it wasn't his fight. Doc quickly replied, "That is a hell of a thing for you to say to me."

The Clantons and the McLaurys walked through the O.K. Corral to the rear entrance on Fremont Street. Frank and Tom went to the Union Meat Market to finish some business, while Billy Clanton and Billy Claiborne turned left, heading toward Third Street. Situated between Fly's Boarding House and Photo Gallery and a building owned by William Harwood, they entered an empty lot to take shelter from the biting wind and wait for the McLaury brothers and Ike. The lot is no more than eighteen feet wide and less than fifty-feet from Third Street. John Behan stopped the McLaurys at the Union Meat Market, where he asked Frank to give him his weapon. Frank refused, saying he would give up his weapon only when "the other party is disarmed." Walking with them to the empty lot, where Ike had joined his brother and Claiborne, Behan did a quick pat down of Ike to learn whether he was carrying a pistol, while Tom McLaury opened his vest or coat to show he was unarmed.

Within twenty minutes, Virgil was told by another man that the group was out on Fremont Street, their weapons in plain sight. Wyatt, Morgan, Doc, and Virgil agreed that they could no longer wait for Behan to return. Virgil exchanged his shotgun for Doc's cane, telling him to hide it under his coat so that they would not appear to be confrontational.

"Come along," he said, as they began walking down the left side of Fourth Street.

It was now about 2:40 P.M.

As the men continued down Fourth Street, some witnesses noticed that Doc Holliday was softly whistling as the wind occasionally blew open his coat, revealing the shotgun underneath. People gathered along Fremont Street, watching the four round the corner of Fourth Street and turn left. Martha King had just entered the Union Meat Market and was trying to get service, but most of the employees were more interested in what was happening outside. She was told that there was about to be a fight between the Earps and some Cowboys.

Turning the corner, the Earps and Holliday, walking four abreast, passed the Capitol Saloon, the offices of the Tombstone *Nugget*, and the Papago Cash Store before crossing the rear entrance of the O.K. Corral. They were now roughly ninety feet from the empty lot.

John Behan looked down Fremont Street from the front of the lot and saw the Earps coming. He told the Clantons and McLaurys to wait in the lot while he went down to stop them. Getting her order filled at the Union Meat Market, Martha King heard someone outside the store yell, "Here they come!" Mrs. King and everyone else in the store ran to the front door in time to see the Earps and Holliday pass under the striped canvas awning.

Behan hurriedly approached the Earps in front of the Union Meat Market, where he told them, "Gentlemen, I am sheriff of this county, and I am not going to allow any trouble if I can help it."[30] As they passed him by, Virgil told Behan that he was there to simply disarm the Clantons and McLaurys. According to testimony by Wyatt and Virgil, the county sheriff claimed, "I have disarmed them."[31]

Hearing what Behan said, Virgil switched his pistol in his waistband from his right hip to his left and placed Doc's cane in his right hand. (None of the Earps were wearing gun-belts that day.) At the same time, Wyatt took his pistol and placed it in the right pocket of his overcoat. Behan followed the group as they approached Fly's Boarding House and Photo Gallery, running through the lot and taking shelter in the landing between the boarding house and photo gallery, as the empty lot came into view for the Earps and Holliday.

Virgil stepped into the lot, with Wyatt only getting as far into it as the corner of Fly's building. Both Morgan and Doc stood out on the street. Upon seeing the Earps and Holliday, Frank McLaury and Ike and Billy Clanton moved deeper into the lot. Tom McLaury stood by the boardwalk with a horse, one of his hands close to the rifle in the saddle scabbard.

"Boys, throw up your hands," Virgil commanded, "I want your guns." Frank McLaury reportedly said, "We will," and his right hand dropped to his gun. Billy Claiborne quickly walked away from the Clantons, ducking behind Fly's Boarding House for cover. Hearing the click-click of a gun cocking, Virgil quickly raised both hands in the air. "Hold! I don't want that!"

In an instant, both Wyatt and Billy Clanton drew their guns, both shots going off instantaneously. Instead of firing his shot at Billy, Wyatt aimed for Frank, hitting him just left of the navel. Billy, cross-drawing his pistol, missed his shot completely. There was a brief lull, as Ike Clanton ran up to Wyatt, pleading for him not to shoot him, causing one of Wyatt's shots to go wild.[32]

Then all hell broke loose.

Morgan drew his gun and his bullet hit Billy Clanton in the left breast, deflating his lung. Frank McLaury, clutching his stomach wound, staggered out of the lot with his horse trailing after him. Turning on the street, Frank fired at Virgil, hitting him in the right calf and knocking him to the ground. Switching the cane to his left hand, Virgil reached for his gun and returned fire at Frank, missing him. Morgan fired again at Billy Clanton and struck him in the right wrist; the bullet continued on to penetrate his stomach.

As Wyatt continued to struggle with Ike, he said coolly, "The fight has commenced. Go to fighting or get away!" and flung him off. Ike ran away, leaving Billy to fend for himself, racing through Fly's Boarding House and eventually getting all the way to Toughnut Street. At that moment, Morgan was hit by a shot, *possibly* from Tom McLaury, that entered his right shoulder, skimming his back and nicking the vertebrae before exiting the left shoulder.[33] He managed to get up and back out farther into the street before tripping over a mound of dirt that had recently covered newly laid water pipes.

Wyatt and Virgil turned their attention to Billy Clanton, who had slid down the wall of the Harwood Building, propping his pistol on his knee and firing wildly before running out of bullets. Wyatt was by now moving out of the lot, heading toward the street. He heard a shot behind him and yelled, "Watch it, Morg! We're getting it from the back." (The shot, possibly a wild one from Billy Clanton, may have ricocheted off a building or piece of metal, giving Wyatt the impression they were being fired at from behind.)

The empty lot quickly filled with smoke from the black powder ammunition. Doc Holliday had not been able to get a clear shot at Tom McLaury because of the horse. Wyatt fired (aiming either for Tom McLaury or his horse) and hit the withers of the animal, causing it to pull away, exposing Tom. Tom was then hit by the shotgun charge, wounding him under his right arm pit. He lurched out of the lot, heading toward the corner of Third and Fremont streets, where he collapsed.

Dropping the shotgun, Doc drew his nickel-plated pistol and followed Frank McLaury into Fremont Street, heading toward Fourth Street from the empty lot. Frank's horse suddenly bolted, leaving him standing in the street confronting Holliday. Holding his pistol in his right hand, balancing it on his left forearm, Frank said to Holliday, "I've got you this time." Holliday replied, "Blaze away, you're a daisy if you have."

Frank's shot hit Holliday's pistol pocket, grazing his hip. "I've been shot clean through," Doc yelled as he shot Frank in the chest.

Lying in the street, Morgan heard Doc cry that he'd been hit. Aiming from his position on the ground, Morgan fired his gun, hitting Frank just below the right ear. The bullet struck the brain stem, pulverizing it, and Frank fell to the ground.[34] Running up to Frank's body, Doc shouted, "The son of a bitch has shot me, and I mean to kill him!"

Thirty seconds. It was over. As the smoke and acrid smell from the black powder ammunition began to dissipate, Wyatt Earp, standing on Fremont Street, was the only one in the street fight to emerge unscathed.

John Behan approached Wyatt, saying he would have to arrest him. Wyatt reportedly replied, "I won't be arrested. You have deceived me, Johnny. You told me they were not armed. I won't be arrested, but I am here to answer for what I have done. I am not going to leave town."[35]

Morgan and Virgil were taken by a wagon to a nearby drugstore, where they were treated for their wounds by Dr. George Goodfellow before being taken to their respective homes. Harry Woods and Wes Fuller carried Billy Clanton to the Harwood house, next to the empty lot, where he was thrashing in pain, calling for a doctor, and saying, "They have murdered me. I have been murdered." Injected with morphine to ease his suffering, Billy Clanton died in less than two hours. Tom McLaury, who was brought into the same room, said nothing before passing away within a half hour. About two hours after the gunfight ended, a wagon took the bodies of the three men to a cabin at the rear of J. O. Dunbar's livery, where the coroner, Henry Matthews, made his examination before they were taken to the Ritter and Reams Funeral Home to be prepared for burial.[36] The *Nugget* described the bodies in the funeral home as lying "side by side, covered with a sheet. Very little blood appeared on their clothing, and only on the face of young Billy Clanton was there any distortion of the features or evidence of pain in dying."[37]

Shortly after the gunfight, Ike Clanton was arrested on Toughnut Street and placed in the county sheriff's jail, mostly as a safety precaution. Later that evening, after going to the funeral home to see Billy's body, Phin Clanton also was placed in the jail under the guard of ten men. (Both would be released the next day.)

The tension of an impending confrontation, which had been growing all morning, had given way to a violent and bloody gunfight and then a sudden rush of relief. But the relief after the day's events soon changed to fear of an attack on the town by the Cowboy faction—a fear happily unrealized. The Earps and Holliday, however, would rapidly see public

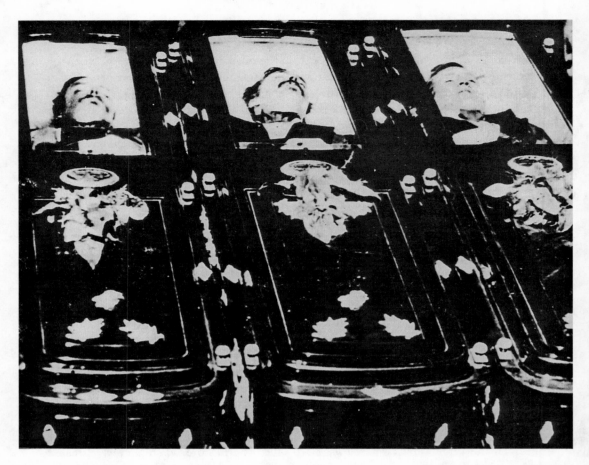

The aftermath of October 26, 1881: Left to right: Tom McLaury, Frank McLaury and Billy Clanton (courtesy of Jeff Morey).

opinion turn on them. A foreshadowing of this was when the bodies of Billy Clanton, Frank and Tom McLaury were displayed, in their black coffins, in the window of the funeral home. The banner above them read: MURDERED IN THE STREETS OF TOMBSTONE.

That night, October 26, 1881, a blanket of snow covered Tombstone.

"Three Men Hurled Into Eternity in the Duration of a Moment" read the headline in the *Epitaph* on October 27. That afternoon, funeral services were held for Billy Clanton, Frank and Tom McLaury before a procession, headed by the Tombstone Brass Band, moved down Allen Street toward the cemetery. The following day, October 28, a coroner's inquest was held, yet none of the Earps were called to testify. Two days later, after the coroner's jury ruled that the three men died from gunshot wounds fired by the Earps and Holliday, the city council suspended Virgil from his office as the city's chief of police.

Ike Clanton filed murder charges against the Earp brothers and Doc Holliday. Behan served the warrants, although those for Virgil and Morgan were waived as they were still recovering from their wounds. Wyatt and Doc were released on bail ($10,000 each), pending an October 31 preliminary hearing held before Justice Wells Spicer, who would determine whether the charges warranted a grand jury.[38] Testimony in the hearing began on November 1, with only one witness at a time appearing in the room. The first to testify was coroner Henry Matthews, followed by others including John Behan. In the following days, others took the stand relating what they saw and the case for the prosecution grew stronger. Will McLaury made a motion that Wyatt and Doc be jailed, without bond, based on the evidence presented. Despite defense objections, Judge Spicer sent Wyatt and Holliday to the jail on Sixth Street, under heavy guard.

Ike Clanton took the stand on November 9 and, in typical fashion, his blustering proved to be his downfall and helped unravel the case for the prosecution.[39] One of the first witnesses for the defense was Wyatt Earp. While it was a highly unusual move, Earp's lawyer used an Arizona law statute that allowed a defendant at a preliminary hearing to make a statement on his own behalf without being cross-examined. Earp read from his prepared statement, explaining the problems he had with the Clantons and McLaurys over time, including the stolen Army mules and his unfortunate deal with Ike. He also detailed the events leading up to the gunfight, including Ike's threats. The defense slowly began chipping away at the prosecution's case. Virgil Earp testified from his bed at the Cosmopolitan Hotel, but unlike Wyatt, he did not read a prepared statement and was questioned by both prosecution and defense. The defense team called two impartial, yet credible witnesses to the case, H. F. Sills and Winfield Scott Williams, who had recently been sworn in as county assistant district attorney. With neither side presenting a closing argument, the preliminary hearing ended on November 29.[40]

In the afternoon of November 30, Justice Spicer rendered his decision. Taking note of Ike Clanton's threats and Virgil Earp's legal duty to disarm anyone who violated the city law by carrying a weapon, Spicer pointed out that Virgil "committed an injudicious and censurable act" when he called on Wyatt and Doc Holliday to help him in disarming the Clanton and McLaury parties. "I can attach no criminality to his unwise act ... he needed the assistance and support of staunch and true friends, upon whose courage, coolness and fidelity he could depend," the judge noted. He went on to say that the Clantons' and McLaurys' act of carrying weapons in town, coupled with the threats by Ike, gave the impression that if they did not plan to kill Virgil and his brothers, they at least planned to resist with force any attempt to be disarmed.

The judge took into consideration the testimony of those witnesses who saw the gunfight from different locations, as well as those involved in the melee. He found that the "weight of evidence" supported the testimony by Wyatt and Virgil. Spicer noted that Billy Clanton's wrist wound was not one he could have received with his hands up in the air, and that Tom McLaury's wound were "not consistent" with a man whose hands were on his coat lapels. He found Ike Clanton's claims that the Earps wanted to kill him were not believable since the Earps could have killed Ike first. The evidence as presented did not support a conviction of the defendants and the judge ordered Wyatt and Holliday released from custody, but left open the option for the Cochise County grand jury to reconsider his decision. The grand jury upheld Spicer's decision on December 16, 1881, officially closing the matter.

After the decision, anonymous letters were sent to the Earps, Judge Spicer, and others, warning them to leave the area. The Earps took the rumors seriously, with Virgil and his wife, as well as Morgan and Louisa, moving into rooms at the Cosmopolitan Hotel, which would provide more safety from a possible attack. John Clum took advantage of a business trip back east to escape any threats—or so he thought. Taking a stage to Benson, Clum found himself caught in a hold-up which was averted by the stage driver. Several miles later, the stage stopped and Clum struck out on his own, walking to Benson.[41] Clum always maintained that the holdup wasn't actually a stage robbery (there was no money or shotgun messenger aboard) but an attempt on his life. The *Nugget* made light of the mayor's paranoia about being marked for death—but no one would be laughing about another murder attempt before the month was out.

Virgil Earp left the Oriental Saloon about 11:30 P.M. on December 28, heading toward his room at the Cosmopolitan Hotel on Allen Street. As he reached the opposite side of the boardwalk, blasts from at least two shotguns punctuated the still night air. Amazingly, Virgil was able to walk back to the Oriental and find Wyatt before collapsing. The brunt of the shotgun blasts hit his left arm, causing a longitudinal fracture between his shoulder and elbow. Virgil was quickly carried to his hotel room, where Dr. Goodfellow worked on saving his arm.[42] George Parsons brought medical supplies to Virgil's room. Virgil's wife, Allie, was troubled by his badly mangled arm, prompting Virgil to reassure her by stating, "Never mind, I've got one good arm to hug you with."[43] Wasting no time, Wyatt wired U. S. Marshal Crawley Dake in Phoenix, apprising him of what happened and requesting the authority to deputize the necessary help. Dake immediately sent the proper papers for Wyatt to take over and pursue the would-be assassins of his brother.

On January 23, 1882, warrants were issued for the arrest of Ike and Phin Clanton. As Wyatt went in search of the Clantons, Ike and Phin turned themselves in, thinking they were to be arrested for mail robbery. Instead, they learned that the warrants were for the attempted murder of Virgil Earp. Charges were dismissed for lack of evidence, and Wyatt quickly realized his chances of arresting and convicting Virgil's attackers were slim. In February, Morgan sent Louisa to stay at the Earp family home in Colton, California, feeling she would be safer there. Wyatt now surrounded himself with a group of men who were not quite the law-abiding type but who could be counted on if things got tough. The men included Dan Tipton, Sherman McMaster, Jack Johnson, and Texas Jack Vermillion. Along with Wyatt's younger brother, Warren, and Doc Holliday, they would soon become well-known in the annals of the American West as the Earp vendetta posse.[44]

On Friday, March 17, Wyatt had been warned by a few people that he and his family might be targets for another attack. Despite the warnings, Morgan, accompanied by Doc Holliday, went to see the play *Stolen Kisses* performed at Schieffelin Hall the following evening. Meeting his younger brother and Doc outside Schieffelin Hall, Wyatt tried to persuade Morgan to return to the hotel. Instead, Morgan managed to talk Wyatt into accompanying him to Campbell and Hatch's on Allen Street for one game of billiards. The saloon and billiard room was between Fourth and Fifth Streets on the north side of Allen, next to the Alhambra Saloon. An alley ran behind the buildings on the north side of the street. The rear doors of Hatch's building had glass windows with the lower half diffused and the upper portion clear. Someone standing in the alley at night would have a perfect view of whoever was inside the illuminated building. The billiard table was near the rear door. Seated inside the room watching the game between Morgan and Bob Hatch, one of the owners, were Sherman McMaster, Dan Tipton, Doc, and Wyatt. At 10:50 P.M., Morgan leaned over the table to line up a shot, his back to the glass doors. A gunshot crashed through the glass windows. The bullet struck Morgan and propelled him onto the pool table. A second shot followed, embedding itself in the wall just above Wyatt's head. Wyatt, Tipton, and McMaster carefully moved Morgan to the card room, where he was placed on a couch. Morgan's wound was fatal.[45] Surrounded by his four brothers—Virgil, Wyatt, James, and Warren—Morgan died shortly before midnight, less than six weeks before turning thirty and the night before Wyatt's thirty-fourth birthday.

"At the front door of the saloon stood a hound, raised by the brothers who, with that instinct peculiar to animals, seemed to know that his master had been struck down.... [It began] whining and moaning, and when the body was taken to the hotel, no sadder heart followed than that of the faithful dog," noted the *Weekly Arizona Citizen*.[46] The fire bell tolled as the funeral procession left Tombstone the following day at 12:30 P.M. Morgan's body was moved to Contention, where James Earp would take the train carrying his brother's remains to the Earp family in Colton, California.

Wyatt would not travel home to attend his younger brother's funeral. Instead, he returned to Tombstone, where Wyatt told Virgil to leave town, as he could not adequately protect his brother *and* go after Morgan's killers. On Monday, March 20, Virgil and Allie, under the protection of Wyatt, Warren, Doc Holliday, Texas Jack Vermillion, Sherman McMaster, and Jack Johnson, left Tombstone.[47] They traveled to the train station at Contention, where Wyatt received word that Frank Stilwell, Ike Clanton, and possibly two others were watching the trains in Tucson with plans to kill Wyatt and other family members.

As the train arrived in Tucson, the group spotted Frank Stilwell and two others, all carrying shotguns, on the train platform. After boarding the transcontinental train, Wyatt saw Frank Stilwell and one other man, possibly Ike Clanton, lying in a prone position on flat cars with shotguns at the ready. Wyatt slipped off the train and doubled back toward the two killers lying in wait. Seeing Wyatt approaching, the two ran, but one fell behind. Wyatt caught up with the man who fell behind—Frank Stilwell, who faced Wyatt in the dimly lit train yard. As Earp approached, Stilwell grabbed hold of the double-barreled shotgun in Wyatt's hands. Wyatt pulled the triggers of both barrels, hitting Stilwell in the abdomen. Wyatt Earp's vengeance had begun.

Wyatt ran along the platform, caught up with Virgil's train car and mouthed to his brother, "One for Morgan."[48] With Virgil safely on his way to California and Stilwell dead, Wyatt and his group rode back to Tombstone. The following morning, workers found the bullet-riddled body of Frank Stilwell. Stilwell's killing, however justified in Wyatt's eyes, began a storm of controversy with the Tucson press quickly calling the shooting a cold-blooded murder. Murder warrants were issued for the arrest of Wyatt, Warren, Doc, Sherman McMaster, and Jack Johnson. Returning to Tombstone on Tuesday afternoon, Wyatt and his group went to his room at the Cosmopolitan Hotel. A friendly telegraph operator showed Wyatt a telegram ordering John Behan to arrest Earp and the others. The operator agreed to withhold it until the posse was ready to leave town. When Behan received the telegram at 8 P.M., he tried to arrest the group as they were leaving the hotel. Behan reportedly said he wanted to see Wyatt. "You can't see me; I've seen you once too often," Earp replied, and the men walked out. Behan later claimed that Wyatt and the other men pulled guns on him and two deputies.[49] Smarting over his inability to arrest Earp, John Behan formed a posse that included Johnny Ringo and Phin Clanton as well as others of the Cowboy faction—to arrest the Earp group on the Stilwell murder charge.

Wyatt and his posse headed to Pete Spence's wood camp in the Dragoon Mountains, a known Cowboy hideout. Arriving in the late morning of March 22, the posse found one of Morgan's killers—Florentino Cruz, sometimes called Indian Charlie. He quickly became the second target of Earp's vendetta.[50]

It was considerably warmer on March 24. Riding in the open sun, Wyatt loosened his gunbelt to ease his discomfort. The posse headed toward a water hole in the Whetstone Mountains called Iron Springs. As the Earp party rode toward the water hole, Wyatt claimed he had a premonition that something was wrong. He took his shotgun from the saddle's pommel strap as he drew closer. Coming into view of the water hole, he was quickly greeted with gunfire. The Earp group had stumbled onto a small party of Cowboys, lead by Curly Bill.

As gunfire erupted, Texas Jack Vermillion's horse went down on top of him. The others in the group—Doc, Jack Johnson, and Sherman McMaster—quickly turned around and headed for cover, expecting Wyatt and Texas Jack to do the same.[51] Wyatt, however, jumped off his horse, threw his reins over his arm, and advanced on Curly Bill. With his horse frantically tugging at the reins, raising a cloud of dust, and with the skirt of Earp's long jacket being peppered with gunshots, Wyatt aimed his shotgun at Curly Bill. Pulling the triggers of both barrels, Wyatt hit his target, "blowing him all to pieces."[52]

Dropping his shotgun, Wyatt went back to his saddle for his Winchester rifle as the remaining members of the Cowboy group took refuge in nearby willows and kept firing. The shooting spooked Wyatt's horse and made it impossible for him to grab his rifle. Reaching for his pistol, Wyatt discovered that as a result of loosening his cartridge belt earlier, it had now slipped down around his thighs, and the two holsters had slid toward his back. He managed to get one gun drawn and quickly fired into the willows, where he wounded Johnny Barnes before attempting to remount his horse and make a retreat.[53]

Attempting to step up into his stirrup, Wyatt could not swing his right leg over the saddle as it was restricted because of the loosened cartridge belt. Hanging onto the saddle with his left hand, and with his horse frightened by the gunfire, Wyatt attempted to pull up his gun belt with his right hand as shots continued to fly around him. One bullet struck the saddle horn within inches of Wyatt's left hand and face. Another clipped his boot heel. (Wyatt thought he had been shot in the leg because his leg went numb with the shot at his boot heel.) Finally getting his right leg over the saddle, Wyatt quickly turned his horse and made a dash for cover, meanwhile picking up Texas Jack, who had managed to get out from under his dead horse.

Once again, Wyatt Earp had emerged from a deadly gunfight without a scratch on his body.

Wyatt's quest for revenge was over. The posse headed for Henry Hooker's ranch, where they rested their horses. By April 15, the Earp group rode to Silver City, New Mexico, taking a train to Albuquerque. Heading to Colorado, the group began to disperse. Doc went to Den-

The only known photograph of Bat Masterson (standing) and Wyatt Earp together. Taken in Dodge City, circa 1876, when Masterson was Ford County sheriff and Earp was a deputy marshal of Dodge City (courtesy of Jeff Morey).

ver, accompanied by Dan Tipton, while Wyatt, Warren, Sherman McMaster, Texas Jack Vermillion, and Jack Johnson went on to the town of Gunnison. It was there that Wyatt had a faithful friend in the town's city marshal—Bat Masterson. Once the group was situated on the outskirts of the town, both McMaster and Johnson went their separate ways. Wyatt, Warren, and Texas Jack kept a low profile in the area. However, Doc Holliday was, as usual, more visible. In Denver, Doc was arrested by a Perry Mallen, who claimed he was deputy sheriff from Los Angeles and had papers ordering Holliday's arrest for the murder of Frank Stilwell, Curly Bill, and Billy Clanton.[54]

Using Bat Masterson's connections, Wyatt got the law authorities in Pueblo, Colorado, to swear out a bogus warrant for Holliday, which would keep him in the state and avoid extradition to Arizona. Meanwhile, in Arizona, Bob Paul was ordered to go to Colorado to arrest Holliday, but the warrants lacked the proper seal and the updated papers would have to be sent to him. Bat Masterson made a last-ditch effort by meeting with Colorado governor Frederick Pitkin. Masterson said Holliday's arrest by Mallen was fraudulent and would result in his being assassinated by members of the Cowboy faction in Arizona. The governor refused to allow Holliday to be extradited based on the fact that the arrest papers lacked the proper seal and that Colorado had priority based on the (bogus) charge in Pueblo. Attempts to serve warrants for Frank Stilwell's death faded, and the days of the Cowboy faction rapidly dwindled. For Wyatt Earp, his time in Tombstone had come to an end.

With the Earps out of Tombstone and the death of Curly Bill, the Cowboy faction seemed to splinter and slowly dissolve.[55] Cattle rustling all but stopped, and stagecoach robberies became less frequent. Silver continued to be extracted from the ground—at least for a while. In May 1882, John Clum sold the *Epitaph* to his rival, the *Nugget*. Later that month a fire broke out and all but destroyed the core of the town, including all the Grand and Cosmopolitan hotels, saloons such as the Occidental, Campbell and Hatch's, and the Golden Eagle Brewery.[56] The offices of the *Nugget* were destroyed and Spangenberg's Gunshop provided a colorful and noisy display as the ammunition went up in flames. Again, the town would quickly rebuild, but Tombstone's decline was on the horizon. Many of the mines, as early as 1881, were hitting water at the 500-foot level. Pumps seemed to control things, but water was soon filling the mines at the 1,000-foot level and lower.[57] Along with the rising water levels, the decline in silver's price spelled the end of the mines. In 1887, the year-end total of silver extracted was below the million-dollar mark.[58] Tombstone's population, which in 1882 was estimated at 5,300, fell to 1,800 in 1890, and the numbers would continue to dwindle.

On July 14, 1882, John Ringo's body was discovered, with a bullet wound to the right temple, his pistol in his right hand, sitting in the bole of an oak tree in the Chiricahua Mountains. Ringo's boots were missing; portions of his undershirt, torn up in sections, were wrapped around his feet. His gun belt was buckled upside down, and his horse was missing. His Winchester rifle was propped next to the body. The coroner estimated that Ringo had been dead about twenty-four hours; the body was buried behind the tree in which it was found.[59] The coroner's report stated that Ringo was a suicide, although there were no powder burn marks alongside the entry wound.

Ike Clanton, who had a habit of showing bravado only to run from a fight, was running again in 1887. This time he got caught. Ike was killed on September 14, 1887, by private detective J. V. Brighton.

After striking it rich in Tombstone, Ed Schieffelin continued to prospect all over the West, including Alaska. He died in a cabin near Canyonville, Oregon, on May 12, 1897, at age 49. His remains are buried on a road outside Tombstone under a monument similar to the kind of marker prospectors built when staking a claim.

John Behan's career as county sheriff ended with the 1882 election. Oddly, he wound up serving as warden of Yuma Territorial Prison, causing some old Tombstoners to comment that he was on the wrong side of the bars. Behan died in 1912.

The members of Earp's posse passed into the pages of history quietly. Little is know of what happened to Dan Tipton after he and Doc parted company in Denver in 1882. In 1890, Tipton was living in El Paso, Texas, and was arrested seven years later for smuggling Chinese immigrants into the country and providing false resident certificates. He was sentenced to twenty months in a penitentiary in Columbus, Ohio, where he died on February 25, 1898, at age fifty-three.[60]

Jack Johnson went on to live in Oak Creek and Yuma, Arizona, as well as in San Diego, California, raising a family of five children. He was reportedly buried somewhere near the Colorado River in 1906. Interestingly, he never went by the name "Turkey Creek" Jack Johnson, but he was occasionally referred to in newspapers as "Mysterious Johnson."[61] Not much is known about what happened to Texas Jack Vermillion in later years except that he returned to Virginia and became a preacher.

Sherman McMaster is another enigma. Some believe McMaster joined the U.S. Army and, during the Spanish-American War, fought in the Philippines, where he died. However, historian Peter Brand carefully checked the military records for the dead in that conflict and found no listing of a Sherman McMaster. What is known is that McMaster's brother, George, and his sister, Janette, stated when they filed a probate claim in Rock Island, Illinois, in 1906 that Sherman died in 1892 in Colorado.[62]

Doc Holliday stayed in Colorado for the rest of his life. In 1883, he moved to Leadville, where he found work dealing faro games. He got into a fight with another gambler and was fired from his job. Broke, prematurely gray at 34, and using a cane for physical support, Doc was eventually ordered to leave Leadville. Doc Holliday became a man without a place to call home. Denver at the time was caught up in a reform movement, and gambling, as well as saloons, became targets. Doc was arrested on charges of vagrancy, but managed to get his case delayed. In late 1885 or early 1886, while staying in Denver, Doc heard Wyatt was in town with Sadie. The two old friends met in the lobby of the Windsor Hotel for one last time. Wyatt supposedly said that he felt it odd that if it were not for Doc, he would not be here today, yet Doc must be the first to go. Parting, Doc threw his reedy arm around Wyatt's shoulder and said, "Good-bye, old friend. It will be a long time before we meet again." Sadie said Wyatt had tears in his eyes when the two men walked away from each other.[63] Doc traveled to Pueblo, before heading to Glenwood Springs, where many tubercular patients were receiving treatment at the sulfur springs. Arriving in May 1886, Holliday's illness had advanced into galloping consumption. It was just a matter of time. On November 8, 1887, at the age of 36, John Henry "Doc" Holliday died in a room at the Hotel Glenwood. Reportedly, his last words, after finishing a drink of whiskey, were, "I'll be damned. This is funny."

Mattie Earp waited at the Earp family ranch in Colton, California, for Wyatt to return. He never did. She eventually left the area, and all that is known is that she drifted into prostitution in Globe, Arizona, still keeping the surname Earp. She died on July 3, 1888, of an overdose of laudanum in Pinal, Arizona. She left no known relatives and was buried in a grave with a piece of sandstone to mark her resting place. During the coroner's inquest, it was stated that Mattie said that Earp "had wrecked her life by deserting her and she didn't want to live anymore."[64]

Morgan's widow, Louisa, remarried in 1885 and died in Los Angeles in 1894. She had not yet turned forty.

Warren Earp followed Wyatt to San Francisco in 1882. By 1900, many believe he was working as a ranch hand in Arizona, although some claim he was a stock detective. On July 6, 1900, near Willcox, Arizona, Warren got into an argument in a saloon with John Boyett. Warren challenged him, and Boyett shot him through the heart. Warren, who was 45, was unarmed, but charges against Boyett were dismissed. Contrary to legend, neither Wyatt nor Virgil avenged the death of their younger brother.

Virgil Earp, accompanied by Allie, went to San Francisco in 1882 to receive medical treatment for his crippled arm. He eventually moved to Colton, where he opened a private detective business and went on to serve as the town constable. In 1893, Virgil and Allie moved in Vanderbilt, California, to follow a silver strike before returning to Prescott, Arizona. In 1898, Virgil discovered that he was the father of a long-lost daughter. Before joining the Union Army, Virgil had eloped with Ellen Rysdam. The bride's family objected to the marriage and, after learning she was pregnant, her parents led Ellen to believe that Virgil had died during the Civil War. Years later, Ellen and Virgil's daughter, Janie, contacted him, and in 1899, Virgil and Allie traveled to Portland, Oregon, for a reunion. A 1903 gold strike in Goldfield, Nevada, led Virgil and Allie to the location, where he was sworn in as deputy sheriff in 1905 and served until his death on October 19, 1905, at the age of 62. He was buried, with Allie's blessings, in Portland, Oregon, at the request of Virgil's daughter. Allie would die in November 1947, twenty-one days shy of her hundredth birthday.

Wyatt's old friend Bat Masterson gave up a life in the West to become a sportswriter. He moved to New York City in 1902, where he became the sports editor for the *New York Morning Telegraph*. Masterson died at his desk while writing a column on October 25, 1921.

James Earp worked a variety of jobs, including running a boarding house, gambling, and operating a saloon in San Bernardino, California. His wife, Bessie, died in 1887, and James passed away in Los Angeles in 1926.

In late 1882, Wyatt left Gunnison, Colorado, for San Francisco. It was there that he became reacquainted with Sadie Marcus, who had left Tombstone in July 1881. The two, who appear never to have

Earp often spent his summer months in Los Angeles throughout the 1920s (courtesy of Jeff Morey).

Pallbearers at Earp's funeral: Left to right: W. J. Hunsaker (Wyatt's lawyer), George Parsons, John Clum, William S. Hart, Wilson Mizner (screenwriter and co-owner of the Brown Derby) and Tom Mix (courtesy of Jeff Morey).

married, would spend the next forty-seven years together. Wyatt followed the gambling circuit of many boom towns throughout the West over the next twenty years. He lived for a time in San Diego, where he dabbled in real estate. He and Sadie moved back to San Francisco in 1890, and this is where Earp would be involved in one of the most controversial events of his life—refereeing the heavyweight championship boxing match between Bob Fitzsimmons and Tom Sharkey. Earp's decision, ruling that Fitzsimmons fouled Sharkey by hitting him in the groin, caused a tremendous uproar. Newspapers claimed that Wyatt Earp was in on throwing the fight to Sharkey, and he was vilified in the local papers, which even unearthed his past in Tombstone.

Wyatt and Sadie followed the 1897 Alaskan gold rush. For four years, Wyatt ran various saloons in Nome from the spring to early fall before returning to winter in San Francisco. The couple would live on and off in Los Angeles and roam parts of the West in search of mining claims for the next twenty-seven years. Toward the end of his life, Wyatt spent his winter months working a copper claim on the California-Arizona border (near present-day Earp, California) and lived in Los Angeles during the summer, either in cheap cottages or with relatives and friends. With the moving picture industry located in Los Angeles, Wyatt struck up friendships with Western movie actors William S. Hart and Tom Mix, and was visited by old Tombstone friends George Parsons and John Clum.

By 1928, Wyatt's health began to fail; he was primarily plagued by kidney problems. Just before the end, in the early morning hours of January 13, 1929, Wyatt, lying in bed, whispered, "Suppose, suppose." Sadie leaned over to him to ask what he said, but there was no reply. The last of the Earp brothers of Tombstone had died at the age of eighty.

2

Hollywood Discovers Wyatt Earp

"This is the West, sir. When the legend becomes fact, print the legend."
—From *The Man Who Shot Liberty Valance* (1962)

Since the movies first flickered on the Nickelodeon screens, audiences have had a love affair with cinematic heroes. Early film producers quickly realized that stories about heroes were profitable assets at the box office. Stories about true-life heroes were an even greater draw because of the built-in name recognition with filmgoers. Between 1915 and 1927, eleven films used Davy Crockett, General George A. Custer, and "Wild Bill" Hickok as main subjects or featured characters, but not one featured Wyatt Earp.[1]

Although silent films ignored him, Earp's exploits in Dodge City and Tombstone had gotten attention from several magazine writers as early as 1919. Unfortunately, the writers played fast and loose with the facts, much to the distaste and embarrassment of Earp. "Notoriety has been the bane of my life. I detest it, and I never have put forth any effort to check the tales that have been published in recent years.... Not one of them is correct. My experiences as an officer of the law are incidents of history, but the modern writer does not seem willing to let it go at that.... My friends have urged that I make this known on the printed sheet. Perhaps I shall; it will correct many mythic writers," Earp wrote in 1925.[2]

It's interesting to note that while he was living part time in Los Angeles during the 1910s and 1920s, surrounded by the movie industry, Earp's life story was ignored by filmmakers. Notables frequently visited movie sets, posing with the stars, and were often photographed by the newsreel cameras, and that film was shown in theaters. Although there is no known newsreel footage of Wyatt Earp on any movie set, he reportedly did visit many, especially those of Tom Mix and William S. Hart. Occasionally directors made offers to Wyatt to appear in their films—but he consistently declined.

The cowboy's way of life was largely gone by the 1910s, much like that of the American Indian before him. And like the Indians, many cowboys ended up on their own form of reservation—Hollywood. Western movies were the bread and butter of all studios in the 1910s and 1920s, from the major studios like Paramount and Fox to the Poverty Row producers.[3] Above all, Westerns needed men to ride horses; and many a cowboy began a new life at wages higher than he had ever earned herding cattle. (A typical cowboy extra could earn between $5 and $10 a day compared to $30 a month working as a ranch hand.) The corner of Gower Street and Sunset Boulevard in Hollywood quickly became known as Gower Gulch, because of the large number of cowboys who would congregate there in hopes of finding work with the various small production companies that had offices in the area. (Both Tom Mix and William S. Hart employed experienced cowboys in their films as extras and wranglers.)

Wyatt Earp—increasingly agitated at the way his life was being treated by authors who paid little attention to the facts—turned to Hart, his friend and a Hollywood heavyweight, for help. Hart was the movie's top Western film star in the late teens, having quickly replaced G.M. Anderson's "Broncho Billy" character in popularity. Hart strove for accuracy in the clothing and sets of his films; however, most of his scripts were pure melodrama. The public didn't seem to care, though, making him one of the most popular stars of the silent era. Hart, born in New York, developed a deep passion for the West, where he was raised. Originally a stage actor (he played Messala in the 1899 Broadway production of *Ben-Hur*), he embraced the Western genre and boasted of being friends with many real westerners such as Bat Masterson, Charlie Russell, and Bill Tilghman.

Wyatt and Hart met in 1920 and quickly became good friends. In a July 7, 1923, letter to Hart, Wyatt expressed his frustration concerning the numerous magazine articles published about his past deeds:

> During the past few years, many wrong impressions of the early days of Tombstone and myself have been created by writers who are not informed correctly, and this has caused me a concern which I feel deeply.... any wrong impression, I want made right before I go away. The screen could do this, I know, with yourself as the master mind. Not that I want to obligate you because of our friendship but I know that I can come to you with this and other things and not feel hurt at anything you may wish to say.[4]

Although a motion picture may have seemed Earp's preferred way to tell his story, Hart suggested it should be put into book form first. Earp turned to John Flood, whom he'd known since 1906 and who handled his correspondence. Flood, who was no writer in any sense of the word, took careful notes from Earp (despite Sadie's unsolicited input) and completed his manuscript in 1926. During the writing process, Earp wrote to Hart several times, usually asking him to be his critic on the final draft. "I know that you would be my earnest critic as readily as you are my friend," he once stated to Hart.[5] The amateurishly written manuscript brought a series of rejection slips, despite the blessings of Hart, who helped submit the material to

Despite old age, Wyatt Earp still had a no-nonsense presence about him (courtesy of Jeff Morey).

publishers. "Please do not be in the least discouraged about the story coming back. It is just a matter of keeping it going until the right one gets hold of it," Hart wrote to Earp on December 6, 1926.

A letter from Anne Johnston of the Bobbs-Merrill Company to Hart reflected the opinions of other publishers regarding the Flood manuscript: "I read the Wyatt Earp manuscript with interest—at least I began it with interest.... I must confess to you that I was deeply disappointed. The material does not strike me as so fascinating as the stories of Wild Bill and Billy the Kid ... but it would show to far better advantage in a more skillfully done setting. The writing is stilted and florid and diffuse. It would be far more effective if it were simple, direct, straightforward."[6] In a letter to Earp, Hart was careful not to come out and say that the reason for the negative reception was because of

Silent film star William S. Hart befriended Wyatt Earp in the 1920s. Earp wanted Hart to do his life story as a movie, but the actor suggested that Earp first publish an autobiography (author's collection).

Flood's poor writing. Hart suggested they discuss the problem, perhaps letting Walter Noble Burns take over the book.[7] Flood readily agreed with Hart's idea, writing to the actor: "It would be a pity to have Mr. Earp's story lost to the world just for the lack of the telling of it. There are several impressions which are not correct and should be cleared up and Mr. Earp justified while he is yet alive. Now is the time, there should be no further delay."[8] Then appeared a man who would, for better or worse, launched Wyatt's story into legendary status—Stuart Lake.

Lake was a former newspaper writer and press agent for President Theodore Roosevelt's 1912 presidential campaign. He credited Bat Masterson, whom he knew from his days in New York, with sparking his idea to write about Earp. In January 1928, Lake contacted Wyatt and began what was to become a lifelong career as Earp's biographer. Lake had many conversations with Wyatt in late 1928, taking notes and following up the stories on his own to make sure the facts were right. As 1928 came to a close, Lake was suffering from the flu and had to put off any further discussions with Wyatt. By the time Lake had recovered, Wyatt's own health was deteriorating. In a January 3, 1929, letter to Earp, Hart notes that he had contacted the San Francisco office of Houghton Mifflin and that "they are very anxious to get a crack at your book. I believe this would be an excellent publishing company to handle it, and this letter shows that they are very interested."[9] In his last letter to Hart, just days before his death, Wyatt replied that he would pass along the information to Lake and keep him apprised.[10]

After Wyatt's death, Stuart Lake had to deal with the increasingly-infuriating Sadie, who realized that Wyatt's story might be her only viable source of income. Filled with illusions that this book could be a big seller, Sadie was determined that the story be told *her* way. She informed Lake that it should be "a nice, clean story." In other words, there would be no mention of Mattie, and Sadie's own past would be carefully reconstructed in the most favorable light. In September 1929, Lake signed a contract with Houghton Mifflin, with the writer splitting the royalties evenly with Sadie. As Lake continued his research, Sadie proved to be an incessant headache, often asking to see sections of the work-in-progress manuscript and dictating her ideas on how the narrative should be written, which caused their relationship to sour. In October 1931, *Wyatt Earp: Frontier Marshal* hit the bookstores. But by that time, Lake was resigned to the fact that he would be lucky to break even, let alone earn any profit from the book for all of his efforts.

Surprisingly, the book touched a nerve in the American reader. Caught in the middle of the Depression, with crime running rampant in many areas of the country, *Wyatt Earp: Frontier Marshal* was a tonic for a weary nation that had little hope. In Lake's book, Wyatt Earp was indeed the white knight who rode into town to restore law and order; democracy and the "American way" prevailed against the evildoers of society. Commenting on the problems of Tombstone, a *New York Times* book reviewer noted that those problems were "not unlike Chicago's predicament, to say nothing of New York's, and what both those cities need seems to be a few Wyatt Earps."[11]

While the book sold out its two initial print runs (more than 7,000 copies) problems with Lake's historical inaccuracies would come to haunt the Earp legend. Two of the most grievous errors were Lake's placing the gunfight inside the O.K. Corral, instead of at the nearby empty lot, and portraying Wyatt as the leading lawman in Dodge City and Tombstone, with his brothers—particularly Virgil—playing second string in all law enforcement details.[12]

Frontier Marshal was a success and provided both Lake and Sadie with monetary comfort in a time when many had no spare change. Still, Sadie was not content. Her unhappiness was exacerbated when Universal Studios announced that they would turn William R. Burnett's novel, *Saint Johnson*, into a film, *Law and Order* (1932), starring Walter Huston. Burnett's book was a thinly fictionalized rendering of the Earps' time in Tombstone, complete with the culminating shootout at the O.K. Corral. (Although Huston's character is named Frame Johnson, there is little doubt that he is patterned after Wyatt Earp.) Much like the boy who cried wolf, Sadie threatened to sue the studio, although no lawyer would take her case. Studios found a legal loophole by simply citing events as historical incidents and changing the characters' names. That same year, Stuart Lake sold the film rights of his book to Fox Pictures for $7,500, which he split with Sadie.[13] The studio immediately went to work on a script, but it also took dramatic liberties with the story. Released in 1934, *Frontier Marshal* featured George O'Brien as Michael Wyatt, because Sadie refused to let Fox use her husband's name.[14]

By 1935, the major studios had come to regard Western films as box office poison.

Opposite: In 1931, Wyatt's biography was published and the legend of Wyatt Earp began (author's collection).

WYATT EARP
Frontier Marshal

STUART N. LAKE

Their opinion was that a Western was not a major moneymaker and was at best merely a filler for the second bill, and were usually produced by B-studios such as Republic.[15] Although Warner Bros. placed their contract stars (including Humphrey Bogart, James Cagney, and Errol Flynn[16]) in Westerns during the 1930s, most of these movies were not considered major A-unit pictures.

The height of Wyatt Earp's status as a mythic figure still lay in the future; Sadie, very protective of Wyatt Earp's public image, would unfortunately not live to see them.[17] Stuart Lake became the guardian of the Earp legend, making a profitable career for himself. Every time a film was released that featured Wyatt Earp as a character, people bought his book.[18] In fact, an argument can be made that every film discussed in this book can trace its lineage and influence to Lake's book.

Like fellow Western figures Crockett, Custer, and Cody, Wyatt Earp would be transformed into a mythic legend by the movies and, later, by television. In fact, between 1939 and 1994—a fifty-five-year span—Wyatt Earp was either the central or a featured character in sixteen films, five television movies, and one television series.[19] In comparison, there were fourteen films, five television movies, and one short-lived television series for Custer. Buffalo Bill Cody was featured in twelve films and nine television movies, while Davy Crockett was the subject of seven films, one television movie, and two television series (both produced by Walt Disney Productions).

Wyatt Earp would be immortalized as a true hero of the American West, becoming the persona of the stalwart, heroic figure moviegoers would come to expect on the silver screen. Earp, because of Lake's book and the subsequent films, served as the prototype of other lawman characters in films and television, notably James Arness' Matt Dillon on the *Gunsmoke* television series. The debut of the TV series *The Life and Legend of Wyatt Earp* in 1955 (debuting the same year and week as *Gunsmoke*) brought

The Life and Legend of Wyatt Earp premiered in September of 1955, running for six years. The TV series, which starred Hugh O'Brian, followed Earp from his lawman days in Kansas to the famous gunfight in Tombstone (author's collection).

Earp into the living rooms of millions across the country. At that moment in 1955, television made Wyatt Earp more popular than any movie featuring him. Stuart Lake, who served as the show's consultant, saw his book reprinted once again, *and* wrote a children's version of the Earp saga. Hugh O'Brian embodied the myth of Wyatt Earp and became, next to Matt Dillon and Paladin (*Have Gun—Will Travel*), one of the most popular television Western heroes of the late 1950s and early 1960s.

Until 1967, Wyatt Earp would be held up as a shining example of everything that was right with the law and those who wore the badge. However, the Vietnam War and the political and social unrest of the late 1960s would alter the way some filmmakers viewed Earp's heroics. Indeed, like many heroes and the West itself, Wyatt Earp would be the

Premiering the same week as the Earp TV series, *Gunsmoke* began a 20-year run on CBS. The character of Marshal Matt Dillon, played by James Arness, was said to be a composite of Earp and other Dodge City lawmen (author's collection).

subject of revisionist filmmakers out to debunk the long-held myths. In the 1970s, the television series *Police Story* aired an episode titled "The Wyatt Earp Syndrome," about a police officer who is too zealous and hard-nosed in his work, which eventually alienates him from society and his family. (The story was originally titled "The John Wayne Syndrome"—the term psychologists at the time used to describe this trait—but changed it when the actor threatened to sue.) Wyatt's exploits, be they good or bad, were fodder for ridicule and demystifying by filmmakers. By the 1970s, the term "O.K. Corral" was shorthand for any type of a conflict, especially one involving gunfire. Even the television series *Star Trek* used the gunfight as an allegory of senseless violence, with Kirk, Spock, and others taking the place of the Clantons and McLaurys.[20]

Yet by the 1990s, serious historians began to uncover more information relating to Earp and his time in Tombstone. Although it was still fashionable to debunk the legend, a balance of sorts was being struck among scholars and filmmakers. Earp was no longer the saint or white knight, but neither was he a cold-blooded, deceptive man behind a badge. A more balanced, honest portrayal of Wyatt Earp was coming to the movie screen.

To understand the creation of a mythical film hero, we have to go back to the beginning. With the United States slowly emerging from the dark clouds of the Depression and another, darker storm brewing in both the Atlantic and Pacific, filmmakers found a story, and a hero, that audiences could look to for strength and hope. The Western genre has always provided that for audiences. The heroes are figures of action. Their word is their bond. When the law is absent, they step in to administer it and vanquish evil. The open spaces of the Western frontier offer hope, imagination, dreams, and the optimism of a new sunrise—or a new sunset. More than any other actual Western figure, Wyatt Earp provided audiences (and filmmakers) those qualities in a film, even if doing so stretched the fabric of truth.

In 1939, the cinematic legend of Wyatt Earp was born.

3

Frontier Marshal (1939)

"You must be all right. If you wasn't, a great fella like Doc wouldn't have liked you."

There will never be another year for motion pictures like 1939. Film scholars and movie buffs readily agree that no year has seen so many movies released that were both critical and box-office successes. In just that one year, audiences saw *The Private Lives of Elizabeth and Essex, Dark Victory, Juarez, Beau Geste, Wuthering Heights, Of Mice and Men, Gunga Din, The Hunchback of Notre Dame, You Can't Cheat an Honest Man, Son of Frankenstein, Babes in Arms, Gone With the Wind, The Wizard of Oz, Drums Along the Mohawk, The Little Princess,* and *Young Mr. Lincoln.*

The Western film also had its share of successes that year. Many film scholars and academics have claimed that it was John Ford's *Stagecoach* that proved to Hollywood that an A-budget Western could earn both critical respect and profits. However, that claim isn't quite true.

A look at the films released in 1939 by the major studios shows that most released one A-budget Western that year. *Dodge City* (Warner Bros.), *Jesse James* (20th Century-Fox), *Union Pacific* (Paramount), *Destry Rides Again* (Universal), and *Stagecoach* (United Artists) were all considered A-budget films by their respective studios. (Both *Dodge City* and *Jesse James* were released in Technicolor, which increased their standing in the A-budget field.) Even MGM jumped onto the bandwagon with *Let Freedom Ring,* a Western melodrama that sported Nelson Eddy singing "The Star Spangled Banner" at the climax! Ford's *Stagecoach* certainly showed that an A-Western could be a critical and box office hit—it was the only Western nominated for Best Picture of 1939. The Western was far from dead.

However, Hollywood studios couldn't survive on A-pictures alone. The B films, or programmers as they were called in the industry, were, for the most part, the bread and butter of the studio system. Each of the major studios released a certain number of programmers, often featuring a single star under contract or one who freelanced. Other programmers featured up-and-coming performers under contract as a way of gauging their talent. One of the bright sides of these programmers (as well as of A-pictures) was their casts of great character actors. Some of these performers, who still rarely get the credit they richly deserve, could make even the dullest picture bearable, giving life and depth to the barest of bit parts.

The programmers, like their A counterparts, worked within the studio system like well-oiled machines. Most of these lower budget productions had shorter shooting schedules, sometimes as few as ten days or as many as thirty, with everyone involved working six days a week. Sets were rarely scrapped; they were simply stored to be dusted off and, with some minor alterations, used for a new film later on. The same was true for a studio's vast wardrobe and prop departments. Everything was recycled, even stories. The term A budget and B

31

budget (or A film and B film) generally referred to the movie's budget, length of time in production, number of stars, and so on. Most major studios had a B unit during the days of the studio system that produced smaller, lower budgeted fare to be teamed on a double-bill. For instance, the *Andy Hardy* series from MGM and the *Blondie* series from Columbia were considered B films. In those days, studios used the block-booking system, by which theatre exchanges were offered perhaps a half dozen A films while being required to take a number of that studio's B films, whose quality could range from very good to awful. This action eventually spelled the end of the studio system when the Supreme Court issued a 1948 ruling called the Paramount Decree. According to the decree, studios had to divest themselves of their theatre holdings. This, along with the birth of television, helped spell the end of B films from the major studios.

With Westerns showing a growing popularity at the 1939 box office, Darryl F. Zanuck, head of production at 20th Century-Fox, dusted off a project the studio had made previously in 1934. The story of Wyatt Earp and his exploits in the mining town of Tombstone was perfect material for the company's programmer unit.

Zanuck had emerged as one of the industry's major moguls by the mid–1930s. Aside from Irving Thalberg, he was considered to be the most hands-on studio head in the business, taking a very active role in story conferences and helping shape completed films in the editing room. Zanuck, born in 1902 in Nebraska, began in movies writing stories for the Rin-Tin-Tin films at Warner Bros. He was extremely prolific, often turning out nineteen scripts in a year under his own name or using one of three pseudonyms. He formed 20th Century Pictures in 1933 and two years later merged with Fox Pictures, with the new corporation known as 20th Century-Fox.[1]

Frontier Marshal was turned over to Sol Wurtzel, the producer who oversaw all of the B-unit films at the studio.[2] Wurtzel's choice for director was veteran Allan Dwan, who began his film career in 1911. Dwan was one of the most respected directors of the silent era, helming many of the best Gloria Swanson and Douglas Fairbanks films.[3] By the mid–1930s, Dwan was working at Fox on mostly B pictures, although he did direct such A pictures as *Suez*, *Heidi*, and *Rebecca of Sunnybrook Farm*, the latter two starring Fox's biggest star, Shirley Temple. Dwan told film historian Kevin Brownlow that Wyatt Earp once visited the set of his 1915 film, *The Half-Breed*, which had starred Douglas Fairbanks:

> As was the custom in those days, he was invited to join the party and mingle with our background action. I think there was a trial of some kind. A group of people demanded that the half-breed be sent out of town. In that group was Earp; he only stood there and nodded his head.... I think he was timid about being photographed, about acting and pretending. He knew inside himself that he wasn't an actor and had nothing to offer. I remember he saw Fairbanks bouncing around in the trees, and he said, "Oh no, I'd like not to do that." And I think for that reason he just finally took one last look and left.[4]*

With Dwan on board, the script, by Sam Hellman, quickly took shape. Using the 1934 script as a guideline, Hellman changed much of the storyline and gave more attention to the relationship between Doc Halliday (with an "a") and Sarah Allen.[5] *Frontier Marshal* opens with the discovery of silver—and a new boom town, Tombstone, is born. Ben Carter, a man of dubious reputation, has just opened his Palace of Pleasure saloon, but the competing Bella Union proves to be more popular. The Palace doubles as a base of operations for robbing

Both Earp historian Jeff Morey and this author have independently reviewed The Half-Breed *and there is no one who even remotely resembles Wyatt Earp in the courtroom scene.*

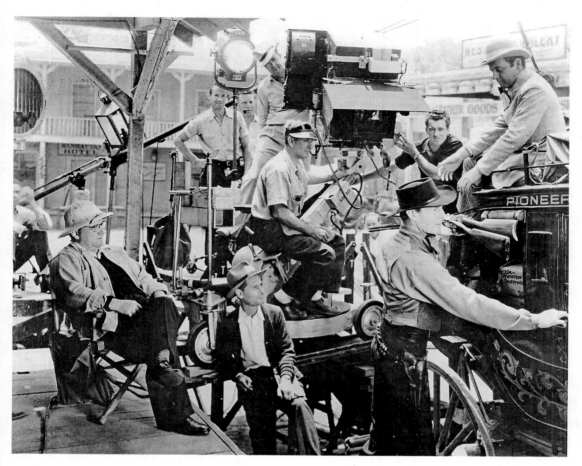

Director Allan Dwan (left, sitting in chair) watches Randolph Scott (right, in dark hat) and Eddie Foy, Jr. (seated on top of stagecoach), during a rehearsal for *Frontier Marshal* (courtesy of the Academy of Motion Picture Arts and Sciences).

the stagecoach line of its silver shipments, with Carter's assistant, Curley Bill, usually carrying out the robberies. A drunken Indian Charlie begins to shoot up the Bella Union. When the town marshal refuses to enter and disarm him, Wyatt Earp steps in to handle the job. Earp is offered the now-vacant position of town marshal but refuses. Earp is a threat to Carter's operations, and after being kidnapped, beaten, and left to die on a mesa by some of Carter's men, Earp changes his mind about the job offer. As marshal, he quickly cleans up the town. Catching Jerry, a dance hall girl, helping a gambler cheat during a poker game, Earp dumps her into a horse trough. Jerry begs Doc Halliday, a former physician and deadly gunfighter, to defend her and kill Earp. However, Earp and Doc quickly become friends. Sarah Allen, Doc's former fiancé, arrives in town. When Doc pleads with Sarah to leave, she reluctantly agrees.

Brooding over his lost relationship with Sarah, Doc begins to drink heavily, eventually firing his gun in the saloon. Wyatt buffaloes Doc and takes him to his room, then asks Sarah to stay, telling her that she is the only person who can save Doc's life. Jerry, meanwhile, tips off Carter that Wyatt will be riding shotgun messenger on the next day's stagecoach with a valuable silver shipment. The stage leaves the following morning with Wyatt and Doc, who

Mayor Henderson (Harry Hayden) pins the marshal's badge on Wyatt (Randolph Scott), as the former town marshal (Ward Bond, standing behind Hayden), Pete (Chris-Pin Martin, center), and Dave Hall (Dell Henderson, right) look on. Both Ward Bond and Chris-Pin Martin appeared in other film versions of the Earp–O.K. Corral story (author's collection).

get into a gun battle when Carter's gang attempts to rob the stage. Carter is killed, and Wyatt and Doc return to Tombstone with the silver shipment.

Walking across the street, Wyatt is caught in an ambush by several of Carter's men. During the gunfight, a young boy is severely wounded. With the town's doctor away, Doc is forced to operate on the boy, with the aid of Sarah. The surgery is successful, but as Doc and Sarah walk out of the saloon, he is killed by Curley Bill and some of his men. Curley Bill challenges Wyatt to a showdown at the O.K. Corral down the street. Wyatt engages in a gunfight, killing all but Curley, who is shot down by Jerry. Sarah chooses to stay in Tombstone after Doc's death, while Jerry leaves the now-civilized town.

Hellman's script played fast and loose with the facts, and the overall story bears little resemblance to Lake's book. Among the factual errors are renaming Holliday as Halliday and omission of any of the Earp brothers from the story. In *Frontier Marshal*, Wyatt is a former U.S. Army scout for General Nelson A. Miles, with no mention of Earp's serving as a law officer in any town. The gunfight takes place at night, with Wyatt against five men. There is no Ike or Billy Clanton, no McLaury brother; only Curley Bill from the Cowboy faction is named. (Ben Carter and his gang were fictional characters.) Nor is there any vendetta ride. Hellman has mainly used the bare basics of the Earp-Tombstone saga to create a purely fictional story. Although Zanuck and Wurtzel may have been happy with the script, others were not—mainly Stuart Lake and Sadie Earp.

Lake stated in a letter to Fox that when he made his deal in 1932 with the studio, he had been orally promised that he would "be employed on the adaptation and screenplay.... They sent for me a half-dozen times to come up and talk over things.... Then, to my amazed disappointment, *Wyatt Earp* [the original title for the 1934 film] was thrown as a sop to Sol Lesser and George O'Brien.... I was left out of pocket and time. But from the first day I talked to Wurtzel, I had sense enough not to tell him, or his help, all that I knew [about Earp]."[6]

Even more unhappy with the studio was Sadie. In a very dramatic letter to Wurtzel, dated June 17, 1939, she complains that the script she read was not the life story of the Wyatt Earp she knew. Among her complaints were that Doc Holliday was more prominent a character in this script version and overshadowed Earp (which is partly true) and that he was a frequenter of saloons, a brawler, and an associate of cheap individuals. She also objected to Wyatt's slapping Jerry and dumping her into the horse trough, something she contends he would never have done. Sadie went on to bemoan the missing Johnny-behind-the-deuce incident, no gunfight at Iron Springs, and no stories from Wichita or Dodge City. In a truly melodramatic sentence, Sadie claims that, in retrospect, she believes that it was Providence that made Earp a man and placed him in that hour of winning the West. Ending the letter, Sadie writes, "You can produce the script that you handed me to read, if you choose; that is within your charge—but you cannot use the name of Wyatt Earp, my husband!" She signed it *Mrs. Wyatt Earp*. The studio sent a carefully worded letter saying that there would be nothing in the film that would be deemed derogatory to the memory of any person portrayed in the movie.

Director Allan Dwan recalled to Peter Bogdanovich that Sadie wanted to sue because "we had given Wyatt Earp a love affair with Nancy Kelly [who played Sarah in the film] and all that. She said it was misrepresentation, that it never happened—and she was right. We never meant it to *be* Wyatt Earp—we were just making *Frontier Marshal*, and that could be any frontier marshal."[7]

The June 1, 1939, script draft of *Frontier Marshal* mirrors the completed movie fairly closely, although some things were changed during filming. The movie opens with a montage sequence of Ed Schieffelin making his silver discovery and crowds of people rushing to the new site as it grows into a town. In the scripted montage were scenes that were cut from the final print. In one, a man rushes to the doctor to help his wife with the delivery of a child, followed by a scene with a buxom woman who runs a boarding house. A miner asks her about a room; she tells him that if he's willing to sleep six to a room for $10 a day, as well as furnish his own bedding, space is available. Another deleted scene shows a wagon dropping a load of lumber, then an assay tent opening for business. One man in line emerges jubilant, while another is downcast. The happy man says he has $20,000 to a ton, but the other man has only lead. The following scene shows the tent of the Tombstone *Epitaph*, where the editor reads his article about the death of Big Nose Jackson. "If the town can stay ahead of burial ground, Tombstone will flourish," he states. (In the finished movie, this scene actually takes place in a building, where we see a sign reading "Tombstone *Epitaph*" in the window.)[8]

Other sequences in the June 1, 1939, script that were missing or changed in the final cut include these:

• After Wyatt shoots Indian Charlie, several "dead bodies" lying on the saloon floor get up and run out. Carter and Curley Bill watch Wyatt leave the saloon and Curley Bill draws his gun to shoot Wyatt, but is stopped by Carter.

• When Wyatt gets up from a gambling table, he gestures for Jerry to follow him. As they go near the door, he grabs her wrist, pulling her outside. In the film, Wyatt grabs her wrist at the gambling table and takes her outside the saloon.

• Halliday confronts Wyatt at the gambling table. As he's about to challenge him to a gunfight, he starts coughing. Blackmore, another gambler, draws his derringer and, as Earp grabs it, a shot goes off harmlessly. In the film, his derringer just drops on the table as Wyatt stops him.

• When Eddie Foy is kidnapped and taken to the Palace of Pleasure, the people in audience yell "Kalamazoo!" as Foy comes on stage. The script notes that "Kalamazoo in Michigan" was one of Foy's most famous songs, but does not describe Foy's act. It simply notes: "Shots of Foy and audience as he does his stuff—as much as we desire."

• When Doc is shot outside the Bella Union, Jerry runs up and sobs uncontrollably. The script notes that Doc opens his eyes and "there is trace of a faint smile on his lips," as he says "It's better—this way" before dying.

The gunfight in the script is vastly different from the one in the film. In the June 1 draft, Mayor Henderson tells Wyatt that there is a great deal of silver in the Express office and urges him to cover the building with two deputies. After Doc's death, Curley Bill is told by one of his men that Earp is in the Express office. Looking out the window, Wyatt sees something and tells the deputies, "Let 'em have it." They open fire, killing two of Curley Bill's men, while other men shoot into the Express office. One of the deputies is shot in the throat. As the shooting continues, Jerry and Sarah try to move Doc's body into the Bella Union. Back in the Express office, the second deputy is shot and dies.

Mayor Henderson joins in the fight from the Bella Union, shooting at Curley Bill's men. Earp is grazed on the forehead and takes cover behind an iron safe in the Express office. Curley Bill orders three men to attack the rear of the building while he and two others rush the front. As Curley Bill's men try to force the front door of the Express office, Wyatt uses a ceiling trapdoor to get onto the roof, then drops to the ground. Taking a position at the end of the street, he waits for the men to exit the Express office, then fires into them. Wyatt shoots at Curley Bill as he tries to mount a horse; the animal rears up and runs off. As Curley tries to mount another horse, Jerry grabs a gun from the body of one of the bandits and fires several times, killing Curley Bill. She shouts to Doc's lifeless body, "I got him for you, Doc! I got him for you!" The sequence fades out.[9]

Obviously not entirely happy with the gunfight as it was originally written, Hellman revised the entire gunfight on June 28. As Halliday and Sarah walk out of the saloon, he is shot by Curley Bill, who calls Earp out, telling him they'll wait for him at the O.K. Corral. Mayor Henderson offers to form a posse to help, but Wyatt says, "No, this is my fight." Taking a shotgun from behind the bar and borrowing an additional pistol from a man in the saloon, Wyatt heads to the confrontation. As he comes out of the saloon, he looks at Doc's body and says, "Sorry you can't come along, Doc, but this fight's all for you." (This was cut from the final print.)

Taking a position at the corner of a building next to the O.K. Corral, Wyatt places the shotgun on top of some crates and fires. He then leaves, giving the impression he is still there while he slips into the building. Coming out the back, Wyatt is now in the corral and sneaks up behind Curley Bill, getting the drop on him. He orders the other men to drop their guns and come out. Indian Charlie, who is on top of some sacks of grain behind Wyatt, throws his knife at Wyatt but misses. Wyatt fires at Indian Charlie as Curley Bill makes his escape. Looking at his body, Wyatt says, "So they got you out of jail, Charlie? I guess that saves us the trouble of hanging you." (This line was cut from the film.) Two more men shoot at Wyatt. He kills them as Curley Bill pulls a rifle from a saddle and fires at Wyatt. Jerry grabs Doc's gun and kills Curley, saying, "I got him for you, Doc! I got him for you!" Before the sequence fades out, Wyatt walks up to the body of Curley Bill and says, "I wanted you alive, Curley, but maybe it's better this way." (This line also was cut from the film.)[10]

Once the script for *Frontier Marshal* was completed, it was submitted to the Production Code Authority for approval. Censorship of motion pictures had begun almost as soon as movies first flickered on the screen. Actions by church and civic groups, concerned that films would corrupt the morals of the public, led to each state forming its own censor board. These boards deemed which films or story elements were or were not offensive. In some cases, one state censor board would take exception to certain scenes in a film and order them removed, while a neighboring state board would allow those very same scenes to be shown. This situation created a headache for the filmmakers. In 1922, with the federal government threatening to oversee the censorship of movies because of pressure from church and social groups, the film industry quickly agreed to police itself.[11] The supervision of the Motion Picture Producers Distributors Association (MPPDA) was given to the former postmaster general, Will Hays, who drafted a set of rules for the producers to follow. (This organization was often called simply called the Hays Office, and Hays was dubbed "The Czar of All the Rushes.") The MPPDA managed to calm the critics—for a while.

On March 31, 1930, the MPPDA board adopted the Code to Maintain Social and Community Values. Producers were not required to follow the Code—and many did not. Many of the movies made during the years 1930–33 contained suggestive dialogue and situations, which led to another call for censorship of films. (This period in film history is known as pre–Code, as are the films.) This time the Hollywood studios couldn't ignore the threats. In 1934, the Legion of Decency, a Catholic-based group, promised to launch a nationwide boycott by all Catholics against the film industry unless a more rigid code of censorship was established. Facing another serious challenge to their business, Hollywood studios agreed, and a new code was drafted. The Production Code Authority took effect on July 1, 1934, headed by Joseph Breen. (It was often referred by the industry as PCA or the Breen Office.) Under the agreement, all producers who were members of the MPPDA (which included all major studios in Hollywood) had to submit scripts as well as the finished movie before being issued a certificate of approval. Without such a certificate, the film could not be shown in theaters.[12]

Breen wrote a letter to Jason Joy, a Fox executive, on June 1, 1939, concerning *Frontier Marshal*. The PCA was "happy to report that it seems to meet the basic requirements of the Production Code."[13] However, Breen did issue some "minor" points of contention with the script. During a fight between Curley Bill and another man, it was suggested the filmmakers eliminate Curley kicking the man on the floor. Breen also suggested that when Wyatt hits Doc over the head with the gun barrel, it should be done out of frame to avoid deletion. He also suggested that the operation on young Pablo be done by suggestion and not show any detail. "Please bear in mind the British censor board will probably delete the whole operation sequence," Breen wrote. As far as the final gunfight, Breen asked that they "please keep down the number of killings" and "avoid any showing of unnecessary slaughter." He also recommended that they omit the scene of Curley Bill's horse being shot out from under him "and any scenes of horses falling."[14]

Not only did the script have to receive PCA approval, but also any song used in a film had to have the lyrics approved. On July 3, Fox requested approval for three songs for the film: "Down Went McGinty," "Frontier Marshal," and "For I Was Born in Kalamazoo." The studio was given approval that same day.[15] (The latter two songs were replaced by the time the film was released.)

One final issue held up *Frontier Marshal* from receiving its PCA approval seal. On July 14, Breen wrote to Joy at Fox that they would have to eliminate a line Halliday delivers to a saloon girl as he pushes her aside: "Not tonight, Josephine." Until the studio notified the PCA in writing that this had been cut, the PCA would not give its seal of approval. On July 19, a PCA form was filed that the line had been cut, and the approval seal was issued.[16]

With the script completed, Wurtzel and Dwan turned their attention to casting the film. Randolph Scott was chosen to play Earp. Scott, who had entered films in 1927 doing bit parts, eventually landed roles as a romantic lead before moving on to Westerns. During this period in his career, he was playing leading roles in top-grade B films and supporting leads in many A pictures. His film credits up to this point varied from playing an uncredited "beast" in *Island of Lost Souls* (1932) to appearing in a Fred Astaire and Ginger Rogers musical, *Follow the Fleet* (1936) and in plenty of Westerns, including the 1936 version of *The Last of the Mohicans* and *Jesse James*. From 1945 until 1962, all of Scott's films were Westerns, including several made in the 1950s with director Budd Boetticher. With his last film, *Ride the High Country* (1962), Scott retired from films. He passed away in 1987.

Cesar Romero, who was under contract to 20th Century-Fox at the time, was given the role of Doc. Romero started out as a ballroom dancer and then moved to Broadway before entering films in 1933. He was under contract to Fox for many years, appearing in a variety of movies, including *Clive of India* (1935), *Wee Willie Winkie* (1937), and *Captain From Castile* (1947), as well as playing the Cisco Kid in five B films. One of his most famous roles was as the Joker in the *Batman* television series (and feature film) of the 1960s. He retired in 1990 and died four years later at the age of 87.

For the role of the saloon girl, Jerry, Sol Wurtzel and Allan Dwan considered several actresses including Claire Trevor, Kay Francis, Ann Sothern, Frances Farmer, and Dorothy Lamour, before giving the role to Binnie Barnes. The role of Sarah went to Nancy Kelly, who was a contract player at the studio. John Carradine, who would have made a great Doc Holliday, was signed to play Ben Carter. Dwan filled the rest of the cast with the familiar faces of such character actors as Chris-Pin Martin, Lon Chaney, Jr., Joe Sawyer, Dell Henderson, Hank Mann, Dick Elliott, and Philo McCullough. Two actors who appeared in *Frontier Marshal* hold the record of appearing in three films based on Wyatt Earp and the famous gunfight: Ward Bond and Charlie Stevens. Bond, a respected character actor, appeared in the 1934 and 1939 versions of *Frontier Marshal* (he plays the town marshal who refuses to go after Indian Charlie in the 1939 version) and as Morgan Earp in *My Darling Clementine* (1946). Charlie Stevens, who was reportedly a grandson of Geronimo, played the same role of Indian Charlie in three versions: *Frontier Marshal*, *Tombstone: The Town Too Tough to Die* (1942), and *My Darling Clementine* (1946).[17]

For the role of Eddie Foy, Dwan looked no further than Eddie Foy, Jr., the son of the famous entertainer and a well-known actor and comedian in his own right. This marked the first of six times Foy would play his father in films and television.[18] Interestingly, the senior Foy

Doc (Cesar Romero, left) gets the drop on Pringle (Lon Chaney, Jr.), while Eddie Foy (played by his son, Eddie Foy, Jr.) is rescued by Wyatt Earp (Randolph Scott) (courtesy of the Academy of Motion Picture Arts and Sciences).

claimed in his 1928 autobiography that he played the famous Bird Cage Theatre in Tombstone just weeks before the famous gunfight. This claim seems to be more fanciful than factual, however, because neither Foy nor his act was mentioned in any of the Tombstone newspapers when he was supposed to be there (summer of 1881). What adds to the suspicion is that the Bird Cage Theatre did not open until December 1881, when Foy was performing in San Francisco.[19]

On Monday, June 5, Allan Dwan headed a company of 50 people up to Lone Pine, California, for four days of location work.[20] Lone Pine had been a favorite location for filmmakers ever since the silent era. The rugged locations served as a perfect backdrop for the Westerns that were filmed in the area, especially around what is known as the Alabama Hills. (Randolph Scott would film several of his 1950s Westerns in this area.) Aside from numerous Westerns, Lone Pine has also served as the location for such films as *Gunga Din*, *High Sierra*, *Bad Day at Black Rock*, *King of the Khyber Rifles*, *The Charge of the Light Brigade*, *Brigham Young*, and *The Great Race*. For the company of *Frontier Marshal*, the location would provide background footage as well as the location for the stagecoach robbery shootout, the sequences of Earp being beaten by Curley Bill and his men, and Earp's retribution fight with Curley. The latter two scenes required Randolph Scott to rush up to location for a day's work and then return to Columbia Studios to finish his work on *Coast Guard* before reporting for work on *Frontier Marshal*.

The company returned from location on Friday, June 9, and the following day began filming the montage sequences on a Western street set on the Fox back lot. Dwan had a cast of 250 bit players and extras for the montage sequences, which were all shot in one day. Before shooting could begin, however, a mess had to be cleaned up. When Dwan was making *Suez* (1938) for the studio, he had put many tons of sand in one area of the back lot to make it look like a desert. When he finished the film, someone asked him what they should do with the sand. Dwan later told Peter Bogdanovich, "I said, 'Well, some sucker will have to move it out of here.' When *Frontier Marshal* came along, I induced Zanuck to let me build a Western street back there but in order to do that, the sand had to be moved. So *I* was the sucker!"[21] Building a set for a B budget was unheard of. However, Dwan had a plan: "I told Zanuck I'd put one up for peanuts if he'd let me do it my way. I knew where there were all kinds of Western fronts around the lot from way back in the time of Tom Mix—I'd used them in the old days. So I got a regular moving company to come over at night with their trucks, and we dragged all the sets over and put them up in two cross streets. This wonderful Western street lasted there quite a while."[22]

With Randolph Scott still tied up with *Coast Guard* at Columbia, Dwan had to rearrange the shooting schedule, filming around him. Despite this setback, Dwan managed to complete principal filming on July 8, 1939, ahead of schedule and saving $40,000 on the $500,000 budget.[23] *Frontier Marshal*, which was shot in 33 days (including the Lone Pine location), not only set a record for speedy completion of movies its size, but it is also a testimony to the productivity of the studio system. With photography completed on July 8, the film was edited and sound effects, optical effects, musical score, and main titles added before its public release on July 28, 1939!

Zanuck had originally wanted to title the film *Frontier Marshal: The Story of Wyatt Earp*. However, both Zanuck and Wurtzel agreed that a title change was necessary to avoid any legal headaches from Sadie Earp. They came up with *Frontier Marshal: The Saga of Tombstone, Arizona*, but then shortened it to simply *Frontier Marshal*.

Upon its release, the film garnered positive reviews. The industry trade paper, *Variety*, commented, "Picture unfolds as acceptable and lusty melodrama of the early west for general audience appeal.... A fast shooting, six-gun type of melodrama, it carries particular appeal for general audiences.... Picture is chockfull of dramatic action, neatly seat up in the script and transferred to the screen by vivid and fast-paced direction."

Motion Picture Herald, a trade magazine for the industry and theatre owners, noted, "A roaring melodrama with guns blazing lethally from start to finish and the story of Tombstone, Arizona, in its untempered youth, told in terms of a personal story well worth telling. Brought to the screen without benefit of bombastic ballyhoo, it stacks up with anything in kind recently released.... Allan Dwan's direction is as swift and sure as the heroic sheriff's six-gun, which is lightning." *The New York Times* was equally full of praise for the film: "The story of Wyatt Earp, who brought law to Tombstone, Ariz., belongs to frontier folklore; to have touched it at all and not to have made a great Western out of it would have been a cinematic crime.... With a grand cast, and excellent job of directing by Allan Dwan, Mr. Earp's screen biography becomes entirely worthy of its fabulous subject.... The players fit their parts with such perfection that it is hard to know whether to credit the actor or the casting director.... In short, *Frontier Marshal* is a cracking good Western, and in the movies there's nothing much better than that."

Looking past the historical inaccuracies, *Frontier Marshal* is indeed an enjoyable Western, reminiscent of the genre shown at the local movie theatre on a Saturday afternoon. It has a stalwart hero, loyal friends, comic relief, good versus evil, and lot of action. Is it as insightful as Ford's *Stagecoach*? Not at all. Is it accurate about Earp's life or the events leading up to the gunfight? Hardly. But *Frontier Marshal* entertains, which was its main (and some say *only*) purpose. Allan Dwan has taken historical folklore and fashioned it into a rousing, energetic Western. It has a gloss and workman-like quality one expects from a major Hollywood studio during the golden years. Even though the budget was modest, there is no skimping on the visuals. The set of the main street of Tombstone, which would be featured in other Fox Westerns, looks fresh and vibrant. For a B picture, there is a lot of action on the street, which is in part the result of the director's touches. Dwan knew from his years of experience how to take a little and make it look like a lot. The montage sequence has a vibrancy and energy to it that is seen in many of the classic films (Western and non–Westerns) from the period. We get a strong sense in just a few quick shots of what the frenzy to build Tombstone may have been like. This sets up the energy of the film.

The introduction to the lawless element in Tombstone begins during the montage, as we see men shooting at each other, and carries into the scene in which Curley Bill arrives with stolen money from a recent stage hold-up. By being introduced to the criminal element this way, the audience knows almost immediately who the villains are in this story. This is a simplistic way of looking at a film, but in B films, unlike their A counterparts, time was of the essence to tell the story. Audiences of a B film, especially the Western or a crime melodrama, came expecting the basics of the plot to be set up within the first fifteen minutes. From there, the audience could watch the story progress to the inevitable conclusion. That is not to say that a genre film could not have its own twists and turns, but the audience had certain expectations, with the hero besting the villain before riding off into the sunset at the final fade out. (This is also the case with most dramatic television series.) Dwan displays a nice, albeit melodramatic, touch to illustrate the lawlessness in Tombstone. We see a young mother holding her baby in the comfort of her small room, singing a lullaby. Suddenly gunshots ring out, startling the mother, as the camera pulls back and out onto the main street of Tombstone. The gunfire causes horses to rear, and panic erupts in the streets.

This sets up the entrance of the hero. The mayor, town marshal, owner of the Bella Union and other citizens gather on the steps of the hotel veranda to tell the marshal to do his duty and arrest Indian Charlie. However, the marshal is a coward. He knows the reputation of Indian Charlie and will not risk his life. From off camera we hear a strong, clear voice, "Nice lot of law you got here." All look up to the second-story balcony, where we see the film's hero, Wyatt Earp, looking down at them. The composition of Dwan's shot has the town members looking up at Earp, as if he's their salvation or savior. (Heroes in most films, but especially Westerns, are usually established with the camera looking upward at them, indicating a dominance of character.) Earp descends to the porch by climbing down from the balcony, which could be viewed as another metaphor of the hero stepping down off his great steed and coming onto common ground. Earp does not put on a gun belt; he sticks the gun under his waist belt. This sets up the belief that Indian Charlie will best him, but the audience knows better. It also makes Earp's actions all the more heroic because he is at something of a disadvantage (no gunbelt to holster his gun) for a gunfight. Besting Indian Charlie by grazing him with a bullet, Earp drags the body out as if it weren't a difficult job. (In the other films with the Indian Charlie character, Earp hits him over the head.) The screenwriter has established Earp as the man who can handle lawlessness but is a reluctant hero. He refuses the job of marshal, claiming he wants to open a stage line, one of the few accurate facts about Earp in this movie.

Wyatt checks a body during Indian Charlie's rampage in the Oriental Saloon (author's collection).

In a story that features a reluctant hero, some action must occur (such as the killing of an innocent woman, child or a best friend) that forces the protagonist into action. In this case, it is Earp who is kidnapped and beaten up by Curley Bill and two other men. Left out on the mesa, Earp is forced to walk back to town. Hearing the laughter of Curley Bill and his men from Carter's saloon, he makes his decision to pin on the badge. Earp, with the assistance of the mayor, takes Curley Bill and the two men back out to the mesa, where Earp has a one-on-one fistfight with Curley Bill—a typical action of the Western hero defeating his opponent without any aid. After beating Curley Bill, Earp tells the men they'd better leave, and he rides off. The stage is now set for a confrontation.

Another aspect common in the Western genre is a conflict between two men who may or may not be good friends. This motif can be seen in numerous Westerns, such as the relationships between John Wayne and Montgomery Clift in *Red River*, James Stewart and Stephen McNally in *Winchester '73*, Joel McCrea and Randolph Scott in *Ride the High Country* and John Wayne and Robert Mitchum in *El Dorado*, not to mention all of the films featuring the Earp-Holliday bond. In *Frontier Marshal*, this situation develops when Wyatt catches Jerry, the saloon girl, helping a gambler cheat at poker. After Wyatt dumps her in a horse trough, Doc Halliday confronts Earp, challenging him to a gunfight. The confrontation is interrupted when Wyatt protects Doc, who has a severe coughing fit, from a gambler trying to draw a derringer on Doc. The two adversaries quickly become friends and

Wyatt catches Jerry (Binnie Barnes, standing) helping the gambler (Arthur Aylesworth, left), while two other card players (Eddie Dunn, center, and William Pawley, right) look on (author's collection).

share a drink—with Doc drinking milk! The bond in this version is quickly established, with Scott and Romero developing a real warmth between their Wyatt and Doc.[24] In this film, Wyatt acts as Doc's conscience, something that will be reversed in later versions.

Doc's illness is never established in the film. We know he coughs, and the bartender tells Wyatt that if Doc ever wanted to end his life, he'd start drinking heavily. There is no mention of his having tuberculosis, although it's *hinted* that he may have heart trouble. The illness is what has made him a feared killer and what drove him away from his only love, Sarah, who has tracked him down. The memory of what Doc once was has come back to haunt him. This subplot takes on great weight in the story, overshadowing the Wyatt Earp character. Sarah is determined not to give up on Doc, until a coughing fit brings Jerry to comfort him. Sarah, realizing the truth, will leave. The romantic triangle between Doc, Sarah ("the good girl"), and Jerry ("the bad girl") will set up Doc's reformation before the final reel. Sarah's arrival starts Doc's downward spiral, with awareness of what he could have been. Looking at himself in the mirror behind the bar at the Bella Union, he says, "I don't like you," and shoots at his reflection.[25]

Wyatt is the one to realize that Doc's only chance of survival (from whatever he's suffering from) is if Sarah stays, which she agrees to do. She reminds Doc in a later conversation of his love of medicine and begs him not to run away from whatever is wrong. When young Pablo is seriously wounded, Doc is forced to return to his former career, and in the end, it regenerates and reforms his character. With the town's doctor away, he must perform a delicate surgery despite being wounded in the arm. Sarah and he work as a team, although Jerry's character displays her hidden decency when the child's life is in danger by getting Sarah to help and by obtaining medical supplies. The surgery is successful, and Doc's redemption takes hold—from being a cold killer to becoming a lifesaver. Leaving the Bella Union after the surgery, Sarah asks Doc, "Isn't it better to save a life than take one?" Doc agrees—and as they step outside, he is gunned down by Curley Bill. Although Doc tries to draw his gun, he cannot return fire. It would be counter to the reformation of Doc for him now to take a life, no matter how evil Curley Bill may be. (The censors would also demand that Doc die to pay the price for his past killings.)

It is up to Wyatt Earp to administer justice. He will do it on his terms, without help. The only one he would have trusted has just been shot down, so he must face his adversaries by himself. (Heading to the O.K. Corral, he says to Doc's body, "Sorry you couldn't be around for this.") Although Wyatt dispatches three of the bad men, it is Jerry who kills Curley Bill and in effect redeems herself. (Sarah, the good girl, certainly could not take revenge on Doc's killer, especially after her lecturing Doc that taking a life was wrong.) By taking up arms against Curley Bill, Jerry displays her good side—she is, after all, saving Wyatt's life—and it is the only way she can show her love for Doc.

After Doc's death, Sarah decides to stay in Tombstone. She tells Wyatt that in this way, she can be close to Doc, and she will probably do something positive for the town, such as providing medical comfort for those in need. Jerry, who represented the lawless and wild times, is moving on. The town is now civilized, with a bank taking over the building that housed the Palace of Pleasure. Jerry tells Earp, "When people start saving money, it's time for me to leave." As she gets into the stagecoach, Jerry extends her hand to Wyatt, and he takes it. "You must be all right," she tells him. "If you wasn't, a great fella like Doc wouldn't have liked you." As the stagecoach rides off, it passes the town cemetery, and she says good-bye to Doc one more time. Wyatt watches the stage leave, then adjusts his tie as he looks back at the hotel. It's hinted there may be a relationship with Sarah when the time is right. In the end, the hero has brought law and order to a reckless town.

Dwan handles the film in a workmanlike fashion, keeping up the pace throughout. He manages to capture the vibrancy of the town in the exterior shots, with extras moving here and there (something lacking in most of the films except the later *Tombstone* and *Wyatt Earp*). Even the gunfight, which is not at all accurate to the facts, has a sense of energy and tension. (The gunfight in this version runs one minute and twenty-two seconds.) Randolph Scott, minus a mustache, makes a good effort to show Earp as the stalwart hero. (Interestingly, the character of Earp could have had an entirely different name without hurting the story.) Scott's Earp is a solid, fearless man. In a street fight, he stands tall, firing his gun calmly. He also shows a good-naturedness when he talks Doc out of making a fight (something Henry Fonda wonderfully captures in *My Darling Clementine*), creating a very likable Earp for the audience. Cesar Romero's Doc Halliday tries to be a smoldering, angry man, yet the effort falls short. Once he and Wyatt hit it off, the anger dissipates until the arrival of Sarah. From there, he alternates from being an occasionally angry man to one accepting

Opposite: TV Guide ad for *Frontier Marshal*. **In the early 1950s, 20th Century-Fox licensed their film library through NTA, which set up syndicated packages to various television stations (author's collection).**

TV's Best...Tonight

ONE TOWN WAS
THE WICKEDEST,
WILDEST, DEAD-
LIEST IN THE OLD
WEST...till the law
came in at the shoot-
ing end of Wyatt
Earp's six-guns!

FRONTIER MARSHAL

with

RANDOLPH   NANCY
SCOTT · KELLY

CESAR ROMERO
BINNIE BARNES
JOHN CARRADINE

Executive Producer Sol M. Wurtzel
Directed by Allan Dwan

20th NTA
CENTURY-FOX TV FILM RELEASE

his fate to one achieving his ultimate reformation. Romero's Doc is not the darker, complex character we will see in *My Darling Clementine, Gunfight at the O.K. Corral, Tombstone,* or *Wyatt Earp.* Both Earp and Doc in this film veer toward the stereotyped protagonists we would expect in a B film. Wyatt and Doc are the lead characters; they revolve around the more interesting supporting characters, who give the film some depth. This is not to slight the talents of Scott and Romero; it is merely an observation of what the B Western genre generally required of its leads.

Nancy Kelly is given the thankless role of the good girl and handles it well, but she has little to do with such a one-dimensional part. Binnie Barnes, who made a career of playing the hard-edged, tough-talking girl, gives a vibrancy to her role of Jerry. While hers is a basic stock character, Barnes manages to give Jerry some dimension. Eddie Foy, Jr., provides the comic relief in the film as well as giving us a glimpse of his famous father's act. The numerous character actors show why they were so important to movies and, sadly, point out something that is lacking in many modern films. Whether it is Hank Mann's drunk in the Bella Union, Chris-Pin Martin crying over his wounded son, or Lon Chaney, Jr., as one of Carter's gang, they give their roles (and ultimately the film) profundity.

Frontier Marshal introduced movie audiences to Wyatt Earp and the famous gunfight, albeit on a purely superficial level. Wyatt Earp, at this juncture in his cinema history, was the representative of good over evil. In *Frontier Marshal,* Earp is presented much as he was in Stuart Lake's novel: a white knight in the wild West. He will intervene in Doc's relationship with Sarah for his friend's own good. He will fight it out with Curley Bill and his men on his own terms. Wyatt even displays a kindness to Jerry, the "bad girl," at the end of the story. He realizes that deep inside there is goodness in her, and as she leaves town, he takes her hand as a gesture of friendship. The Wyatt Earp in *Frontier Marshal* is the kind of hero that children at the movies would look up to. Audiences, and the Western genre, needed that in 1939. World events were beginning to make many nervous; spending a few hours in a movie theatre watching a story about an actual person who vanquished lawbreakers gave audiences a sense of hope and welcome relief. The cinematic myth of Wyatt Earp, upholder of law and order, was just beginning.

Frontier Marshal

A 20th Century-Fox Release. *Released:* July 28, 1939. *In Production:* June 10, 1939, to July 8, 1939. 7 reels, 6,429 feet. *PCA Certificate Number:* 5487.

Executive Producer: Darryl F. Zanuck. *Producer:* Sol Wurtzel. *Director:* Allan Dwan. *Screenplay:* Sam Hellman, based on a book by Stuart N. Lake. *Cinematographer:* George Clarke. *Camera Operator:* Lou Kunkel. *Camera Assistants:* Eddie Collins and Paul Garnett. *Film Editor:* Fred Allen. *Assistant Film Editor:* William Claxton. *Script Supervisor:* Stanley Scheuer. *Costume Design:* Herschel. *Wardrobe:* Robert Martin, Gertrude Kirkwood, Viola Richards. *Makeup Department Supervisor:* Ben Nye. *Makeup Artist:* Raymond Lopez. *Hair Stylist:* Wilma Ryan. *Musical Director:* Samuel Kaylin. *Assistant Directors:* Gordon Cooper, Aaron Rosenberg and Tom Dudley. *Dialogue Director:* Herbert O. Farjeón. *Assistant Sound:* L. B. Dix. *Boom Man:* Art Wright. *Cable Man:* R. M. Braggins. *Art Director:* Lewis Creber. *Production Manager:* William Koenig. *Unit Production Manager:* W. F. Fitzgerald. *Props:* Don Greenwood. *Assistant Props:* Len Tribe and Andy Kisch. *Best Boy:* Charles Wise. *Gaffer:* Paul Rose. *Follow-up:* William Eull. *Casting:* Owen McLean. *Horse Wrangler:* Russ Crane. *Still Photographer:* Emmett Schoenbaum. *Songs:* "Down Went McGinty," words and music by Joseph Flynn; "I've Taken a Fancy to You," words by Sidney D. Mitchell, music by Lew Pollack; "Heaven Will Protect the Working Girl," words and music by A. Baldwin Sloane. *Running Time:* 71 minutes. The film was re-released in 1948. Filmed in black and white. *Filming Locations:* Portions of the film were shot in Lone Pine, California, and 20th-

Century-Fox Studios. *Working Titles: Wyatt Earp, Frontier Marshal; Frontier Marshal—The Saga of Tombstone, Arizona.*

Cast: Randolph Scott (*Wyatt Earp*), Nancy Kelly (*Sarah Allen*), Cesar Romero (*Doc Halliday*), Binnie Barnes (*Jerry*), John Carradine (*Ben Carter*), Edward Norris (*Dan Blackmore*), Eddie Foy, Jr. (*Eddie Foy*), Ward Bond (*Town Marshal*), Lon Chaney, Jr. (*Pringle*), Chris-Pin Martin (*Pete*), Joe Sawyer (*Curley Bill*), Dell Henderson (*Dave Hall, proprietor of Bella Union Café*), Harry Hayden (*Mayor John Henderson*), Ventura Ybarra (*Pablo*), Charles Stevens (*Indian Charlie*), Richard Alexander, Harry Woods (*Curley Bill's Men*), Tom Tyler (*Buck Newton*), Arthur Aylesworth (*Card Player*), Philo McCullough, Ethan Laidlaw (*Toughs*), Fern Emmett (*Hotel maid*), Margaret Brayton (*Mother*), James Aubrey (*Cockney Man*), Hank Mann, Heinie Conklin, Edward Le Saint, John Bleifer, George Melford (*Patrons of the Bella Union Café*), Pat O'Malley (*Customer*), Jack C. Smith (*Man*), Dick Elliott (*Mine Owner*), Tom London (*Deputy*), Harlan Briggs (*Newspaper Editor*), Gloria Roy (*Dance Hall Girl*), John Butler (*Harassed Man*), Ferris Taylor (*Doctor*), Kathryn Sheldon (*Mrs. Garvey*), Walter Baldwin, Harry Strang, Cy Kendall (*Men*), Henry Clive (*Gambler*), Eddie Dunn (*Card Player*), William Pawley (*Cowardly Man*), Jack Stoney (*Drunk*), Si Jenks (*Prospector*), Jimmie Dundee (*Bully*), Post Park (*Stagecoach Driver*), Don Hamilton (*Man*).

4

Tombstone: The Town Too Tough to Die (1942)

"There will never be anything done to cure lawlessness in Tombstone until we can find a man who can stand up to Curly Bill."

It was another three years before Wyatt Earp and the Tombstone saga returned to the silver screen, this time under the title *Tombstone: The Town Too Tough to Die*. Once again, the story was fashioned into a high-gloss programmer produced by Harry Sherman for Paramount. As darkening clouds began to unleash a torrent of war over Europe and threatened to soon spread to the Pacific, the image of Wyatt Earp as a protector against evildoers was one movie audiences appreciated.

Harry "Pop" Sherman, a Boston native, had a love affair with the American West. Beginning his career as a theater owner in the east, he had come to Hollywood in 1913 seeking movies to show in his theaters. During this visit, he met with D.W. Griffith and wound up advancing him money to finish an epic called *The Birth of a Nation*.[1] Sherman went on to produce the first movie based on a Zane Grey novel, *The Light of the Western Stars*, in 1916. In 1935, he formed his own company and produced the first fifty-four *Hopalong Cassidy* films before selling the rights to the film's star, William Boyd. He set up a deal with Paramount that allowed the studio to release the *Hopalong Cassidy* films and permitted Sherman to occasionally produce some higher budgeted B Westerns. Sherman took pride in the fact that his Western heroes never drank, swore, or shot someone in the back. He once said that he received great satisfaction from the letters parents sent him thanking him for the kind of films he made, which gave their children someone positive to emulate. The image of Wyatt Earp as the West's top lawman fit right into Sherman's inclinations.

Tombstone: The Town Too Tough to Die opens with a scenic sunset and vistas of the Arizona mountains, as a voice identifies itself to the audience as "the voice of yesterday ... a voice of a period in American history that is hallowed with memories." Two prospectors, Ed Schieffelin and Tadpole, stumble across a major silver find in the Arizona desert. Tadpole warns Ed that all he will find in this rugged land is his tombstone. "Tombstone or no tombstone, I'm sticking," Ed replies—and the town of Tombstone is born. As the town grows, so does lawlessness. Curly Bill's gang rides into town, shooting their guns and causing a panic. Into the melee ride Wyatt, Virgil, and Morgan Earp. His brothers remind Wyatt that this lawlessness is not his affair and that he's hung up his guns. However, Wyatt's comments on the lack of law enforcement cause Mayor Crane to hand him a badge and order him to arrest the outlaw. After Wyatt arrests Curly, he is offered the sheriff's job, but he refuses it. Gunfire again erupts on the street, and Ike Clanton accidentally kills a young boy. Wyatt decides to take the job as law officer.

Ike Clanton (Victor Jory, center, holding two pistols) and Curly Bill (Edgar Buchanan, back to Jory) take delight in causing a ruckus in Tombstone (author's collection).

Coming into a saloon in Galeyville for a meal, Johnny Duanne meets Curly. The outlaw likes the kid and offers him a job posing as a tax appraiser from Tucson. Johnny is to accompany Wyatt on his rounds collecting taxes and help kill the lawman. Doc Holliday arrives in Tombstone, and Wyatt asks his old friend to help him enforce the law. Later, at the Bird Cage Theatre, Wyatt is introduced to Johnny, posing as the tax appraiser. The following day, they begin collecting taxes, and Wyatt suspects that Johnny is working for Curly. During a conversation, Wyatt tells Johnny that he thinks the young man's good side is fighting against his bad side. Curly had told Johnny to shoot Wyatt in the back while he was sleeping, but the young man cannot do it. Johnny rides back to Curly, tipping him off about a silver shipment they can rob.

After the robbery, Johnny learns that Wyatt wants to see him in town. Johnny is reunited with Ruth, the girl he left behind. He realizes that Wyatt set up the reunion and rebuffs Ruth's affection. Doc follows Johnny into a saloon and starts a fight with him, causing the young man to be arrested. Upon his release from jail, Johnny goes to see Earp at the Bird Cage, where he runs into Ruth, posing as a dance hall girl. Upset with her new job, Johnny pulls Ruth into a back room, and the two young people realize they love each other. Johnny promises to make good and stay out of trouble, finding a job at a local mine.

With Curly away rustling cattle, Ike Clanton decides to have it out with the Earps. In a saloon, Ike boasts that he will have a showdown with the Earps. Meeting with his younger

Morgan (Harvey Stephens, left) and Virgil Earp (Rex Bell, center) arrest Johnny Duanne (Don Castle), as Doc Holliday (Kent Taylor) watches (author's collection).

brother, Billy, and the McLowerys, Ike orders Mayor Crane to tell the Earps that they will be waiting for them at the O.K. Corral. The confrontation with the Clantons and McLowerys erupts into a gunfight. Following the gunfight and trial, Wyatt enters a saloon, where Morgan is playing pool and Doc is dealing faro. Wyatt says that he was fired as town sheriff by Mayor Crane and plans on leaving town for California. Morgan is shot by Indian Charlie, who has been standing outside the rear door. Wyatt is now appointed U.S. marshal and sets a trap to arrest Curly Bill and his gang.

Curly Bill offers Johnny a chance to join in on a robbery of silver shipment, but the young man declines. Later, Curly and his gang rob the wagon carrying silver, only to find that they have been tricked. Wyatt's posse, which has been watching, drives Curly's cattle into the gang, crashing the wagon and forcing the outlaws to take refuge in some rocks. During the shootout, Johnny kills Ike Clanton, who was about to shoot Curly in the back. Wyatt kills Indian Charlie before cornering Curly Bill and killing him. Wyatt then boards a stage to California, saying good-bye to Ruth and Johnny, who is now town sheriff.

Credit is murky as to who wrote the script. On October 2, 1940, *The Hollywood Reporter* stated that Harry Sherman had purchased an original script by Dean Franklin entitled *Tombstone, Arizona*. The following month, it was announced that the script was written by Dean Reisner; yet the script's first draft, dated August 25, 1941, credits Albert Shelby Le Vino and E. E. Paramore as the screenwriters (both would get screen credit). Another interesting item is that the August 25, 1941, draft marks the first time the script is credited as being based on the Walter Noble Burns book, *Tombstone: An Iliad of the Southwest*.[2] Oddly, there is no mention in the industry trade papers of Sherman's buying the screen rights to the Burns book, although announcing the fact would have helped the movie's publicity. It is possible that Sherman may have made a quick deal to buy the rights to Burns's novel as a way to avoid any legal contention from Stuart Lake or 20th Century-Fox that his original script could have "borrowed" material from either Lake's book or the previous films produced by Fox.

The August 25 draft contains no opening narration. Instead, there are a few establishing shots of the rough Arizona countryside. We then see Ed Schieffelin and Tadpole making their discovery of the silver strike. Prior to Wyatt's arrival in town, we are inside Hatch's saloon, where Curly Bill pulls the badge off Sheriff Crane and flings it onto the floor. He then grabs the former officer, pins the badge on the seat of his pants, and pushes him out the door. Outside the saloon, Wyatt dismounts and picks up the lawman as Curly and the mob move on. After this draft, the sheriff character would be dropped and rewritten as Mayor Crane.

Another scene dropped after this draft occurs once Wyatt takes Sheriff Crane into another saloon. Curly Bill and his gang enter the Crystal Palace, and immediately a hush comes over the room. He yells at some miners, "Get out of the way, you maggots!" One miner replies, "Let's heave them cow-chips out," and a fight beings, spilling into the street. (The PCA objected to the "cow-chips" line, demanding it be cut.) The fight reaches a crescendo when Ike fires at a man and accidentally kills a young boy.

The scene of Wyatt and Johnny collecting tax money from Curly included a bit of business that was dropped from the final print. Johnny gives Curly a receipt with a note reading, "Don't worry. I'll handle him when the time comes." In the film, we never see a close-up of the note, although Curly makes a comment to one of his men that Johnny would handle things and bring back the money. The movie also includes Wyatt telling Johnny that he saw him give Curly a sign, yet the audience never sees anything like that in the film. Also, a montage sequence in the first draft, which was scrapped, begins when Wyatt and Johnny ride from a watering hole after collecting money from Curly. The script describes the montage as a constant shot of "Wyatt's saddle bags getting heavier and fuller. Across this in rapid succession come scenes of Johnny and Wyatt riding across deserts—among mountains. Two or three night camps, STOCK SHOTS of smelters, mines, sawmills and ranches where taxes are being paid."

The script then takes Wyatt and Johnny to the Clanton Ranch, where the action differs from that in the film. The script has Ike calling for a young Mexican boy to bring out the money while he's tied up. Wyatt doesn't wrap Ike and Billy around the tree but rather waits for Johnny to make good his escape, then simply lets the rope go off his saddle horn before riding away. As he's riding off, Phin arrives and fires at Wyatt, missing him. Wyatt returns fire and hits Phin in the leg. The rest of the men on horseback chase Wyatt and Johnny. The script notes that Johnny lets go of the pack horse and "turns off the road in some daring, stunty jump."[3]

After Johnny fails to kill Wyatt at the night camp, the first draft had a sequence in which the camera is looking in the window of the *Epitaph* newspaper, where Wyatt's saddle sits with a card propped up against it reading: "To collect $14,619 in taxes WYATT EARP rode 1,650 miles in this SADDLE—The Tombstone Epitaph cordially invites Dan Crane, Curly Bill and The Tombstone Miner to KISS IT!" This scene was dropped from the final draft as the PCA demanded the cut because of the "kiss it" reference. Another scene dropped because of expected PCA complaints of suggestive sexual innuendo happens when Johnny takes Ruth back to the private room and they finally embrace. Wyatt, Doc, Tadpole and Queenie, the head hostess at the Bird Cage, are smiling as they look through the curtains at the couple before walking off. The script direction had Tadpole coming back and placing a sign that read "Closed for Repairs" on the closed curtains.

After former Sheriff Crane tells Wyatt he'll have him arrested for murder, there is an insert of a headline in the *Tombstone Miner* (standing in for the *Nugget*): "Wyatt Earp Indicted for Murder! Claim McLowerys and Clanton Killed While Hands Were Up." Right after that, an insert of the *Epitaph*'s headline reads, "Court Dismisses Charges Against Wyatt Earp and Brothers. Judge Holds Shooting of Outlaws Service to Community." This was dropped in the final script draft in favor of the two scenes of John Clum reading his headlines to his printer.[4]

After Morgan is killed, Wyatt sits shotgun while Virgil and Doc ride inside a stage-coach bound for Tucson. Arriving in Tucson in the evening, they chase Frank Stilwell and Indian Charlie, but the two get away. Wyatt tells Doc to go on the train with Virgil to California while he goes back to Tombstone. In Tombstone, Wyatt visits Ruth, who is working in a hat store. She asks him if he is going to take the U.S. marshal position, but Wyatt says no. "It'd tie my hands. I want to be free to get every one of that gang of murderers if it's the last act of my life." Ruth admonishes him, saying that is simply revenge and that his people "brought you up to respect the law. You've got to make them respect it here. Then quit if you want to. But not for revenge, Wyatt, you're too big for that." A similar theme of dialogue would appear in *Gunfight at the O.K. Corral, Hour of the Gun*, and *Wyatt Earp*, only with Doc Holliday speaking these sentiments to Wyatt.

Harry Sherman submitted the August 25 draft to the PCA for its approval. In a September 2, 1941, letter to Sherman, the PCA outlined its concerns with the first draft. They stressed that there be "no apparent cruelty to animals" in the scene in which the wagon driver whips Curly's horse as they are riding through town. When Wyatt tells Curly that "I'll take a few of you to *hell* with me," the PCA warned that censor boards would delete the word "hell." "May we suggest the substitute 'hades?'"[5] Another concern was drinking in the film. The PCA requested that alcohol consumption be kept to a minimum, noting, "As you know, audiences object not so much to the presence of liquor in saloons and like places as to the actual guzzling. This is particularly true with regard to the lead, Wyatt."

The final script draft was submitted to the PCA on September 8, 1941. There was no opening narration (that would be added in December), but a sequence in the final gunfight raised eyebrows at the PCA office. Indian Charlie is sneaking around the rocks, rifle in hand. Wyatt comes up behind him and says, "Turn around, rat!" Charlie turns, dropping his rifle, and raises his hands (he still has his pistol in his gunbelt), pleading for his life. "I'm giving you a chance you never gave my brother. Now draw!" Wyatt commands after holstering his gun. Charlie refuses to draw. Wyatt turns his back on him, saying he'll fight Charlie's way. Watching Indian Charlie's shadow on the face of a rock, he sees him reach for his gun. Wyatt draws and wheels in a lighting movement, shooting Indian Charlie dead. In a letter to Harry Sherman, the PCA stated: "We cannot approve this new scene ... as written since your lead, Wyatt, actually provokes Indian Charlie to draw his gun so that he can kill Charlie, an action which is murder. Some business must be substituted wherein Wyatt does not provoke Indian Charlie to draw. Otherwise, this scene could not be approved in the finished picture."[6]

Aside from their concern about the way Wyatt kills Indian Charlie, the PCA cautioned

Wyatt Earp (Richard Dix) gets the drop on Indian Charlie (author's collection).

Sherman that the dance hall girls, wearing black stockings, had to be shown full length; "otherwise, we could not approve shots showing the bare legs of the girls above the stockings."[7] Additional concern was the way two Mexican characters would be portrayed. In a September 12 letter to Sherman, Addison Durland of the PCA requested that "the two Mexican characters in the story be presented in the best possible light, as far as speech, makeup and costume are concerned. This, we believe, will not affect your story adversely, and will serve to minimize the possibility of offending sensibilities of our Latin American neighbors."[8]

As the PCA script concerns were being worked out, Sherman signed Lesley Selander to direct; he had directed many of the *Hopalong Cassidy* movies for Sherman. Beginning his career as a lab technician in the silent era, Selander moved up to become an assistant cameraman in 1920 and cinematographer two years later. In 1924, he began working as an assistant director at MGM, before getting his chance at directing from his friend, actor Buck Jones. Selander went on to direct many of Jones's later films, as well as scores of B westerns.[9]

Casting announcements began in November 1940, with Sherman stating he had signed Preston Foster for the role of Wyatt Earp and was hoping to sign Ellen Drew for the role of Ruth.[10] This was probably a "publicity plant" by Paramount studios because Foster was under contract at the time. It was not uncommon for studios to plant stories that would appear not only in the industry trade papers but also in dozens of national newspapers.

Planted stories about a star's being signed for a specific film were a way of keeping his or her name in the public's eye, even though the star never had actually been considered for the movie. The most well-known example of a publicity plant occurred in 1942, when Warner Bros. announced that Ronald Reagan and Ann Sheridan would star in *Casablanca*! The role of Wyatt Earp ultimately went to veteran actor Richard Dix. Born Ernest Brimmer in St. Paul, Minnesota, in 1894, Dix originally intended to become a surgeon, but that plan changed after he took some theatrical courses in college. Dix made his Broadway debut in 1919, and in 1921 was signed to a long-term contract by Paramount, where he quickly became one of the silent era's leading male stars. In 1929, he signed a contract with RKO and two years later received a Best Actor Oscar nomination for his performance in *Cimarron*. He went on to play Wild Bill Hickok in *Badlands of Dakota* (1941) and to star in a series of B films based on the popular radio drama *The Whistler*. He died in 1949 at the age of 56.[11]

Kent Taylor, who starred in many B films in the 1930s and 1940s, was signed to play Doc Holliday. Philip Terry was originally signed for the role of Johnny, but by August 20, 1941, he was replaced by Don Castle. Castle, like several other actors, turned out to have an incestuous relationship with movies about the gunfight at the O.K. Corral. In this film, he played the younger leading man; in *Gunfight at the O.K. Corral* (1957), he played a drunken cowboy who pulls a gun on Wyatt Earp. Frances Gifford was cast as Ruth, and Edgar Buchanan was signed to play Curly Bill.[12] The rest of the cast was filled with such well-known character actors as Victor Jory, Clem Bevans, Chris-Pin Martin, Beryl Wallace, Charles Halton, Wallis Clark, and Tom London.

The film would be shot on a tight schedule of 21 days, which also included some location work in Tucson, Arizona, and Long Valley, California. The town set of Tombstone was located on the Paramount Ranch in Aguora, California, about forty-five minutes north of Los Angeles.[13] Harry Sherman announced on August 15 that he was going to take his company to Tucson, Arizona, for several weeks of location work. "Tucson officials will cooperate with Sherman, permitting the use of vacant buildings for set interiors and artificially sanding the main street for reproduction of a typical Arizona street in 1879," *The Hollywood Reporter*s stated.[14] This probably was another publicity story to make the movie sound like a major production, considering that filming wouldn't begin for another month and that the Tombstone town set was located at the Paramount Ranch, not Tucson.

While Harry Sherman was very familiar with Lesley Selander's previous directorial work, he wasn't happy with some of the director's choices for this picture. In a brief press release, it was announced that Sherman and Selander "couldn't see eye to eye on how some roles in *Tombstone* should be characterized, so the director has gone off the picture."[15] Selander, who would direct several more films for Sherman, was replaced with William McGann, who had just recently handled Sherman's *Parson of Panamint* (1941). McGann, like Selander, had begun his career in the silent era as an assistant cameraman. His directing credits consisted of mostly B films from 1930 until 1944, when he took over as head of Warner Bros.' special effects department.

With a new director in place, filming commenced on September 16, 1941, with location work. The first two days' work consisted of Ike spotting the silver shipment from Mason's mines, Wyatt's posse finding Curly Bill and his gang with the stolen wagon, and the final shootout. The next three days had the company filming at various locations for the smelter mine, the Clanton and Sparkman ranches, and Wyatt and Johnny being chased by the Clantons. The next day, the robbery of the stagecoach and the scenes of Schieffelin and Tadpole discovering silver were filmed. The first part of the second week was taken up with Curly

Bill and his group shooting up the town, the Earp brothers' entrance into Tombstone, Wyatt's arresting Curly, and the Earps' walk to the O.K. Corral. According to the shooting schedule, the twelfth day of production was devoted to filming the gunfight. The last day of filming, October 9, covered the scenes of Wyatt and Ruth talking in her store (this was cut from the final print), Johnny and Ruth in a room at the Bird Cage Theatre, and the campfire sequence between Wyatt and Johnny.[16]

With production completed, the film was quickly assembled and underwent a title change to *The Bad Man of Arizona*. After editing was finished, the film was submitted to the PCA for its certification, which was granted on December 23, 1941. The film's title was changed once again in January 1942 to *Tombstone: The Town Too Tough to Die*.[17] Released on July 27, 1942, the movie received fairly positive notices. *Variety* commented, "It is made to order for a multitude of customers familiar with the Harry Sherman product.... The picture's ferocious action and its general quality set it up for solid competition with the war-slanted films.... It is produced for entertainment rather than accuracy.... Richard Dix, best since his peak in *Cimarron*, fits his restrained performance perfectly.... Dix plays it hard and tough and with the competence of the marshal he impersonates.... The fighting, sustained suspense, the deadly foreboding is [*sic*] packed solid for exciting entertainment in William McGann's direction. He handles gun battles, the challenging encounters, the explosions of wounded pride and vanity with socking vigor and expert craftsmanship. The rides and the fights have meaning and sense, are not merely tossed in for noise and spectacle, although they have both these ingredients, too."

The New York Times wrote that the film "stacks up as a tidy Western. That it is supposed to be based on the life of Wyatt Earp, famous frontier marshal, doesn't matter greatly. What does matter is that Harry Sherman, who specializes in outdoor dramas of strong silent men, has produced another lickety-split yarn of frontier laws vs. the bad hombres, and that the bad hombres die like dogs in the last reel. Mr. Sherman has a strong sense of justice and he likes it to happen fast." *The Hollywood Reporter* praised the film, calling it "one of [Harry Sherman's] big-budget pictures, and its success is a feather in his sombrero.... There is plenty of fast action and shooting in the tale.... William McGann does a bang-up job of direction.... Richard Dix is his excellent self as Wyatt Earp, and Edgar Buchanan has a rip-roaring good time as Curly Bill."

As *Variety* noted in its review, the movie was made as entertainment, not for historical accuracy. However, the gunfight *is* fairly accurate. The width of the lot (which has horse stalls on one side, thus literally making it the O.K. Corral) is very close to the real empty lot in the 1881 gunfight. The order of position of the Earps and Holliday as the gunfight begins is fairly accurate, although they are grouped closer together than was actually the case, and the shootout is not drawn out. (The gunfight in this movie runs one minute and thirty-one seconds.) Wyatt tells the Clantons and McLowerys that they are under arrest and to put up their hands. "Like this?" asks Frank McLowery, before he draws his two guns. As the firing begins, Frank goes down, and Billy is hit. Lying against the wall of the corral, Billy wounds Morgan, who tells Wyatt the shot got him. In a very even tone, Wyatt says, "Behind me, Morg, and take it easy." We see Ike cowering near a horse stall as Tom hits Virgil in the shoulder. Doc fires his small sawed-off shotgun at Tom, killing him. Ike stands and yells at Wyatt that he has no gun. "You started this. Now get to shooting or get out," Wyatt tells Ike, who runs into a nearby building. He breaks a window in the door to fire at the Earps, but Tadpole (who has followed the Earps and Holliday) fires at Ike, causing him to flee. As the shooting ends, Tadpole walks up to Billy Clanton, who asks him to take off his boots because he promised his mother he wouldn't die with his boots on!

The screenplay tries to follow some historical facts, but many aspects were either omitted or glossed over. For example, Wyatt, as in Lake's biography, is the central law officer instead of Virgil. The fictitious character of Crane, the crooked mayor, was a replacement for Johnny Behan. This was the first film to feature Curly Bill as the leader of the outlaw gang (it wouldn't happen again until the 1993 *Tombstone*), while the McLaurys (misspelled McLowery) simply fill in as part of the outlaw element without any character development. Wyatt's brothers are relegated to minor supporting roles, with neither having any wives (nor does Wyatt) and only Morgan being killed.

Like its predecessor *Frontier Marshal*, Sherman's movie follows a standard outline found in many B Westerns. Opening with a narration instead of titles, the film uses a montage to set the tone. The narration thanks the one man who had the courage to stand up to the bad men. This is a unique way of introducing Wyatt Earp, as we already are told what he has done for this town before his arrival. This type of story introduction was common in many of the B Westerns of the day (especially those geared to the Saturday matinee crowds), with either a narrator or character in the opening of the film warning the villains or sharing their thoughts with fellow townspeople that a certain man will fix the problem. It builds the audience's expectations of the hero's arrival and helps viewers to immediately recognize the protagonist when he makes his first appearance.

Wyatt's arrival, with his two brothers, comes in the midst of Curly Bill's shooting spree. The three Earps ride calmly into the town that is being hurrahed, as if this were nothing new to them. Even their horses are not skittish. An older man bumps into Wyatt's horse, and Earp steadies him with one hand while sitting in the saddle. Earp is quickly shown as a man who is cool and calm in the most turbulent situations. Dismounting, Virgil and Morgan express little interest in the town's problems, but Wyatt comments that Curly Bill has a growing disrespect for the law. His brothers remind Wyatt that he has hung up his guns. Dix allows his character to feel around his waist where his guns used to be, indicating that Earp's old habit is hard to break. Once again, Wyatt Earp is the reluctant hero. He is pressed into service and does what is expected of him before relinquishing his duties. It is the code of the hero to step up when a guileless person is being taken advantage of or is physically harmed. Remaining the reluctant hero until something contradicts his code justifies the hero's vengeful actions and wins the audience's approval.

Wyatt Earp also is once again portrayed as a man of steely resolve with a good heart. He shows no fear when he comes up to arrest Curly. With the shotgun in his hands and a gun around his waist, Richard Dix gives Wyatt a cold, nervy outline. There is little doubt in the audience's mind that he will unleash that shotgun if he has to, but he would rather avoid any gunplay. Dix also gives Earp a quiet dignity as he goes about his job. When he talks to Johnny and tells him his good side is fighting his bad side, it isn't a lecture. It is laid out matter-of-factly for Johnny to see. He doesn't force the right-vs.-wrong lecture onto Johnny (or onto the audience), but his performance tells us (and Johnny) that he's right. Dix's performance of Earp is that of the quintessential Western hero.

Tombstone: The Town Too Tough to Die follows the genre plot structure of two protagonists who start off as adversaries and eventually become friends. In this case, it is Wyatt and Johnny who form a father-son or older-younger brother bond instead of focusing on Wyatt and Doc. Through the first three-quarters of the film, Wyatt attempts to persuade Johnny not to follow in Curly's footsteps, but the young man resists. However, the narrative dictates that some sort of action, either the death of one of the two friends or the unconditional love of a woman or child, will force one of the two protagonists to take action and

Curly Bill's gang hurrahs the town of Tombstone. The exterior streets of Tombstone were filmed at Paramount's ranch in Agoura, California (author's collection).

make a moral decision. With Johnny, it comes from his love for Ruth and from Wyatt's lecturing about his good instincts fighting his bad ones. Because of Ruth, Johnny forgoes following Curly and instead takes an honest job. When he is tempted by the outlaw with money from a previous stage robbery and Ruth asks him what he's going to do, we are left for a moment wondering whether Johnny will go back to Curly. Only in the next scene do we learn that he's turned the money over to Wyatt and offers to help in capturing his old companion. Even doing this, however, Johnny's feelings for Curly are split. He knows that what Curly does is wrong, yet he genuinely likes the man. In the final gunfight, he saves Curly's life when Ike Clanton attempts to shoot him. Looking at Johnny, Curly waves to thank him. Later, with Curly's death, Johnny feels regret over losing his friend, and Wyatt tells him that out of the entire gang, Curly was the only one he respected. At the conclusion of the film, the friendship and respect between Wyatt and Johnny, as well as the boy's love for Ruth, transform the younger man. He is now able to step up and take over the job as town sheriff from his mentor. Don Castle does little to endear himself to the audience in the role of Johnny. Early in the film he appears smug, almost cocky to the point of irritating the audience. He shows little interest in being a good fellow, although there are a few instances in which his good side (according to the script) comes through. Unfortunately, Castle's overall performance is bland, and he doesn't really show a strong transformation in his character.

There is little interplay between Wyatt Earp and Doc Holliday in this movie. Their friendship must be taken at face value because there are only a few scenes with the two of them together, and nothing really demonstrates a bond between them. Instead, the character of Doc is relegated to a supporting role, giving Kent Taylor little to work with. We never see Holliday coughing, and the only reference to any illness is when he tells Wyatt that he plans to stay in Tombstone for a while because his doctors said "the fine Arizona air might do him some good." Taylor appears to be just walking through his paces as Doc, but this it really isn't his fault; the role gives him little to build on other than playing a familiar name in history. In this film, Doc Holliday is simply a secondary cardboard character.

Edgar Buchanan is completely miscast as Curly Bill. His performance lacks any sense of menace, with the actor relying on a laugh that comes across as forced, hitching up his gunbelt, and rolling his eyes. We cannot believe that this man could be the leader of a gang of killers and rustlers. Buchanan as the adversary is the film's weakest link. A picture such as this needs a strong antagonist to go up against Wyatt Earp, someone who will instill fear in the audience. With Buchanan in the role, the fear and intimidation the villain is supposed to bring to a film is nowhere to be found. Victor Jory, who plays Ike Clanton and often played villains, would have been a better choice. With Jory there is a sense of danger, even as he plays Ike Clanton as a blustering coward who would shoot Curly in the back. Jory gives depth to his role in the limited time he's onscreen. Other character actors, such

A staged publicity picture of Curly Bill (Edgar Buchanan) being held at gunpoint by Wyatt (Richard Dix). In the movie, Earp kills him during a cat-and-mouse game in the rocky terrain (author's collection).

as Clem Bevans as Tadpole, Chris-Pin Martin as Chris Charles Halton as Mayor Crane, and Beryl Wallace as Queenie, make the most of their roles, giving them a spark against the flat and tired dialogue they utter.

William McGann's direction is competent but not outstanding. He handles the scenes with craftsmanship, yet he adds nothing special to the film. A perfect example happens in the Bird Cage Theatre when Queenie Fontaine is singing a traditional tear-jerker of a song. McGann cuts back to a couple sitting at a table, drinking beer. The man, a long-faced, stolid chap, sits at the table, never drinking and staring into space. He is totally oblivious to the fact that his wife is crying over this song. The crying is badly dubbed, and the actress doesn't really try to make anything of this moment. McGann cuts to the couple three times, with the last time supposedly the capper to a gag: As the song ends and the woman is crying, she whacks the man on the side of the face, causing him to innocently ask, "What did I do?" It could have been a funny gag (one audiences have seen over and over), but its execution and the performance of the actress make it fall flat, with no payoff for a laugh.

McGann does do a good job building tension as the Earps and Holliday walk to the O.K. Corral. The first shot, in a low angle from the street, shows the Earp brothers and Holliday exiting the saloon and coming down the boardwalk. We see the reaction of people as they watch the procession. The lawmen walk down the street in pairs, Wyatt and Virgil in the lead followed by Doc and Morgan. Billy Clanton comes up to tell Ike and the others that the Earps and Holliday are coming. There is another shot of the Earps and Holliday walking down the street as the orchestra plays a slow, deliberate tempo. The film's score, which overall is awful, does help build tension in this sequence.[18] Tom McLowery pulls his rifle from his saddle as the Earps keep moving. There is another shot of Ike, Billy, and Frank waiting, watching. A close shot features the boots of the Earps and Holliday walking along the boardwalk as the music continues to build. Tom McLowery reholsters his rifle as the footsteps are heard by the men in the corral. Ike backs up against a fence as the Earps and Holliday move in.

This sequence is solidly directed and composed, building the necessary tension. In comparison, the final scene, in which Wyatt leaves Tombstone, appears to have been shot quickly, with little attention to detail. It is done in one master shot, with the camera and the principal actors standing on the porch (and in the shade, making it hard to see them). Wyatt enters from right of the frame, his arms around Ruth and Johnny. They stand together, with Wyatt in the middle. He tells Ruth to make sure Johnny shines his badge. (The director does not feature a close-up of Johnny wearing the badge.) He bids them goodbye and makes his way to shake hands with Doc. They have a very brief exchange of words before Wyatt climbs onto the seat with the driver and the stagecoach rides off. McGann doesn't bother to cover this shot with close-ups or even medium shots with the principal players, giving us the feeling he was rushing to shoot this to finish the day's work. The final scene, with the hero riding off into the sunset, lacks the emotional impact the end of the movie needs.

Tombstone: The Town Too Tough to Die was made in the months preceding the attack by Japan on Pearl Harbor, which plunged America in World War II. One could theoretically argue that this film is an allegory of what was happening at the time of its 1942 release, but that certainly wasn't primarily on the minds of the filmmakers. (By the time the movie came out, American and British troops were fighting the Germans in the desert of North Africa.) No doubt, however, audiences did see the violence in Tombstone as reflecting the horrors occurring on the battlefields of Europe and in the Pacific. Tombstone could be viewed as a stand-in for beleaguered Europe and North Africa, with Curly Bill and his gang Hitler's army. Then comes Wyatt Earp to administer justice, his arrival reflecting the American's beginning involvement in the war. Once the villains are vanquished from Tombstone, Wyatt leaves—which could be read as the armies of America and Britain driving the Germans out of North Africa before moving on to Italy.

This would not be the first time that Wyatt Earp and the gunfight would be looked upon as a symbol to reflect the era in which the film was made. It would be another four years before a filmmaker would once again tackle the Earp saga. This time, it would not be relegated to B-movie status. Instead, a three-time Oscar-winning director would take the Earp story and fashion it into a mythical, visually stunning Western.

Tombstone: The Town Too Tough to Die

A Paramount Pictures release. *Released:* July 27, 1942. *In Production:* 21 days, September 16, 1941, to October 9, 1941. 8 reels, 7,164 feet. *PCA Certificate Number:* 7984.

Producer: Harry Sherman. *Associate Producer:* Lewis J. Rachmil. *Director:* William C. McGann. *Screenplay:* Albert S. Le Vino and Edward E. Paramore, Jr., based on "Tombstone" by Walter Noble Burns. *Cinematographer:* Russell Harlan. *Musical Score:* Gerard Carbonara. *Musical Direction:* Irvin Talbot. *Art Director:* Ralph Berger. *Set Decoration:* Emile Kuri. *Supervising Film Editors:* Sherman A. Rose, Carrol Lewis. *Sound:* Charles Althouse. *Assistant Director:* Glenn Cook. *Technical Advisor:* Fred Gilbert. *Running Time:* 79 minutes. Filmed in black and white. *Filing Locations:* Portions of the film were shot in Tucson, Arizona, Long Valley, California, the Paramount Studios Ranch and Paramount Studios. *Working Titles: The Badmen of Arizona, Tombstone.*

Cast: Richard Dix (*Wyatt Earp*), Edgar Buchanan (*Curly Bill Brocious*), Frances Gifford (*Ruth Grant*), Don Castle (*Johnny Duanne*), Kent Taylor (*Doc Holliday*), Clem Bevans (*Tadpole Foster*), Charles Halton (*Mayor Dan Crane*), Victor Jory (*Ike Clanton*), Chris-Pin Martin (*Chris*), Rex Bell (*Virgil Earp*), Wallis Clark (*Ed Schieffelin*), Beryl Wallace (*Queenie Fontaine*), Charles Stevens (*Indian Charlie*), James Ferrara (*Billy Clanton*), Paul Sutton (*Tom McLowery*), Dick Curtis (*Frank McLowery*), Harvey Stephens (*Morgan Earp*), Donald Curtis (*Phineas Clanton*), Hal Taliaferro (*Dick Mason*), Roy Barcroft (*Henchman*), Edward Brady (*Sour Man*), Bob Card (*Charley*), Murdock MacQuarrie, Merrill McCormick, Charles Middleton (*Townsmen*), Bill Nestell (*Barfly*), Jack Rockwell (*Bob Paul*).

5

My Darling Clementine (1946)

"Mac, you ever been in love?" "No, I been a bartender all me life."

At the end of *The Man Who Shot Liberty Valance* (1962), Ransom Stoddard (James Stewart) tells a newspaper editor the true story of the man responsible for killing the vicious title character, Liberty Valance. Learning the truth, the editor tears up the notes he had prepared for his article and throws them into a pot belly stove. Answering Stoddard's question as to whether he'll print the real story, the editor replies, "This is the West, sir. When the legend becomes fact, print the legend." This sentiment certainly applies to John Ford's 1946 classic, *My Darling Clementine*. Although cinema historians and critics have praised the film's artistic value, even calling it one of the finest Westerns ever made, many Earp scholars are less than kind with their criticisms, some opinions bordering on rabid distaste.

What is it about this movie that causes some Earp specialists to become so enraged? One answer is that Ford played fast and loose with the historical facts of the events in Tombstone. Perhaps another is something Ford once said about Earp and the gunfight. Ford related to director Peter Bogdanovich, "I knew Wyatt Earp. In the very early silent days, a couple of times a year, he would come up to visit pals, cowboys he knew in Tombstone; a lot of them were in my company. I think I was an assistant prop boy then and I used to give him a chair and a cup of coffee, and he told me about the fight at the O.K. Corral. So in *My Darling Clementine*, we did it exactly the way it had been. They didn't just walk up the street and start banging away at each other; it was a clever military maneuver."[1]

Although Ford loved history, he was never bound to the exactness of literal detail when making a movie. As Henry Fonda noted, "Jack used history, he didn't feel he was married to it."[2] The legend and the heroic tradition of the character were more important to Ford than facts. In all of Ford's films, the personal story is played out within the perspective of the time in which it takes place. This is very true of *My Darling Clementine*.

Based on Ford's own comments, it is easy to see why some Earp historians would hold his version of the gunfight in such disregard. Unfortunately, those that dismiss the film may not understand John Ford or his approach to his work. To begin with, Ford was a complex man who fashioned an image of a movie director who was both feared and loved. In reality, he was extremely shy, loved literature and history, and hid his sentimental side from coworkers by using his biting Irish wit to keep them at a distance. He was able to overcome his shyness when he became a director, projecting the persona of a person whom few dared to cross. One typical story that illustrates his ability to impose his will on a set happened when he fell behind in the shooting schedule. A producer was sent to the sound stage to tell him he was three script pages behind. Ford promptly called for the script. He tore out three pages and told the befuddled producer, "Now, we're on schedule!"[3]

Ford's cantankerous persona as a director often belied a gifted artist who could paint pictures with a movie camera. He dismissed any claims of artistic inclination, stating that he was just a hard-nosed, hard-working director who made Westerns. Ford relished the impression that his work looked as if he simply walked onto the set, set up the camera, and had the actors speak their lines. To believe that is akin to saying that Shakespeare was a decent writer or Charles Russell an average painter of the American West. Through the dark-tinted glasses he wore, Ford was able to construct visual images that no other director has yet to equal.[4] He would tell the story more by using images than dialogue, something he learned during his days directing silent films. His characters convey in looks and actions more than they could with mere words. A perfect example of this approach can be found in *The Searchers* (1956), when Martha gently holds and caresses Ethan's coat before giving it to him. This action, and the looks between the two characters, express more about their unspoken love for each other than any dialogue ever could.

John Ford was born to an Irish family in Portland, Maine, in 1894. His older brother, Francis, left home to become an actor and eventually found his way into motion pictures. By 1914, Francis was a prominent star with his own production company at Universal Studios. After finishing high school, John immediately went to Hollywood and found work with his brother's company as an assistant prop boy. He got his chance at directing in 1917: a Western, *The Soul Herder*, starring Universal's leading western star of the time, Harry Carey. The two men would make more than 20 movies together and Ford would later feature Carey's son, Harry Carey, Jr., as well as his widow, Olive, in many of his films. In 1920 Ford moved to Fox studios, where he made the epic Western *The Iron Horse* (1924). He won his first Oscar for Best Director for 1935's *The Informer*. He went on to win three more Oscars for directing (*The Grapes of Wrath*, 1940; *How Green Was My Valley*, 1941; and, *The Quiet Man*, 1952) yet he never received an award for his Westerns.[5] During World War II, Ford joined the Navy and his photographic unit served in the European and Pacific theaters. He took a leave of absence to make *They Were Expendable* (1945) at the behest of Secretary of the Navy James Forrestal; while Ford was

Henry Fonda as Wyatt Earp (author's collection).

filming this movie, World War II came to an end.[6] Ford was mustered out of military service and returned to Hollywood.

Prior to the outbreak of World War II, Ford had one film remaining on his contract with 20th Century-Fox Studios, and he agreed to be paid $150,000 for the remaining picture.[7] Darryl F. Zanuck was keen on remaking *Frontier Marshal*, and the idea of a Western—Ford's first since *Stagecoach* (1939)—appealed to him.[8]

The story of *My Darling Clementine* opens with the Earp brothers driving a herd of cattle through Arizona, bound for the family ranch in California. Wyatt meets Old Man Clanton, who offers to buy the cattle, but Wyatt declines. Later that night, Wyatt and his brothers, Morgan and Virgil, ride into Tombstone, leaving their younger brother, James, to watch the herd. Indian Charlie starts shooting up Kate Nelson's Boarding House and the town marshal quits. After Wyatt captures Indian Charlie, he refuses the marshal's job. Riding back to camp, the Earp brothers find their cattle stolen and James murdered. Wyatt returns to town to accept the job of marshal.

Days later, Wyatt meets Doc Holliday and they quickly become friends, much to the annoyance of Chihuahua, a Mexican dance hall girl and Doc's lover. Arriving on the stagecoach is Clementine Carter, who is looking for her fiancé, Doc. Later that night, Doc tells Clementine that the man she once knew no longer exists and she should return home to Boston. After Clementine agrees, Doc starts drinking heavily, until Wyatt knocks him out. The following morning, Wyatt learns from Clementine that she intends to go, but instead, she allows Wyatt accompany her to the church social, where the two dance. When Doc sees that Clementine is still in town, he orders her to leave. He warns Wyatt to start carrying a gun, then rides off on the stagecoach. When Wyatt finds Chihuahua wearing the cross that belonged to James, she tells Wyatt that Doc gave it to her. Wyatt sets off after Doc and catches up to the stage, ordering Holliday to return to Tombstone.

Wyatt and Doc confront Chihuahua, who admits it was given to her by Billy Clanton. Clanton, who is standing outside her window, shoots her and rides off. Virgil Earp chases after Billy, while Doc is forced to operate on Chihuahua. Arriving at the Clanton ranch, Virgil learns that Billy has died; as he leaves, he is shot in the back by Old Man Clanton. The Clantons ride into Tombstone and dump Virgil's body, saying they will be waiting for Wyatt at the O.K. Corral. As dawn breaks over Tombstone, Doc joins the Earps. He tells them that Chihuahua died during the night. Wyatt walks up the street toward the O.K. Corral while Morgan and Doc come up behind the Clantons. In the brief but deadly gunfight that erupts, the Clantons and Doc are killed. A few days later, Wyatt and Morgan leave for California to see their father. Clementine says she will be staying on as the new schoolteacher. Wyatt tells her, before riding off into the distance, that he will come back to see her.

On November 6, 1945, Zanuck sent a memo to Ford stating that he had held a conference with producer Samuel Engel and writer Thomas Job ("I told them all the things we have discussed as to characterizations, historical background"[9]), but ultimately Winston Miller was assigned as the writer for the project. Although Miller had never written a screenplay for Ford, the two men previously worked together in 1924, when Miller played the lead character as a young boy in *The Iron Horse*. Miller, who was the brother of silent screen actress Patsy Ruth Miller, began his career as a screenwriter in 1937 at Republic, scripting many B Westerns before serving with the U.S. Marine Corps in World War II. (He reportedly was one of many uncredited writers who worked on the screenplay for *Gone With the Wind*.[10]) After the war, his agent called with an offer to work for John Ford. Miller said that he and Ford sat around for five to six weeks kicking the story around and that they disregarded the previous versions of *Frontier Marshal*, adding, "We just started from scratch and made up our own story."[11]

Miller's memory is not exactly accurate. While it is likely that he and Ford did adapt their own version, many aspects of *My Darling Clementine* can be traced to the 1939 version of *Frontier Marshal*. For example, the scenes of Wyatt catching Chihuahua telling the gambler what cards Wyatt is holding, then dumping her into the horse trough, come from the 1939 version, as do Doc saving a life before he is killed and the use of a theatrical performer for comic relief. The two men quickly worked out the story points and, after that was done, Ford left Miller alone to write the screenplay. Once the first draft was completed on February 22, 1946, a story conference was held with Miller, Ford, and Darryl F. Zanuck. Out of that conference came a series of interesting notes that show how the film was crafted before going into production.

In the opening of the film was a sequence with the four Earp brothers riding side by side, driving the cattle and having a conversation about whether they should make camp or keep moving on. In the conference notes, Zanuck suggested the brothers should not be bunched together but separated, with Wyatt at the head of the herd and Morgan and Virgil on either side, with James riding drag. "Because of the impossibility of carrying on a conversation with this arrangement, the dialogue which we now have in the script will have to take place later on when they make camp."[12] After subduing Indian Charlie, the first draft had the town mayor thanking Wyatt and asking his name. When he tells him, the mayor replies, "The famous gunfighting marshal from Dodge City?" Zanuck was not happy with the mayor uttering this line; he suggested that the mayor could tell a second man who Earp is. (In the film, the mayor says, "You're not by chance the marshal from Dodge City?")

After discovering James dead and the cattle gone, Wyatt and Morgan ride back to Tombstone, where they meet the mayor in the Silver Strike Saloon. Wyatt takes the job of marshal and is sworn in at that moment. As Wyatt is about to leave, the Clantons enter the saloon. "They are jubilant. They shake the rain from their hats and coats, and start for the bar. Wyatt is staring at them. He asks someone who they are, and is told, 'The Clantons.' Wyatt strolls up to them at the bar and they have a scene along the lines which we now have in the script."[13] In the film, Wyatt goes to Tombstone alone and wakes up the mayor in his hotel room. When he leaves, the Clantons are coming into the hotel and meet Wyatt. He tells Old Man Clanton that he has lost his herd and is now taking a new job as marshal.

When Doc rides off on the stage (after the hotel brunch scene, in which he tells Clementine to leave town), the original draft had Doc yanking the driver from his place on the coach. Zanuck suggested that Doc should not do this because "When we come to the coach later ... the driver should be there, almost dead from fright because of the wild ride Doc has given him."[14] The script also had the stagecoach overturning as Wyatt rides up to it. Instead, Zanuck felt that Wyatt should bring the stage to a stop and order Doc out. "They should not make an issue of the brooch here. Wyatt merely tells Doc he's taking him back to town, and when Doc refuses and orders him to draw, Wyatt wounds him."[15] Zanuck also suggested that, after the operation on Chihuahua, the Clantons ride by, dump Virgil's body, and issue their challenge. The next scene had Doc coming to the jail to offer his help to the Earps, saying that Chihuahua is dead. (The characters of the mayor and Simpson, the town's unofficial church deacon, were not in this sequence in the first draft.[16])

After the gunfight, there is a funeral for Doc, Virgil, and Chihuahua. "We see townspeople trudging up the hill towards the graves. Kate and her girls in one group; Simpson and his followers in another, etc." In the first script draft, Ford had a scene at the funeral in which Wyatt and Clementine each learn the other will be staying on in Tombstone. Zanuck suggested an alternative scene with Morgan driving a buckboard; he says goodbye to Clementine at a spot at the edge of town. Wyatt rides up, and she says she is staying. "The last scene between Wyatt and Clementine should be very touching. He looks at her and says, 'Well, goodbye, Miss Clementine. I may be coming this way again sometime.' Clementine: 'If you do, I'll be here.' He looks at her again, then says softly, 'I sure like that name—Clementine.' He rides off into the sunset, with Clementine looking after him." (This is the way the film ends, with some minor changes.[17]) This is one point on which Zanuck was right and Ford was wrong. The ending as Ford shot it, with Wyatt simply shaking Clementine's hand goodbye, was a disappointment to the audience, inviting laughter. There needed to be a touching goodbye kiss between the two.

During one of their script conferences, Ford told Miller that he wanted to do a scene of a whore's funeral in a small Western town. Ford related how the casket would be carried through town on a wagon toward the cemetery, with only the madam and her girls walking behind it. As the small procession goes through town, we would see the town banker watching from his office; he eventually goes out and follows the wagon. One by one, Ford said, people would fall into line so that, when the procession gets to the cemetery, it has become a parade. A few weeks later, Ford asked Miller how the scene for the whore's funeral was coming. Miller said the problem with that scene was the character, Chihuahua, was not a whore with the heart of gold. Ford told Miller he didn't know what he was talking about because "on screen it's going to look a hell of a lot like a whore's funeral." Ford knew the idea would not work, Miller later said, but he had to have the last word, and the decision to eliminate a specific scene had to be his and his alone.[18] (Ford would later use this idea in *The Sun Shines Bright* in 1953.)

The first draft was sent to Joseph Breen at the PCA for comments and suggestions. Rarely did a first draft past muster and get approval from the PCA. In fact, many studios sent their first drafts in to judge what they could and could not get away with. Breen's reply, dated February 22, 1946, noted his concern that the character of Kate Nelson and her girls must be changed "as to get away from the inescapable inference of prostitution. It must be established *affirmatively*, that these girls are engaged in a lawful and gainful business, and that the boarding house at which they reside is strictly this, and nothing more." Breen was also concerned with the long speech John Simpson gives at the church meeting. During his sermon, he states that neither "Kate Nelson [nor] her girls, can stop Your word from being heard in Tombstone." Breen noted that revisions in the speech would be needed "in the light of the necessary changes to be made in the characterization of Kate and her girls." (Ford would drop Simpson's entire sermon before filming began.[19])

When it came to the role of Cactus (later to be renamed Chihuahua), Breen was adamant that there be no reference to an illicit relationship with Doc Holliday ("which seems to us to be the inescapable inference in the present script") and that there not be a secondary illicit affair with the character of Billy Clanton. Breen cautioned that "we assume that the 'passionate kisses' between Billy and Cactus will not be excessive or lustful in nature." Another concern was the consumption of liquor in the film. "It seems to us that there is an *excessive* emphasis on this factor, throughout the script.... In line with this same problem, we request that you consider the possibility of changing somewhat, the character of the 'town drunk,' so as to make him a 'character' on some different basis."[20] With Breen's comments in hand, Miller went back to rewriting the script, while Zanuck sent a letter to

Breen stating, "We have no intention of offending the morals of anyone, and many of your ideas in your letter will be automatically taken care of."[21]

In the March 11 draft of the script, Miller added several changes, some of which would be eliminated because of PCA concerns or Ford's simply trimming material while filming.[22] Miller's additions to the March 11 draft included the following.

Posed publicity photograph of Henry Fonda, Linda Darnell and Victor Mature. These types of pictures were not only used in publicizing the movie, but also served as a guide for artists who would design the film's posters (author's collection).

- After Virgil covers James's body with his slicker, the three brothers talk about how his death will affect their father and Nancy (James's fiancé, later changed to Cory Sue). From that scene, Wyatt rides into town to tell the mayor he will take the marshal's job. (Ford dropped this idea before filming.)
- When Wyatt meets the Clantons in the hotel lobby, Old Man Clanton offers his assistance, saying, "Well, if you need any help, call on us. Us cattlemen gotta stick together." As Wyatt walks out of the hotel, Ike, his rifle cradled in his arms, walks to the door and "looks ominously into the dark street." (Ford trimmed the dialogue and action during the filming of this scene.)
- Doc's entrance into the Oriental Saloon had him walking up to the gambler at the table and pulling out a silk handkerchief. Holding one corner, he tells the gambler to take the other end and draw. (He would repeat this gesture with Wyatt at the bar later in this sequence.) As the gambler leaves, Doc fires his gun and laughs loudly as the bullet hits the wall. (Ford scrapped all of this before production began.)
- When Wyatt and Doc go after the missing actor, Granville Thorndyke, the scene remained in Doc's booth, with Billy Clanton walking into the booth, kissing Chihuahua, and giving her a pearl necklace. As Wyatt and Doc head toward the other saloon, Doc tells Wyatt he knows Chihuahua is "a two-timing coquette," but will look great at his funeral. (This was cut due to PCA demands.)
- Wyatt sends Thorndyke back to the Bird Cage Theatre, and he finds Doc in the Oriental Saloon. He comments that parts of Shakespeare he understood, "especially about one's conscience making cowards of all of us." The following morning we see Thorndyke, before he leaves on the stage, reading a review of his performance. He was too drunk to remember any of it, and his missing skull (a stage prop for *Hamlet*) is brought in by Kate Nelson. The missing skull was something of a running joke in the March 11 draft, with Thorndyke always misplacing it and getting the nickname of Yorick by the Clantons and others. (Ford deleted most of this material during filming.)
- After the church services, Wyatt takes Clementine to James's grave. She breaks down, crying, and says how much help Wyatt has been to her. He urges her not to give up on Doc. As they ride back to town, Clementine is awed by the landscape, as Wyatt softly hums "My Darling Clementine," telling her that James used to sing it all the time. (Ford shot these scenes but cut them during editing.)
- When Doc rides off on the stage and leaves Chihuahua behind, she runs up to Clementine's room, and a fight between the two women breaks out. Wyatt, who is playing poker downstairs, hears the commotion and stops the fight. Wyatt notices the cross that belonged to James on the floor. (The PCA voiced concerns about the two women fighting and Ford restaged the whole scene, eliminating most of the fight.)
- After Doc performs surgery on Chihuahua, Clementine and Doc talk, and she tells him he should go back to practicing medicine. Doc admits that he does feel some pride in himself and his former work. (This is similar to the scene between Doc and Sarah Allen in the 1939 *Frontier Marshal*; Ford cut all of this dialogue during filming.)
- Before the gunfight, only Wyatt, Morgan, and Doc are in the jail. The characters of the mayor and Simpson are not present. The gunfight is much different from that in the film. Both Morgan and Doc are successful in sneaking up behind the Clantons, killing Phin. Morgan is then wounded, and Doc pulls him to safety and is wounded. Doc manages to kill Sam Clanton before he dies. Wyatt kills Ike. (Unlike the scene in the film, Ike does not advance toward Wyatt as the stagecoach goes by before being killed.) Old Man Clanton runs

John Ford shot a scene where Wyatt and Clementine visit the grave of James Earp. Zanuck ordered it cut from the preview print. The scene was filmed at the studio, using a rear-screen projection of Monument Valley (author's collection).

out of ammunition and Wyatt tells him to ride away and get out of the territory.[23] (Ford added the characters of the mayor and Simpson to the sequence before filming. Old Man Clanton is killed because of PCA demands.)

Again, the PCA reviewed the script and suggested additional changes. Breen once again urged that Kate Nelson and her girls be identified as dance hall girls much sooner. He also felt that any dialogue showing Kate and her ladies in the Bird Cage Theatre box "be carefully revised to avoid presenting objectionable flavor." Breen once again cautioned against too much excessive drinking in scenes. He urged that they change the town drunk into another type of character, as well as recast some lines in which characters suggest taking a drink. "The character of Thorndyke as addicted to the bottle seems legitimate, but here again, the treatment of him as such, should be restrained."[24]

When it came to dealing with Old Man Clanton in the final scene, the filmmakers had two ideas of handling it: one was to have him arrested, the other simply to set him free, with Wyatt telling him never to come back. Breen was not happy with the latter idea and noted that "in view of the fact that Clanton deliberately, premeditatedly, and cold-bloodedly kills Virgil (scene 184, page 124), it is our carefully considered opinion that, for the finished picture to be approved under the Code, it will be essential that due process of law prevail."[25] In the film, Wyatt lets Old Man Clanton ride away, but Clanton draws his gun and is killed by Morgan.

In addition to the script's being approved, all songs and women's costumes had to receive the PCA's blessing before production could begin. Breen had suggested in his letter of March 27 that the filmmakers hold the fight between Clementine and Chihuahua to a minimum, adding, "Particular care should be exercised in all of these scenes to avoid anything offensive. This, of course, includes any undue exposure of the girls." Breen wrote to Jason Joy at Fox about his concerns over the female costumes. "We wish to extend a general caution regarding these costumes. It seems to us that some of them may possibly photograph badly, depending on the camera angles during actual filming of the picture.... We wish to remind you that these dresses should be arranged and worn in such a manner as to completely cover the breasts of the girls at all times."[26] With the PCA finally signing off on the script, attention to casting the film took priority. Zanuck told Ford in a November 6, 1945, memo that "we are trying to get Henry Fonda as Wyatt Earp, James Stewart as Doc Holliday, Linda Darnell as the Mexican dance hall girl and Jeanne Crain as the young nurse."[27]

This marked the fourth of seven films Henry Fonda would make with John Ford.[28] Fonda was born in Grand Island, Nebraska, in 1905 and began his acting career with a community theatrical troupe under the direction of Dorothy Brando (mother of Marlon Brando). He worked on Broadway for many years before making his film debut in *The Farmer Takes a Wife* (1935). He went on to become one of the most popular stars in the cinema, starring in *The Lady Eve* (1941), *The Ox-Bow Incident* (1943), *The Wrong Man* (1957), *Fail-Safe* (1964), *Once Upon a Time in the West* (1969), and *On Golden Pond* (1981), his last film before his death in 1982 at the age of 77. Fonda and Ford had a serious falling out during the filming on *Mister Roberts* in 1955. Fonda, who had originated the role on Broadway, was not happy with Ford's direction and one evening while on location in Midway expressed his opinions to Ford. The discussion ended with Ford hitting Fonda. Tension on the set between the two men was quite noticeable, with Ford often asking Fonda in front of the crew if his direction met with his approval. Mercifully for cast and crew, Ford's gall bladder needed to be removed once the company returned to Hollywood, and Mervyn LeRoy took over directing the film.[29] After their fight and Ford's leaving the film, the two men did not speak to each other for almost fifteen years. Yet whatever rift there was, it appeared to have healed by 1971, when the two men were reunited during the filming of the CBS special *The American West of John Ford.*

Fox studios attempted to get MGM to loan out James Stewart for the movie; however, the idea of casting Stewart as Holliday was quickly dropped.[30] Ford then thought of using Tyrone Power as Holliday but, as with Stewart, that idea was quickly dismissed. The director then came up with the idea of using Douglas Fairbanks, Jr., and urged Zanuck to think the idea over, adding "He might be really terribly good in it. He would look about the same age as Henry [Fonda] and as it's a flamboyant role it is quite possible he could kick the hell out of it."[31] Zanuck was not thrilled with the idea, mainly because Fairbanks, Jr., would be a free agent and cost more in salary compared with a studio contract star. Vincent Price was another Ford suggestion that was met with silence by Zanuck. Ford was not at all happy with Zanuck's suggestion—Fox contract star Victor Mature. Eventually, Ford came around and agreed to use Mature for the role, which Zanuck happily noted in a memo to the director. "I am pleased you like Victor Mature. Personally I think the guy has been one of the most underrated performers in Hollywood.... A part like Doc Holliday will be sensational for him as I know you will get a great performance out of him and I agree with you that the peculiar traits of his personality are ideal for a characterization such as this."[32]

Zanuck notified Ford that Jeanne Crain would not play Clementine because "the part is comparatively so small that we would be simply crucified by both the public and the critics for putting her in it. She is the biggest box-office attraction on the lot today."[33] Ford finally cast Cathy Downs, a Fox contract player, in the role.[34] Nor did Ford get Anne Baxter or Donna Reed for the role of Chihuahua. Instead, he had to use Linda Darnell, who was also under contract to the studio. Veteran character actor Walter Brennan was hired to play Old Man Clanton, while Grant Withers (loaned out from Republic Studios) played Ike Clanton. John Ireland was set as Billy Clanton.[35] Ford peppered his film with players who were quickly becoming known as members of his fabled stock company. Jane Darwell was cast as Kate Nelson; Ward Bond as Morgan Earp; J. Farrell MacDonald as Mac the bartender; Russell Simpson as John Simpson the church leader (who bears a tremendous resemblance to an older Wyatt Earp wearing a dark suit, hat and mustache!); Jack Pennick as the stagecoach driver; Fred Libby as Phin Clanton; Mae Marsh as John Simpson's sister; William Steele as Indigo, the wrangler at the Wells Fargo corral; and Danny Borzage as an accordionist.[36]

One actor he was unable to cast was black actor Stepin Fetchit. Fetchit, who had worked

During a break in filming *My Darling Clementine*, cast members posed for a picture on the town set in Monument Valley. Standing, from left: Cathy Downs, Roy Roberts, Grant Withers, Fred Libby, Walter Brennan, Francis Ford, Mickey Simpson (standing behind Ford), Linda Darnell, Tim Holt, Don Garner, unidentified woman, Ward Bond, Henry Fonda and John Ireland. On top of the stagecoach: John Ford (center, with sunglasses), Victor Mature, Jack Pennick (author's collection).

with Ford in the early 1930s, was in severe financial trouble and needed work. He had been a very popular performer, but by 1946 his dim-witted, shuffling, bug-eyed performances, despite their excellent comedic timing, were viewed as a degrading stereotype. Zanuck agreed with Ford that Fetchit would be great in the film, but he told the director that the current president of the increasingly militant NAACP had warned studio heads that casting Fetchit in films would result in heavy criticism and financial boycott at the box office.[37] Instead, Ford cast his brother, Francis, in the role of Old Dad.

Zanuck felt the film needed a new title to replace *Frontier Marshal*. That title struck him as ordinary, and he didn't want something that sounded as if it had previously been made. Nor did he want something that sounded too much like a Western. "If possible I would like to get more or less of a neutral title and not be tied down to *Boom Town* or *Tombstone* or anything that sounds like a typical western. Our picture is far too important for this," he noted.[38] Zanuck told Ford that he had no problem using a fictitious name for the Earp and Holliday characters, although he admitted using the real names would give the film an authenticity and not make it so generic. Zanuck contacted the studio legal department to see whether they had had to deal with any lawsuits with the 1939 version. Other than Sadie's complaints and the studio's not advertising Wyatt Earp's name in the ads or movie posters, the legal department had had no problems so it was decided to use the real names in the Ford film. They did have to obtain permission from Wells Fargo to use that name in the movie, as well as the Tombstone *Epitaph* for the use of its name for newspaper headlines in the film, although Ford discarded many newspaper headlines once filming began.

Ford planned to film interiors at the Fox studio, and then to spend almost four weeks in Monument Valley, his first return to the area since *Stagecoach*. How he found this unique location has always been debated among Ford scholars. Actor George O'Brien said he originally told Ford about the area, as did John Wayne. Ford himself claimed he found the area in the late 1920s while driving back to Los Angeles. The most credible story is the one told by Harry Goulding's wife. Goulding and his wife, "Mike," bought 640 acres in 1923 and began to trade with the Navajos, ultimately building a two-story trading post, which still stands today.[39] Harry heard that a film company was scouting locations for a Western in nearby Flagstaff, Arizona, in 1938. He and his wife took several photographs of the Valley area and headed to Hollywood, where he was able to meet with *Stagecoach*'s location manager and show him his pictures. Once Ford looked at the photographs, he fell in love with the location and eventually shot seven pictures in Monument Valley between 1939 and 1964.

The decision to film *My Darling Clementine* in Monument Valley was a financial godsend for the Navajo tribe. The studio built the set of the town, at a cost of $250,000, on a stretch of road that leads into the famous Valley. It was the "biggest and most expensive location jaunt since before the war" for the studio.[40] Construction on the town set began March 20, 1946, with a crew of twenty laborers sent out by the studio and the rest supplied by the Navajo tribe. When film companies typically build sets on location, most of the companies often cheat and build only what shows up on film, leaving many buildings with only three walls and half a roof. However, in Monument Valley, the town set (which numbered close to 40 buildings, including an exterior recreation of the Bird Cage Theatre) were fully enclosed (four walls and a roof). The logic for this decision was to have housing for the film equipment as well as to provide a wardrobe, makeup, and hair styling areas for the performers. This also allowed Ford to use long, sweeping shots of the area without having to worry about moving cumbersome trucks and equipment every day. Fox sold the set to the Navajo tribe in 1948 for $5, and it remained there until 1951, when it was torn down and sold for

John Ford returned to Monument Valley to film portions of *My Darling Clementine* in 1946. It was the first film he made in the Valley since *Stagecoach* (1939). Henry Fonda strikes an impressive pose with the famous East and West Mittens behind him (author's collection).

scrap. (Part of the town set is briefly seen in Ford's 1949 film *She Wore a Yellow Ribbon*.) The studio paid the Navajo tribe $25 for every day they filmed in Monument Valley, and over 450 Navajos were hired by the studio in various job capacities. Unskilled Navajo laborers were paid $6.60 an hour, while skilled laborers received $9.50 an hour. Any Navajo mounted riders used in the film were paid $9 for an eight-hour day, and feed was supplied for their horses. (The studio also employed ninety families from the Mormon town of Bluff, Utah, northeast of Monument Valley, to play townspeople in several scenes.) Fred Yazzie and Frank Bradley were paid $100 a month to provide security for the Monument Valley set; Bradley and his brother, Lee, also worked as translators for Ford. After this movie, the two brothers worked on every film Ford made in the Valley.

Ford had a smaller version of the town set built on Stage 1 at Fox studios for the night scenes in Tombstone. Filming night sequences in Monument Valley would have been nearly impossible because of the number of lights needed to illuminate the sets and surrounding area. With an interior set, Ford had complete control over lighting (and no weather related worries). This was especially important for the rain sequences. Some night shots, such as that of the Earps looking over Tombstone for the first time and the chase between Virgil and Billy Clanton, were shot in the daytime. (The cinematographer used a filter over the lens that gave the appearance of evening. This type of shot is referred to as "day for night.")

Stuart Lake once again reared his head, sending a letter to the legal department at Fox. The correspondence clearly suggests that he was trying to get involved with the production. In his letter, he throws out some bait by saying that Ford should have gotten in touch with him "because the real story is a honey." He goes on to say that he had to leave key material out of his book and he's the only one alive who knows these things. He also notes how steadily his book continues to sell, claiming a rate of several thousand copies a year, and even suggests a special edition being published as a tie-in to the film's release. The letter was forwarded to Ford, who chose to ignore Lake. He would make his own film on Earp and needed no advice.

Filming began on April 16, 1946, at Fox studios. A little less than three weeks into production, on May 8, the company left for Monument Valley. Taking a train from Union Station in Los Angeles, they arrived the following day in Flagstaff, Arizona, where the cast and crew either took a bus or a chartered plane to the Valley. The film company built an X-shaped landing strip near Goulding's lodge, which allowed planes to make daily flights with supplies and to take the day's footage back to Hollywood. The plane was also on stand-by in case of any injuries to the cast and crew.[41] Ford and the main cast members would stay in cabins next to Goulding's lodge, while the rest of the cast and crew were put up in tents on the valley floor below the lodge. There was also a large building set up for dinner, and a 55,000-gallon water tank constructed for the showers.

Making a film in Monument Valley could be difficult. One morning the company was greeted with a light dusting of snow. By that afternoon, a huge sandstorm could hit, and during dinner there would be a cloudburst, blowing down some tents in the camp.[42] During the horseback chase scene between Tim Holt (playing Virgil Earp) and John Ireland (playing Billy Clanton), Holt's horse took a spill, with the actor under it. He got up, remounted the horse, and rode on. It wasn't until after Ford yelled cut that it was discovered that Holt had broken four ribs.[43]

Evenings on location were something to look forward to, as Henry Fonda remembered. "Ford knew that there were 150 to 200 people in the company and a large cast and crew that would be stuck on this location with nothing to do at night. And we were there for three weeks. Every night after chow ... there would be a campfire and there would be something different happening every night. And he [Ford] put me in charge—as a matter of fact, I was the camp director of Camp Junalusca we called it.... There would be a program every night, and during the day when you're on the set, between takes you'd be talking about it, planning and organizing it. Anyway, it was something that people got to looking forward

Filming *My Darling Clementine* in Monument Valley. The Earp brothers (Ward Bond, Henry Fonda, Tim Holt) stand outside the hotel. Note the wood plank to allow the camera dolly to move easily. Camera dollies have been around since the early 1910s and are still in use today. The round white ball at the end of the microphone boom is designed to cut down the amount of wind noise that would be picked up while recording sound (courtesy of the Academy of Motion Pictures Arts and Sciences).

to. And I remember at the end—the end of the program—whatever it was each night, Ford would give the cue to a bugle player.... when nobody could see Ford give it and he would disappear.... and suddenly when it got to the last song, he would blow taps from way back ... and, I tell you, people would cry. It was nostalgic. It was being a child again at camp."[44]

From May 10 to 12, Ford shot the opening scenes of the film with the cattle drive and the introduction of Old Man Clanton and Ike. From May 13 to 17, Ford shot various scenes which took place on the street set, including the famous chair balancing sequence. "More people have asked me about this balancing act then almost anything else I've done. It wasn't in the script, but Jack figured it was something Wyatt Earp would do. So I did it," Fonda later recalled.[45] This sequence shows Ford's inspired direction, adding touches that were not in the script but that became memorable moments on the screen. Fonda's Earp makes a habit of sitting in a chair outside of the hotel, watching the vast expanse of the desert before him. His two brothers, Morgan and Virgil, stop to talk before they walk down the porch, passing Chihuahua, who is carrying a pitcher of milk. Morgan gives a loud whinny as she walks by, and she tosses the contents of the pitcher into his face. Morgan walks off stunned, wiping his face. Wyatt, who is now sitting in his chair, leans his foot against the porch post. He slowly performs a balancing act, changing one foot to the other on the post and extending his arms out, ignoring Chihuahua's predictions of what Doc Holliday will do to him for hitting him over the head the previous night. As she leaves, Wyatt lets his foot down and smiles after her.

None of this action was in the script. Morgan's horse whinny (something Ward Bond also did in Ford's *The Searchers*) was planned, although Chihuahua's response of throwing the milk was a pure Fordian touch. No doubt making Bond the butt of a joke delighted Ford to no end, as Bond was one of his favorite targets for "being in the barrel," and the actor's ego loved the attention from Ford, no matter how caustic. The balancing act was not in the script, either. Fonda told director Peter Bogdanovich, "As we got ready to do it, Ford said 'Turn your chair a little bit,' so I did. He said, 'Lean back in it.' There was a veranda post there and he said 'Put your foot up on it.' So I put one

Ford came up with the idea of Fonda balancing himself on the building post while filming this scene. It became a memorable moment in the movie. Note the two Navajo Indians in the background (author's collection).

foot up and then he said, 'Put your other foot up there' and I leaned back. 'Change the position.' It became a little choreographed dance with pushing away and changing the position of my feet. It became a little moment that was not indicated until then and everyone remembers and comments about. Again, it's so typical. You don't know when he thought of it, whether it was at that moment or driving to the location in the morning. He never gives you a clue until that moment."[46]

From May 18 to 20, Ford filmed the sequence of Wyatt and Clementine walking to church and the church dance. Over the years, many film scholars have offered countless theories about this sequence, attempting to explain what Ford was expressing with Earp and Clementine going to church and the dance. Some have suggested it represents Earp's indoctrination into a civilized society. This is just a lot of theoretical hot air uttered by those who have no clue about Ford's talent or taste. Winston Miller recalled, "I have read things about My Darling Clementine where people read things into it that weren't there. I knew because I wrote it. What you saw was what you got. There [were] no tertiary motivations."[47] As for the long shots of Fonda walking, which many film theorists have read a lot into, Ford simply loved Fonda's slow-pace stride and let the camera capture it (much like Howard Hawks loved Wayne's unique walk in his films). The dance between Wyatt and Clementine was never originally planned, but Ford remembered Fonda's knee-high dancing done in Young Mr. Lincoln (1939) and decided to add it into this film. "I did that dance in three [Ford] pictures," Fonda said. "He just loved it. I did it just joking the first time and he laughed it up and embroidered it."[48]

Home movies shot on location show everyone having a good time and sharing a lot of laughs. Although most people had fond memories of working on the film, one actor did not enjoy his experience working for Ford. Although the exact reasons are not known, Walter Brennan was not happy with Ford's caustic wit and prodding of actors. (The home movies show a very sedate Brennan on the set.) According to Ford biographer Scott Eyman, Brennan was having trouble mounting his horse in one shot. Ford yelled at the actor, "Can't you even mount a horse?" Brennan quickly replied, "No, but I have three Oscars for acting."[49] Brennan later told Ford he never wanted to work with him again, and he never did.

The gunfight sequence took three days to film (May 21 to 23). In The American West of John Ford, Ford and Fonda discuss the movie and how Earp told Ford the shootout occurred. Again, the Ford blarney is laid on thick, and it is obvious that both Ford and Fonda know he's telling a tall tale. Ford relates that Wyatt Earp lived north of Pasadena and that his wife was a very devout religious woman. A couple of times a year, she'd attend religious retreats in Utah and northern Arizona, and Wyatt would take the streetcar to Universal. This is where Ford met Earp, and the old lawman told him how the fight happened. (Needless to say, none of this is true; it is just Ford enhancing a story.) He claims that the stagecoach that rides past the O.K. Corral in the film at a crucial time during the gunfight actually happened and that it was timed by Wyatt. "That is the way it exactly happened," Ford proclaims on camera as Fonda looks off. Once again, it was the heroic legend that mattered more to Ford in his cinematic storytelling.

Friday, May 24, was devoted to filming Wyatt and Morgan's departure from Tombstone and Wyatt's final goodbye to Clementine. The next day involved the horse chase between Virgil and Billy Clanton as well as scenes on the front porch of the Clanton ranch, which were shot in front of Goulding's trading post. On Sunday, May 26, Ford shot the scene in which Wyatt goes alone to James's grave (this would later be reshot at the studio) as well as scenes (later deleted) of Wyatt and Clementine at James's grave and riding in a buckboard.

The last two days in the Valley consisted of Wyatt chasing Doc's stagecoach and their confrontation. The company wrapped filming in Monument Valley on May 28 and headed back to Los Angeles. Filming resumed on May 31 at Fox studios, with the day devoted to the night campsite sequences. The interior scenes involving the jail set and Wyatt coming to the mayor's hotel room were shot on June 3 on Stage 7. The following two days were spent filming scenes inside the hotel lobby, on Stage 1; on June 6, Ford filmed the night rain scenes on the interior set of the street. On Stage 1, Ford had not only a portion of the Tombstone town set built but also the interiors of the Oriental Saloon, the barber shop, the hotel lobby, and dining room. This would allow Ford to turn the camera around and shoot looking out towards the windows for night sequences. This was a quite common aspect used in filmmaking, and even the *Gunsmoke* television series had an interior set of the main street with key sets (Matt Dillon's office, the Long Branch Saloon, Dodge House, and so on) furnished inside for filming certain scenes.

The next three days were spent on Stage 7, where Ford shot scenes involving the hotel rooms of Doc, Clementine, and Chihuahua, including her being shot by Billy Clanton. June 11 saw the company filming the Earp campsite in the rain, where they discover James's body. The next day, Ford shot additional scenes of Wyatt and Clementine at James's grave, as well as of Doc telling Clementine to leave town. These were shot as a rear-screen process, which involved a moving image being projected onto a translucent screen from behind the screen, with the actors, and possibly a portion of the set, placed in front of the screen. The entire action, and the background footage projected onto the screen, are photographed by a camera synchronized with the rear screen projector. This is the method used when we see Wyatt

Cut from the final print was a scene with Wyatt (Fonda, on horseback) and Morgan (Ward Bond, driving the buckboard) riding out of Tombstone after the gunfight (courtesy of the Academy of Motion Pictures Arts and Sciences).

alone at James's grave, as well as when we see close shots of Doc on the stagecoach. The last day of filming, June 14, involved the scenes of Wyatt subduing Indian Charlie at Kate Nelson's boarding house.

With principal photography completed, Ford turned the film over to his editor, Dorothy Spencer. Once it was assembled, Zanuck viewed the film. Ford's version is laconic, with passages of scenes that have little to do with the overall story (such as the Earps vs. the Clantons) but which add wonderful texture and nuance to the film. Winston Miller stated that the movie has a lot of flaws in its construction. "Earp stays in town to get his brother's killer, and we vamp for sixty pages with what we hope are interesting scenes. We don't get back onto the brother's killer until way late in the script."[50] Miller admitted that if they didn't vamp, the picture would have been wrapped up in two reels, so they needed to add other things.

After watching Ford's cut of the picture, Zanuck sent him a letter on June 25, 1946: "I didn't tell you the truth last night when I gave you my reactions to the film.... You have in the film a great number of outstanding individual episodes and sequences. You have a certain Western magnificence and a number of character touches that rival your best work, but to me the picture does not come up to our anticipation. I know we can cut it down and make a number of adjustments and these will probably represent a definite improvement.... Many of my recommendations in the editorial handling of the film are radical. I believe we have sufficient film and that you have provided ample protection to make 95 percent of the changes possible.... It is my opinion that in this picture we have to be *big time* all the way. We cannot be big time only in certain outstanding episodes." Zanuck goes on to ask that Ford suggest to producer Samuel Engel that Zanuck be given the film to edit, and he reminds the director that he took over editing duties on Ford's *How Green Was My Valley* and *The Grapes of Wrath*, which won them both Oscars.[51]

Zanuck did take over editing the film and ordered a new scene shot with Wyatt at James's grave. Many believe that he did this to change the date of James's death on his headstone, which now reads 1882! (James, the second oldest brother, lived until 1926.) The scene is wholly reminiscent of one in *Young Mr. Lincoln*, in which Lincoln visits the grave of his first love and makes the decision to practice law. It is such a typical Ford scene that not many realize it was actually directed by Lloyd Bacon. Zanuck sent Bacon a memo on July 13, noting, "I thought the rushes that you did for *My Darling Clementine* were excellent, particularly the scene at the grave. This should be a very effective sequence."[52] Bacon also reshot some scenes between Doc and Clementine in their first meeting.

For years, many people believed the print they saw of *My Darling Clementine* was the only version in existence. However, in the 1990s, a 35mm nitrate print from Fox was found at the UCLA Film Archive. When it was compared to the original release print, archivists realized that they had in their possession a preview print of the movie. From this, they learned that although Zanuck made many cuts, these were not as radical as he let on in his June 25 letter to Ford. The following compares the preview print and the final release print:

- *Preview Print:* Chihuahua leaves Mac at the bar and goes outside to watch the stage arrive. Billy Clanton comes up and tells her that Doc is not on it and kisses her. She does not respond but says, "Be a good boy," before walking off. Chihuahua goes back into the saloon and begins singing "Under a Broad Sombrero" with the saloon's musical group before she walks off and looks out the door behind Earp, seated at a poker table. She then looks at Wyatt's cards and gives the gambler the sign with her fingers.

Final Print: After Chihuahua leaves the bar, she goes back to look out the door behind Wyatt at the poker table. She then looks at Wyatt's cards and gives the gambler the sign with her fingers.

• *Preview Print:* After Doc has chased off the gambler in the saloon, Wyatt walks up to him and they introduce themselves. Doc offers him a drink, and Wyatt asks for whiskey. Doc insists he have champagne. Wyatt agrees and takes a drink. Wyatt says, "Ya know, Doc, if I weren't your guest—mind you, I said if I weren't—and you didn't take so unkindly to marshals, I'd say this drink tastes like fermented vinegar."

Final Print: After Doc runs the gambler off, Wyatt walks up to Doc and they introduce themselves and talk. The line about the champagne tasting like fermented vinegar has been cut.

• *Preview Print:* The interior of the Bird Cage Theatre has several shots of people milling around, men greeting Kate Nelson and her girls, and a Mexican woman selling tamales. We see Doc come in, sporting bandages on his face. As he sits with Wyatt in their booth, Wyatt looks at Doc's face and asks what happened. "Shaving," Doc says. We then see the barber, holding a glass of beer, standing on the floor of the theatre and telling Doc, "I got it working good now, Doc!" We come back to a medium shot of Wyatt and Doc. Doc says to Wyatt, "Chair." "What?" Wyatt asks him. "Barber chair. New. Try it!" Wyatt just nods. Chihuahua comes into the box seats and kisses Doc before looking at Earp. Doc introduces her to Wyatt.

Final Print: We see the interior of the Bird Cage, with people milling about, men greeting Kate Nelson and her girls, and a Mexican woman selling tamales. Doc and Wyatt are sitting in their chairs when Chihuahua comes into the box seats and kisses Doc before looking at Earp. Doc introduces them. All the talk of shaving and the chair have been eliminated.

• *Preview Print:* We hear the sounds of Wyatt's boots as he walks down a sidewalk. He looks around and doesn't see Old Dad bringing out his chair. The hotel clerk comes out with the chair and apologizes for Old Dad's absence. Wyatt sits down and makes a comment to the clerk that the stage is late. Two of the hotel waitresses come out, greet Earp, and hit the triangle as the stage arrives. The driver calls out to the passengers, and a gambler gets off the stage and looks at Earp. Wyatt asks how things in Deadwood are, tells him to go eat, then get back on the stage. The clerk helps Clementine Carter down. Wyatt gets up and retrieves her luggage from the stage. They go inside, where she asks the clerk about Doc. She takes a room right across the hall from Doc's. Pushing open his door, she looks at some photos and we hear the theme song, "My Darling Clementine."

Final Print: Long shot of the town. We see Wyatt already sitting as the two women from the hotel come out to hit the triangle and greet the guests. The gambler and Wyatt exchange their dialogue. As Clementine gets off the stage, the theme song "My Darling Clementine" begins and plays through the entire scene in Doc's room, until Clementine leaves and closes the door.

• *Preview Print:* As Doc is about to start operating on Chihuahua, he asks if she's ready. Chihuahua nods and Kate Nelson gives her a napkin to bite on. Doc calls out, "Miss Carter!" Clementine replies, "Ready, Dr. Holliday." As she walks out of frame, the camera holds on Wyatt (deep in shadows) at the bar for a moment before cutting to a long shot of the saloon where people are clustered around the operating table. We hear Chihuahua cry out, "Oh, Ma!"

Final Print: As Doc is about to start operating on Chihuahua, he asks if she's ready. Chihuahua nods and Kate Nelson gives her a napkin to bite on. Cut to a long shot of the saloon where people are clustered around the operating table, and we hear Chihuahua cry out, "Oh, Ma!"

• *Preview Print:* At the end of the gunfight, Morgan comes up to Wyatt and simply says, "Wyatt..." He asks, "Doc?" Morgan replies, "Yeah," as Wyatt swings over the fence and they walk to Doc's body. They look at Doc, and then Wyatt says, "I'll get his boots." As he walks off, Simpson and the mayor come in before the scene fades out. As the next scene fades in, people are standing outside the hotel saying goodbye to Wyatt and Morgan, who is driving a buckboard. Two girls from the hotel give Wyatt a basket of food. As Wyatt steps into his saddle, he looks at Doc's room with curtains blowing in the wind. He turns his attention to the people around him and says, "Goodbye, folks. Me and my brothers, we're ... we're obliged to ya." They ride out but stop at the edge of town, where Clementine waits. Morgan bids her goodbye and drives off. Wyatt gets off his horse and tells her they are headed for California to see their father. She tells him she is staying on in town and will be the new schoolteacher. Wyatt mentions that he might come east and get some cattle and stop by. She asks if he'll stop by the school house and he says yes. They shake hands and he gets back into the saddle. "Ma'am, I sure do like that name. Clementine," he tells her before riding off.

Final Print: At the end of the gunfight, Morgan comes up to Wyatt and simply says, "Wyatt..." He asks, "Doc?" Morgan replies, "Yeah" as Wyatt swings over the fence and they walk to Doc's body. They look at Doc, and then Wyatt walks off as the scene fades out. As the next scene fades in, Wyatt and Morgan stop at the edge of town where Clementine waits. Morgan bids her goodbye and drives off. Wyatt gets off his horse and tells her they are headed for California to see their father. She tells him she is staying on in town and will be the new schoolteacher. Wyatt mentions that he might come east and get some cattle and stop by. She asks if he'll stop by the school house and he says yes. They shake hands and he gives her a quick kiss on the cheek. Stepping back into the saddle, he says, "Ma'am, I sure do like that name. Clementine." Wyatt rides off as Clementine watches.

A sneak preview of Zanuck's cut of the picture went fine until the final scene. Zanuck summed up the problem in a memo to producer Samuel Engel: "I liked the ending of *My Darling Clementine* exactly as it is. It is completely satisfactory to me from every standpoint. Unfortunately 2,000 people who saw the picture at a preview did not agree. You were present and you know what happened and you have read the cards.... You will recall that the last scene was perfect up to where Fonda reaches out to shake hands with Cathy Downs. It was such an obvious build-up for a kiss or for some demonstration of affection that the audience felt first amused and then completely cheated.... I do feel that it will be honest, legitimate and reasonable if Henry looks at the girl, smiles, leans over and kisses her on the cheek. It is a good-bye kiss and nothing more. He *does* like her. The audience *knows* he likes her. Now is no time for us to get smart."[53] In mid–September 1946, Fonda and Downs came back for a quick reshoot of the end scene, with Wyatt saying, "Yes, Ma'am, I sure will," and then kissing her on the cheek before stepping back, and the cut back to the original footage. (Looking at the scene it is obvious that this was added and shot on a soundstage.)

Before the film's release, producer Samuel Engel petitioned for a writing credit. Winston Miller did not go on location, but Engel did and made some minor dialogue changes, which allowed him to request the shared screen credit. Neither Ford nor Miller was happy,

Wyatt and Clementine say goodbye. When Ford shot this scene in Monument Valley, he had Fonda shake hands with Cathy Downs. After a preview screening, Fox's studio head, Darryl F. Zanuck, went back and shot an insert of Fonda kissing Downs on the cheek. Ford was very unhappy and refused to sign another long-term contract with Fox (author's collection).

and Miller even asked Engel why he did it. Engel reportedly said that everyone knows a producer credit means nothing on a John Ford film, since he's his own producer, but a writing credit was different.[54]

Released on October 16, 1946, the film garnered praise from the critics. *Time* called it "[a] rattling, good movie full of gusto, gunplay and romance.... Director Ford has accomplished more than an intelligent retelling of a hoary yarn. His camera sometimes pauses, with a fresh, childlike curiosity, to examine the shape and texture of a face, a pair of square-dancing feet, a scrap of desert landscape or a sunlit dusty road. The leisurely lens.... makes some of Ford's black-&-white sequences as richly lifelike as anything ever trapped in Technicolor."[55]

"When John Ford is handling a subject he likes, he has no peer as a director in the entire motion picture industry.... The photography ranks with the best ever achieved by Joe MacDonald, many compositions actually breath-taking.... Fonda's work is of his most delightful caliber. He has many moments that are especially enjoyable.... Victor Mature has never been seen to such advantage as in what he makes of Doc Holliday," commented *The Hollywood Reporter*.[56]

Variety felt the film "reproduces vividly and excitingly on the screen the melodramatic life and atmosphere of one of the toughest, wildest towns in the old West.... The film is tops in acting, direction, and authenticity of background.... If this one misses at the box office then both westerns and melodrama are out.... Henry Fonda's interpretation of Wyatt Earp makes the famous marshal of Tombstone a gentle mannered soul of stern purpose.... Victor Mature's portrayal of Doc Holliday is a standout acting job."[57]

"My Darling Clementine proves that Ford is a master of combining art and action.... John Ford has created a remarkable film—remarkable for its imaginative handling of raw and sometimes brutal material to create a moody, almost poetic, picture.... Surprise of the picture is Victor Mature's performance. Cast as the renegade doctor, Mature turns in an excellent performance that should completely erase his earlier, pretty-boy performances.... My Darling Clementine is a quiet, down-to-earth film that pulls you into its time and place and keeps you there, getting to know the folks, until the final fadeout," wrote the Motion Picture Herald.[58]

The film earned $4.5 million, which allowed it to just about break even because of its high production costs. Despite the lack of a huge profit, Zanuck offered Ford a contract for $600,000 a year to stay at the studio. But Ford had had enough. Years later he said he was disappointed with the cuts Zanuck made to his film and that those actions prompted him to form his own company, Argosy Productions, to satisfy his need for autonomy. Although he would return on occasion to Fox studios, the collaboration Zanuck and Ford enjoyed during the 1930s was definitely a thing of the past.

In the years that followed, Ford never regarded My Darling Clementine as one of his favorite films. Zanuck's recutting the movie hurt Ford deeply and he would not admit to anyone that the film was any good, let alone one of his favorites. Despite Zanuck's recut, however, My Darling Clementine is one of Ford's best pictures. He filled it with lyrical moments that embrace the heroic image of Wyatt Earp. As much as Stuart Lake made Earp a hero in the literary world, John Ford elevated Earp to that same stature in cinema. Yet Ford's Earp is a reluctant hero. He, like many protagonists in the Western genre, is pressed into service when violence strikes close to home. Once Earp responds, there is no doubt of his enforcing the law, yet it is done in a slow-paced way (possibly to match Fonda's own easygoing pace). Ford's Earp is not as hard-edged as in later portrayals in other movies. He is more willing to win a fight by using his placid manner than drawing a gun. Like the real Earp, this cinematic version will use a gun only as a last resort.

Ford opens with the Earps driving cattle, and we are introduced to each character with quick shots. We then see Old Man Clanton and Ike pull up in a buckboard. By showing them against a gray, cloudy sky, Ford indicates that they are the villains (as does Cyril Mockridge's obvious score). When we get our first close look at the two Clantons, their eyes are heavily shadowed by the brims of their hats; they are ominous. Old Man Clanton imposes his rule over his family with a whip; his gun is a secondary weapon. (One could suggest that Old Man Clanton is a cousin to Liberty Valance, who uses his quirt to unleash his violence.) Within the opening minutes, before anything else has happened, we know that conflict will arise between these two parties.

A theme commonly found in Ford films is the family, be it the army in his Cavalry trilogy, the Welsh family in How Green Was My Valley, the political associates in The Last Hurrah, or the Joads in The Grapes of Wrath. The same is true in My Darling Clementine. In the brief dinner camp scene, he conveys the close bonds between the four brothers by showing us their good-natured teasing of James who has bought an expensive cross necklace for his fiancé. Ford succinctly captures the warmth and feeling of kin among the four men.

Although this is a posed picture, it captures Joseph MacDonald's wonderful chiaroscuro lighting. This scene, an interior set of the town's exterior, was shot on Stage 1 at Fox studios (author's collection).

My Darling Clementine has some of the most strikingly beautiful and dramatic photography of any black-and-white Western. (Oddly, the movie was originally planned to be filmed in Technicolor, but this was dropped because of costs.) The lighting and composition give some scenes a film noir aura. Certainly one of the most striking shots in the film uses chiaroscuro: the three Earp brothers riding to the edge of Tombstone. (The effect is doubly amazing when one realizes that Ford and cinematographer Joe MacDonald shot this as day for night.) Wyatt is in the middle, flanked by Virgil and Morgan, as they pull up their horses. Wyatt's horse stops on a small rise, making him stand out as the dominant figure. Ford has the three men pause for a moment, looking over the town as if they are surveying their destiny, before Virgil says, "There it is. Tombstone." After a brief pause, Wyatt flatly says, "Let's go." As they arrive in Tombstone, Ford shows a wild and woolly town with plenty of cowboys carousing. The way the town set is lit for evening, is very reminiscent of the way Ford shot the sets of Lordsburg in *Stagecoach* (1939). Despite having filmed this scene on a soundstage, Ford conveys a realistic quality to Tombstone.

While the town may be wild and woolly, Tombstone has some sense of sophistication in the form of the barber shop. The three Earp brothers dismount in front of the building, and the barber welcomes them to the "Bon Ton Tonsorial Parlor." Wyatt asks if it is a barber shop, and the proprietor, defeated in his attempt to sound cosmopolitan, sullenly gives in with, "If you want to call it that." Ford injects further comedy into the scene as Wyatt reclines in the barber chair and almost topples over. The barber admits he has not gotten used to the chair, noting that it came all the way from Chicago. Ford uses the barber chair as a running gag in the film, but the one scene where it adds a great deal of humor—Doc pointing to his facial bandages—was eliminated in the final print. Again, Ford finds comic relief in attempts at being worldly in a Western town.

When the brothers discover James's body, Ford uses brief cuts to build the tension before actually showing the body. We see the Earp brothers ride in the rain (all of this was shot on a soundstage) and exclaim that the cattle are gone. They do not mention James at all. There are three quick shots—the empty chuck wagon, the rained-out campfire, and pans and pots filling with rainwater—before we see James lying in the mud. Ford adds a unique touch to this shot by having James's right foot turned in his stirrup, his body lying in the mud with his horse next to him. Ford's Wyatt treats the deceased with some gentleness by shielding James's face from the rain with his hands. After Virgil covers the body with his slicker, Ford simply has the three men stand there in the rain, saying nothing. By having them stand silently over the body in the rain, and with the effective use of lighting, Ford manages to say what dialogue could never have accomplished.

When Wyatt comes face to face with the Clantons at the hotel (after accepting the marshal's job), Ford uses the same technique to create tension. The viewer is inside the hotel lobby looking at the main doors, which are quickly opened by two of the Clanton boys. With something befitting a military officer, each boy stands at his door and waits for Old Man Clanton to enter, followed by his other two boys. They stop as they see Wyatt descend the stairs. Ford uses close-ups of the Clantons' reaction to Earp's presence before cutting to a reaction close-up of Wyatt. As Wyatt relates that he has taken a new job, Ford remains on a two-shot of Old Man Clanton and Ike at the hotel counter. Old Man Clanton says, "Well, good luck to you, Mr.... ?" Wyatt replies, "Earp. Wyatt Earp." Instead of using a close-up of Wyatt uttering his name, Ford remains on the two Clantons and uses their reaction to stress the importance of his name. As Wyatt walks out, with the other four Clanton boys watching, Ford cuts to a long shot of Wyatt walking along the boardwalk as the rain continues. It is a symbolic shot of the hero walking alone, facing his enemies and his destiny.

Although the scene of Wyatt at James's grave was later reshot by another director, there is such a seamlessness that few ever would suspect that someone other than Ford had handled the duty. In many of Ford's films, the protagonist sits at a grave, talking to the departed: Fonda in *Young Mr. Lincoln* (1939), John Wayne in *She Wore a Yellow Ribbon* (1949), Carroll Baker in *How the West Was Won* (1962). Ford uses these scenes to convey a character's feelings and emotions (aside from its being a very Irish trait). Sitting at his grave, Wyatt comments that James didn't get much of a chance at life. He tells James that he and their brothers will be staying in Tombstone for a while. "Can't tell—maybe when we leave this country, young kids like you will be able to grow up and live safe," he says before riding off. We can speculate that these lines were ruminative of those who served in World War II who spoke similar words over their fallen brethren's graves. Certainly one could see that the filmmakers, who had all recently been discharged from active duty (Ford, Zanuck, Miller, Fonda, and many more), would have had such feelings—sentiments easily transferred to this scene.

Ford always used humor as a way of easing the tension of a scene that was overly sentimental or dramatic. It was his way of giving the audience a break and allowing himself to continue to build on the story. A humorous scene is placed next to a dramatic scene in most of his movies. The example often cited is when John Wayne's character is given a silver watch by his cavalry troop before his retirement in *She Wore a Yellow Ribbon*. To read the inscription, Wayne has to pull out a pair of spectacles, and he shyly looks around before donning them. Ford felt that such gestures eased the sentiment of the scene for the audience. In *My Darling Clementine*, he has toned down his usual boisterous comedy, yet he still displays touches of humor throughout. From the barber chair to Morgan's getting hit in the face with a pitcher of milk to the patrons of the Bird Cage Theatre wanting to run the owner around town on a rail, Ford allows moments of humor to populate the film without taking away from the dramatic content. One of the more obvious comedic scenes involves the traveling thespian, Granville Thorndyke. Although the drunken actor is humorous, he is also a tragic figure. When he is forced to perform in another saloon by the Clantons, the years of drinking, and age itself, cause him to forget lines from *Hamlet*'s soliloquy. True to his policy, Ford comes up with another humorous moment when the actor bids farewell to the town citizens—and skips out on his hotel bill!

There is a wonderful example of Ford's using comedic moment without going overboard when Wyatt has been given a haircut with a new hairstyle (another attempt at sophistication in the West). Sitting in a straight-back chair at the barber shop, Wyatt looks at his new hairstyle with some concern that he is too "dandified." As he stands up, the barber says he is getting a new chair, this one from St. Louis. The gag is somewhat lost in the final print, as we miss the banter between Wyatt and Doc at the Bird Cage Theatre about the new barber chair. Looking out the door, we hear the peal of church bells and see people heading to services. (Ford even has the bartender closing up the saloon to attend church.) The barber sprays some perfume on Wyatt's neck, saying it is "sweet-smelling stuff." Wyatt's look of disdain says it all. As he and his brothers stand outside the hotel and watch everyone head to church, Virgil comments that he can almost smell the honeysuckle blossoms from their hometown. Wyatt says, with some embarrassment, "That's me. Barber." Ford again uses this joke when Clementine and Wyatt stand on the hotel porch and she states she can smell the catus blossoms.

One disappointing aspect of the film is the lack of any real bond between Wyatt and Doc. While the interaction between the two here is better developed and played out than in the previous films, the relationship between Wyatt and Doc still appears to be more restive, almost bordering on the adversarial. Although we get a feeling from Wyatt in some scenes that he likes Doc, there is little display of warmth between the two men. However, in the preview print, we see a friendlier alliance come across when they meet at the Bird Cage Theatre and Wyatt sees the bandages on Doc's face.[59] The interplay between the two actors in that missing scene gives their characters a warmth that, to a large degree, is missing throughout the rest of the picture.

In his film, Ford paints Holliday as a tragic character. He is a man on the run from his past (and possibly the law). This Doc Holliday is angrier than in the other performances up to that time. He is living a lie, posing as a deadly gunfighter, afraid of no one. (It was in this film, and later ones, that the image of Holliday as a cold-blooded killer with a death wish began to take shape.) Doc, much like John Ford the director, builds a persona for himself that hides his past, although we are offered glimpses of it. Doc likes champagne, he can recite Shakespeare, and he was once a medical practitioner. Although Doc has given up his medical practice, he hasn't completely cut the ties to his past. Inside his hotel room are medical books and his doctor's bag; diplomas adorn one wall. His carefully crafted image is shaken when Clementine Carter, his abandoned fiancé, comes to town searching for him. After telling her that the man she once knew no longer exists, she agrees to return to Boston.

Holliday walks into his hotel room, and Ford creates one of his most striking scenes in the film, one not in the original script. The room is illuminated only by the outside street light. Holliday, heavily in shadow (reflecting his dark emotional mood), enters and stands before his medical bag, diploma, and a bottle of whiskey. He fills a shot glass. The only sounds we hear are the shouts and yelling coming from people in the various saloons. Doc sits on the edge of his bed and takes a drink. Ford cuts to an over-the-shoulder shot with Doc's reflection caught in the framed glass of his diploma. With great bitterness, Holliday looks at the parchment paper and says, "*Doctor* John Holliday!" After a brief second, he throws the shot glass into the framed diploma, shattering the glass.[60]

Ford uses the scene of Doc reciting *Hamlet*'s soliloquy to reflect the character's feelings. As Doc quotes, "The undiscovered country, from whose bourne no traveler returns, puzzles the will and makes us rather bear those ills we have than to fly to others that we know not of. Thus conscience makes cowards of us all," he is actually looking inwardly at himself. The fact that Ford allows Doc to suffer a coughing fit and hastily exit the saloon is a subtle way of focusing on Doc's own fears. The coughing fit also prevents Doc from further personal reflection. When we see Doc urging the stagecoach to go faster and faster, it can be seen as a reflection of Doc's anger at Clementine's coming back into his life and of his capricious way of rushing against his limited time on earth. Again, there is no mention

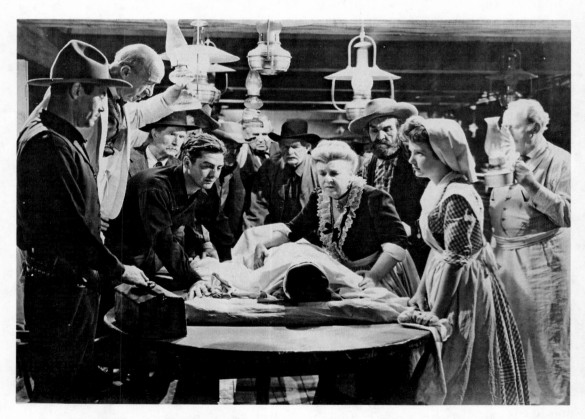

Doc (Victor Mature) is forced to operate on Chihuahua (Linda Darnell). Left to right: Fonda, J. Farrell MacDonald (holding lamp), Mature, Russell Simpson, Jack Curtis (center, in background holding lamp), Jane Darwell (right, at table) and Cathy Downs (right) (author's collection).

of Doc's having a disease of any kind, although it is suspected he may have tuberculosis. The only reference to an illness is when Clementine asks the chef if Doc's coughing happens often, and he replies that it gets worse every time. When Chihuahua is shot, Doc is forced back into his profession. He can no longer run from his past and, when pressed into service, he is all business. Ford and cinematographer Joe MacDonald captured some astounding shots in this scene when Doc operates on Chihuahua. With the foreground of the saloon in deep shadow, only the gambling tables, where Doc operates, are heavily illuminated. The scene is further enhanced by distant jubilant voices yelling and singing, as well as the sounds of a tinny piano. In this one long shot, Ford shows the dichotomy of life and death at the same moment. Completing his surgery, Doc's pride in his profession has come back. He feels it, and others do as well. When Kate Nelson asks if she can take Chihuahua to her place to care for her, she addresses him as "Doc ... I mean, Doctor." He is no longer a gambler but a respected surgeon. Even Wyatt addresses him as "Doctor Holliday" when they stand at the bar for a drink. When Clementine compliments him on his work, he cannot accept praise from her. All Doc can say before he walks out of the saloon is that Chihuahua was a brave girl.

Wyatt Earp is portrayed in Ford's version as the reluctant hero. Some writers have suggested that the Earp in this film reflects the mindset of those returning from World War II service, who wanted only to avoid any further conflict in their lives. In Wyatt's case, all he wants is a quiet shave in Tombstone, yet his life is turned upside-down, first with Indian Charlie's rampage and then with the murder of James and the stolen cattle. In this movie, Wyatt Earp has no gray shading to his character. His actions are clear cut. When he goes after the Clantons for the murder of his two brothers, he will arrest them if he can, but when it comes to a fight, Wyatt is quick to see that justice is meted out. He is a fair administrator of justice in a lawless town. He orders the gambler on the stagecoach to leave, but first to get something to eat. Wyatt is not above hitting Doc on the jaw to prevent him from causing trouble in a saloon or getting himself killed. Even at the gunfight, he displays a unique brand of justice when he orders Old Man Clanton to leave town and live with his actions.

Although the Wyatt Earp in Ford's film can handle himself in a fight, he displays a boyish charm, especially around Clementine. Next to her, he is respectful, yet nervous. This is obvious when he escorts her to the church service. As they walk, there is a stiffness in Wyatt's gait; he walks rigidly next to Clementine, her arm on his. Standing at the church foundation as people dance, he is uneasy as we see him slowly work up the courage to ask the young lady for a dance. Enhancing this moment is Clementine's side glances at him and her attempt to hide her smile, knowing he wants to ask her. When he does make up his mind, Wyatt tosses his hat aside (something repeated at the end of the 1993 *Tombstone*), showing the audience that he is taking a stand, much to Clementine's delight.

In many of Ford's films, especially his Westerns, there is always a dance of some sort. Ford loved to use dances as a way of showing how people associated in these periods and to illustrate a community coming together in the wilderness. Examples are the small wedding group in *The Searchers* (1956), the officer's party in *Fort Apache* (1948), and the Mormon wagon train in *Wagonmaster* (1950). One of the most touching yet humorous scenes in *My Darling Clementine* takes place after Doc has finished operating on Chihuahua. As Doc walks out of the saloon, Wyatt stands at the bar, illuminated by a lamp, with the bartender, Mac. In the background at the saloon doors is Clementine, who follows Doc outside. Wyatt taps his fingers on the bar and turns the whiskey glass in his hand as he thinks for a moment.

Looking at the older Mac, he asks, "Mac, you ever been in love?" "No," Mac replies. "I've been a bartender all me life." As he walks away, Mac takes the lamp with him and the saloon falls into semi-darkness, with Wyatt, the hero, striding along the length of the bar alone.

The last scene of the movie is reflective of both the Western genre and Ford's Westerns. Standing on the edge of town, Clementine waits to say goodbye to Wyatt. Morgan briefly bids her farewell before riding on in the buckboard. Wyatt, dressed like a typical cowboy (hat, chaps, rough clothing), dismounts his horse and takes his hat in hand. The two of them stand apart, not knowing what to say. Clementine says she is staying on in Tombstone and will be the new schoolteacher. Wyatt explains that he and his brother are going back to California to explain events to their father; then he may get another herd of cattle and pass through this way again. Clementine suggests that he might stop by the school house, and Wyatt replies, "Yes, ma'am, I sure will." There is hesitation before he leans over and kisses her on the cheek, then shakes her hand goodbye. Stepping into his saddle, he looks at her and smiles. "Ma'am, I sure like that name. Clementine." He takes his hat off in a short sweep and then begins to ride after his brother down a lonely stretch of road as Clementine watches. There is a reverse long shot of Clementine watching him go, and the song "My Darling Clementine" begins softly. The final shot is over Clementine's shoulder as we see Wyatt riding away, becoming more and more distant as the song grows louder. In this scene, Ford celebrates the myth, not only of Wyatt Earp, the lawman, but also of the lone hero riding into the sunset. It is a typical ending for the Western genre, but Ford makes it distinctly his own. It is not corny or clichéd; it is real. It also reflects the women in many of Ford's Western movies (especially his Cavalry trilogy), who watch silently as their loves disappear down a road or over a hill.

Factually, the film barely resembles history, other than using the participants' names and the town of Tombstone. There is no reference to the town being a major mining center, nor is the Cowboy faction ever mentioned. The fight between the Earps and the Clantons is based on the Clantons' murder of James and Virgil and stealing the Earps' cattle—a unique story twist, having the Earps involved in the cattle business! By paring down the facts and limiting the villains to the Clantons, Ford has made the conflict more of a personal matter, yet it is cloaked in law and order because Wyatt tries to arrest the Clantons.[61]

When it comes to the gunfight, Ford's claim that it is portrayed exactly the way it happened, as related to him by Earp himself, is more fiction than fact. Ford made his own version of what really happened, enhancing the Earp legend. As many filmmakers have learned, a thirty-second gunfight does not register as dramatically on film as it may have in real life. The gunfight in Ford's movie, which runs three minutes and thirteen seconds, is extremely well staged and shot, despite its bearing little resemblance to history. Dawn begins to rise over the O.K. Corral and Old Man Clanton slowly awakens from leaning on a fence; Ford creates the effect by simply having the camera's iris slowly open, giving the effect of the sun rising. As Wyatt walks up the main street (with the mayor and Simpson walking behind him, posing as Morgan and Doc), Ford frames it in a wide shot, showing the street and sky, with only the occasional sound of a dog barking. The shot is reflective on two counts. First, the three men are dwarfed by the vista of the area, a theme found in many of Ford's pictures of the personal story placed against the bigger story, be it history or the natural landscape. Second, Ford allows the tension to build with this long shot, using no music, only a few natural sounds. Wyatt, dressed in dark colors, stands out against the bright sky as he walks down the street. Fred Zinnemann would echo this with Gary Cooper in *High Noon* (1952).

When the shooting starts, the gunfight, much like the real one, happens quickly and is not drawn out. Doc, even before getting a shot off, climbs a rail fence in the corral and begins to cough, giving away his position. Although he is fatally wounded, he is able to dispatch one of the Clantons before dying. Ford frames Doc leaning against the wooden rail gate, holding his gun in one hand and his white silk handkerchief in the other. He kills Phin before dropping out of frame, leaving only his handkerchief on the rail fence, blowing in the wind.

Not only did Ford ignore the facts of the story, he also wasn't terribly concerned with some inconsistencies when it came to continuity. For instance, as Wyatt lies back in the barber's chair, his face has not been lathered, yet when the camera angle changes and shows the stray bullet hitting the mirror, his face is fully lathered. The set for Kate Nelson's Boarding House is nowhere to be seen in any of the exterior shots filmed in Monument Valley. The set, which was built on a Fox soundstage, is never again seen in the film. Nor does Wyatt ever seem to get his cattle back, even after killing the Clantons. Doc's trips are equally a mystery. There is no explanation why he goes to Tucson or Mexico or what he really does. A big continuity mistake happens at the Earp night camp, where, for the first time, we see a chuck wagon. The opening scenes of the cattle drive had all four Earp brothers riding horses with no sign of a chuck wagon following them. These inconsistencies did not bother Ford. He felt that most viewers would not catch the mistakes and that it was the story that mattered most.

Henry Fonda, who many feel gives one of the best performances of any actor playing Earp, displays a quiet dignity and a boyish charm. He is not afraid to handle trouble, but he can disarm someone with the ease of a simple comment. Fonda's unique ability makes his performance appear so effortless that many tend to overlook the complexities he instills into the role. His glances at Clementine say more about his feelings than any words, and the impassive look he gives those he's confronting, such as the gambler or Old Man Clanton, have a tacit strength. It is one of the actor's finest performances. Victor Mature is surprisingly good as Doc Holliday, although he hardly looks as if he's suffering from tuberculosis. Mature's performance is one of the best he ever gave. His Holliday is filled with smoldering anger, like a volcano about to erupt. Yet he often comes off as extremely likable, notably the scene in the preview print at the Bird Cage Theatre with Wyatt. Mature plays Holliday as a man filled with conflict who is forced to confront his past when Clementine arrives in town. His disgust with himself and his inability to save Chihuahua's life leap out in a few lines in the jail scene. Mature was never better in any other role. It is amazing that he did not receive an Oscar nomination for his work in this movie.

Ford had less success with Linda Darnell and Cathy Downs. Darnell, who was a Fox contract star with a limited range of talent, tried to give her role some distinction, but there was little to build on. Unlike Dallas in *Stagecoach* or Denver in *Wagonmaster*, Chihuahua is not a bad girl with a decent side but a conniving, deceitful, childish woman. When she is shot, most viewers feel she got what was coming to her, and her death earns her little sympathy from the audience. Cathy Downs had the misfortune to be cast in the typical stalwart good girl role. Like Darnell, Downs had a limited range and the role required minimal emoting. For what was demanded of her, Downs did a decent job, but nothing stands out.

Walter Brennan, despite his personal problems with Ford, is chillingly effective as Old Man Clanton. Brennan has never been better as a villain than he is in this film. His Old Man Clanton manifests a cold darkness, ruling his sons, and anyone else, with his whip. Many of the character actors in the film showed what they could do with a small part to

Doc's last moments in the gunfight (author's collection).

make it their own. J. Farrell MacDonald is a perfect example as Mac, the bartender. In his scenes with Doc, we sense a deep caring, and the look on his face after he begs Doc to stop drinking is almost heartbreaking. Jane Darwell makes her minimal role of Kate Nelson, the madam, stand out. Ward Bond and Tim Holt give Fonda strong support as his brothers, and Bond, of course, excels in the few comedic scenes Ford gives him. Ben Hall gives a dandy performance as the barber. Alan Mowbray as the thespian Thorndyke made the most of his scenes, including his breakdown in the saloon.

There has never been enough praise given to Joe MacDonald's camerawork. The images he created with chiaroscuro lighting are nothing short of stunning. A great deal of credit given to Ford for making this an A picture, belongs to MacDonald's imagery, which gives the movie a life of its own. Amazingly, his work never even received an Oscar nomination.

Unfortunately, the same cannot be said for Cyril Mockridge's score. Ford always liked to infuse many of his films, particularly his Westerns, with songs from the specific period. He even chose "Ten Thousand Cattle" for this film. When one compares the preview print (the closest to Ford's directorial cut) and the released version (with Zanuck's cuts and additions), the difference in the music is terribly obvious. For example, in the preview print, when Clementine gets off the stage, we do not hear the "My Darling Clementine" theme until she goes into Doc's room and looks at the pictures. In the release version, the theme starts the moment she gets off the stage and continues until the scene fades out. (This was Zanuck's choice.) The result is that the emotional impact of an abandoned love who returns has been diluted. Similarly, the scene in the release version in which Chihuahua watches

Doc ride off on the stagecoach, and his throwing a bag of money at her, loses its dramatic impact with Mockridge's stentorious scoring. As Chihuahua watches Doc ride by on the coach, the score becomes bombastic, hitting a crescendo as we see a close-up of the bag of bank money in Chihuahua's hand. The crescendo is carried through as she runs down the street and only softens as she enters the hotel. In the preview print there is no music, just the sounds of the stagecoach rolling by and Chihuahua's running down the street. The bombastic score overemphasizes the drama of the scene and actually minimizes any histrionic impact.

Although he ignored most of the facts surrounding the 1881 gunfight (much to the dismay of many Earp historians), John Ford fashioned a memorable Western, filled with impressive images and performances. *My Darling Clementine*, created by a major Hollywood studio and an Oscar-winning director, elevated the Earp saga to A-picture status. The story of the famous gunfight and the legend of Wyatt Earp was now shown to be viable material for A-list actors and producers to pursue. Ford had baptized the Earp legend, giving it a legitimacy beyond the B Western potboilers.

My Darling Clementine

A 20th Century-Fox release. *Released:* October 16, 1946. *In Production:* April 16, 1946, to June 14, 1946. *Reshoots:* July 11 and 12, 1946, and mid–September (one day), 1946. 10 reels, 8,728 feet. *PCA Certificate Number:* 11591.

Executive Producer: Darryl F. Zanuck. *Producer:* Samuel G. Engel. *Director:* John Ford. *Screenplay:* Samuel G. Engel and Winston Miller, from a story by Sam Hellman. Based on a book by Stuart N. Lake. *Cinematographer:* Joe MacDonald. *Musical Score:* Cyril Mockridge. *Film Editor:* Dorothy Spencer. *Art Direction:* James Basevi, Lyle Wheeler. *Set Decoration:* Thomas Little, Fred J. Rode. *Costume Designer:* Rene Hubert. *Makeup Supervision:* Ben Nye. *Makeup Artist:* Harry Maret. *Assistant Directors:* William Eckhardt, Jack Sonntag. *Production Manager:* R.A. Klunel. *Location Manager:* Ray C. Moore. *Sound:* Eugene Grossman, Roger Heman. *Special Photographic Effects:* Fred Sersen. *Musical Director:* Alfred Newman. *Music Arranger:* Edward B. Powell. *Running Time:* 97 minutes; preview version is 104 minutes. Filmed in black and white. Filmed in Monument Valley, Arizona, and 20th Century-Fox Studios.

Cast: Henry Fonda (*Wyatt Earp*), Victor Mature (*Doc Holliday*), Linda Darnell (*Chihuahua*), Cathy Downs (*Clementine Carter*), Walter Brennan (*Old Man Clanton*), Tim Holt (*Virgil Earp*), Ward Bond (*Morgan Earp*), Alan Mowbray (*Granville Thorndyke*), John Ireland (*Billy Clanton*), Roy Roberts (*Mayor*), Jane Darwell (*Kate Nelson*), Grant Withers (*Ike Clanton*), J. Farrell MacDonald (*Mac, the barman*), Russell Simpson (*John Simpson*), Don Barclay (*Opera House Owner*), Danny Borzage (*Accordionist*), Francis Ford (*Dad, the Old Soldier*), Earle Foxe (*Gambler*), Don Garner (*James Earp*), Fred Libby (*Phin Clanton*), Mickey Simpson (*Sam Clanton*), Mae Marsh (*Simpson's Sister*), Arthur Walsh (*Hotel Clerk*), Ben Hall (*Barber*), Louis Mercier (*Francois*), William B. Davidson (*Owner of the Oriental Saloon*), Charles Stevens (*Indian Charlie*), William Steele (*Indigo, man at Wells Fargo corral*), Jack Curtis (*Bartender*), Harry Woods (*Luke, Tombstone Marshal who quits*), Aleth "Speed" Hansen (*Townsman playing Guitar*), Frank Conlan (*Piano Player in Saloon*), Charles E. Anderson, Kermit Maynard, Duke R. Lee (*Townsmen*), Margaret Martin, Frances Rey (*Women*), Hank Bell (*Opera House Patron*), Jack Curtis (*Bartender*), Frank Conlan (*Piano Player in Saloon*), Robert Adler, Jack Pennick (*Stagecoach Drivers*).

6

Gunfight at the O.K. Corral (1957)

"There are a hundred more Tombstones on the frontier all waiting for the great Wyatt Earp!"

In the early 1950s, Westerns were not only popular at the movies, they were also quickly becoming a major staple in the new medium called television. By 1955, there were seven Western series on television, including the debut of *The Life and Legend of Wyatt Earp*.[1] For the next six years, the show was watched by millions of viewers, ensuring the continuation of the image of Wyatt Earp as a fearless enforcer of law and order.[2] By the fall of 1959, the TV series moved Earp to Tombstone, and the final two seasons led up to the gunfight. The show ended its last season with a five-part storyline based on the gunfight.[3] To give the series a sense of legitimacy, the producers hired Stuart Lake to serve as a creative and historical consultant.

The story of Wyatt Earp was not relegated only to the small screen, however. A year before the series debuted, producer Hal B. Wallis expressed interest in obtaining the film rights to a magazine article about Doc Holliday written by George Scullin. "While both of these men [Earp and Holliday] have been dramatized to one extent or another in various Western pictures, I don't think the relationship between the two men, which makes this article interesting, has ever been done before," Wallis wrote to his story editor, Irene Lee.[4] Paul Nathan, Wallis's long-time associate producer, commented to Wallis that while the story was interesting, the subject matter of Doc Holliday begged the question, "[a] ruthless beast killing while dying of consumption. Is this a good movie?"[5]

Wallis was a shrewd and very talented filmmaker whose movies garnered many Oscar nominations and awards. He was assistant head of publicity for Warner Bros. in 1923. In 1933, Wallis took over as head of production of the studio, overseeing many notable films, including *The Adventures of Robin Hood* (1938), *Yankee Doodle Dandy*, and *Casablanca* (1942). In 1944 he formed his own independent company at Paramount Studios, where he produced many of the early Elvis Presley pictures, the Martin and Lewis comedies, and John Wayne's *True Grit* (1969).[6]

Although Nathan had doubts that a film about Doc Holliday could be a popular draw at the box office, Wallis listened to his instincts and proceeded with his idea. He bought the rights to Scullin's story for $500; then he began looking for a writer for the project. Wallis quickly registered the following titles for his proposed movie: *Doc Holliday*, *Saga of Doc Holliday*, and *Gunfight at the O.K. Corral*. (In an undated memo, Nathan noted that Wallis liked the last title best.) Among the list of writers Nathan suggested to Wallis in January 1955 were Winston Miller, David Dortort, James Warner Bellah, Oscar Brodney, Dudley Nichols, and Leon Uris.[7]

Another writer they considered was Stuart Lake. At first, Lake was somewhat appealing to Nathan because he had supplied stories for Western films and was currently a consultant for the upcoming *Wyatt Earp* TV series. In a memo to Wallis, Nathan stated that Lake would read the Scullin story (without being paid), then meet with Wallis and Nathan to discuss their story. If they agreed, Lake would write a detailed step outline for $2,500. Wallis had a 14-day option to let Lake proceed with a detailed treatment for an additional $5,000. Upon completion of that, there was a 30-day option for the writer to complete a detailed screenplay and polish for $17,500.[8] After meeting with Lake, Wallis agreed to pay him $2,500 for a detailed step outline, which was due on April 8, 1955. Lake asked to push the date to April 28, as his agency, William Morris, needed to check with the producers of the Earp TV series to avoid any conflict. The headaches in dealing with Lake were just beginning.

By April 26, 1955, Lake had cashed the check for the first half payment for the outline, yet he had delivered nothing. Nathan noted to Wallis that the best they could do was to wait it out, adding that they had legal grounds to get out of the deal and ask for their money back; Wallis agreed to wait. Lake delivered an eight-page outline on May 5, noting his delay was due to a bout with the flu. The following day, Nathan sent a terse memo to Wallis about Lake's outline. Nathan was angry ("Judging from these eight pages, I would say we are going to get nothing from this man"), stating he could not believe Lake took so long to draft eight pages. "I am pretty sick about this long waste of time with this character. He is obviously a sick, tired old man—and a big phoney to boot," he wrote.[9]

Wallis felt the eight pages was not a step outline at all and that Lake had "failed to fulfill his obligation." He suggested to Nathan that if the rest of Lake's material did not improve or if the writer did not give them more to work with, Nathan should turn the matter over to Lake's agent and Paramount's legal department.[10] Lake sent more material to Nathan, indicating that his thirty-page outline would be more of a treatment. Both Nathan and Paramount's legal counsel, Mike Franklin, sensed that Lake was trying to get more money by delivering an outline. Lake's agent told Nathan that the writer was simply trying to avoid more work. Obviously, Lake thought he was a shoo-in to write the screenplay, something he had been hoping for since selling the film rights to his book to 20th Century-Fox.

By June 16, Lake's continued delays pushed Nathan's patience to the brink. "I don't know what to say about Stuart Lake.... I told him it has been months and every time I talk to him he tells me he will finish it up by the end of the week, but nothing happens." Nathan goes on to note that Lake stated he would finish the outline by that weekend, delivering a 105- or 110-page step outline. Lake hoped Wallis would not want him to do a treatment since the outline was so detailed, feeling he could just jump into writing the screenplay. Lake added (probably as a sales pitch for himself) that his chapter on the O.K. Corral was required reading in many colleges, including Oxford, Yale, and Lake's alma mater, Ithaca, "and not for its historical content alone."[11]

One has to wonder what Lake was thinking while writing his outline for Wallis; it is simply full of mistakes. For instance, he states that Wyatt Earp was the marshal of Dodge City. Lake has Doc staying at the Cosmopolitan Hotel, not at his room at Fly's Boarding House the night before the gunfight. He has Doc leave Tombstone on the stage after the Spicer hearing, leaving Wyatt, Virgil, and Morgan to round things up! Eighteen double-spaced pages contained introductions for Wyatt and Doc, explaining who they were and what they were like. There was no story information. Little wonder Wallis and Nathan were unhappy with his work.

Wallis signed Leon Uris on June 28, 1955, at $750 a week to write a thirty-page story treatment. If they engaged Uris to write the screenplay, he would be paid $1500 a week. Meanwhile, getting anything from Stuart Lake continued to be a struggle. In a July 4 letter to Nathan, Lake says the delay in finishing his outline is due to problems he is having with his publisher, and then he proceeds to boast about a new printing of his book, as well as the release of a children's version. Lake added, "If I seem slow I can say that haste is the Hallmark of 'B' pictures." Wallis suggested that they pay Lake the additional $1,250 to fulfill their obligation and have Lake sign a release, which he did. With the release in hand, Wallis and Nathan thought they had seen the last of Lake.

Leon Uris went to work on writing a story treatment. Within a month of signing a deal, Uris turned in his completed treatment to Wallis. The producer was happy with Uris's job of compressing principal incidents into the storyline, but cautioned him that in doing so the story was more episodic instead of the "free-flowing continuity" he had hoped for. Wallis also suggested that when Uris came to write the screenplay, he must be aware of this problem and make certain that one incident lead into another. Wallis stressed the most important thing in any revision is to "further develop the unique relationship" of Wyatt and Doc.[12] He also urged Uris to make his portrayal of Holliday "a more sinister character with the deadly menace which was ever present whenever he was on the scene."[13] Uris quickly replied to the memo, stating he felt Doc's role was just as big as Wyatt's and that he was attempting to create a sort of "interdependence and inevitability" between the two men. Director Michael Curtiz, a long-time colleague of Wallis' from the Warner Bros. days, read the script and wrote to Wallis that Uris had done a splendid job. He even suggested that the character of Earp came off "conventional, seems modern and sophisticated."[14]

Gunfight at the O.K. Corral opens as three riders arrive in Fort Griffin, Texas. Ed Bailey has come to seek revenge on Doc Holliday, who killed his brother, and waits for him in John Shaughnessy's saloon. At the same time, Marshal Wyatt Earp rides in, trailing Ike Clanton. Wyatt learns that Sheriff Wilson let Clanton leave town without holding him. Stopping in Shaughnessy's saloon, he is told that Doc Holliday might know Clanton's location, but Holliday refuses to help. Later, Holliday confronts Bailey, who tries to shoot him but is killed by Doc. Holliday is arrested and locked in his hotel room. Kate, Doc's lover, begs Wyatt to save Doc from the lynch mob and he agrees. On a signal from Wyatt, Kate sets fire to a stable, allowing herself and Doc to flee Fort Griffin on horseback.

In Dodge City, Wyatt finds that Doc has arrived in town. Doc gives his word to Wyatt that he will not cause any problems. A lady gambler, Laura Denbow, arrives in Dodge and begins playing cards in the Long Branch Saloon. Wyatt arrests her for causing a disturbance, but Doc manages to convince Earp to release her. Wyatt agrees, partially because he is attracted to Laura. After chasing bank robbers with Wyatt, Doc learns that Kate has taken up with Johnny Ringo, who tries to goad Doc into a gunfight. Doc refuses, remaining true to his promise to Wyatt.

Falling in love with Laura, Wyatt plans to quit his marshal's job and marry her. However, a telegram arrives from Wyatt's brother, Virgil, the town marshal in Tombstone, saying that he needs his help to quell Ike Clanton's cattle rustling. Wyatt pleads with Laura to understand why he must put off their marriage and go. Doc joins Wyatt on his trip to Tombstone. When they arrive, Virgil explains to Wyatt that Ike Clanton is using hired gunmen to move his stolen cattle through the town to market, but as long as the Earps control the law in Tombstone, Ike can do nothing. Wyatt is appointed U. S. marshal for the territory, and he tells Clanton to take the stolen cattle back to Mexico.

Advertising poster for the movie (author's collection).

Kate Fisher arrives in Tombstone and again takes up with Johnny Ringo, who is now working for Clanton. Jimmy Earp, the youngest brother, is gunned down by the Clantons as he makes his nightly rounds of the town. Wyatt is given a message that Ike wants to meet the Earps at the O.K. Corral at sunrise. Doc joins Wyatt and his brothers as they walk to the O.K. Corral and a gunfight ensues.

Days later, riding up to the Alhambra Saloon, Wyatt bids Doc a farewell. He says he is headed to California and, he hopes, a reunion with Laura. "I want you to know, I never would have made it without you," Wyatt tells Doc. Wyatt rides out of town and past Boot Hill, headed for California.

While the script was being written, Wallis and Nathan began to consider a director for the project. Several names were discussed, including Anthony Mann and John Ford. Nathan told Wallis that Ford had a picture pending at MGM, but there was no definite deal. Part of the problem was that Ford was trying to get John Wayne for the lead role in the MGM picture and contractual deals had not been worked out. (Wayne would ultimately star in the project, entitled *The Wings of Eagles*.) Nathan suggested that if they got Burt Lancaster and Richard Widmark for the lead roles, Ford might find this casting and box office combination appealing. However, Nathan added, "If it is a lesser cast, then Ford undoubtedly would not be interested."[15] Michael Curtiz wrote to Wallis on January 31, 1956, that Paramount studio head, Frank Freeman, had suggested to the director that he might be a possible choice for directing the film.[16] Ultimately, John Sturges was chosen to direct.[17]

Sturges began his film career in 1932 in the design department at RKO Studios, where he eventually moved into film editing. (One of the movies he worked on, uncredited, was George Stevens' 1939 *Gunga Din*.) During World War II, as a captain in the U.S. Air Corps, he edited and directed more than 45 training films. After the war, he directed his first film, *The Man Who Dared* (1946). Two of his early Westerns, *Escape from Fort Bravo* (1953) and *Bad Day at Black Rock* (1955; a modern, Western-themed story) were well received and he went on to direct a variety of films, including *Last Train From Gun Hill* (1959), *The Magnificent Seven* (1960), *The Great Escape* (1963), *Ice Station Zebra* (1968), *Marooned* (1969), *Joe Kidd* (1972), *McQ* (1974) and *The Eagle Has Landed* (1976; his last picture). Sturges died in 1992 at the age of 81.

With the director signed, Wallis turned his attention to casting the two main roles as well as the supporting and bit parts. His leading choice for the role of Wyatt Earp was Burt Lancaster, whose contract owed Wallis one more film. But Lancaster did not want the role. Wallis began to consider other stars such as Gary Cooper, William Holden, Alan Ladd, Glenn Ford, Charlton Heston, Gregory Peck, Robert Mitchum, Henry Fonda, Kirk Douglas, John Wayne, and Jeff Chandler. The likelihood any of these stars would take the role was slim, and Wallis was still hoping to sign Lancaster. He knew he needed a "hook" to interest the actor, which lay in the casting of Doc Holliday.

Richard Widmark, Robert Mitchum, Jack Palance (who was "terribly upset" at not getting the role), Jose Ferrer, Robert Ryan, Yul Brynner, Wendell Corey, Kirk Douglas and Ben Gazzara were looked at as possible choices for Doc Holliday. Two of the more unusual casting considerations for the role were Frank Sinatra, who politely declined, and Humphrey Bogart.[18] Wallis asked Nathan to contact Lancaster and ask him "would he go with Kirk Douglas. Important casting might intrigue him."[19] Douglas claimed that Lancaster called him and said if he'd play Holliday, it would get Lancaster out of his contract with Wallis. The actor said that Lancaster was paid $90,000 for his role, while Douglas agreed to a $300,000 salary.[20] (In reality, Lancaster was paid $125,000 and Douglas got $200,000.[21]) In

10209-110

Burt Lancaster and Kirk Douglas brought a strong chemistry to their performances as Wyatt Earp and Doc Holliday. This still, used for publicity purposes, was shot on the Western street at Paramount Studios (courtesy of the Academy of Motion Picture Arts and Sciences).

playing Holliday, Douglas realized he would have to cough a great deal in the film, and that matching the severity of his coughs could become a continuity nightmare. He planned ahead of time how light or hard he would cough in certain scenes, while in others he didn't cough at all.[22]

With Lancaster and Douglas set, attention turned to casting the two feminine leads. Nathan told Wallis that Lauren Bacall was available, but Wallis's reply was a firm "No!" (As was Nathan's suggestion of Barbara Stanwyck for Kate Fisher.) By March of 1955, they had not made a choice for the Laura Denbow character, although actresses Joanne Dru, Arlene Dahl, Ida Lupino, Yvonne de Carlo, Nancy Olson, Polly Bergen, Betsy Palmer, and Maureen O'Hara were considered. Nathan noted that Rhonda Fleming "is beautiful in color and can act well enough for this [part]." Evidently Wallis agreed and signed the actress for the role at a salary of $20,000.[23] Wallis passed on Nathan's suggestion of Bette Davis for Kate Fisher.[24] The list of actresses under consideration included Jean Hagen, Ruth Roman, Shelley Winters, Ida Lupino, Gwen Verdon, and Gena Rowlands. Jo Van Fleet, who had recently earned a Supporting Actress Oscar nomination for *East of Eden* (1955), won the role of Kate.

For the role of Ike Clanton, actors Sheb Wooley, Frank de Kova, James Westerfield, Robert Middleton, Lee Marvin, Raymond Burr, Richard Boone, Lyle Bettger, and DeForest Kelley were discussed.[25] In a memo to Wallis about Kelley, Nathan wrote, "You particularly liked DeForest Kelley when he played this part on TV, and I want to bring him in as soon as I can."[26] The role of Ike went to Lyle Bettger, who had also been under consideration for Johnny Ringo. Ralph Meeker, Richard Boone, Tony Franciosa, Lee Marvin, Neville Brand, Tom Tryon, Scott Brady, George Macready, Wendell Corey, and George Raft were some of the performers up for the role of Johnny Ringo, which went to John Ireland.[27] Don Castle, who played Johnny Duane in *Tombstone: The Town Too Tough to Die* (1942), was originally considered for one of the Clanton gang members but was instead used instead to play the drunken cowboy in the Long Branch Saloon who draws a gun on Wyatt.[28]

Uris, who completed his first draft on September 6, 1955, divided the script into three acts, with the first act taking place in Fort Griffin, Texas. Act Two takes place in Dodge City, and the final act is set in Tombstone. To connect the acts together, the film cleverly uses a ballad that also acts as a form of story narration. The ballad idea was developed before any composer had even been hired, with the lyrics in this draft written by Uris and Milton Raskin. The ballad begins,

> O.K. Corral—O.K. Corral; there the outlaw band made their final stand at O.K. Corral!/Guns blazed–guns roared, men fell—dear lord!/What a gory sight, Wyatt Earp's big fight at O.K. Corral![29]

In this first-draft script, Ed Bailey arrives in Shaughnessy's saloon, and we see a knife going into a wall, as the camera pulls back to reveal Doc seated in a chair in his hotel room. After Kate leaves to go to the saloon, Doc looks at his pocket watch. (In it is a picture of his parents with the inscription, "To Our Beloved Son, Doctor John Holliday.") Doc looks at himself in the mirror. The script direction notes, "a whiskey bottle, a gun belt and knives in the wall are very much in evidence. Doc hates what he sees now." After a violent coughing seizure, he stares into the mirror and says, "Doctor John Holliday!" He flings the watch at the mirror, smashing the glass, and the watch rolls to the floor. Picking up the watch, he "caresses it apologetically," and tears fill his eyes. (Sturges would end this scene with Doc simply looking at himself in the mirror because the rest of the scene, as written, was too similar to the one in *My Darling Clementine*.[30])

At the beginning of Act Two, the script had another version of the ballad, which sets up the action for this portion of the story. We see Wyatt walking along the railroad tracks toward his office, as deputy Charlie Bassett tells him that Bat Masterson is in Wyatt's office. The script direction notes that "through the large plate window we can see the Dodge House where the stagecoach is unloading." Reading a letter from Virgil, Wyatt's face becomes rigid. Wyatt says that Virgil has arrested Ike Clanton, but Ike's father managed to get a judge to drop the charges. Through the office window, Bat and Wyatt see Laura Denbow exit the stagecoach. There is a brief scene of dialogue between Laura and the stage driver, who tells her where she can hire a buckboard.[31]

After Laura is released from jail, the first script draft had a scene in which Wyatt walks along with Laura after she leaves the saloon. Wyatt tells her that a lady such as Laura does not belong in a gambling hall, but she replies that working as a schoolmarm or in a general store or being a farmer's wife does not appeal to her. "My life is mine," she tells him. She vows never to be bound by old-fashioned ideas about womanhood. Wyatt notes that she plays her "cards real well, skirts and all." She bids him good night. All of this would be dropped in the subsequent script revision.

When Wyatt deputizes Holliday in the saloon, there was a brief scene in Doc's room, where he changes into rough clothes. Kate asks him where he's going and he simply says, "Out." When she realizes he is going with Earp, she asks why. "I owe him a debt of honor and I'm going to pay it," he replies. Kate asks about his honor to her, but Doc says nothing. He gives her his pocket watch and tells her to take care of it for him while he is gone. Instead, she smashes it into the mirror. The script direction notes, "With a murderous look Doc slaps her across the face and she falls sprawling on the bed." He puts the watch into a dresser drawer and leaves as Kate yells, "You're dirt! Nothing but dirt!" This scene was dropped from the next revision because it would never have been acceptable to the PCA.

The first-draft script described the action during the camp scene when Wyatt and Doc kill the robbers with Doc firing from under his blanket as Wyatt shoots from the ground. Sturges was obviously not happy with this direction, because he has written in the margin of his script, "Fix this—talk to Kirk and Burt." Sturges was also aware that some inoffensive words would not translate well in other countries. At the Social Hall dance when Shanghai Pierce's men barge in, a merchant tells Pierce, "You'd better get those no-good bums of yours south of the deadline." Next to the line, Sturges has written, "Check bums for England."[32]

Moving into the Tombstone sequence of the film, there is another ballad refrain that sets up the action for the final act. The script describes Wyatt and Doc as "bearded, grimy and haggard" when they pull into the O.K. Corral, where an old timer welcomes them. The old timer points out that this was the spot where Curly Bill shot Sheriff White.[33] Wyatt goes to Virgil's home while Doc heads to the Cosmopolitan hotel. Sturgis rewrote the scene, with Wyatt and Doc pulling up to the Alhambra saloon. Doc says to sell his horse and get a good deal, as Wyatt starts to warn him. "I know. No guns, no knives, no nothing," Doc says

When Wyatt takes the drunken Billy Clanton to his home, the script had him draping the young boy across his saddle outside his office. Next to all this direction, Sturges has written, "Stay inside." In the film, James and Morgan drag Billy into the office, and Wyatt puts Billy over his shoulder and walks out. When he takes Billy home, the conversation at the table is different than in the finished film. In the script, Billy confides to Wyatt that he wants to be a veterinarian, but his brothers Ike and Finn tell him it's a stupid idea. Wyatt says he doesn't think it is, and Billy asks if he could come talk to Wyatt sometimes ("Ike and Finn don't seem to understand too well"). Wyatt says he will talk to him any time and offers to help him find a veterinarian school.[34] In the film, Wyatt relates that he knows how hard it is to live up to older brothers. Billy says he really doesn't want to be a gunfighter, but he gets lonely. "All gunfighters are lonely," Wyatt tells him. Billy agrees that he will cause no more trouble. The script had a scene in which Wyatt returns to his office, where his brothers and John Clum greet him with grim expressions. Wyatt tells Clum to get his safety committee ready because it looks as if a war with the Clantons is imminent. Wyatt asks where Doc is, but no one knows. Sturges cut this scene, feeling it was too talky.

Immediately after James is killed, the script had Virgil, his wife, Morgan, and Wyatt looking at the body. Virgil, remorseful over his brother's death, asks himself why he sent for James. Morgan tells him that he cannot blame himself. Wyatt stares at the body, then walks away and leans against a building. The script action describes a hand reaching out and pressing Wyatt's shoulder, then the camera pulls back to reveal Doc.[35] On the evening before the gunfight, after leaving Doc's room, Wyatt returns to his room and tries to open a whiskey bottle. In frustration, he smashes it open and takes a big drink, half of it going down the front of his shirt. There is a knock on the door and it is Laura Denbow. She tells Wyatt that while she was in Tucson, she heard about what was happening. Wyatt embraces her and tells her he is scared. ("Someone told me this would happen. I didn't believe him.") He tells her he needs her and she agrees to stay. ("Stay? Yes, I'll stay ... tonight you need me and I'll be here ... but tomorrow—tomorrow you will be the great Wyatt Earp again and you will be ashamed you called to someone for help. Or dead.") As morning dawns, Wyatt straps on his gunbelt as Laura watches. He says nothing as he walks out of his room, and we hear his footsteps disappearing down the hallway. The script action describes Wyatt walking down the stairs; he "grabs the rail very tightly, half closes his eyes and sucks in a deep uneven breath." A door closes and Doc is standing at the top of the stairs. He slowly walks down until he is beside Wyatt and nods to him. Wyatt returns the nod and both of them exit.[36] Sturges would delete Laura in Wyatt's room, partially due to objections raised by the PCA. Another reason was that it seriously slowed the dramatic impact of Doc joining Wyatt, as well as the need to get to the upcoming gunfight. The first draft has Kate sitting in Doc's room, very distraught, as Laura stands in the doorway. She sits next to Kate, who begins to cry on her shoulder. Later, as the gunfight erupts, Kate, hearing the shots, rushes out of the room, with Laura following. Sturges scrapped all of this because it took away from the gunfight and, in some ways, was too similar to the scene in *High Noon* in which Grace Kelly hears the gunfire and runs off the train toward town.

As the Earps get close to the O.K. Corral, Wyatt tells Ike and the others to throw down their guns because they are under arrest for the murder of James. Doc sees Tom McLowery in the wagon aiming a rifle at them and yells out to hit the dirt. The shooting begins. Finn Clanton wounds Morgan as he tries to flank the corral, but Wyatt and Doc fire back at Finn, killing him. Morgan, despite his wound, makes his way from the open street to behind some sheds. Ike sees Morgan is still moving and tells Ringo that he will cover their rear. Ringo tells him to stay put, but Ike is gone.

When Wyatt fires his shotgun at the wagon, he hits a lantern hanging above the tailgate, setting the wagon's canvas on fire. Tom McLowery, sitting in the wagon, is caught in the fire.[37] Wyatt, Virgil and Doc shoot at Tom's burning body as Frank goes mad and returns fire. One of his bullets hits Virgil before Wyatt and Doc kill Frank. Ringo tells Billy that he wants cover fire so that he can sneak up and kill Wyatt. As six horses break loose, Ringo is suddenly exposed, leaving him to face off with Doc. Doc kills Ringo before his body is trampled by the horses. Doc is shot in the arm by Billy and Wyatt drags Doc to safety. Billy pleads for Ike to help him, but the older brother rides out the back of the corral, where Morgan kills him. Billy staggers deep into the corral, clutching his stomach, as Doc takes aim at the boy, only to be stopped by Wyatt. After checking on Morgan, Wyatt follows Billy Clanton, who has broken into Fly's Photo Gallery. Wyatt begs Billy to throw his gun down and not force him to shoot. As Billy takes aim, Doc fires and mortally wounds the boy.[38] Wyatt walks up to Billy, who asks him to pull his boots off. (There was a note in the script to make an alternate shot, with Wyatt's hands coming in and pulling Billy's boots off, with no dialogue.)

Doc tells Wyatt he will finish off Ringo during the gunfight (author's collection).

In the script description, we see Wyatt's body from the waist down (his face is never seen from this angle) as he unbuckles his gunbelt, dropping it to the ground over Billy's boots. The camera would pull back enough to show Wyatt's chest (his face still not seen) as his hand reaches for the tin star and rips it from his shirt. There would then be a close-up of Wyatt's fist holding the badge as it "closes over the tin star, crushing it with such force that his hand shakes and the edges of the star bite into his flesh, forcing blood." The next shot would be of Wyatt with tears on his face as he walks out of the building, passing Mrs. Clanton. The script described them facing each other like statues before she sees Billy on the floor and begins wailing and crying. Laura shows up and tells Wyatt that his brothers are going to be fine. The script action notes that she "takes his hand quietly and leads him through the crowd."

The final scene was written to take place outside the Cosmopolitan Hotel, with Doc standing next to Wyatt, who is saddling his horse. The script notes that the street is hauntingly deserted. Wyatt says he's heading to "California or Timbuktu. It doesn't matter where. Any place where there's peace." He says that he thought it best for Laura to wait for him in Tucson until the inquest was over. (This is the only mention of an inquest being held in any script drafts.) As Doc coughs, Wyatt pleads for him to go to Denver. Doc refuses, saying he has a lucky streak at the gaming tables. The horse is saddled and the two men stare at each other awkwardly. Wyatt finally says, "I don't think either one of us can rightly put it in words, Doc." "No ... I guess not," he replies. "I'll see you around ... pal." "So long, Marshal." The two exchange a long, formal handshake. Wyatt tries to speak again but cannot, and he quickly mounts his horse, moving down Allen Street. Doc stands frozen and tight-lipped, before walking into the Alhambra Saloon. Walking up to some men sitting at a poker table, he asks, "What's the name of this game?" Kate comes up behind him, complaining that he was to take her to Bisbee and if he gets into the game, they'll never go. Without looking at her, Doc reaches in a vest pocket and withdraws some money, handing it to her. As Wyatt rides by Boot Hill, he looks over and "raises his hand in a salute and, turning his horse, moves off at a canter, the camera panning with him into a limitless vista of desert and distant mountains."[39]

The completed first draft was sent to the PCA for its approval. Geoffrey M. Shurlock told Wallis his concerns with the script, including Shaughnessy's saloon being portrayed as a pub and brothel. "Some revisions will be necessary to make it quite clear that these B-girls are not prostitutes." Another problem was when Wyatt is greeted by one of the saloon girls who asks if he remembers her. His reply, "Sadie's, Wichita," was deemed unacceptable "since it obviously refers to a house of prostitution." Shurlock also expressed concern that the scene showing Bailey being knifed in the heart "will have to be handled with great discipline not to be excessively gruesome and brutal."[40]

The PCA felt there were "several instances in this story where the mistress relationship between Kate and Doc is too explicit." Kate's line to Doc, "I'll make it right for you. I can be awful good," was found to be "offensively sex suggestive, and should be changed or eliminated." The scene with the townspeople yelling "Fire!" after Kate sets fire to the barn was considered a specific Code violation and had to be cut. The PCA felt that the scene in which Doc tracks down Kate to another room in Dodge City and begins to take her dresses out of the closet suggested "too specifically" a mistress relationship between the two characters; it was ordered cut. When Cotton Williams makes the comment to Wyatt that Ike Clanton "owns a United States Congressman," they recommended it be deleted.[41]

The PCA felt the scene with Laura sitting in Wyatt's room prior to the gunfight must have "no suggestion that they have slept together." They also noted that "scenes of people burning to death always border on excessive gruesomeness. For this reason we ask that the human torch [Frank McLowery in the film] in Scene 288 be handled with great restraint. Also, the business of Doc pouring gunfire into the flaming body is unacceptably brutal and gruesome." They recommended that the scene of Ringo being trampled by horses be done by suggestion "in order to avoid excessive gruesomeness."[42]

Uris completed his second draft on November 16, 1956, and it too was sent to Shurlock at the PCA for approval. In a letter to Wallis, Shurlock was adamant that there be no hint that the ladies' parlor in Shaughnessy's be a brothel. Uris had revised the dialogue between Wyatt and the girl in the saloon who asked if she remembered him. Wyatt's revised line read, "Sadie's, Wichita. How could I forget?" Shurlock said it was still unacceptable "since it obviously refers to a house of prostitution." The scene of Doc yanking dresses from Kate's closet and throwing her trunk out the door was still viewed as establishing the two were "having an illicit sex affair. We believe that, within the framework of this story, such a relationship can be told; however, in its present version it is too specific and too detailed." The PCA still demanded the line about Ike Clanton owning a Congressman be cut. "Under the heading of good and welfare of the industry, we ask that Ike's line, 'I don't know what we're paying that Congressman for' be eliminated," Shurlock wrote.[43]

Another bone of contention with the PCA was the scene of Laura in Wyatt's room prior to the gunfight. "On the basis that this story is not geared to handle an illicit sex relationship between our romantic leads, we ask that you revise this sequence accordingly." Shurlock also reminded Wallis that the burning man was gruesome, adding it was needlessly brutal for Virgil, Wyatt, and Doc to shoot at the man's body. After some revisions to pacify the PCA, the script was once again submitted for review. In a February 28, 1956, letter to Wallis, Shurlock still complained that the scene of Doc throwing Kate's clothes from her closet should be eliminated, despite revisions to the scene. He also noted that scenes of Wyatt and Laura having a number of "fierce kisses" avoid any open-mouth kissing. ("We should like to remind you that open-mouthed kissing is unacceptable.") The PCA was also concerned over the tone of the relationship between Wyatt and Laura, suggesting an illicit affair.[44]

The following day, February 29, Wallis sent a strongly worded letter to Shurlock, noting, "I think your objections and criticisms have now reached the picayunish stage.... You have a note concerning Page 61 where Doc takes Kate's dresses from a closet and you state that this establishes that Kate is living in the same room with Doc. If you will refer to page 60 you will note in the directions, that Doc goes through a door to Kate's room and all subsequent action takes place in Kate's room. We added the extra room because of your objections.... You do not have to remind me about open-mouthed kissing not being acceptable. You have had no trouble with my pictures on this score, although I have seen flagrant violations of this rule in other pictures.... I do not agree with your interpretation in your comment on Page 81. This is not an illicit sex relationship, as is evidenced by the scene immediately following, when Wyatt tells Doc that he and Laura are getting married. Has marriage between our romantic leads become an illicit relationship? I do not know what you mean when you state that this story is not geared to handle an illicit sex relationship. None is so indicated."[45] (Wallis and Sturges would simply scrap the scene of Laura in Wyatt's room prior to the gunfight.) Shurlock eventually gave the PCA's approval on the final draft.

With the script approved, the team began to gear up for production. One major decision was choosing a location. Paramount had a Western street set they would use in the film, but Sturges would have to carefully pick and choose his camera angles because the street set would double for both Dodge City and Tombstone. Another set would have to be chosen for Fort Griffin, Texas, as well as the hilly plains of Kansas and Texas. In considering locations, the studio locations department would look at various areas that fit the locale of the picture and then run detailed weather predictions for the various areas. They would list how many days of sunlight, rain and wind a specific area was likely to get; and this would allow the producer and director to choose the most beneficial site. Some of the biggest concerns in picking a location for a movie, especially a Western, are how many days of sunlight will be available, what kind of clouds are likely (and if there is cloud coverage), rainfall averages, and wind, altitude, and other factors. Wallis and Sturges considered places like Prescott, Wickenburg, Phoenix, and Tucson, Arizona. St. George, Utah, was also looked at but was deemed too cold and possibly snowy when they would be starting production. In California, they looked at Indio, Painted Canyon, Lone Pine, Borego Springs, Warner Hot Springs, and Julian. Ultimately, they chose areas of Elgin and Tucson, Arizona. Elgin was no stranger to film companies, having served as location for Howard Hawks' *Red River* (1948); it would later be used in *Tombstone* (1993). The breadth of hilly and brown, grassy terrain surrounding Elgin would double perfectly for the opening credits as well as for the Kansas plains. The sets of Old Tucson would carefully double both Fort Griffin and parts of Tombstone.[46]

As details were being worked out on locations, the budget was set at $1,975,000, based on a 40-day shooting schedule, which included one Saturday and one Sunday of location filming.[47] On April 12, 1956, the budget was revised to $2,025,000, raising it $50,000 over the initial projection. (The final budget cost, as of December 28, 1957, would be $2,245,996.60)[48] A total of $474,502 went to salaries of the principal actors, while $11,880 was spent on bit players and $19,705 for extras. The film's wardrobe budget, which also included Edith Head's salary (she was the studio department head), came to a total of $30,502.[49]

Aside from budgetary concerns, numerous other details had to be worked out. Paul Nathan discussed with Wallis whether they could use a soundtrack of Eddie Foy, Jr., from the Paramount film *The Seven Little Foys* (1955) or would have to bring him in for a new recording. Wallis decided he wanted Foy to do a song.[50] Wallis and Nathan also began considering a composer for the film. Dimitri Tiomkin, Leonard Rosenman, and Alex North were prime contenders, with Wallis and Nathan leaning toward Tiomkin, who was asking $17,500.[51] Wallis chose Tiomkin, who also brought aboard his lyricist Ned Washington to help write the ballad for the film.[52]

Prior to principal filming, Wallis wanted to see the actors who would work on location in their wardrobe before the company left for Arizona. This was a cost-saving measure which would allow Wallis to make any changes without delaying production. On March 5, Lancaster and Douglas shot wardrobe tests on a stage and on the studio's Western street, as well as makeup tests. As the filming date approached, another problem arose—Stuart Lake. Lake had contacted the Screen Writers Guild stating that he wanted to contest the solo screen credit given to Leon Uris. Quickly retaliating, Uris filed a complaint with the Writers Guild and sent Nathan a telegram stating, "I hereby protest tentative credits on *Gunfight at the O.K. Corral*. Credit should read original story and screenplay by Leon Uris."[53] After reading the script, Lake sent a telegram to Wallis on March 16, stating that he was concerned with the quality of "his" picture. He also commented that the script had many of the principals' identities badly mixed up, saying Wallis's film would be "the laughing stock of hundreds of thousands who care more for accuracy than you may think." Lake offered to straighten things out for no charge, but Wallis ignored the offer.[54]

Two days later, Wallis received a letter from Lake that can only be described as professional suicide. Discussing the final script, Lake commented that the dialogue sounded too modern. He also cited other faults such as having gas lights in Fort Griffin and large plate glass windows in Dodge City ("Don't think that hundreds of thousands of motion picture fans don't know better"). Lake goes on to say Uris is "woefully ignorant" about the time, places and people he is writing about. He even suggests that Uris has no clue how a heroic man would act in a showdown, adding, "I'm just guessing that he's spent too much time on 'the couch.'" Lake went on to say that his material "gets held over for weeks and runs and re-runs for years." He reminded Wallis that the producer will be the one who takes a "beating for another person's lack of ability."[55] He offered to tackle a tackle a salvage job—for a fee—to help Wallis save face. One can only imagine Wallis's reaction, considering that the producer was responsible for many Oscar-winning films, as well as the recipient of two Irving G. Thalberg Memorial Awards given by the Academy of Motion Pictures Arts and Sciences for "excellence in filmmaking." Paul Nathan's description of Lake as a "sick, tired old man—and a big phoney to boot" was certainly proving to be true.

In a letter to the Writers Guild, Lake stated that he was due full credit for the original story.[56] Nathan spoke to Joseph Hazen (Wallis's partner and legal counsel) and Mike Franklin of Paramount's legal department on March 21 about Lake's credit demands. The shared opinion was to ignore Lake, who had a "long record of being a trouble maker." Nathan felt they should drop the matter and Wallis agreed. The Writers Guild sided with Leon Uris, who received sole screen credit.

Filming began on location in Old Tucson on March 12, 1956. The day was devoted to shooting Ed Bailey and his gang riding into town, as well as Wyatt's arrival. The following day the company moved to Elgin, where they shot sections of the opening credits. Also in Elgin, they filmed scenes of Wyatt walking by the Dodge City train tracks and the sequence between Charlie Bassett and Doc, although the company had to contend with high winds all day. On March 15, the company moved to the Empire ranch, where all outdoor scenes between Wyatt and Laura were filmed. Final shots for the opening credits were done on March 17, before the company moved to Phoenix, where they filmed exteriors of the Clanton ranch near the Superstition Mountains. Location filming was completed the next day, March 19, and the entire company traveled back to Hollywood that evening.[57]

The next day, scenes between Wyatt and Doc in their respective Tombstone hotel rooms were shot on Stage 4. The company then moved into the set of Shaughnessy's saloon for three days of work. During Doc's confrontation with Ed Bailey, a special effects trick developed in the late 1940s was used when Doc throws a knife at Bailey. This special effect, which allowed filmmakers to show a knife, arrow, or spear actually hitting its target on camera, was accomplished by using wires and camera angles. In the movie we see Holliday standing at the bar in Shaughnessy's Saloon, making comments about Bailey's brother (whom he killed). As Bailey starts to stand up and pull a derringer from his boot, Doc pulls a knife from behind his neck and throws it, hitting Bailey in the chest and killing him. A careful viewing of the scene shows that, just before Kirk Douglas throws the knife, he reaches down with his right hand between the bar and railing, where an open knife has been placed. He palms the knife in his right hand as he turns, bringing his right arm up to the back of his neck. Douglas makes the gesture of pulling the blade from the back of his neck, then throws it. There is a direct cut to a medium shot of Lee Van Cleef (playing Ed Bailey) getting hit in the heart with the knife. Van Cleef's chest area has been padded so that the knife can hit him without any danger. The knife is run on a wire attached to the actor's chest (another reason for the padding). When the knife hits him, Van Cleef makes a grimace of being stabbed. As he pulls the knife out, one can quickly see the knife hover in midair before it falls to the ground. March 29 and 30 were spent filming interiors in Wyatt's Dodge City office set, including Laura's jail scenes, as well as Wyatt and Laura's love scene after the buckboard ride. The Dodge City social hall dance, which is taken over by Shanghai Pierce's gang, was filmed over two days, April 6 and 7.

The following week was spent filming the scenes between Doc and Kate in the Fort Griffin hotel room before moving to the sequence where Wyatt helps Doc escape. The last two days were spent filming various scenes in the Long Branch Saloon. The week (April 16–21) was spent shooting the campfire sequence between Wyatt and Doc, scenes in Virgil's kitchen set and the interior of the Clantons' ranch. On April 30, the daily production report shows they were dropping one day on the schedule due to slow progress because of bad weather in Hollywood. The company had been forced to shoot interior scenes instead of filming on the outdoor Western street set. The night sequence involving Ike Clanton and his group riding up to Schieffelin Hall was shot over a three-night period (April 28 to 30), when the rain ceased.[58]

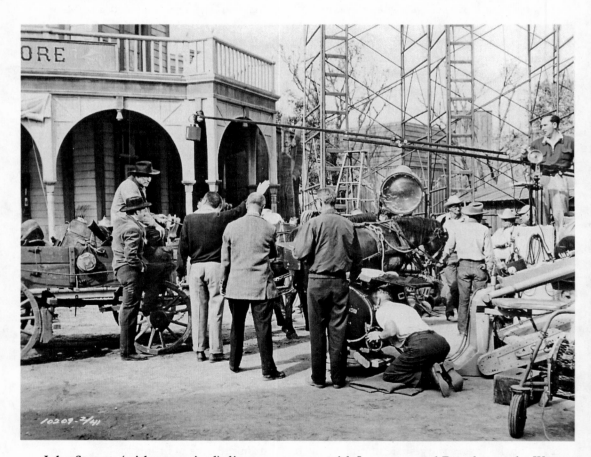

John Sturges (with arm raised) discusses a scene with Lancaster and Douglas on the Western street at Paramount Studios. The large VistaVision camera can be seen on the ground, while two wranglers hold the horses (courtesy of the Academy of Motion Picture Arts and Sciences).

The first two days in May were spent filming Wyatt coming into Doc's room and attempting to revive him, as well as the night scene in which James Earp is killed by the Clantons. The final goodbye between Doc and Wyatt in the Alhambra Saloon was shot on May 4. Production was idle on May 6 due to Kirk Douglas calling in sick. He returned the next day to film the hotel room scene in which Doc tells Kate, "If I'm going to die, then let me die with the only friend I have." While filming the confrontational scenes, Jo Van Fleet, a method actress, asked Douglas to slap her before the cameras rolled. Douglas asked if she was sure about this and she said yes, so Douglas slapped her. This continued with every take, much to his amazement. When Lancaster was told about it, he watched dumbfounded as Van Fleet asked Douglas to really hit her before a take.[59]

On May 10, the entire company left Hollywood to return to Old Tucson, where they began filming portions of the gunfight the following day. Wallis said in an interview that they had given thought to filming at the actual site, but "we would have been cramped for angles." He claimed that the set they used was a close duplication of the real thing, with minimal changes.[60] Obviously Wallis was spinning some good publicity; the sets for the film in no way represented the reality of Fremont Street or the empty lot. Wallis also knew that for dramatic and storytelling purposes, their gunfight had to be longer than thirty seconds, saying, "We needed to build the sequence for maximum suspense."[61] Sturges spent the next three days, May 12 to 14, filming the gunfight. During those three days he managed between 22 to 27 camera setups a day while working no more than ten hours a day, including an hour lunch break! On May 14, location work was completed at 4:55 P.M., and the entire company returned to Hollywood that evening.[62] The next morning, May 15, they began filming Billy Clanton breaking into Fly's Photo Gallery. Gunfight at the O.K. Corral completed filming, eleven days behind schedule, at 5:40 P.M. on May 17, 1956.[63]

Wallis, Nathan, and composer Dimitri Tiomkin discussed several singers for the ballad in the film. Tennessee Ernie Ford and Frankie Laine were prime contenders (both were asking $15,000). Another singer briefly considered was Elvis Presley. Although Wallis produced many of Elvis's early films, he felt that Presley was the wrong choice. Eventually, they settled on Frankie Laine.[64] While the ballad for Gunfight at the O.K. Corral was a hit for the film and for Laine, it failed even to garner an Oscar nomination for either Best Song or Best Musical Score. (However, Gunfight at the O.K. Corral did earn nominations for Best Sound and Best Editing, marking the first time any film on the gunfight was honored by the Academy of Motion Picture Arts and Sciences.)

Reviews were positive when the movie was released July 1, 1957. Newsweek said, "Richly furnished and lovingly photographed, Gunfight fairly swims in sumptuous color.... Lancaster as Earp, and Douglas as a knife-throwing gambler with a tragic cough, seem to enjoy themselves. Some of this enjoyment may rub off on the spectator. Summing Up: Fun with two men on a boy's errand." The Hollywood Reporter labeled the film as "certainly the best western of the year.... John Sturges paces his story so that not a minute or a second of this time is extraneous. The excitement kindles in the opening frames and it is relentless throughout.... As for the performances, they demonstrate vividly why there is such a thing as a star system.... What a pleasure it is, too, to watch two strong and able stars such as Douglas and Lancaster play together, not dueling for prominence but achieving a fusion of extraordinary talent that supercharges the screen. They are both superb."

Life headlined its review, "Cash in the O.K. Corral," calling the movie a "western that has everything. It has Burt Lancaster as the noble Earp and Kirk Douglas as the law-hating Holliday fighting the evil Clantons.... It has lonely riders against purple skies, long bars with mirrors over them so drinkers can see who is about to shoot them in the back.... It has sad and fateful music by Dimitri Tiomkin..... And it all leads to a soul-satisfying moment when guns roar and anger and justice triumphs."

"Hal Wallis has a strong money picture in this film based upon what is probably the most famous gunfight in the history of the old west, and consequently a highly exploitable product.... [The] film is further enhanced by the pictorial values provided by VistaVision and a haunting title song.... Both stars are excellently cast in their respective characters, Douglas perhaps edging out Lancaster for honors due to the greater demands made upon him," commented *Variety*.

However, not all reviews were positive. The Legion of Decency gave the film a Class B rating for its "low moral tone." The Protestant Motion Picture Council rated the film for adults and mature young people. They noted that "wholesale consumption of liquor is grossly exaggerated." Trade journal *Harrison's Reports* said it was not suitable for children. When the film was released overseas, several cuts had to be made. In Britain, all shots of a man on fire had to be eliminated. In Australia, it was demanded that the producers "reduce considerably view of Kate drinking at saloon bar and eliminate the words, 'you slut,' in dialogue between Doc and his wife." Germany set an age limit of 16 to see the film and ordered that it *not* be shown on Holy Days.[65]

One reason for the film's success was the unique chemistry between the two lead actors. Just like the real Earp and Holliday, Lancaster and Douglas were as different as night and day. Lancaster, the son of Irish Protestants, was born in 1913 in the East Harlem area of Manhattan. He was an excellent athlete and, with childhood friend Nick Cravat, formed an acrobatic act. The two performed in circuses and vaudeville for many years. After World War II, Lancaster got his start on Broadway before making his film debut in *The Killers* (1946). The film made him a star, and he was one of the first actors to become a successful independent producer (his company produced *Marty* [1955]). *The Flame and the Arrow* (1950), *From Here to Eternity* (1953), *Sweet Smell of Success* (1957), *Judgment at Nuremberg* (1961), *Birdman of Alcatraz* (1962), *Seven Days in May* (1964), *The Professionals* (1966), *Airport* (1970), *Ulzana's Raid* (1972), *Atlantic City* (1981), *Tough Guys* (1986), and *Field of Dreams* (1989) were some of his major films. Lancaster was nominated three times for an Oscar and won for his performance in *Elmer Gantry* (1960).[66] He suffered a debilitating stroke in 1990 and passed away at age 81 in 1994.

Kirk Douglas was born Issur Danielovitch Demsky in New York to Russian Jewish immigrants in 1916. He worked a variety of jobs to put himself through the Academy of Dramatic Arts in Manhattan and made his acting debut on Broadway in 1941. After World War II service, he returned to the stage and was given a screen test by Hal Wallis when his former drama school classmate, Lauren Bacall, recommended him. Wallis cast him in *The Strange Love of Martha Ivers* (1946), and he played in numerous films before appearing in *Champion* (1949), which earned him his first Oscar nomination for Best Actor. In 1955, he formed his own production company and produced several films, including *Spartacus* (1960). Some of his other starring roles include those in *Detective Story* (1951), *The Bad and the Beautiful* (1952), *20000 Leagues Under the Sea* (1954), *Lust for Life* (1956), *Paths of Glory* (1957), *Lonely Are the Brave* (1962), *In Harm's Way* (1965), and *Greedy* (1994). Over the years, Douglas has written many books, including one about his 1995 stroke, and is still active on behalf many civic causes.

Their styles of acting were equally different. Lancaster was described by Dennis Hopper as "very generous, very involved."[67] He would constantly pick a script apart until he felt

Lancaster was never shy about acting out a scene during rehearsals. Director John Sturges listens as Lancaster makes his point (courtesy of the Academy of Motion Picture Arts and Sciences).

every scene was just right. Sitting in the makeup chair, Lancaster could care less what the makeup artist was doing; he was often more interested in discussing old films or current events. And then there was that Lancaster smile, with the white teeth and his hearty laugh, which many tried to impersonate. While Burt could be kind to many actors, he was forceful in his opinions. DeForest Kelley recounted an incident while filming Ike Clanton's confrontation with Wyatt in front of Schieffelin Hall. He said that in the first rehearsal, actor Lyle Bettger (who played Clanton) "jumps off his horse and walks up to Lancaster and begins to tell him off." Burt walked over to Sturges, Kelley said, and told the director that Bettger "was coming on too strong to suit Burt."[68] Douglas could be just as strong in his opinions as Lancaster, which caused Leon Uris to dub them "the Bobbsey Twins." Many actors can relate stories of witnessing Douglas's "take no prisoners" attitude when it came to camera time, and he was not above upstaging other actors in a scene. Whereas Douglas thrived on the attention on a movie set, Lancaster simply blended in with the crew.[69]

Lancaster once told this author that he felt *Gunfight at the O.K. Corral* really captured the chemistry between the two leading actors.[70] The men found a lot to talk about, often arguing but never bored. On location in Tucson, Burt and Kirk would talk for hours during and after dinner, sometimes until the early morning hours. Hal Wallis, surprised at their ability to talk almost nonstop about various subjects, once asking Douglas what the two men talk about "night after night?"[71] Yet the chemistry between the two did not make for a long-lasting or endearing friendship. Douglas, the more pugnacious of the two, lacked Lancaster's humanistic skill at handling people. During production, Lancaster told a group of people seeking his autograph to ask Douglas for his, providing he was wearing his elevator shoes![72] This was a constant source of kidding on Lancaster's part. During the early days of production on *Tough Guys* (1986), Douglas insisted on having special elevated shoes made for him so that he would have equal height next to Lancaster. "Just like old times," Lancaster told this author, shaking his head. While they may not have always gotten along off camera, onscreen the two actors played extremely well off each other and that chemistry is what gives the film its foundation.

The opening of *Gunfight at the O.K. Corral* sets the tone of the film. Tiomkin's score begins with bombastic notes before we hear the singular whistle accompanying the ballad. The brown, hilly terrain slowly shows three riders making their way across the wide expanse of the American West. Before any part of the ballad is sung, the audience knows that action will be a key element to this film. As the riders come into Fort Griffin, the stares they get from many of the townspeople, including Kate Elder, signify that these men are dangerous and trouble will be forthcoming.

The first main character we are introduced to is Doc Holliday. Sturges uses a master shot of Kate pleading with Doc, who has his back to camera, sitting in a chair. All through her conversation, he simply throws several switchblades into the door of his hotel room. In this scene we are also introduced to the mercurial relationship between Doc and Kate, as she insults his family and his Southern ways. Doc responds by throwing a knife at the wall near her. She grabs it and tries to stab him, but he overpowers her. When she asks what would happen to her if he is killed, Doc coldly replies, "You'd lose your meal ticket." With just as much passion as he demonstrated in throwing his knife at her, he then kisses her, asking her to go tell Ed Bailey that he will be coming. She says she needs money (for a drink) and he peels off a few bills. (This was to be a running gag throughout the film, but was cut down because of PCA objections.) Our first glimpse into Holliday's character is that he is a man with a temper, a drinking problem, and a possible death wish. When Kate speaks of

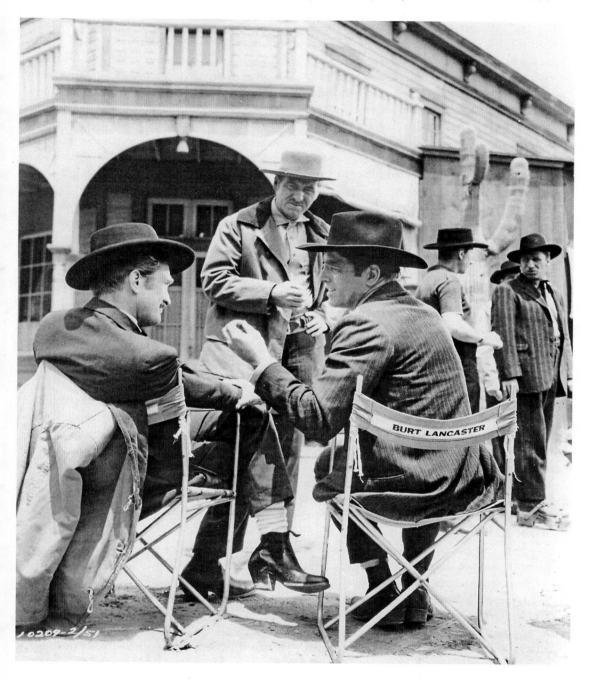

Lancaster and Douglas were never at a loss for conversation during filming. Actor Frank Faylen (center, standing) listens. Note the shoe blocks strapped to Lancaster's stand-in (right), which brought him up to Lancaster's height (courtesy of the Academy of Motion Picture Arts and Sciences).

his family in a mocking way, his anger is quick; Doc grabs her hard and tells her never to mention his family. Shortly after she leaves, Doc looks at his pocket watch and inside we see a photo of what we assume are his parents, based on the picture and watch inscription. This is all we are told of his family background, and the audience is led to believe that there was some form of alienation between them. Without a clear answer, we are left to assume that Doc is carrying a dark secret that, in addition to his disease, is an impulse for his ill temper and violent actions. We see Doc staring at the watch and then at himself in the mirror, before the movie cuts to the entrance of Wyatt Earp. The cut between the two scenes is abrupt, which may indicate that Sturges filmed the scene as it was written (Doc sarcastically calls himself a doctor and flings the watch into the mirror, breaking it), but felt it too closely echoed a similar scene in Ford's film *My Darling Clementine*.

When we first see Wyatt Earp, the view is from ground level, looking up. Riding tall in the saddle on his buckskin horse, he is a lone and solitary figure.[73] The shot conveys to the audience that Earp is the ideal lawman and hero. He is his own man and no one can sway him from the truth. When he learns that Sheriff Cotton Wilson, a man he admired, has let Ike Clanton ride out of town without arresting him, he tells Wilson to give up his badge. Leaving the office, Wyatt says nothing and will not look at the other lawman, who has disgraced the honor of the badge. This Wyatt Earp is a man whose life is the law.

The myth and legend of a man with a reputation is a major touchstone in the Western genre. In this movie the issue of a man's reputation is reflected in a brief scene between Wyatt and John Shaughnessy, who says to Earp, "You know how it is when a man gets a reputation." Wyatt knowingly replies, "I sure do." The same can be said of Holliday in this film. He is painted as a deadly killer of the frontier, and the death wish theme is further enhanced in a scene when Shaughnessy, standing outside his saloon, warns Doc about Bailey waiting for him. Doc ignores his warnings; Shaughnessy asks if he wants to get killed. "Maybe I do," Doc quietly replies. Later in the film, when Wyatt and Doc are trailing bank robbers, Doc explains his feelings about dying. After suffering a coughing fit, he admits that the only thing he's afraid of is dying in bed. "I don't want to go little by little," Doc says. "Some day somebody's got to out-shoot me and it will be over real quick." If any film is guilty of enhancing the myth of Doc Holliday being a lethal killer with a death wish on the Western frontier, it has to be *Gunfight at the O.K. Corral*. Although the previous movies hinted that Holliday was a deadly person to tangle with, it was not as overtly presented as it is in this film. Although done to enhance the dichotomy between Wyatt and Doc for dramatic purposes, the characterization quickly became ingrained in the public consciousness and has persisted for generations.

Despite Wyatt's dislike of Holliday, he will not let him be lynched by an angry mob. Wyatt is not above bending the rules to free a man who was justified in a killing. He is not afraid to hit a deputy over the head to free Doc, nor does he blink at having a stable set afire as a diversion. ("Don't take it personal, Doc. I just don't like lynchings," Wyatt says, as a way of explaining his actions.) This is the first time a movie showed Wyatt Earp, the lawman, helping someone escape from the law, no matter how corrupt the law was. It could be argued that this characterization of Wyatt, and those of others in the film, was something of a reflection of the times (the Cold War, House UnAmerican Activity Committee hearings), when not everything in regard to the law was black and white. Those enforcing the law could be the "bad guys" (such as the Cotton Wilson character), and an enemy might really be a valued friend (Doc Holliday). Wyatt helping a known killer escape would have been unthinkable in a film a decade earlier. Certainly, the Wyatt Earp on the television series wouldn't do such a thing. But in this movie, it became part of the development of the friendship between Wyatt and Doc.

Yet Earp is still shown as basically a straight shooter. When he confronts Doc about his arrival in Dodge City, Earp is all business, telling him to leave on the next stage. We are told, via a ballad refrain, that "Wyatt's word in Dodge was law." He runs a tight city and tolerates no lawbreakers. Holliday, ever the gambler, pleads poverty but offers Earp a deal: He will split his poker winnings 50–50 if Wyatt will stake him some money. Earp gives in on the condition that Doc not become involved in any killings. Holliday gives him his word, and Earp accepts it. In Westerns, the word of a man is his bond. Should he break it, he is worth nothing. Wyatt adds one last condition: He should treat Kate better, or leave her. "Poor old Kate," Doc replies. "She stands for everything I hate in Doc Holliday." In this scene, we again see the dichotomy between the two men and gain a little more insight into Doc's complicated character.

The filmmakers also touch on the myth surrounding Wyatt Earp by showing him holding the Buntline Special pistol. It is a brief throwaway in the scene where Charlie Bassett tells Wyatt about Laura Denbow gambling in the Long Branch Saloon. The incorporation of the Buntline is a tribute to the legend of Earp and may have been influenced by the television series, since Hugh O'Brian carried one throughout its run.

Gunfight at the O.K. Corral makes several references to Wyatt Earp as deliverer of all from evil. Doc often calls him "Preacher," pointing out that the two of them are a lot alike. Doc tells Wyatt that they both carry a gun and kill people, the only exception being that Wyatt has a badge. When Wyatt refuses to accept his analysis, Doc sarcastically asks, "What's the matter, Preacher? Don't you like being preached at?" Wyatt cannot answer, and Doc chuckles at having bested him. When Laura Denbow is about to be jailed by Wyatt, she tells him to buy a new halo, adding, "This one's too tight." Yet Wyatt's staunch beliefs in the law are often bent or broken, as when he frees Doc from a mob, or when he relents and has Doc let Laura out of jail. "Conscience?" Doc asks. "Maybe I like her," Wyatt softly replies. When she is about to walk out of the jail, Laura simply stands there and says, "Marshal...." Wyatt gets up and opens the door for her. There is an unspoken attraction and sexual tension between the two, hinting that a romance may be possible. Their courtship will be a far cry from that of Wyatt and Clementine.

Wyatt rides out to where Laura frequently rides, finding her walking her lame horse. Telling her he'll send out a blacksmith for the horse, Wyatt mounts his and offers Laura a ride back to town. As she sits behind him, she puts her arms around him but quickly withdraws. "Better hold on tight," he tells her. As she loosely puts her arms around him, he orders her to hold on tighter. When she does, a slight smile comes over his face as they ride off. Later in the film, he meets her as she leaves a dance. Wyatt takes her on a buggy ride, and they stop in the country (a rustic version of Lover's Lane, no doubt), where he asks why she came out with him. She confesses she doesn't know, but Wyatt turns her around to face him and says he knows why and firmly kisses her, to which she responds. This Wyatt is the most forceful we have seen in courting a woman.

Doc, however, is not as lucky in his relationship with Kate. Returning after his stint as Wyatt's deputy, Doc asks Charlie Bassett to find Kate and tell her that he needs her. (This is the first admission Doc makes that he actually needs Kate.) When he learns that she has taken up with Johnny Ringo, he goes to her room. Confronting Kate, Doc asks, "So you got homesick?" He says that she couldn't stay away and had to crawl back into the gutter. Sturges subtly suggests with this dialogue, and the action of Doc walking to Kate's room, that she has gone back to prostituting herself. Kate taunts Doc, calling him "the little deputy" as Ringo comes out of another room, presumably having just dressed. Ringo ridicules Holliday, throwing a gun on the table, daring him to shoot. Kate scoffs at Ringo's attempt, saying Doc "promised Wyatt Earp he'd be a good little boy." Ringo further baits Doc by throwing whiskey in his face. Clenching his fists, Doc refuses to fight. His first impulse is to kill Ringo, but his word to Wyatt is too strong.[74]

When Wyatt tells Holliday he is quitting as marshal to marry Laura, Doc is happy for him, although he declines the offer to attend the wedding. ("I am better at funerals.") Wyatt suggests that Doc get out of the gambling racket while he still has time, but his comment is met with an ironic chuckle. Wyatt leaves, and Holliday looks at the deck of cards before him as though they have already dealt his future. Coming back to his hotel room, he finds Kate waiting for him. She begs him to take her back, adding that she doesn't care how he treats her. Doc, reflecting on Wyatt's recent good fortune and his own misfortune, tells her that it is too late. ("It's just the way the cards fall.") Lying on his bed, he tells her to do something for herself while she still has a chance. Kate begs him, saying, "Don't let me go back there," a reference to her prostituting herself. Doc ignores her pleadings and as she walks out, Kate coldly states, "I'll see you dead."

When Wyatt receives Virgil's request for help, he is forced to make a decision between marrying Laura and helping his brother. He pleads with her to understand: "He's my brother." Laura fires back that she is to be his wife. "Don't ask me to let him down," Wyatt begs. Laura says that he shouldn't let *her* down, adding that she will give up anything for him, "but you must meet me halfway." Wyatt walks a few steps, attempting to make up his mind. Turning to her, he says, "I must go to Tombstone!" The decision is made. The law must be enforced, and the brothers must back up each other. Laura tells him to go clean up Tombstone, adding, "There are a hundred more Tombstones on the frontier all waiting for the great Wyatt Earp!" Mounting his horse, he says before riding away that he loves her. "I love you, too," Laura softly replies, watching him disappear.

In Tombstone, the brothers—Virgil, Morgan, and James—agree to let Wyatt act as lead marshal in dealing with the Clantons. Morgan expresses reservations about Wyatt associating with Doc, adding that he's a deadly killer. Wyatt reminds Morgan that Doc saved his life in Dodge City and he does not forget that; besides, Doc is a man of his word. Morgan replies he wasn't aware they were a team. "We're not. It's just a case of a square deal. Holliday stays." Lancaster's Earp will not back away from his friendship with Holliday, despite what others may think. Nor will he accept bribes. Cotton Wilson, who is now county sheriff and working for Ike Clanton, tells Wyatt that Ike will pay him $20,000 to look the other way and let him ship his stolen cattle. Wyatt refuses the offer, even hinting that he may run for county sheriff himself. Wilson is not fazed as he states that he has his own ranch and money in the bank. "Get off your pulpit, Wyatt. Ellsworth, Wichita, Dodge City. What have they got you but a life of misery and a woman who walked out on you and the friendship of a killer?" Cotton barks at him. Wyatt silently hands Cotton back the bribe money. He cannot be bought.

When Ike's younger brother, Billy, is arrested for public drunkenness, Wyatt takes him back to the family ranch and attempts to get the boy to see the error of his ways. He tries to show Billy that if he keeps following in Ike's footsteps, he will end up in jail or dead. Billy just wants to try to live up to his older brothers. Wyatt replies that he did the same thing when his older brothers went off to fight in the Civil War. The two understand each other and Earp, no doubt, sees something of himself in Billy, especially when the boy says he doesn't really want to be a gunfighter, but he just gets lonely. "All gunfighters are lonely," Wyatt replies. There is a touch of knowledge in his voice; gunfighters and lawmen face a lonely existence. Billy promises that he will not cause any more trouble and Wyatt leaves, feeling he's made a difference in saving a life. (This is an important dramatic story point that plays out later.) Wyatt is now seen as a counselor for a wayward youth, a way of perpetuating the myth of Earp as the savior of the young who cannot see their own wicked ways. It also ties in with Doc's calling Wyatt Preacher.

When the Clantons ambush James Earp at night, thinking they have killed Wyatt, the fight becomes personal. Wyatt swears revenge on Clanton, but Holliday urges him not to throw away his badge for vengeance. "The hell with logic!" Wyatt says. "That's my brother lying there!" But Doc has become Wyatt's conscience at this point. Earp cannot and does not want to think clearly. It is Doc who must remind him that he cannot throw away his badge and everything it stands for.[75] Later that night, Billy Clanton finds Wyatt and tells him that Ike wants a showdown at dawn at the O.K. Corral. Billy says he will be there as well. "Ike and Finn are my brothers. You can understand that," he says. "Yes, I can," Wyatt replies. He understands that he cannot pull this boy away, for if he could, he must also step away from seeking his revenge against Ike Clanton. While the battle has become personal for Wyatt and family, the confrontation is justified by Ike's cold-blooded killing and the fact that he is still breaking the law by rustling cattle.

Learning from Kate that she knew of the Clantons' ambush sends Doc into a murderous frenzy, only stopped when a coughing spell incapacitates him. Coming back to his hotel room, Wyatt hears Doc coughing in his room. He tries to awaken Holliday, telling him he needs him. Earlier, Wyatt had told Holliday that he doesn't need anybody, adding, "Certainly not Doc Holliday." We now see that that was just bravado; he truly has come to rely on Holliday. Sitting in a corner of the room is Kate, who says Doc is dying. Wyatt leaves, feeling lost and alone. As dawn breaks, Holliday awakens and Kate begs him not to go, but he refuses to listen. "If I am going to die, at least let me do it with the only friend I ever had." These two scenes demonstrate the bond of friendship that has developed between the two men, and it is the first time any film showed a vulnerable side to Earp's persona. He needs Holliday and relies on him. The audience can relate to their friendship and need for each other, despite Wyatt's earlier protests. We, the audience, know Earp does need Holliday as much as Doc needs Wyatt. Doc has become a surrogate brother to Wyatt, one of the few who truly understands him. Doc needs Wyatt because he is the first person in a long time who has accepted him as an equal, not shying away from his illness or reputation.

Wyatt is standing in his room alone when Doc enters. Walking to the window, Holliday tells Wyatt that his two brothers are waiting outside. They briefly look at each other, and Wyatt goes to load a shotgun. As they step out the door, Holliday pauses and looks at Wyatt. The look between the two men says it all—Doc is standing with Wyatt in his fight. The bond is complete. *They are a team.*

As the gunfight reaches its conclusion, Wyatt has followed a wounded Billy Clanton into Fly's Photo Gallery. He pleads with the young man to drop his gun so that he will not have to kill him ("Don't make me do it, boy!"). In the end, it is Doc, not Wyatt, who kills Billy. Earp's legend will not be sullied by killing a boy led astray by his criminal brother. However, it is readily acceptable to the audience that Doc kill him. He is protecting the one man who was his friend in life. By doing this, the filmmakers have even softened Holliday's penchant for violence, even after his shooting Ringo several times in the corral.

In the final scene of the film, Wyatt rides up to the Alhambra Saloon and finds Doc inside. It is clear, even before any dialogue is uttered, that Wyatt is heading to another place. "I want you to know, I'd never have made it without you," he says to Holliday, adding that he is heading to California in hopes of getting back together with Laura. Wyatt begs Doc to go to Denver to see a doctor for his disease, but the gambler says, "And give up this winning streak?" As Wyatt leaves, Doc says, without looking at Wyatt, "So long, Preacher." Earp stops, slightly turns, and softly smiles before heading out the door. Doc looks straight ahead, holding tightly to his emotions. With a show of bravado, he walks over to a gaming table and sits, asking, "Gentlemen, what's the name of this game?" Riding past Boot Hill, Wyatt stops for a moment to look at the town before riding towards California, tall in the saddle, as the last passage of the ballad swells up. The hero's mythic stature remains as he rides into the proverbial sunset.

John Sturges handles the film with a competent style, giving the movie a steady pace. He allows dramatic moments to build like a roller coaster ride, then slow down a bit to let viewers catch their breath before the next piece of action. He knows how to frame his shots for the maximum effect, such as in Wyatt's entrance into town, announcing the arrival of the hero, or in placing James Earp in the shadowy foreground and the Clantons in the brighter background, yet unrecognizable. He captures the sweep of a Western epic, filling the screen with action and movement. He is not afraid to let the camera linger on a master shot, placing the actors to one side and small bits of action playing off to the side, such as when Wyatt, Charlie Bassett, and Bat Masterson are talking on a Dodge City street on

Leaving Tombstone for California, Wyatt pauses at Boot Hill (author's collection).

one side of the camera frame while the stagecoach action takes place on the other side of the frame. He also has people looking out windows of the Dodge City set when Shanghai Pierce's men ride in. It is a small piece of business, but it gives the film a sense of life that other films lack. Sturges was also able to bring out the chemistry between Lancaster and Douglas that few other directors were able to capture. One scene that illustrates this chemistry takes place when Wyatt needs a deputy to help him catch some bank robbers. With some of his deputies out riding with Bat Masterson, he needs to keep Charlie Bassett in town. Wyatt walks into the Long Branch Saloon and asks the bartender where Luke Short is. Learning he's gone, Doc, sitting at a poker table, offers his services to Wyatt. Declining, Wyatt begins to walk out of the saloon, but stops and returns. He tells Doc to raise his right hand. "Do you solemnly swear to ... oh, this is ridiculous! You're sworn in," Wyatt says. He tells him to get a horse saddled and meet him outside. "Don't I get a badge?" Doc teasingly asks. "Not on your life!" Earp replies as he walks out, and Doc smiles. This scene depicts the beginning of their friendship, and the two actors play with just enough light-heartedness and humor, without destroying the dramatic structure.

Lancaster gives a good performance as Earp. His is not a one-dimensional character

Filming a Dodge City sequence on the Paramount Studio Western Street set. Kenneth Tobey, who plays Bat Masterson, is seated (left) with Lancaster. Actor Earl Holliman (standing, right), playing Charlie Bassett, waits for his cue (courtesy of the Academy of Motion Picture Arts and Sciences).

but has shades of gray, a harbinger of future performances of the Earp character in films. He is not afraid to face down Shanghai Pierce's group unarmed, nor is he hesitant to use his gun when needed. For the most part, Lancaster plays Earp as the stalwart hero, but his personality is layered. He can admit his weakness only to Doc, such as when he tells him to let Laura out of jail or when he relies on Doc in his moment of need at the gunfight. Douglas, who has the more splashy role, gives Holliday a conflicted image. He is obviously carrying a dark secret or failing within him regarding his family. His dental practice has failed because of his illness. Kate Elder is the only woman who cares for him, yet she also despises his existence. Douglas gives his Holliday occasional moments of roguish likeability so that the audience is not completely unsympathetic toward him. Both Lancaster and Douglas complement each other's performances in this film.

The rest of the cast give solid portrayals, with Jo Van Fleet making the most of her role as the trampy Kate Elder. Lyle Bettger is effective as Ike Clanton, although he is limited in a stock characterization as the lead villain. Many of the character actors have limited screen time and yet do some fine word, which gives the film an added depth. Particularly good are George Mathews as John Shaughnessy, Frank Faylen as Cotton Wilson, and Olive Carey as Mrs. Clanton.

As for historical accuracy, one can say that the filmmakers made a decent attempt to be somewhat accurate, but they embellished several facts and overlooked many others. While they brought in Bat Masterson and Charlie Bassett, Wyatt being head marshal was an obvious departure from facts for storytelling reasons. Instead of Mattie or Josie as a love interest for Wyatt, they created a fictional character, again for dramatic purposes. Cotton Wilson is obviously a fictional stand-in for John Behan, while Ike Clanton is shown as the head of the criminal element. Clanton is painted in typical shades of black as the film's antagonist, whereas the facts as to why he and Earp clashed are overlooked in deference to a more superficial plot point (cattle rustling). The inquest, wounding of Virgil and murder of Morgan after the gunfight, and the vendetta ride are all ignored. For the most part, the film touches lightly on some facts, using them as a springboard for a dramatic plot.

It is ridiculous to assume that the gunfight is in any way historically accurate. While the original script had the action happening in close quarters, the film is spread out and runs eight minutes and five seconds. As Wallis noted, the entire movie builds to this big moment, and to simply have a thirty-second gunfight would have cheated the audience. The gunfight *needed* to be enlarged and played out on a wider canvas instead of a small lot because it was being filmed in the wide-screen format of VistaVision. Overlooking the historical inaccuracies, the gunfight is well staged and shot by Sturges. He intercuts with ease between the sets at the Paramount studio and those at Old Tucson, and by using most of the Old Tucson area for the majority of the gunfight, there is a sense of expansiveness and openness not attainable by filming in the confines of a studio outdoor street. His camera angles capture tension and give us a sense of scope in the gunfight.

A major contribution to the film was Dimitri Tiomkin's score. As he did in *High Noon*, Tiomkin relies on a monothematic score, with occasional orchestrations of other music, to set the dramatic tone of the film. Also as in *High Noon*, Tiomkin uses a ballad to set the stage; however, in *Gunfight at the O.K. Corral*, the ballad acts more as a Greek chorus, foretelling and summarizing events in the picture. Opening with bombastic notes, the music slows as we hear a lone whistling (something Sergio Leone would use in his "Man With No Name" trilogy) as Frankie Laine begins to sing the ballad, shadowed by the score and a male chorus rhythmically repeating certain key words from the ballad (such as "Boot Hill,"

"Mighty cold, mighty still"). All of this gives the narrative composition a depth and flow to the film.[76]

From a filmmaking point of view, the movie is a solid A-budget Western with two dynamic stars in the lead roles. The important thing about this film (as in *My Darling Clementine*) is that it continued to carry the Earp-Tombstone saga into the A class of movies. The story was no longer relegated just to B pictures. In some ways, this film, even more than Ford's picture, gave the Earp legend a legitimacy in the eyes of Hollywood producers. However, it also continued to foster the myth of the heroic lawman Wyatt Earp and, once again, the facts about the October 26, 1881, gunfight became even more obscure.

Gunfight at the O.K. Corral

A Paramount Picture release. *Released:* July 1, 1957. *In Production:* March 12–May 17, 1956. Additional filming, July 24, 1956. *PCA Certificate Number:* 18134.

Executive Producer: Joseph H. Hazen. *Producer:* Hal B. Wallis. *Director:* John Sturges. *Screenplay:* Leon Uris. *Associate Producer:* Paul Nathan. *Cinematographer:* Charles B. Lang, Jr. *Musical Score:* Dimitri Tiomkin. *Art Direction:* Hal Pereira, Walter Tyler. *Set Decoration:* Sam Comer, Arthur Krams. *Costume Designer:* Edith Head. *Men's Wardrobe:* John Anderson. *Women's Wardrobe:* Grace Harris. *Makeup Supervision:* Wally Westmore. *Makeup Artists:* Jack Stone, Terry Miles. *Hair Stylists:* Hedi Mjorud, Lenore Sabine. *Unit Production Manager:* R.A. Blaydon. *Assistant Directors:* Michael D. Moore, Clem Jones, Ralph Axness. *Script Supervisor:* Marvin Weldon. *Sound:* Winston Leverett, Harold Lewis. *Special Photographic Effects:* John P. Fulton. *Props:* Bob Goodstein, Dwight Thompson. *Stunts:* Paul Baxley, Jerry Gatlin, Richard Farnsworth. *Supervising Editor:* Warren Low. *Technicolor Consultant:* Richard Mueller. *Song:* "Gunfight at the O.K. Corral" sung by Frankie Laine. Lyrics by Ned Washington, Music by Dimitri Tiomkin. *Running Time:* 122 minutes. The film was re-released in 1963. Filmed in VistaVision and Technicolor. *Filming Locations:* Portions of the film were shot in Elgin, Phoenix and Old Tucson, Arizona, and Paramount Studios.

Cast: Burt Lancaster (*Wyatt Earp*), Kirk Douglas (*Doc Holliday*), Rhonda Fleming (*Laura Denbow*), Jo Van Fleet (*Kate Fisher*), DeForest Kelley (*Morgan Earp*), John Hudson (*Virgil Earp*), Lyle Bettger (*Ike Clanton*), Dennis Hopper (*Billy Clanton*), Martin Milner (*James Earp*), John Ireland (*Johnny Ringo*), Earl Holliman (*Charlie Bassett*), Kenneth Tobey (*Bat Masterson*), Olive Carey (*Mrs. Clanton*), Ted de Corsia (*Shanghai Pierce*), George Mathews (*John Shaughnessy*), Frank Faylen (*Sheriff Cotton Wilson*), Lee Van Cleef (*Ed Bailey*), Whit Bissell (*John P. Clum*), Lee Roberts (*Finn Clanton*), Mickey Simpson (*Frank McLowery*), Jack Elam (*Tom McLowery*), Joan Camden (*Betty Earp*), Nelson Leigh (*Dodge City Mayor Kelly*), Frank Carter (*Hotel Clerk*), Edward Ingram (*Deputy*), Don Castle (*Drunken Cowboy in Saloon*), Bing Russell (*Bartender in Ft. Griffin, Texas*), Dorothy Abbott (*Girl*), Henry Wills (*Alby*), William S. Meigs (*Wayne*), Ethan Laidlaw (*Bartender*), John Benson (*Rig Driver*), Richard J. Reeves (*Foreman*), Frank Hagney (*Bartender*), Roger Creed (*Townsman/Deputy/Killer*), Robert C. Swan (*One of Shaughnessy's men*), Len Hendry (*Cowboy*), Trude Wyler (*Social Hall Guest*), John Maxwell (*Merchant*), Tony Merrill (*Barber*), Harry B. Mendoza ("*Cockeyed*" *Frank Loving*), Charles Herbert (*Tommy Earp*), Tony Jochim (*Old Timer*), James Davis, Joe Forte, Max Powers, Courtland Shepard (*Card Players*), Danny Borzage (*Accordionist at Social Hall Dance*), Gregg Martell, Dennis Moore (*Cowboys*), Morgan Lane, Paul Gary (*Killers*).

7

Hour of the Gun (1967)

"If you're gonna kill like me, you might as well drink like me!"

A decade had passed since the release of *Gunfight at the O.K. Corral*. During that time, the Western genre as well as the country itself had gone through changes that would affect how people viewed American icons. In the time between the releases of *Gunfight at the O.K. Corral* and *Hour of the Gun*, the United States experienced an escalation of the Cold War with Russia, a presidential assassination, and the nation's increasing involvement in an unpopular war in Vietnam. At the same time, the issue of civil rights for minorities was quickly approaching the forefront of national awareness, including the treatment of Native Americans.

Historical revisionism was becoming commonplace. Custer's defeat at the Little Big Horn, once considered a heroic stand, was now viewed as a disastrous failure resulting from the general's ego. "Buffalo Bill" Cody was no longer the hero of the Plains, but a flashy showman who had stretched the truth for publicity. Heroes of the American West were no longer looked upon as white knights—but instead were regarded as less than heroic. The Western film genre was beginning to show signs of change as well. By 1967, there were only thirteen Western television series on the fall schedule, compared with seventeen a decade earlier.[1] Although Western movies were still made, they were done on a much smaller scale than previously. With the growing popularity of the "Spaghetti Westerns," especially in Europe, the hero was likely to be less than pristine.[2]

Since making *Gunfight at the O.K. Corral*, John Sturges had several hit films under his belt, such as *The Magnificent Seven* and *The Great Escape*. The director decided to revisit the story of the famous gunfight, this time focusing on the events after the shootout.[3] After reading two chapters of Douglas D. Martin's *Tombstone Epitaph* that focused on the aftermath of the gunfight, Sturges was convinced that there was another story to tell. He bought the rights to Martin's book and hired two-time Oscar winner Edward Anhalt to write the script.[4] The original title of the project was *Tombstone Law*, but that was soon changed to *The Law and Tombstone*. Shortly after production was completed it was announced that the movie would be called *Day of the Guns*, but finally *Hour of the Gun* was settled on.

The movie opens on October 26, 1881, with the Earps and Holliday walking to the O.K. Corral to disarm the Clantons and the McLowerys.[5] Following the gunfight, the Earps and Holliday are charged with murder, and a hearing is held before Judge Spicer. The Earps and Holliday are exonerated, but soon after, Virgil is ambushed and crippled. Morgan decides to run in Virgil's place for the post of city marshal against Pete Spence, a candidate fronted by Ike Clanton. While the election ballots are being counted, Morgan is killed as he plays a game of billiards. Wyatt is appointed deputy U.S. marshal, with the authority to arrest those involved in the attack on Virgil and in Morgan's murder.

The three Earp brothers and Doc Holliday walk toward the O.K. Corral. Left to right: Sam Melville, Frank Converse, Jason Robards and James Garner. Bill Fletcher, playing Sheriff Ryan, can be glimpsed behind Converse (author's collection).

In Tucson, Wyatt is greeted by Sheriff Sherman McMasters, who warns him that Frank Stilwell and others are in town, possibly to kill him and Virgil. While seeing off Virgil and his family on a train to California, Wyatt spots Frank Stilwell in the shadows. Slipping off the train undetected, Wyatt stalks Stilwell and kills him as Doc watches. McMasters joins Wyatt and Doc as part of the posse formed to arrest the others. Returning to Tombstone by train, Wyatt learns that the law is after him for killing Stilwell. To avoid being arrested, Wyatt agrees to meet Doc and McMasters at another train stop down the line. In the meantime, Doc gets Texas Jack Vermillion and Turkey Creek Jack Johnson to join the posse.

Ike Clanton, unhappy that Earp hasn't been killed, orders Spence, Andy Warshaw and Curly Bill to disappear until he can take care of Earp. Spence is told to go east on business, but Clanton refuses to give him any money. Curly Bill is told to go to Texas, and Warshaw agrees to hide out in a line shack on Clanton's property. The Earp posse comes across a stagecoach that has been robbed. Before dying, the driver identifies Pete Spence as the shooter. Wyatt tells the others to meet him at a cabin; he then tracks Spence to a stage stop, where Wyatt finds the stolen stage money in Spence's valise. Forcing Spence into a showdown, Wyatt kills him. Meeting the others at a cabin, Wyatt explains that Spence wouldn't submit to arrest and is dead. While drinking in a saloon that evening, Doc learns that Curly Bill is in town. Doc confronts him and, as they draw their weapons, Wyatt, who has followed Doc, kills Curly Bill.

Once again the Earp posse is on the move. They head to the line shack, owned by Clanton, where Andy Warshaw is hiding out. Warshaw admits to Wyatt that he was paid $50 to serve as a lookout while others murdered Morgan. Wyatt challenges Warshaw to earn more money by drawing on him, and guns down Warshaw. The killing of Warshaw ends any chance the posse may have had to collect a reward. Wyatt apologizes to McMasters, Johnson and Vermillion, who ride off, leaving Wyatt and Doc. Realizing that Wyatt never intended to arrest any of the wanted men and that the warrants were simply his license to kill, Doc's anger builds. "Well, here, if you're gonna kill like me, you might as well drink like me!" Doc yells at Wyatt. Wyatt lashes out and hits Doc, knocking him to the ground. A coughing spell overcomes Doc and Wyatt offers to take him to Denver for treatment of his tuberculosis.

In Denver, Wyatt meets with members of Tombstone's business community, who tell Earp that they have secured a U. S. marshal's position for him, along with an opportunity to become adjutant-general of the Arizona Territory. Wyatt also learns that Clanton has fled to Mexico and that the townsmen bought off Sheriff Bryan and others in Clanton's employ. Wyatt goes to visit Doc at a Denver sanitarium, where he says he is heading to Tombstone to take the marshal's job. On a southbound train, Doc joins Wyatt, knowing that Earp is headed for Mexico to get Clanton. Doc refuses to return to Denver. With the help of Mexican officers, Wyatt tracks down one of Clanton's men herding stolen cattle and captures two men who say they were working for Clanton. Later, Wyatt is informed that the two men were killed while sitting in their jail cells. Clanton once again has escaped criminal prosecution.

Riding into a small village, Wyatt and Doc find Clanton and some men in a church courtyard. When Wyatt walks into the courtyard, the other men back away. He unpins his badge and throws it to Doc. Clanton and Wyatt square off for the final showdown, and Wyatt kills Clanton. Back in Denver, Wyatt visits Doc in a sanitarium. Struggling for the right words, Doc says, "Go on, get outta here." Outside the sanitarium, Wyatt meets Dr. Goodfellow. He tells the doctor that he has turned down the marshal's position and that he's through with the law. With that, Wyatt rides off in a buckboard as Doc watches him go, knowing that Wyatt has told him a friendly lie.

The first draft of the screenplay, dated May 25, 1964,[6] is basically the same as the released film. The opening in the 1964 draft has conventional titles without background or musical score. Over the credits, the script noted, would be the sound of wind blowing and the occasional rumble of wagon wheels and clomp of horses' hoofs, which became more specific, eventually suggesting the audience is "listening inches away." Sounds of horses galloping, slowing down and men dismounting would also be heard before the director's credit was flashed on the screen and the wind "dies down to a hiss" and the screen goes black. Hammers of weapons click open, then gunfire explodes. "The screen comes alive in flame and smoke—short brutal cuts of a gunfight. Then silence."[7] We would then see people coming out to witness the carnage and Sheriff Bryant stating he will arrest the Earps. (Ike Clanton is not in this sequence at all.) As Wyatt helps Morgan and Virgil to the doctor's office, Sheriff Bryan tells Wyatt that his badge won't help him this time. Doc hands his own badge to attorney Horace Sullivan. "Then it sure won't as hell help me, will it? Here. Halloween's over," he says. (In the film, Sullivan isn't present and Wyatt and Doc ignore Bryan's claims of arresting him.)

Inside Dr. Goodfellow's office, we see Virgil taping his leg wound, while Goodfellow tends to Morgan. Sullivan asks why they went down to the corral. Wyatt replies that it was to disarm them. Doc states that it was the challenge to his badge that made him go down

Director John Sturges and James Garner discuss a scene during location filming for *Hour of the Gun* (courtesy of the Academy of Motion Picture Arts and Sciences).

to the corral and needles Wyatt by saying that they cannot have authority undermined, even if it means a gunfight. "No matter what kind of a gunfight it means, so long as the reasons are right," Wyatt replies. Goodfellow comments that he could never understand why those in dirty shirts automatically vote for a cattle thief or claim jumper the minute he runs for office. "That's easy," Doc says. "They'll never *have* clean shirts, so they vote for a man who has the guts to steal yours." He has a coughing fit and takes a drink of alcohol from one of Goodfellow's medicine bottles. The doctor reminds Holliday that alcohol is not good for someone with tuberculosis. Doc says he knows that and leaves. Before the Earps leave the office, Goodfellow warns them that Clanton will try to get even. Sturges shot this scene, but deleted it during the editing process, feeling that the scene slowed the film's pacing.

Ike Clanton arrives at the funeral parlor not only to view the bodies but also to lay out his plan to eliminate the Earps. The script then has a scene in Judge Spicer's courtroom in which the defense attorneys (John Clum and Sullivan) and the prosecutor (Octavis Roy) bicker over a ruling requiring a closed courtroom for the hearing. Spicer sets a date for the hearing and orders Wyatt and Doc each held on $25,000 bail. Stilwell turns to Sheriff Bryan and says, "Let them find *that* on a Saturday afternoon"—as Anson Safford comes in with a valise of money for their bail.[8]

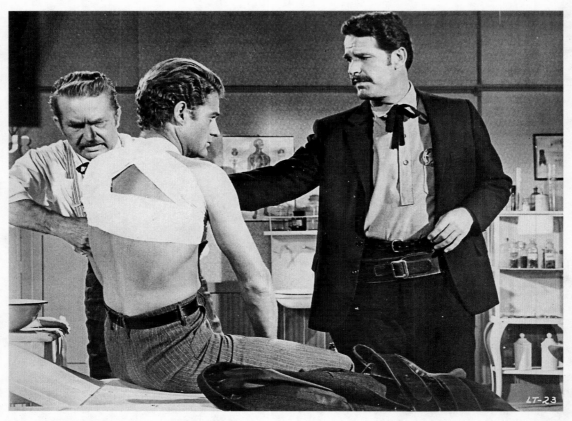

Another scene that was cut from the final print: Dr. Goodfellow (Karl Swenson, left) tends to the wounded shoulder of Morgan (Sam Melville) as Wyatt helps (author's collection).

During the funeral procession, Wyatt and Doc stand in front of the courthouse, watching. The script had a sequence of shots of their point-of-view of the funeral on Boot Hill and of hearing the preacher deliver his sermon. Across the street from the courthouse, Doc sees several prostitutes and their madam watching and listening to the funeral from the veranda of their building. Doc waves to them, but the girls avoid his looks while the madam glares. As the funeral ends, Doc asks, "What's so special about death?"[9]

Anhalt had written a brief courtroom scene between John Clum and Prosecutor Roy, in which he asks Clum whether he's an objective reporter, and Clum replies affirmatively. Roy then reads a quote from Clum's newspaper and asks whether the comment is objective. Clum replies that it was "an editorial against anarchy." (Anhalt used an actual newspaper quote from Clum's paper stating that the Earps' actions were right. However, it was cut from further script drafts.) After Wyatt and Doc are acquitted, Holliday asks when they will kill Clanton. Wyatt states they'll get him at the election with ballots. "You are dreaming. Get him before he gets you," Doc warns.[10]

A street parade for Pete Spence's election, complete with a trick rider and Indians, proceeds down Allen Street. People are carrying placards that read: "Keep our daddies safe on the streets of Tombstone" and "Vote for Spence for City Marshal." The parade passes the Oriental and the Alhambra saloons. We see Spence inside the Alhambra watching the event, while Clanton drinks coffee at a table. Spence is impressed with the turnout, only to learn

Sturges filmed a sequence where Pete Spence (Michael Tolan, standing in buggy) takes part in a parade for his bid as city marshal. The scene was cut before the film was released (author's collection).

that Clanton paid for the whole thing. It is indicated that Virgil will be attacked, and Spence asks why he has to be part of Virgil's ambush. "So I know I can be sure of you once you're city marshal," Clanton calmly says.[11]

When Virgil is ambushed, Harry, a waiter at the Oriental Saloon, witnesses the shooting from his room and rushes to Virgil's aid, as Wyatt and others arrive. In this draft of the scene, when Harry refuses to name the killers, Wyatt slams him against a post, telling Harry that he has as much to fear from him as he does from Clanton. The waiter agrees to talk as long as it is just between him and Wyatt. Wyatt agrees to the deal, they walk away from the gathering crowd and Harry tells him what he saw. (In the movie, there is no crowd other than Wyatt, Doc, Morgan, and Dr. Goodfellow.)

The sequence of Wyatt and Doc escorting Morgan's remains and Virgil's family to Tucson by train includes a scene in which Wyatt gets a telegram telling him that he has authority to arrest Stilwell, Spence and Curly Bill. Doc notes that the warrants do not include Clanton; Wyatt tells him there isn't enough evidence. "Then that proves you can't play this by the rules for sure," Doc replies. Wyatt claims he will be busy with the warrants, causing Doc to reply angrily, "I thought you'd be convinced by now, Wyatt. *Nail Clanton!* Virgil didn't and he's crippled. Morgan didn't and he's dead." Wyatt's face becomes rigid. Doc doesn't push the matter but offers to be his first gun for the posse. "It isn't worth it. Not if I have to listen to you telling me all about myself," says Wyatt. "Someone has to," says Doc.

Although this scene appears in the finished production, Sturges has eliminated the dialogue between Wyatt and Doc (Doc's urging Wyatt to nail Clanton, Wyatt's reply that he doesn't want Doc around if he has to listen to him). Instead, Wyatt tells Doc that no funds are available and that the warrant is for arrest and conviction. "Not your style, Doc," he says. Holliday reminds him of the $20,000 reward put up by Clum and others, adding, "For that kind of money, I can be as law-abiding as you are."

After finding the stagecoach robbed and the driver dead, Wyatt's posse follows horse tracks that lead them to a mine shaft, where they spot Spence and two other men. Wyatt has Doc and the others keep the two men pinned down while he chases Spence back into the mine. Inside the mine shaft, Spence finds himself at a dead end. Wyatt sees a weakened, rotting timber and shoots at it, causing the shaft to cave in on Spence.

As Wyatt comes out of the mine shaft, McMasters comments to Doc that the reward is getting smaller and smaller. When Turkey Creek Johnson asks where Spence is, Wyatt flatly says, "Rock hunting." As they ride off, Doc asks, "Now—Clanton?" Wyatt tells him they'll hole up at a house of a U.S. marshal in Contention until Sheriff Bryan's posse has moved on. "Well, you've already had a full day," says Doc. When Wyatt asks him what he said, Doc replies flatly, "Nothing."

Later, as the Earp group rides toward Clanton's line shack, Wyatt has Turkey Creek Johnson open a barbed-wire fence with wire cutters. Once they have passed through, Wyatt tells Johnson to mend the fence. Johnson says he doesn't mind if Clanton's cattle stray, but Wyatt is adamant. Doc asks Wyatt if he thinks riding up and just arresting Florentino Cruz will be easy.[12] Earp tells him that no one will be expecting them, thinking they have gone to Colorado instead. "Stop pressing, Wyatt. Nobody blames you for wanting this, this badly," Doc says. Wyatt tells him it is the law, "not what I want or you want." Doc sardonically replies, "I'm no lawman and I don't have to pretend that to myself." Wyatt grabs Holliday's reins and says he means it. Looking at Wyatt, Doc says, "I almost believe you." (Sturges would drop all of this scene during production.)

In the script when Wyatt arrives at the Denver hotel, Anhalt has a brief bit of business as Earp gets into the elevator after being told some of his friends are waiting for him. Inside the elevator, Wyatt opens his bag and takes out his pistol and loads it. The bellboy is so fascinated he misses the intended floor. When Wyatt reaches the room and discovers Sullivan, Clum, Stafford, and others, he hands the gun to the bellboy and asks him to put it back in his bag.[13] All of this was dropped from the final print.

After meeting Clum and others, Wyatt goes to see Doc at a sanitarium. He tells him about the job offer and that he is heading back to Tombstone. The next scene has Wyatt boarding a train, with Doc following him through the train station. The script notes that Holliday's clothing appears "too large for him." Doc sits next to Wyatt on the train, telling him he didn't believe for a minute that Earp was going to take the marshal's position. "It's Clanton, still Clanton." Wyatt says nothing and gets up and goes outside to stand on the platform. The script describes Wyatt as looking "suddenly tired." Holliday joins him, and Wyatt admits he had no intention of arresting Cruz or the others. Doc tells him Clanton is different. "You're planning this one. That's no reason to tear off your badge and start shooting wild. If you have to do it, do it legally," he says. Holliday urges Earp to go to the Mexican authorities for help, saying they'll give him warrants to make anything legal. Wyatt says he's not that much of a hypocrite. "The whole thing's hypocrisy. The words are 'Thou shall not kill.' But the rules they've tacked on say unless you're wearing a tin badge or a soldier's uniform you can't kill. I know you, Wyatt. The rules are hypocritical but they're the only rules there are and they're more important to you than you think." When Wyatt doesn't respond, Doc replies, "It must be hell to have a conscience."[14]

In Mexico, Wyatt and Doc, with the help of Mexican Federales, catch some of Clanton's men with stolen cattle. Returning to the hotel, Wyatt is greeted by a doctor who says Holliday's heart is giving out. Wyatt goes to see Doc, who asks Wyatt not to let him die in Mexico. He tells Holliday he's not going to die, when a nurse notifies Wyatt that a Federale captain is waiting for him The captain tells Wyatt that the two witnesses were shot while in jail and without them, there can be no trial. Wyatt comes back into Doc's room, straps on his gun belt and walks out, ignoring Doc's questions. The nurse tells Holliday what she overheard, and Doc replies, "I guess he's just found out they break the rules in Mexico, too."[15]

At the border town of Nogales, Wyatt approaches two vaqueros (with a riderless horse between them) in front of a Mexican bank. Ike Clanton watches Wyatt talking to the vaqueros, who quickly leave. Clanton goes to a bank official and arranges for a horse at the rear of the bank. Wyatt sees Clanton and follows him to a bullfighting ring, where they stalk each other. Clanton runs through the grandstand seats, while Wyatt tracks him from below. Wyatt shoots at Clanton, hitting him in the back. Clanton sprawls into the ring as Wyatt empties his gun into the man's body. Sitting on a horse at the entrance of the ring is Doc, holding Wyatt's horse. It is now obvious that Doc is a dying man.

As they ride off, Doc tells Wyatt to go back to Tombstone and take the marshal's job. Wyatt says they both will go back to Tombstone, Doc replies, "You never could lie to me, Wyatt." Doc falls off his saddle and dies.[16] The final scene takes place at the Nogales train station, where Wyatt watches Doc's casket being loaded onto a baggage car. As the train leaves, a young Mexican boy holds the reins of a well-stocked wagon and team. Wyatt tips the boy, who asks him where he's going. In a barely audible voice, Wyatt says, "California," as he rides off.[17]

Anhalt's second draft of the script, dated August 15, 1966, has a few minor changes, including two different versions of the final showdown between Wyatt and Clanton, but the overall script remains intact. Other changes include a new opening. This draft has a group of riders, the McLowerys, Billy Clanton, Billy Claiborne, and Curly Bill, approaching the outskirts of Tombstone. We then see a buckboard, driven by Ike Clanton, with Pete Spence and Andy Warshaw riding alongside. (The script refers to Clanton's clothes as "cut with style and elegance.") As they turn past the courthouse and down Fremont Street, we see a "tall man in a dark suit pause as he watches Clanton go by, then he continues walking up the street. This is Wyatt Earp."[18] Earp meets Doc Holliday outside the Oriental saloon. Over this shot a title would have read: "The gunplay lasted only a few seconds but it set in motion events that uprooted and twisted those involved for the rest of their lives." Instead, Sturges has written: "This is what actually happened." As the credits begin, people join Clanton by the O.K. Corral. Wyatt and Doc are joined by Morgan and Virgil, and they begin their walk into destiny. Sheriff Bryan tries to stop them without success. As the credits conclude, the Earps and Holliday pause opposite Fly's photo studio before the gunfight begins.[19] Sturges would slightly modify the opening scenes during production, using this draft as his guideline.

Another change takes place with Morgan's death. In the script, he looks up at the others and says, "I guess this is my last game of pool." (These were Morgan's actual words.) In Sturges' personal script, he has scratched this out. Instead, he has Morgan, lying on the billiard table, looking up at Clum and the others and say, "I won, didn't I?" He then

John Sturges sits atop a Chapman camera crane while filming the opening sequence for *Hour of the Gun*. Camera operator David Walsh (center) and camera assistant Terry Meade run the Mitchell 35 camera (courtesy of the Academy of Motion Picture Arts and Sciences).

calls Wyatt over and quietly says something to him before dying. (The audience doesn't hear it.)[20]

As Wyatt rides off in pursuit of Pete Spence, Bryan's posse quickly approaches the rest of Earp's group. Doc tells McMasters, Vermillion, and Johnson to take a position in one area and they will catch Bryan's posse in a crossfire, holding them down. After a few minutes, the four men sneak off, leaving Bryan's posse shooting at nothing. (In the final print, the sequence of Doc and the others pinning down Bryan's posse has been eliminated.[21])

Following the Denver hotel sequence, the scene between Wyatt and Doc on the train has been pared down. We no longer see Doc following Wyatt in the station, but simply entering the passenger car and taking a seat next to Wyatt. He says he knows Wyatt wouldn't leave him in a hospital just because Earp was offered a job. Wyatt tells him to let it go, but Doc continues to needle him, adding that the only reason Wyatt would leave would be to go after Clanton. Rising suddenly, Wyatt says, "Talk to yourself," and he goes to stand on the outside platform. Doc follows him. Wyatt says they have laws in Mexico as well and that is how he'll get Clanton. (Sturges would use most of this dialogue in the film, but shot the scene entirely in the passenger car.[22])

The first of two versions of the showdown between Wyatt and Clanton has Earp and Holliday riding into a Mexican village where they are greeted by gunfire. The two men slowly move to a plaza where they kill Clanton's men who are shooting at them. Wyatt goes ahead, as Doc, whose health is ebbing away, covers him. Wyatt passes a door that opens, revealing Clanton holding a shotgun. Doc sees this, but cannot hold his gun to shoot at Clanton. He grabs his whiskey bottle and throws it, causing it to break. Hearing this, Wyatt spins around to see Clanton fire the shotgun. Jumping aside just in time, Wyatt rushes into a large room and circles behind Clanton. Coming up behind Ike, Wyatt holsters his gun and the two men stare at each other before drawing their pistols. Wyatt's shot fires true, and Clanton is killed.[23]

The second alternative ending has Wyatt going into the Mexican hotel where he learns of Doc's illness. He then speaks to the Federale captain about the two witnesses being killed. Back in Doc's room, Wyatt tells him about the two dead witnesses. He also admits to Doc that he was right about Warshaw and the others, and he would be right about Clanton. As he is saying this, Wyatt takes off his badge and leaves it on the dresser. They have the same conversation in which Wyatt admits he is not that much of a hypocrite and Doc tells him the whole thing is laden with hypocrisy, unless one has a badge or a military uniform. Wyatt says, "I can't let Clanton walk the earth anymore," and leaves the room. Doc's nurse returns to ask what is wrong, and Holliday says that Earp has learned that rules get broken in Mexico as well. As he takes a drink and looks outside his window, he sees Clanton standing in an archway across the street with a shotgun. Doc throws his whiskey bottle out the window and yells at Wyatt. At that instant, Wyatt, on his horse, sees Clanton and jumps out of the saddle as Clanton fires.[24] Seeing two men holding horses, Doc grabs a gun and goes out the back door. Holliday kills both men as Clanton and Wyatt stalk each other through an arcade. Wyatt comes up behind Ike, who turns around to find Earp staring him down, gun in holster. The two square off and, as Clanton aims his shotgun, Wyatt kills him. The final scene is identical to the 1964 draft, except that Earp does not tell the young Mexican boy where he is heading.[25]

With the script completed, Sturges renegotiated the contact he had with the Mirisch Corporation. The deal, announced in July 1966, would allow Sturges to make two additional pictures under his original contract, including *Hour of the Gun*.[26] The following day it was announced that Sturges had decided upon James Garner to star in the film as Wyatt Earp. Garner, whom the director had worked with previously in *The Great Escape* (1963), recalled matter-of-factly, "I knew John, so I guess he wanted me."[27]

Garner, who began his acting career with a small role in the Broadway production of *The Caine Mutiny Court Martial* in 1954, is no stranger to the Western genre, having starred in the popular television series *Maverick* (as Bret Maverick) for three seasons (1957–60) before leaving over a contractual dispute.[28] Over the years, Garner has appeared in several Westerns, including *Duel at Diablo* (1966), *Support Your Local Sheriff!* (1969), *The Skin Game* (1971), *The Castaway Cowboy* (1974) and *Maverick* (1994), in which he played the father of Bret Maverick. His performance in *Murphy's Romance* (1985) won him a Best Actor Oscar nomination, and in 1990 he was inducted into the Hall of Great Western Performers of the National Cowboy and Western Heritage Museum. Garner is also the only actor to play Wyatt Earp in two movies: *Hour of the Gun* and *Sunset* (1988).[29]

With Garner set as Wyatt, Sturges chose Jason Robards for the role of Doc Holliday. Robards, the son of famous stage actor, Jason Robards, Sr., had started his acting career on the stage, avoiding motion pictures until 1959, when he was 37. His Broadway performances in such plays as *The Iceman Cometh, Long Day's Journey Into Night* and *A Thousand Clowns* earned him much critical acclaim. He went on to win two Best Supporting Oscars for his work in *All the President's Men* (1977) and *Julia* (1978).[30] In his last film role, *Magnolia* (1999), Robards played a man dying of lung cancer, a disease he himself died from in 2000.

For the role of Ike Clanton, John Sturges chose veteran actor Robert Ryan, who had previously worked with the director in *Bad Day at Black Rock* (1955). The rest of the cast featured many familiar character actors including Larry Gates as John Clum, Monte Markham as McMasters, and Lonny Chapman and William Windom as Turkey Creek Johnson and Texas Jack Vermillion, respectively. *Hour of the Gun* also marked the feature film debut of a young actor named Jon Voight. Even screenwriter Edward Anhalt played a small role, that of Holliday's doctor in the Denver sanitarium.

One of the mandates from United Artists, which was producing the film in association with the Mirisch Corporation, was that none of the actors who appeared in Sturges's 1957 film about the gunfight should be cast in any major role. Sturges had wanted to use both John Hudson and DeForest Kelley in the same roles they had played in 1957 (Virgil and Morgan Earp respectively), feeling that their appearances in the previous version were so small that an audience would not be aware of it. However, Hudson had no interest in traveling to Mexico and Kelley was co-starring in the *Star Trek* television series. The roles went to two young actors, Frank Converse and Sam Melville.

With casting completed, Sturges turned his attention to choosing locations. Sturges said he needed a location that would, among other things, offer ideal weather and access to a railroad line. Looking first in Arizona, Sturges found nothing that would suit his needs, so he turned his attention to Mexico, where he had filmed *The Magnificent Seven* in 1959. In September 1966, Sturges chose Torreon as his principal filming site. Torreon, 550 miles northwest of Mexico City, was considered a wealthy city, boasting numerous cotton fields and vineyards, with a population of about 180,000. This is where Sturges would build the town set of Tombstone. Using more than 75,000 native pines from the nearby Durango area for lumber, over 30 buildings were erected, including exteriors of the Oriental Saloon, Fly's Photo Galley and the O.K. Corral. The construction crew built a 500-foot railroad siding, complete with station and platform. This allowed the train used in the film to pull off the main line, which was not far from the set, during peak rail line hours. A 250-foot-deep well was dug and a 25,000-gallon reservoir built to wet down the streets and keep dust to a minimum. Bulldozers widened nearby dirt roads to allow the heavy production trucks to reach the location.[31] Despite the remoteness, sightseers would number close to two thousand, clogging the highway from Durango to Mazatlan.[32]

The production company rented the railroad engines from the Mexican government; two passenger coaches were bought for $4,800 and refurbished for the film. A train station in La Goma, Mexico, would serve as the Tucson station, and additional rail tracks, aside from the two existing tracks, were built for the night sequences. The company also hired reserves from the Mexican Army to serve as guards during production. While filming certain scenes in the ancient pueblo of Atotomilco, the filmmakers removed the only telephone and power line into the small village, but later replaced it with a more technically advanced line. In a letter to the cast and crew who would be traveling to Mexico, Sturges noted that the weather in Torreon during November would generally be dry and warm, although the mornings and evenings could get cold. He stated that shortly before Christmas, the company would move to Mexico City, where they would film all the interior sets at Churubusco Studios, the largest studio in Mexico. In January, the company would move to San Miguel de Allende, a three-hour drive north of Mexico City, for the final weeks of production. "We've all worked hard to organize every angle of the location, but it is an imperfect world and if something gets goofed up let us know and bear with us until we can straighten it out," Sturges added.[33]

Filming began on November 9, 1966, in Terreon, with the interior set of the line shack in which the Earp group takes refuge from Bryan's posse. After completing those scenes, the company moved to the Tombstone set and filmed the interior of a saloon set, with Doc swearing in Texas Jack as a deputy, before returning to the line shack set for the exterior scene of Doc leaving to get a drink in Contention. November 10 and 11 were spent filming in La Goma aboard the passenger train. The prevailing way to film scenes on a passenger train at this time was to rig a set on a stage and use the rear-screen projection process of the countryside going by. While this offered a filmmaker control over the elements and lighting, it also looked distinctly unreal. Instead, Sturges actually had a train engine pull the passenger cars along the track as they shot the various scenes. An additional three days in La Goma, November 14–17 (they didn't film on Sundays), were spent filming night scenes of the Tucson train yards and the death of Frank Stilwell. The following day, the company had off, calling it a "conversion day," allowing the crew a day's rest and to get back on a daytime shooting schedule.[34]

The company returned to Torreon on November 22 to begin filming the opening credits and gunfight sequence. They would spend a total of ten days shooting all of the scenes, with two days off for celebrating the Thanksgiving holiday, even though Mexico had no such holiday observance.[35] December 9 and 10 were devoted to filming the scenes on the Tombstone street after the gunfight before Sturges went on to complete other exterior scenes on the Tombstone street set, including the scrapped election parade for Pete Spence and the funeral procession. On December 20, the company completed filming in Torreon and moved to Mexico City for interior scenes at Churubusco studios. The following day, Sturges began Morgan's death scene in the billiard hall. The company was idle on Christmas and the following day, and then began filming the courtroom scenes on December 28. These sequences continued through New Year's Eve, before taking a three-day break. The company returned to the courtroom set on January 4, 1967, for four additional days. Moving to the studio's Western street on its back lot, Sturges spent three nights, January 9 to 11, filming the Contention City saloon scenes, Curly Bill's death, and Virgil's ambush. The following day was another conversion day for the company, which then moved to a location just outside Mexico City to film the Denver sanatorium set. It is here that Sturges filmed the final goodbye sequence between Wyatt and Doc. On January 16, the company moved to San Miguel De Allende, where they would film over the next four days the sequences of Wyatt catching Clanton's men with stolen Mexican cattle and the final showdown with Clanton. Production on Hour of the Gun was completed on January 22, 1967.[36]

Returning to Los Angeles, Sturges began cutting his film with his long-time editor, Ferris Webster.[37] During this process, Sturges eliminated many scenes that he felt hurt the flow and heart of the story. Garner remembered Sturges as "a wonderful, wonderful director." When it came to directing, Garner said that "John knew me. I knew him. I knew pretty much what he wanted, and John was pretty good at casting and then let them [the actors] do their job. Only if you were missing a point he was trying to make, he didn't say a hell of a lot." Garner felt that Sturges was a very underappreciated director, but that his biggest strength was in the editing of a film. "His forte was editing. He was a great editor.... He and Ferris Webster. And he kept Ferris with him and they did a lot of things," the actor recalled.[38]

Released in early October, *Hour of the Gun* received mixed reviews, with many critics pointing out the problems when dealing with fact versus fiction. "Genuine zip and interest in first half eventually dissipates into talky, telescoped resolution.... Unfortunately for any filmmaker, probing too deeply into the character of folk heroes reveals them to be fallible human beings—which they are, of course—but to mass audiences, who create fantasies (and have fantasies created for them) to fulfill inner needs, such exposition is unsettling. Reality often makes poor drama.... Robards and Garner play well together, the former supplying an adroit irony in that he, an admitted gambler as much outside the law as in, becomes more moral as Garner lapses into personal vendetta," wrote *Variety*.[39] *The Film Daily*, another industry trade paper, noted that the film was "a bristling western, with formula touches here and there, that should do well in the market.... In the three dominant roles Garner, Robards and Ryan handle their assignments with authority.... Sturges' direction of this Mirisch-Kappa picture keeps the action boiling with Western-style excitement."

The Hollywood Reporter stated that the "potentially strong film emerges as a big, routine and curiously static western, which fails to answer questions it raises, takes its time in the inevitable liquidation of remaining members of the Clanton gang and concludes with Earp riding off with the knowledge that he has subverted the letter of the law into a license to kill. Legend augmented by top billing of James Garner, Jason Robards and Robert Ryan should prompt moderately strong grosses in multiplexes."[40] The *Los Angeles Times* felt that "while both films [Sturges' 1957 film and *Hour of the Gun*] bear the stamp of Sturges' crisp masculine style, the second is not as satisfying as the first.... [The movie] commands respect but never really engages the emotions. As an expression of timeless truths about human nature, the myth is ever more persuasive than the documentary. Yet there is much to admire in *Hour of the Gun* in the way of good acting.... Garner and Robards have been balanced very well.... Their final leave-taking, not on the dusty streets of their triumph but on the porch of a convalescent home where Doc has come to die, is especially poignant."[41] Despite the mixed reviews, the National Association of Theatre Owners at their Fall Film Fair commended the film as one of four movies for excellent entertainment.

Hour of the Gun opens with a shot of Wyatt, dressed in black clothes, alone on the street, as he walks toward the camera. This shot is a typical motif in Westerns, the hero standing alone on the street before the showdown; another example is the famous shot of Gary Cooper walking the street alone in *High Noon*. Each main character—Wyatt, Doc, and Ike Clanton—is introduced in medium shots as the credits begin. Over the rest of the opening credits, we see the cowboys ride into the O.K. Corral and gather across the street at Fly's Photo Gallery (where Clanton is standing) and the Earp brothers talking and swearing in Doc. As Wyatt walks away from them and stands alone on the street, a credit comes up saying this exactly the way the story happened. The two other brothers and Doc join Wyatt on the street. Wyatt pauses, obviously understanding the complications of what they are about to do, and exhibits a quiet sense of resignation. He takes a deep breath before they all start walking down the street.

As they stop by the corral, Wyatt notes the people around Fly's Photo Gallery. Without taking his eyes off them, he asks Virgil to tell him who is in the corral. It is a small piece of business, but it shows how Wyatt and his brothers worked as law officers. Virgil commands the men to give up their guns, as Ike (who is wearing a gun belt) and others around Fly's get out of the way. Just then, shooting erupts, and the gunfight is underway. When it is over, Clanton emerges from the photo gallery without his gun belt, giving the viewer an indication of how he will use the legal system to his advantage.

When Ike comes to view the bodies at the funeral home, he is more concerned with getting the Earps out of the way than with the death of his younger brother. Clanton is shown as a cold, calculating man who is out for personal gain. He reminds the viewer of a Western-era syndicate man. He even tells his people in the funeral home that if this situation were back east, he could make law. Out here, he notes, the best thing he can do is own the law. Clanton wants to expand his cattle and range holdings before the area becomes too settled, but the Earps, and their enforcement of the law, stand in his way. When he is called to view the bodies of his brother and the McLowerys, he glances at them and then rides off. The dead bodies serve a purpose for his gains and nothing more.

During the hearing in Judge Spicer's courtroom, Doc Holliday verbally spars with the prosecution attorney, Octavius Roy. Doc displays a dark, sardonic sense of humor. When Roy asks him why he killed a man he didn't know, Holliday replies, "I killed a lot of men I didn't know between 1861 and 1865. Nobody said anything about it." (This was obviously dramatic license on the part of the writer. Holliday was eleven when the Civil War began.) When he hears Ike Clanton explain that he uses an armed Andy Warshaw as a scientific stock breeder, Doc loudly offers, "Maybe he has to force the stock to breed." Wyatt is cool and calm under cross-examination, not letting the questions ruffle him. When prosecutor Roy asks if Wyatt selectively enforces the law, he replies, "I would arrest General Ulysses S. Grant if he were carrying a firearm on the streets of Tombstone." From his statement, Wyatt

Wyatt and Doc await Judge Spicer's decision on their murder charges. Karl Swenson and Austin Willis sit immediately behind James Garner, on the left and right respectively (author's collection).

comes across as the supreme law enforcer. This is done to show the audience how his character's moral foundation will change during the course of the film. Ike Clanton comes across
as a very calm, soft-spoken man during his testimony, totally unlike the real Ike Clanton.
Interestingly, it is the character of Sheriff Jimmy Bryan (a stand-in for Johnny Behan) whose
angry testimony helps to sink the prosecutor's case.

Running to Virgil's aid after he's been ambushed, Wyatt is all business. He tells Morgan to check the alley and quickly sees to his other brother's needs. When he questions
Harry, the waiter who witnessed the shooting, he knows immediately the man is lying.
Wyatt, foreshadowing his darker side, grabs the man's hand and begins to twist his wrist to
get a truthful answer. For the first time we see the cold, intimidating side of Wyatt, and it
is not comforting. Wyatt gives his word to Harry that he will not reveal him as his source,
and after the man names the attackers, Wyatt pats him on the shoulder as a way of thanking him and apologizing. In court, despite Spicer's attempts to allow them to present the
evidence needed for a conviction, Wyatt remains silent. His word is his bond. He will not
yet bend those rules for justice. With charges dismissed against Stilwell, Spence, and Curly
Bill, Dr. Goodfellow reminds Wyatt that Virgil will be a cripple for life. The words hang
heavy on Wyatt's conscious, but he cannot break his promise. Stafford asks who will now
run against Spence for city marshal. Morgan speaks up and Wyatt is obviously proud of his
younger brother, gently touching his upper arm as a way to express his feelings. Leaving the
courtroom, Wyatt looks at Doc, telling him not to say anything. "I'm just educating myself,"
Holliday says. "I've never been on the right side of the law, I wanted to see how much good
it did you."

After Morgan's murder, as he and Virgil's family board the train, Wyatt tells Clum and
others that he will take legal action when he gets back from Tucson. Again, he is calm and
shows no signs of anger or grief. Inside the train, he sees Doc sitting a few seats away from
Virgil. When Wyatt asks him what he's doing here, Doc replies, "I'm crazy about trains."
Both Wyatt and the audience know why Doc is there, and his reply is the only way he can
express his feelings. After Wyatt receives the telegram granting warrants for Morgan's killers,
Doc volunteers his gun. Wyatt reminds him that it is for arrest and conviction, not dead
or alive. "Not your style, Doc." Noting the reward of $20,000, Doc says that for that sum
of money, he can be as law-abiding as Wyatt. The way Doc speaks this line foretells Earp's
future actions.

In Tucson, as he is saying goodbye to Virgil and his family, Wyatt spots Stilwell. He
quickly moves to stop him and the others. Catching one man, Wyatt just shoots him. He
comes up behind Stilwell, stating that he is under arrest and ordering him to drop his gun.
As Stilwell grabs Wyatt's pistol, Earp fires several times. His expression is cold. No emotion,
no second thoughts. As the train moves out, Wyatt sees Doc looking at him. There is no
need to say anything; Doc's expression speaks volumes. He is slowly realizing that Wyatt
does not intend to enforce the law but rather to eliminate those who attacked Virgil and
killed Morgan.

Returning to Tombstone, Wyatt learns there are warrants out for his arrest for killing
Stilwell. At the Tombstone train depot, he sees that Spence has sworn in deputies and that
they are merely standing there, taking no action to arrest him. Wyatt is reminded by Clum,
Stafford, and others that if the deputies wanted to arrest him, they would. Wyatt understands the meaning: They plan to kill him. It is here that Wyatt's ethics begin to change.
The law, which he has always upheld, will not punish the guilty, and those wearing the badge
will use it for their own gain. Wyatt, too, will use his badge to dispense justice.

After stopping the stagecoach and learning of the robbery, Wyatt goes alone to track Pete Spence, refusing Doc's offer of assistance. Wyatt wants to go alone so that no one, especially Doc, can remind him of his oath to uphold the law. Tracking Spence to a stage stop, Wyatt appears very calm when he finds the man waiting for the stage. By comparison, Spence is uneasy and nervous. In relating the facts of the stage robbery to Spence, Wyatt's tone is conversational. Spence falls for the trap. His anger slowly rising, Wyatt asks Spence if he knows what it's like to look down a shotgun at a man's back, referring not only to the stage driver but also to his two brothers. Spence's ineffectual attempt to explain any involvement only fuels Wyatt's anger. Taking his gloves off, we know that Wyatt is preparing for a gunfight. Spence's declaration that he was already acquitted (and that he would be again of any involvement with Virgil's attack or Morgan's death) only solidifies Wyatt's belief that he must dispense justice in his own way. Even if Wyatt chose to rationalize that he would arrest the wanted men, this comment of Spence's becomes the catalyst for his revenge. As Wyatt opens the man's valise and sees the stolen money, Spence's guilt gets the better of him. Grabbing his shotgun, he fires at Wyatt, who ducks behind an adobe wall. Firing his pistol, Wyatt kills Spence.

Meeting with his posse at a shack, Wyatt is now resigned to his actions. He offers little information to the other men about Spence, only that he's dead. Doc needles Wyatt about Spence, observing that there was no formal chance for an arrest. Wyatt's tone of "That's right, Doc" has a biting edge. He knows what Doc is attempting to say, and he doesn't want to hear it. As Wyatt goes into a bedroom, Doc casually says, "Well, you already had a busy day." Wyatt challenges him about his comment, but Doc drops the matter. Wyatt looks at Doc with contempt, which really is directed more toward himself than to Doc. His failure to properly arrest Spence has put him outside the law and that very fact gnaws at him. Later, after Doc confronts Curly Bill in Contention and Wyatt kills the Cowboy, Wyatt angrily tells Doc that he has ruined any attempt to use surprise on their part to arrest the others. Doc knowingly says, "Everybody has bad luck. I cough when I drink. You come up against sneaky people who get you to commit suicide."

Trailing Andy Warshaw to Clanton's line shack, Wyatt's dark side completely overtakes his reason. When Wyatt learns that Warshaw was paid $50 to be a lookout for the attack on Virgil and the murder of Morgan, it is all he can do to contain his anger. "A man's life. Fifty dollars," he says with contempt. Getting off his horse, Wyatt squares off against Warshaw, telling him that Clanton might even give him another $50 if Warshaw kills him. Warshaw tries to back out, but he has nowhere to run. Wyatt tells him he will count to three. Warshaw can draw on two and Wyatt will wait until three. Warshaw pleads that he only watched, which simply angers Wyatt further. He starts counting and even with the edge, Warshaw cannot get his gun out in time. The anger in Wyatt's voice is equaled by the report of his gun firing six shots into the man, as if his fury is propelled through him into his gun.

As some of Clanton's men drag Warshaw's body away, Wyatt slowly looks at his gun before holstering it. Walking to his horse, he catches Doc's gaze and says nothing. No words are necessary between them because he knows he has crossed the line. The feelings of the other men in the posse (McMasters, Vermillion, and Johnson) range from understanding to disappointment because of the loss of the reward money. Wyatt realizes this and does his best to apologize, but Johnson tells him, "You don't hear any complaints, do you?" The three men ride off, leaving Doc and Wyatt alone.

Leaning against his saddle, Wyatt is lost in thought. Doc, with his typically biting wit, says, "Boy, you sure gave him a chance." He offers Wyatt a drink from his flask, which is

Wyatt's posse tracks down one of Morgan's killers at a Clanton line shack. Left to right: Monte Markham, Jason Robards, James Garner. William Windom sits on a horse behind Garner (author's collection).

declined. Doc contemptuously says that Wyatt needs that drink to keep this morning down. His anger at Wyatt, who hid behind his badge to kill the wanted men, grows as Doc remarks how Wyatt knew he would never get a conviction in court and used his promise to a man to remain silent as his way of getting warrants to hunt down those responsible. "You didn't want to be cheated out of this! Those aren't warrants you got there. Those are hunting licenses.... You're gonna kill Clanton the same way I would and you don't need a warrant for that. So go on. If you're gonna kill like me, you might as well drink like me!" Wyatt's anger at Doc's words builds and he hits him, knocking his friend down. Almost immediately, he realizes he has done the wrong thing as Doc has a coughing spasm. Wyatt says that he will take Doc to Denver for treatment for his tuberculosis. "Sorry to spoil your party," Holliday replies.

In Denver, Wyatt is told by Clum, Safford and Sullivan that Clanton has run off to Mexico and that they bought off the rest of Clanton's men, including Sheriff Bryan. They want Wyatt to take the position of U.S. marshal in Tombstone, with its opportunity of his becoming the adjutant-general of the Arizona Territory. Wyatt is more interested in learning Clanton's location in Mexico and he tells the men he will have to think about the offer. We now know that Wyatt's personal quest for revenge supersedes everything else in his life.

He will even the odds and eliminate the man who managed to evade the law. On the train to the border, Wyatt is joined by Doc, who notes that Wyatt is still obsessed with getting Clanton. Wyatt tells him that they have laws in Mexico, and he will use those laws to arrest Clanton. Although Wyatt sounds believable, the audience knows that he is hoping to have his own chance at getting Clanton.

After two of the witnesses in Mexico are killed by Clanton's group, Wyatt realizes that even south of the border Clanton has managed to elude punishment. At this point, Wyatt removes his badge, as if abdicating his law enforcement career. What he will now do, he'll do without wearing the badge. He knows he is going to step outside the law to kill Clanton, and he will not use the law to justify his actions. Trailing Clanton to a small village, Wyatt finally faces him down. Before the gunfire erupts, Wyatt tosses his badge to Doc, who has been his conscience throughout most of the movie. By giving the badge to Doc, Wyatt signals to Doc (and the audience) that Holliday was right. Still, he will go through with killing Clanton no matter what. Thus, by giving his badge to Doc, even though it may be merely a symbolic gesture, Wyatt has no contact with the law. He has forsaken the law in order to mete out justice.

The final scene takes place back in the Denver sanatorium.[42] Doc has returned to be treated for his disease when Wyatt arrives. The two men are left alone on the porch of Doc's room, and there is an awkward silence. Doc finally says that he was wrong about saying that Wyatt couldn't go back to law enforcement after what he did in Mexico. This is his way of saying he was sorry, and he wants to believe that Wyatt will remain with the law. Wyatt merely smiles, as if trying to assure him it doesn't matter. Doc asks him if Wyatt's going back to Tombstone to accept the marshal's job, and Wyatt says he will. "Don't lie to me this time," Doc replies. When Wyatt firmly says he will be going back, Doc is relieved. "That's what I wanted to know," and he hands Wyatt his badge. The two men are silent again, at a loss for words. Doc tries to muster up a brave front and tells Wyatt to do him a favor and "get out of here." As Wyatt says goodbye and turns to leave, Doc calls after him. Again there is a moment of silence as the two friends look at each other. They both know there is nothing they can say. Doc limply waves and says so long. Wyatt bids goodbye and leaves. Outside the sanatorium, Wyatt talks with Dr. Goodfellow, who came to see Doc. Wyatt tells Goodfellow that he's turning down the marshal's position in Tombstone. "I'm through with the law," he says before riding off in his buckboard. Seated on his porch playing cards with his male nurse, Doc watches Wyatt ride away. He realizes that Earp has told him a friendly lie and that won't be taking the lawman's job. Doc hesitates for a moment as he watches Wyatt ride off, before taking a gulp of whiskey. Reacting to the taste, he says to his nurse, "God, that's terrible. Where do you get that stuff?" Doc watches for one last time as Wyatt's buckboard climbs a ridge and disappears.

Hour of the Gun was the most accurate film about the gunfight and the aftermath produced up to that time. It was the first film to deal with the Earps being tried for murder and to show the attacks of Virgil and Morgan happening at different times. For dramatic and storytelling purposes, certain events or people were either combined (such as Ike Clanton serving as the head of a criminal element), deleted (any reference to Johnny Ringo), or dramatized (Wyatt going to Mexico to kill Clanton). It was necessary for the story to have a lead antagonist and Ike Clanton served the purpose, although he was portrayed as a guileful and treacherous man who would stop at nothing for his own benefit. This also provided the conflict between Clanton and Wyatt Earp. In this film, Clanton's ability to subvert the law and get away with various crimes, including murder, further compels Wyatt's desire to see justice served. With Clanton undermining the law and not being held accountable for his actions, Wyatt is compelled to take matters into his own hands. Thus his inner conflict begins to develop. Wyatt watches his belief in the law slowly erode as lack of evidence, alibis and corrupt officials stop him from seeking equity. When one brother is maimed and another is killed, he is hindered by a promise in the former case and met with bogus excuses

Hour of the Gun was the first film to deal with the events following the famous gunfight, and to show Wyatt Earp with a darker side. The poster for the film asks viewers if Earp was a hero or a killer (author's collection).

in the latter. Using legal documents (in this case, arrest warrants), Wyatt slowly comes to realize that the only means to bring about justice is through the use of a gun—his gun. It is imperative in such stories, especially in the Western genre, that the protagonist seek a final retribution with the lead antagonist. Most Westerns allow the antagonist to get away with numerous crimes (including murder), but at the end of the story, these actions cry out for justice, usually dispersed by the protagonist in a final showdown. That is what we have here in *Hour of the Gun*. Despite the fact that Wyatt never faced down Ike Clanton in reality, it was necessary, as well as demanded by the structure of the genre itself, that he and Clanton square off. It would not satisfy the audience if the movie had Clanton getting away with his crimes or being killed by anyone other than Wyatt Earp. Although we see a different version of Earp from those portrayed in previous films, he is still viewed by the audience as the hero, and it is the hero who must vanquish the villain.

Despite dramatic liberties with the story, *Hour of the Gun* is a well-made and audience-involving film. Much of the credit goes to director John Sturges, as well as to the cast. Sturges handles his film with great authority and an economy in filmmaking. Shots are not wasted on things that do not move the story forward and build tension. Indeed, Sturges eliminated many scenes of dialogue, during production and in the editing room, that he felt hindered the progression of the story and slowed the pace of the film.

His staging of the gunfight, compared to his 1957 film, is brief, yet it captures the violence of the moment. (Interestingly, the gunfight in this film runs a mere 15 seconds, half the time of the real incident.) Although the staging is not entirely accurate (Fly's gallery is across the street from the O.K. Corral), it does recreate most of what happened. In the famous walk to the gunfight, Sturges has Wyatt at the right of frame, with Doc next to him. Next to Doc is Virgil and then Morgan on the left side of the frame. Placing Wyatt and Doc next to each other could have been Sturges's decision to emphasize the bond between the two men, as well as a directorial choice when both Morgan and Virgil are wounded in the fight.

There is no dialogue during the gunfight, such as Ike's plea not to shoot, Wyatt's reply to fight or get away, or Doc telling Frank McLowery to blaze away. The two Earp brothers, Virgil (who does not carry a cane) and Morgan, are shot early but continue to return fire. After the shooting ends, Wyatt and Doc are the only ones standing, signifying their dominance in the story and possibly suggesting their isolation as the only two who will completely survive the events. Sturges gives the audience the feeling of what the gunfight must have been like, framing the action in wide shots to capture the action quickly.

As the Earps and Holliday approach the corral, Ike Clanton and others who have been standing by Fly's Photo Gallery quickly take refuge inside or around the building, leaving the McLowerys and Billy Clanton on their own. These men, the McLowerys and Billy Clanton, remain standing inside a three-pole corral throughout the entire gunfight. One could make a theoretical argument that their placement represents a form of prison, indicating they will never get out alive from that location. It could also be argued that because the Earps and Holliday shot at the men while they were in the corral, they took advantage of that location as they had no other cover and could not avoid being shot, thus making it easier for them to be killed. Or it could be that their placement in the corral, without any real form of protection, indicates they were deliberately sacrificed by Clanton to advance his own agenda.

In the role of Wyatt, James Garner gives one of his best performances and, in the opinion of many Earp historians, one of the most accurate and moving portrayals of Earp. (Garner told this author that he felt that Henry Fonda was the best Wyatt Earp on film.[43]) One of Garner's strengths as an actor is his ability to play a believable, grim character. He does this in *Hour of the Gun*, and we see the slow development of Earp's unforgiving determination to seek out justice. The viewer understands Wyatt's reasons for taking the law into his own hands, and, in many ways, for justifying his actions as reasonable. This is achieved because Garner has a way of making a connection between his character and the audience that resonates as truth, in the same way that audiences responded to John Wayne's dark performance as Ethan Edwards in *The Searchers* (1956). *Hour of the Gun* was the first film to show Wyatt Earp as willing to sacrifice the law in favor of his own personal brand of justice. Here, Earp has evolved from the shining white knight to a more complex and dark character; yet he remained someone the audience could respect. Much of the credit for this goes to Garner, who, under Sturges' direction, gives a tightly controlled, yet sympathetic performance as Wyatt. Garner recalled his approach to the role: "I didn't do a lot of research. I let [screenwriter Edward] Anhalt do that. I just went with the script. I didn't try to come out with, you know, 'I heard this wasn't true or that wasn't true,' whatever. We're making a movie and I didn't get in too heavy with it. You know, everybody knows about Wyatt Earp anyway.... Wyatt Earp was one of our Western heroes, you know, on the cusp. As kids we looked up to him. He was a great Robin Hood of our day, we thought."[44]

James Garner as Wyatt Earp. Many feel that Garner's performance came closest to mirroring the real Earp (author's collection).

Another strong performance is that of Jason Robards as Doc Holliday. In this movie, Doc is something of a conscience for Wyatt, keeping him from straying too deeply into the dark abyss of revenge. (The concept of Holliday serving as a conscience for Wyatt began in *Gunfight at the O.K. Corral* and would later be seen, to some degree, in both *Tombstone* and *Wyatt Earp*.) In this film, Holliday is still referred to as a deadly killer, something many historians dispute. However, this character angle was needed for the story structure, as Doc warns Wyatt that he can't kill "like I do." Robards jumps into the role with great relish, giving Holliday a tired and sardonic outlook on life. His delivery of dialogue contains a biting wit, coupled with an underlying resignation of the hand that life has dealt him. Robards is at his best in this role when he has dialogue that allows him to look at Wyatt's actions. Whether it is the scene in which Doc's anger builds to a climax over Wyatt's killing of Andy Warshaw, or the scene in which he quietly points out to Wyatt that killing Clanton will mean he's throwing away everything he believed in, Robards brings an honesty to the words that ring true.

One of the most moving scenes, and possibly the best scene in the film, takes place at the end, when Wyatt comes to say goodbye to Doc at the sanitarium. Having killed Clanton, Wyatt and Doc have returned to Denver, where Doc's months are numbered. Walking out onto the porch, Wyatt greets Doc, who casually says as the nurse wraps a blanket around him, "I'm surprised I'm feeling better." As the nurse leaves, the two men are left alone. The awkward silence between the two of them is deafening: they know this is their final goodbye. Both Garner and Robards play this emotional scene with careful understanding, avoiding the pitfalls of overplaying the moment. With few words, the two men convey their characters' deep affection for each other simply by their visual looks. Jerry Goldsmith's moving music for this scene expresses the great emotion of their farewell. Robards's reaction as he watches Wyatt leave, knowing he was told a friendly lie, captures Doc's sardonic humor.

John Sturges (left), Robert Ryan (center, playing Ike Clanton) and an unidentified crew member discuss a scene (author's collection).

Robert Ryan serves the purpose of the antagonist, giving Ike Clanton a quiet, conniving trait that fits the story. Although he wasn't given much to work with, Ryan imbues his performance with a quiet menace, playing Clanton as a man who will stop at nothing to achieve his goals. The rest of the cast provide solid, dependable supporting performances. The entire cast compliments each other, with no one attempting to out-perform anyone else. "That's the way an ensemble piece should be done. You know, you don't try to outdo everybody else," Garner noted.[45]

In discussing *Hour of the Gun*, one cannot ignore Jerry Goldsmith's wonderful score. Goldsmith, who began his career composing for radio shows and later television series before doing his first movie score in 1962 (*Lonely Are the Brave*), was one of the geniuses who created vibrant, moving film scores over the last forty years. Goldsmith's work spanned all types of films, and earned him 17 Oscar nominations; he won in 1976 for *The Omen*. He often used a variety of things to achieve a different musical effect (he used steel bowls for the 1968 film *Planet of the Apes*), and his scores were as varied and different as the genres he wrote for. With more than 170 film credits, he passed away in 2004, at the age of 75.

With *Hour of the Gun*, Goldsmith once again displayed his unique ability to capture the dramatic moments and enhance the emotional ones. Opening the film, Goldsmith does not use a bombastic score. Instead, the score begins with the soft chords of a guitar, accompanied by an accordion playing the main theme. This continues as the score builds in strength, overtaking the guitar and accordion with trumpets, drums, trombones, and a tambourine. Goldsmith increases the score by using a snare drum and trumpets, which hit and end their notes harshly. As the Earps and Holiday arrive next to the corral, the music suddenly ends, with violins taking over in a staccato style. This dissolves into a slow playing of the main chords, gradually building with a base drum to a crescendo, and abruptly ends as the gunfight begins.

Throughout the film, Goldsmith skillfully uses the main theme in a variety of sequences to achieve specific emotional responses from the audience. For example, when the Earp posse is riding along, the music captures the vast openness of the Arizona territory as the score is played full out, with dominant use of trumpets, trombones, violins, a tambourine and even an electric guitar. Played in this manner, the score sweeps the viewer along with the posse as it gallops through the desert. When Morgan is shot and dies on the billiard table, Goldsmith turns the main theme into a slow, mournful tune, enhancing the emotional loss of a brother. Equally effective is Goldsmith's final piece when Wyatt and Doc meet for the last time. Using the main theme as an undertone, Goldsmith uses the soft sounds of a violin, clarinet, and flute to capture the awkward moment between Wyatt and Doc, both knowing that this is the last time they will ever see each other. With Doc fighting to find the right words, the violins take on a somber and melancholy tone, while soft trumpets enhance a reprise of the main theme. As Wyatt rides off, and Doc realizes his friend has told him a lie, the score changes to reflect this by using a few heavy chords from an electric guitar and a xylophone. In doing so, Goldsmith lightens the emotional moment and offers the audience a transition. The flutes and the accordion, which were first heard in the opening titles, return. The main theme becomes stronger as the trumpets and trombones swell, taking over the score for the final shot of Wyatt riding off.

Hour of the Gun explored new territory in the Wyatt Earp–gunfight saga. For the first time, a film dealt with the events after the gunfight, not to mention offering a slightly different perspective of Wyatt Earp. Four years later, another film would offer a complete revisionist look at Earp and the famous gun battle, echoing the political and social strife that engulfed the country.

Hour of the Gun

A United Artists release of a Mirisch Corp. Presentation. *Released:* October 4, 1967. *In Production:* November 9, 1966–January 22, 1967.

Producer and Director: John Sturges. *Screenplay:* Edward Anhalt. *Cinematographer:* Lucien Ballard. *Musical Score:* Jerry Goldsmith. *Film Editor:* Ferris Webster. *Makeup Artist:* Charles Blackman. *Wardrobe:* Gordon Dawson. *Art Director:* Alfred C. Ybarra. *Set Decorators:* Victor Gangelin, Rafael Suarez. *Camera Operator:* David Walsh. *Assistant Camera:* Terry Meade. *Production Manager:* Nate H. Edwards. *Unit Production Manager:* Jack Lacey. *Production Supervisor:* Allen K. Wood. *Assistant Directors:* Thomas Schmidt, Robert Jones. *Sound:* Jesus Gancy. *Gaffer:* Joe Edesa. *Key Grip:* Bud Gaunt. *Crane Grip:* Robert Schunke. *Script Supervisor:* John Franco. *Props:* Joe Labella. *Casting:* Lynn Stalmaster. *Construction Coordinator:* William Maldonado. *Music Editor:* Richard Carruth. *Sound Effects Editor:* Frank E. Warner. *Special Effects:* Sass Bedig. *Leadman:* William C. Linder. *Still Photographer:* Jack Harris. *Assistant Editor:* Jorge Azcárate. *First Aid:* James Moffet. *Ramrod:* Bill Jones. *Head Wrangler–Mexico:* Chema Hernandez. *Assistant Wrangler:* Bruce Galbraith. *Wranglers:* Wayne Cutlip, Corky Randall, Buddy Sherwood. *Transportation Captain:* Robert Edwards. *Running Time:* 101 minutes. *Filming Locations:* Filmed in Torreon, La Goma, San Miguel de Allende, Mexico. Interiors filmed at Churubusco Studios, Mexico City. *Working Titles: The Law and Tombstone, Day of the Guns.*

Cast: James Garner (*Wyatt Earp*), Jason Robards (*Doc Holliday*), Robert Ryan (*Ike Clanton*), Frank Converse (*Virgil Earp*), Sam Melville (*Morgan Earp*), Jon Voight (*Curly Bill*), Lonny Chapman (*Turkey Creek Johnson*), Larry Gates (*John Clum*), Monte Markham (*Sherman McMasters*), William Windom (*Texas Jack Vermillion*), Charles Aidman (*Horace Sullivan*), Austin Willis (*Anson Safford*), Richard Bull (*Thomas Fitch*), Karl Swenson (*Dr. Goodfellow*), Bill Fletcher (*Sheriff Jimmy Ryan*), Robert Phillips (*Frank Stilwell*), Michael Tolan (*Pete Spence*), Steve Ihnat (*Andy Warshaw*), William Schallert (*Judge Herman Spicer*), Albert Salmi (*Octavius Roy*), Edward Anhalt (*Denver Doctor*), Walter Gregg (*Billy Clanton*), David Perna (*Frank McLowery*), Jim Sheppard (*Tom McLowery*), Jorge Russell (*Latigo*), Roydon Clark (*Stunt Double for James Garner*).

8

Doc (1971)

"Oh, you'd be surprised what you can accomplish with a gun."

As the 1970s began, America was witnessing another revolution. The country was involved in an unpopular war, soldiers were unjustly dubbed "baby killers" and spat on when they came home from service in Vietnam, police officers were called "pigs," minorities were fighting for their civil rights, and a young generation was "turning on and dropping out" with the use of illegal drugs. Bell-bottom jeans, love beads, men growing their hair as long as women's, and free love without commitment were popular. And historical icons were being deconstructed during this wave of revisionism.

Motion pictures were undergoing their own radical change during this time. The studio system was gasping its last breaths, with the old guard giving way to a new breed of studio head, men with law degrees or former talent agents. Some studios became subsidiaries of even larger companies that had little or nothing to do with the film industry. Both MGM and 20th Century-Fox studios held massive auctions of their property and possessions, including props, sets, and wardrobe. Fox sold off three-quarters of its real estate, where such films as *Young Mr. Lincoln*, *The Ox-Bow Incident*, and *In Old Chicago* had been filmed. (The land became a huge commercial and residential development known as Century City.) MGM's numerous back lots were sold off to developers. Today, where *Meet Me in St. Louis*, *Showboat*, and the *Andy Hardy* series were shot stand a condominium complex and a housing tract.

Western films were not immune to the changes. In 1971, there were only four Western series on television, compared to the fourteen a decade earlier.[1] The studios released just 16 Western features in 1971, which is only slightly ahead of the 14 released in 1961.[2] Even John Wayne, who had become the perennial Western star of the 1960s and early 1970s, made changes. In *True Grit* (1969), he bellowed his first curse words in a film ("Fill your hands, you son of a bitch!") and, in 1971, *Big Jake* became his most graphically violent film. The Westerns changed, some say for the worse, with the release of *The Wild Bunch* in 1969. The use of blood squibs showing bullets impacting the human body, slow-motion camerawork capturing this bloodshed, and the four leading protagonists portrayed as anti-heroes brought a savageness to the Western film genre it had not previously seen. Buffalo Bill Cody and General Custer were subjects of revisionist filmmaking. The legend of Wyatt Earp would be no different.

Doc began as an idea for a novel by *New York Post* columnist Pete Hamill after visiting Vietnam in 1966. Hamill said he began to look at Indochina as some sort of Dodge City and the Americans as a "collective version of Wyatt Earp."[3] While attending a party on Long Island, Hamill struck up a conversation with director Frank Perry and told him of his idea

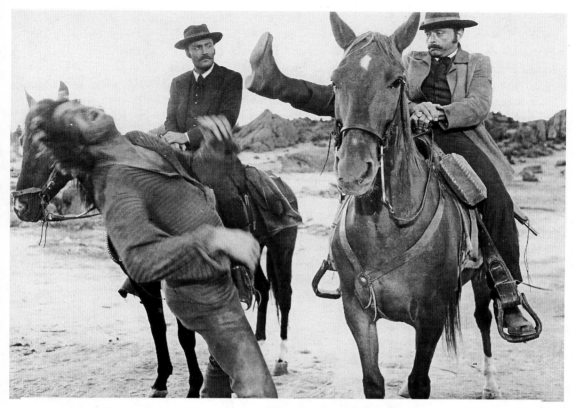

Wyatt (Harris Yulin) administers his own brand of justice, kicking Ike Clanton (Mike Whitney) in the face, as Doc (Stacy Keach) watches (author's collection).

for his novel. A week later, Perry suggested to Hamill that he skip writing his novel and instead write a screenplay. Perry said he would pay Hamill for his effort and attempt to get financing for the project if he liked the screenplay. Hamill, who had no prior experience in writing screenplays, read a few books on writing for the screen, which he claimed were useless. After studying a few scripts, Hamill began with a twenty-page outline, which he presented to Perry. The director liked what he read and gave Hamill the go-ahead to write the screenplay. Hamill proudly noted that he finished the script in a mere nine days, a claim that many film and Earp historians say shows in the finished product.

The film opens with a brutal wind storm and a lone rider, Doc Holliday, making his way through the desert night. He comes into a small cantina, where he sees Ike Clanton and "the Kid" sitting at a table. Ike has his arms around a woman, Kate Elder, and is pawing at her breast. Holliday plays a game of five-card stud with Ike. If Ike wins, he gets Holliday's horse. If Holliday beats Clanton, he gets the woman. Doc wins the game and as Ike is about to draw his gun, Holliday pulls a derringer. It goes no further. The next day, Doc, with Kate, rides to Tombstone, where he meets his friend Wyatt Earp. Earp tells Holliday that the town is ripe for the taking and, with his plans to run for sheriff, he would control the town and Doc could control the gambling. "We sound like a couple of bad people, Wyatt," Doc comments. "We are," Earp replies.

Doc's frustrating on-again, off-again relationship with Kate causes him to barge into the whorehouse one night, telling Kate she is retired. They settle down in a small shack in town and appear to be happy, as Wyatt watches them with disapproval. When a stage is robbed, Wyatt gets Doc to help him track down the highwaymen. Wyatt and Doc arrive at Ike's ranch and a fistfight between Wyatt and Ike takes place, with Clanton severely beating Earp. Returning home, Wyatt tells his brothers to find Ike and offer him a deal: He can have the reward money for the stage robbery if he will turn over Johnny Ringo so that Wyatt can arrest him, get the credit, and win the upcoming election.

Days later, the Kid meets Holliday and a friendship begins between the two. After the Kid kills a man in a saloon, Wyatt arrests the boy as a way to force Ike to carry out his part of the deal. Later that night, Doc bails out the Kid, asking him why he killed the man. "Because I want to be like you, Mr. Holliday," he replies.

With Holliday bailing out the Kid, Wyatt's deal with Ike falls apart. Earp hatches another plan to arrest the Kid and Ike for the stage robbery, knowing full well that this will provoke an armed confrontation between the Earps and Clanton. The Clantons and McLowerys ride into town. The Kid finds Holliday in a saloon and warns him of the impending shootout. Doc joins the Earps as they head down to the O.K. Corral. The gunfight begins and all of the Clantons and McLowerys are killed, as well as Morgan Earp. The Kid is the only one left standing, and he aims at Doc. Recognizing him, the Kid holsters his gun and begins to smile as Doc shoots him. Riding out of Tombstone, Wyatt asks Doc why he killed the Kid. "I guess he reminded me of too many things," he says.

Doc (Stacy Keach, left) confronts Wyatt (Harris Yulin) over the arrest of the Kid (author's collection).

Hamill's screenplay is based very loosely on the facts and are twisted to suit the mind-set of the writer and director, who felt "the more we looked at the evidence, the clearer it became that the myth of the West, the whole legend of its heroes, all of that was a lie."[4] Although Hamill may have hoped to unmask the uglier side to the Western heroes and myths, his script is simply dreadful, filled with stilted and insipid dialogue by someone who obviously did not understand how a film script is constructed. The screenplay is a series of lurching starts and stops with no narrative flow. The dialogue is some of the most amateurishly written (and performed) material in any film, let alone a Western. While camping on their way to Tombstone, Kate Elder awakens Doc and asks for something to eat. He tells her there is a pan of beans and salt beef. Kate tells him that beans will make her fart. He tells her to stay away from him. She calls him a bastard, he replies calling her a whore. Later in the scene, as he's rolling over to go back to sleep, Doc tells Kate, "If you gotta break wind, turn the other way. You aim at the fire, you might blow us both up, and I gotta get to Tombstone." Kate replies, "Suck grass."

There is an example of Hamill's interesting approach to the friendship of Doc and Wyatt when the two men are after stage robbers. Camping along the way, Wyatt asks Doc why he's moved in with Kate (he calls her a slut), claiming he isn't the same Doc Holliday he knew in Dodge City. Wyatt suggests that "maybe the whole thing between men and women ain't really normal.... Maybe men love each other better than men love women, or vice versa." He goes on to suggest that he and Doc just keep riding, heading out to California where they could buy a ranch together. Doc reminds him that they could never be ranchers; they are what they are. Doc adds that he cannot go anywhere as he's dying.[5]

In Hamill's original script, the film opened with a shot of a stark mesa and Doc Holliday, dressed in black, sitting at a small card table. He greets the camera with a narrative, talking about losing at cards and losing oneself in the vast wilderness. He goes on to say that purgatory is a form of a prison, where "the brain becomes a cell, tied in by bars of despair.... Here, in the prison of purgatory, you fear nothing." Holliday then ends his speech by taking the viewer to the year of 1881, and the story shows him making his way through the desert storm. (This opening was dropped and the film begins with Holliday making his way through the storm.[6])

The discovery of the stagecoach robbery was a bit more elaborate in the script, with the coach driving wildly through town to be stopped by Wyatt and others, who find that the missing strong box was carrying $80,000. Wyatt mounts his horse and takes another one to Doc's shack, where he tells Holliday they have to go after the robbers. Doc is reluctant to go until Wyatt pleads that he cannot trust anyone else.[7] The script also had a montage showing Doc and Kate on a picnic, lying in an open field, and making love as a series of dialogues between the two takes place during the action. (In the film, the director cut all this down to one scene of the two lying in a field talking, taking place after Doc has returned with Wyatt from the Clanton ranch.) Another scene following this montage was shot, but it was cut from the film. In it, Doc leaves after dinner, telling Kate he has to work. She asks him to take her to the Alhambra Saloon, but he refuses, saying respectable women do not go there. As he leaves, she hits him in the face with a pie. He retaliates by pouring a bottle of wine over her head as well as breaking a few eggs on her head. The two wind up kissing each other and the scene dissolves to them sitting in a tub together.[8]

After the scene in which Kate sets fire to the opium den, the script had Doc running up to Boot Hill, where he spends the night sleeping among the graves. In the morning, he heads back to the shack, where he is confronted by Kate. She asks him to leave town now with her, but he cannot. He gives her $3,000 and tells Kate to take the stage and open a dress shop. The following scene had her and Doc saying goodbye at the stage depot, but she follows him to the Alhambra Saloon. In the saloon, Doc agrees to help the Earps, much to Kate's disgust. After the gunfight, Doc says that he and Kate can start anew, but she tells him that death is around him and leaves. The end of the script had Doc once again talking to the audience, saying Wyatt lost the election and died in Los Angeles in 1929. He then hears "a faint whisper of music" and calls out Kate's name. He dances a waltz by himself as the scene fades out.[9]

Director Frank Perry had made *David and Lisa* (1962), a low-budget film featuring relative unknowns. It caught the eye of critics and earned Academy Award nominations for direction and screenwriting. Perry, who was born in New York City in 1930, worked in theatre before directing films. His success as a director (he made only 20 films) was checkered at best. Many of his movies, among them *The Swimmer* (1968), *Last Summer* (1969), and *Diary of a Mad Housewife* (1970), were popular with critics yet failed at the box office. He died in 1995 at the age of 65.

Doc was set up to be released by United Artists and was produced by Perry's own company. It was originally to be filmed in Southern California and Mexico in April 1970.[10] Instead, Perry chose Almeria, Spain, for his location. As with many Westerns made at that time, it was less expensive to make a film outside the United States, and Spain was a favorite choice of location, especially for the producers of Westerns.[11] A half-hour drive from Almeria, seven acres of land would be transformed into Tombstone, with eighty-six buildings, many of them built with four walls and roof.[12] Several interiors would be shot in these buildings, including the Alhambra saloon, Doc and Kate's shack, the barber shop, and the bordello.

To play the role of Doc Holliday, Perry eschewed a big name star in favor of a lesser-known actor. Stacy Keach was a classically trained stage actor before gaining critical attention in *The Traveling Executioner* (1970). He is probably best remembered for playing Frank James in *The Long Riders* (1980) and the lead in the television series *Mike Hammer, Private Eye* (1997–98). For the role of Wyatt Earp, Perry picked Harris Yulin, who had previously appeared in only two minor films. The role of Kate Elder went to Faye Dunaway, who had gained stardom after her lead role in *Bonnie and Clyde* (1967). She would go one to become one of the most favored actresses of the 1970s, with such film credits as *The Thomas Crown Affair* (1968), *Little Big Man* (1970), *Chinatown* (1974), *The Towering Inferno* (1974), *Network* (1976) and *Eyes of Laura Mars* (1978). Perry filled the rest of the cast with other unknowns and newcomers, including Denver John Collins (the brother of singer Judy Collins) playing "the Kid," and New York writer Dan Greenburg as John Clum. Perry announced in the industry trade paper *Variety* that he was looking for "wildly interesting, offbeat, freaky faces" for roles in the film.[13]

Filming began on August 17, 1970. Temperatures at the stark location would quickly rose above 110 degrees during filming. Dan Greenburg recalled the blistering conditions while filming one scene in the afternoon. In addition to the heat from the four carbon arc lights lighting the scene, the temperature climbed to 120 degrees. The discomfort was further exacerbated by a dust storm that drove sand into the actor's face.[14] The gunfight sequence began filming on September 17 and would continue for five days. Many of the performers playing members of the Clanton gang in this scene had varied backgrounds, including one who had been in the French Foreign Legion for 15 years. Four of the men had never ridden a horse, which provided the Spanish wranglers with many laughs. One rider put his right foot

The Earps and Holliday prepare to confront the Clantons and McLowerys at the O.K. Corral. Left to right: Harris Yulin, John Bottoms, Phil Shafer and Stacy Keach. Dan Greenburg, who played John Clum in the film, can be seen leaning against a column in the background (author's collection).

into a left stirrup, swinging himself onto the saddle backward, while another was so scared of horses that he took too many tranquilizers and had to be lifted into his saddle by the assistant director.[15] Production ended in early October, and by then, Perry had decided to seriously cut close to an hour out of the film.

When it was released in August 1971, reviews were nothing short of appalling. *Newsweek* felt that the film "fails so abysmally in its pretensions to be cerebral anti–Western.... *Doc* is so callowly conceived, poorly written and flaccidly directed, that it provokes laughter only at its own shortcomings.... Perry and Hamill hint that Earp was not only vicious and corrupt, but a latent homosexual as well.... Reportedly Harris Yulin, who plays Wyatt, declined to recite the lines that would have delineated the relationship. He would have been wiser still to refuse the role altogether." *The Hollywood Reporter* noted that "the newest full-blown trend in American movies, it seems, may be the de-mythologization of the Western.... Frank Perry has leapt aboard, as producer-director of United Artists' *Doc* ... and a poorer leap he's never made.... What he and Hamill fail to do is to provide characters we can believe in or care about.... Keach's Doc is consumptive and an opium smoker.... The role is an utter waste of his explosive talents. Yulin's Earp spouts Nixonion rhetoric and gives a Johnson barbecue and, not surprisingly, the entire conception of his character is an embarrassment." *Playboy* stated, "[Perry and Hamill's] theme seems to be that all our mythic heroes were sick, dirty, violent, decadent and otherwise far-from-perfect creatures.... Keach and Yulin ... utter each line in measured cadences, *sotto voce*, their eyes fixed in the middle distance.... Somehow they even manage to *walk* in slow motion, which is plumb crazy.... John Wayne won't like any of this, nor do we. Too goddamn boring."

There is little positive to say about this film. Basically it is a complete mess because of the amateurish script, lackluster direction and performances, and harsh editing required once filming was completed. It is a complete waste of time. The Wyatt in this film is a mumbling, shifty type who cares only for personal ambition. Harris Yulin is sadly miscast as Earp and his performance (if it can be called that) is weak and reduced to speaking in a soft, slow delivery. He resembles Wyatt Earp about as well as John Wayne looked like Genghis Khan in *The Conqueror* (1956). This Earp wears two guns on his belt, including a replica of the Buntline Special.[16] No doubt a theorist could have a field day analyzing the Freudian aspects of the gun's length and its relationship to Earp in this film! More than a few have noted that both Frank Perry and Pete Hamill envisioned the Earp character as based on President Richard Nixon.

The director and screenwriter also viewed the fabled gunfight as an allegory to the Vietnam War, with the Earps and Holliday representing the United States and the Clantons and McLowerys as the Vietnamese. In the gunfight, members of the Clanton group, which

Wyatt (Harris Yulin) arrests the Kid (Denver John Collins), as Doc (Stacy Keach) and James Earp (Ferdinand Zogbaum, right) watch. In this film Wyatt Earp wears two guns, including a Buntline Special (author's collection).

numbers seven, have only pistols, while the Earp faction all carry shotguns. The Earps and Holliday begin firing on the opposition once they walk into the corral; the Clantons wanted only to talk. In the gunfight, the Earps dispatch the Clanton group in short order, with even Morgan being killed. (The gunfight is completely inaccurate and runs one minute and nine seconds.) Wyatt hardly displays any emotion over Morgan's death; instead, he turns to the crowd of people who have gathered and delivers a speech saying that even though his brother died, it won't be in vain, and they will be able to build a bigger and better Tombstone. The speech is met with polite applause by those gathered.

Stacy Keach, who is a fine actor, is completely wasted in this film. He delivers his dialogue in such a quiet, hushed manner that one has to strain to hear what he is saying. Faye

The poster for *Doc* attempted to sell movie audiences the idea that this movie would shatter the images of Earp, Holliday and Kate Elder. The film flopped at the box office (author's collection).

Dunaway's role was heavily cut once the film was completed. It leaves us with little by which to judge her performance and wondering why a star of her standing at the time took on such a project. The rest of the actors are simply dull and amateurish. Denver John Collins as "the Kid" tries to underplay his character, and in doing so gives nothing to his role. Dan Greenburg as Clum is equally clumsy in his performance. Perry evidentially thought Greenburg had an interesting face and cast him based on that, regardless of any potential acting ability. Given the appalling script and inept direction, the remainder of the cast do nothing with their roles besides simply uttering their lines. The Clanton group all look the same—dirty and unkempt. There is no attempt to given any of them any type of character distinction or dimension. They are portrayed as dirty, foul-mouthed cowboys who are the villains because Wyatt Earp, in the film, says so.

The direction by Perry is so incompetent that it appears the actors were left to direct themselves. There is no sense of flow to the film, and the hatchet job done in the editing room hurts the film instead of helping it. Although both Perry and Hamill claimed to have done an enormous amount of historical research, little resembling the facts comes across on the screen. In fact, they appear to have ignored history altogether, using only minimal information to place their story in the context of the times. The musical score by popular song composer Jimmy Webb adds nothing to the movie.

One has to wonder who at United Artists approved this project. Perhaps Perry's status as one of the new up-and-coming directors with a few critically praised films (despite their poor performances at the box office), as well as the fact that a New York newspaper writer of some note was penning the screenplay.[17] In some newspaper ads, the headline read, "*High Noon—A Fistful of Dollars—Hang 'Em High*. There Has Never Been a Western Like *Doc!*" Below the headline banner was artwork of Stacy Keach with his gun drawn and several bodies falling down. The other ad banner read, "For the Past 90 Years These Three People Have Been Heroes. Until Now." The artwork shows three drawings of Keach, Dunaway, and Yulin, with their faces cracking and crumbling. But nothing helped this film, and it was quickly forgotten.

It would be twenty-two years before another filmmaker tackled the subject matter, this time coming much closer to presenting the historical facts. The movie would have drama behind the scenes to equal the story being filmed.

Doc

A United Artists release. *Released:* August 5, 1971. *In Production:* August 17, 1970–October 1970.
Producer and Director: Frank Perry. *Screenplay:* Pete Hamill. *Cinematographer:* Gerald Hirschfeld. *Musical Score:* Jimmy Webb. *Production Designer:* Gene Callahan. *Art Director:* Malcolm Bert. *Film Editor:* Alan Heim. *Costume Designer:* Sandy Cole. *Wardrobe Master:* Agustín Jiménez. *Sound:* Derek Ball. *Camera Operator:* Enrique Bravo. *Assistant Camera:* Alec Hirschfeld. *Camera Loader:* Juan Antonia Aguilar. *Second Camera:* Rual Perez Cubera, Mario Pacheco. *Unit Production Managers:* Tom Pevsner, José María Rodríguez. *Assistant Directors:* Stefano Capriati, Luis G. Valdivieso, Antonio Tarruella. *Boom Operator:* William Burgess. *Chief Electrician:* Enrique La Jara. *Chief Grip:* Antonio Sanchez. *Assistant Art Directors:* Jose Maria Alarcon, Vicente Sempere Sempere. *Props:* Jaime Rubio. *Sound:* Derek Ball. *Special Effects:* Kit West, Antonio Parra. *Assistant Costume Designer:* Clara Toro. *Makeup Artists:* Mariano García Rey, John O'Gorman. *Casting:* Marion Dougherty. *Still Photographer:* Antonio Luengo. *Script Supervisor:* Judy Tucker. *Running Time:* 96 minutes. **Filmed in Almeria, Spain.**
Cast: Stacey Keach (*Doc Holliday*), Harris Yulin (*Wyatt Earp*), Faye Dunaway (*Katie Elder*), Mike Whitney (*Ike Clanton*), Richard McKenzie (*John Behan*), John Bottoms (*Virgil Earp*), Phil Shafer (*Morgan Earp*), Fred Dennis (*Johnny Ringo*), Denver John Collins (*The Kid*), Dan Greenberg (*Mr. Clum*),

Penelope Allen (*Mattie Earp*), Hedy Sontag (*Alley Earp*), Bruce M. Fischer (*Billy Clanton*), James Greene (*Frank McLowery*), John Scanlon (*Bartlett*), Antonia Rey (*Concha*), Ferdinand Zogbaum (*James Earp*), Marshall Efron (*Mexican Bartender*), Mart Hulswit (*Reverend Foster*), Gene Collins (*Hotel Clerk*), Gene Reyes (*Wong*), Vivian Allen, Sharon Fruitin, Lucy Tiller (*Whores*), Per Barclay, Henri Bidon, Dan van Husen (*Clanton Cowboys*), Mart Hulswit (*Rev. Foster*).

9

Tombstone (1993)

"There is no such thing as a normal life, Wyatt. There's just life."

The Western genre celebrated its ninetieth anniversary in 1993. By then, the genre, battered and worn, was hardly the workhorse of the industry; the oft-heard comment was that "Western films are as rare as hen's teeth." Westerns were dead. The sentiment was taken at face value throughout Hollywood studios despite the fact that Clint Eastwood's *Unforgiven* (1992) had won a Best Picture Oscar that year.[1]

However, 1993 saw the release of a film that proved the Hollywood naysayers were wrong about a Western being box-office poison. It reflected more of the truth about the famous gunfight than any other, and it had as much controversy and drama behind the scenes as did the events that really happened in Tombstone in 1881. The film was *Tombstone*.

The movie opens with clips from early silent Westerns, including what film historians call the first Western film, Edison's *The Great Train Robbery* (1903). The narration sets up the story, introducing Wyatt Earp and Doc Holliday, before explaining that the Cowboy faction, identified by the red sashes they wear, is the major criminal element in the area. "They call themselves the Cowboys," the narrator intones as the image of a Cowboy fires at the audience. Suddenly a rush of riders gallops past the screen and enters a Mexican village, where a Mexican police captain's wedding is taking place. As the newlyweds exit the church, they are confronted by Curly Bill, along with Ike and Billy Clanton, Johnny Ringo, and Sherman McMasters, over the killing of two Cowboys. Curly Bill and the men open fire, killing the other Mexican police officers in attendance, as well as some innocent bystanders and the newlyweds.

Wyatt Earp arrives on a train in Tucson and is asked by U.S. Marshal Crawley Dake to take a marshal's position for the Tombstone area. Wyatt declines. Meeting Wyatt and his common-law wife, Mattie, are his brothers, Virgil and Morgan, and their wives. They all head to Tombstone where they hope to make their fortune. While playing cards in a Prescott saloon, Doc Holliday gets into an argument with Ed Bailey over his winnings, and Doc kills Bailey with a knife. He and his lover, Kate, leave town, heading for Tombstone.

Arriving in the newly established mining town, Wyatt enters the Oriental Saloon, where he learns that the business is suffering because of an abusive faro dealer. Wyatt throws the man out and takes over dealing the faro game. Outside the saloon, Wyatt and his two brothers meet Doc Holliday. As they talk, a stage arrives carrying Josephine Marcus and a theatre troupe. The following day Wyatt meets Josephine while out riding. The two engage in a spirited ride before coming to rest; it is apparent they find one another attractive. Returning home, Wyatt finds Mattie under the influence of laudanum.

Marshal Fred White is killed as he attempts to disarm a drunken Curly Bill. Wyatt hits

Clockwise from left: Doc Holliday (Val Kilmer) Wyatt Earp (Kurt Russell), Morgan Earp (Bill Paxton) and Virgil Earp (Sam Elliott) in *Tombstone* (courtesy of the Academy of Motion Picture Arts and Sciences).

Curly Bill over the head and holds back a mob that wants to kill him. Wyatt, aided by Virgil, Morgan, and Doc, breaks up the crowd. Charges against Curly Bill are dropped and
Wyatt loses any interest in seeing law enforced, despite the pleadings of Mayor John Clum.
Virgil, however, decides to take the job of city marshal, along with Morgan as his deputy,
ignoring Wyatt's pleas not to get involved.

During a marathon poker game at the Oriental, a drunken Ike Clanton gets into a verbal fight with Virgil. Wyatt defuses the situation, as Doc collapses and is taken to his hotel
room. Ike, carrying his guns, threatens to will kill Holliday and the Earps next time he sees
them. Virgil overhears and buffaloes Ike, carrying him off to jail. The next day, Ike is released,
but he promises the Earps that a fight is coming. The Earps learn that Ike Clanton and the
McLaurys are making death threats against them and Holliday, and that they are gathered
in an empty lot near the O.K. Corral. Doc joins the Earps; they decide to disarm the Clantons and McLaurys. When they confront the men in the lot, a gunfight erupts. Billy Clanton and the McLaury brothers are killed, while Virgil and Morgan are wounded.

Months after the gunfight, on a stormy night, Virgil is ambushed walking home, and
an hour later Morgan is killed while playing billiards. The devastated Earp family leaves
Tombstone. While they are waiting for a train in Tucson, Ike Clanton and Frank Stilwell
attempt to ambush the Earps. Wyatt kills Stilwell and a bloody vengeance begins, with Wyatt
and his posse killing several members of the Cowboy faction. Doc's health is failing, however, and Wyatt's posse takes refuge at Henry Hooker's ranch, where Wyatt is briefly reunited
with Josephine, whose stagecoach has stopped. McMasters, who has left the Cowboys, is
summoned by Ringo and Clanton to a meeting. They invite him to rejoin their group, and
when he refuses, he is killed. Leaving Doc behind at the Hooker ranch, Wyatt goes to face
down Ringo, but Doc arrives first and kills Ringo. Wyatt decides to finish the job and the
Earp posse breaks up the Cowboy faction for good.

In Glenwood Springs, Colorado, Wyatt visits a dying Doc at a sanitarium. Doc tells
him to go away, find Josephine and enjoy life. Leaving, Wyatt says, "Thanks for always being
there, Doc." At a theatre in Denver, Wyatt finds Josephine and promises to love her for the
rest of her life. As the two of them dance in the snow, the narrator says that Earp died in
1929 in Los Angeles and that famed Western movie star Tom Mix wept at his funeral.

Tombstone was the brainchild of screenwriter Kevin Jarre. Jarre, the adopted son of film
composer Maurice Jarre, had written the highly praised *Glory* (1989), about the historic
black 54th Massachusetts Union regiment. Based on his success with *Glory*, Jarre was given
a deal to write and direct a film with Universal Studios. He chose to revisit the legend of
Dracula and was proceeding with that story when Francis Ford Coppola announced that
he would make a version of the vampire tale based on the Bram Stoker novel. Universal,
fearing that two competing Dracula movies would hurt each other's box office chances,
dropped the project. Jarre was given the option of coming up with another idea for a film.

Jeff Morey, a Wyatt Earp historian, had met Kevin Jarre at a party, where he gave him
a copy of a photograph of Earp and others taken outside a Tombstone firehouse. "Kevin
claimed that after *Dracula* was cancelled, he was trying to figure out what other film he
could do. He said he looked up and saw the picture and that is what gave him the idea to
do a film on Earp," Morey recalled.[2] Jarre and Morey met again at director John Milus's office,
where the two talked for almost ninety minutes about Earp and the incidents in Tombstone,
yet Jarre never let on that he was even remotely thinking about a film on the subject. This
meeting was only the beginning of a long road to bring Jarre's story of Earp, the Cowboys,
and the gunfight to the screen once again. Jeff Morey recalled that the next day,

Kevin called me and said he wanted to hire me as historical consultant. He told me that my take on Earp [Wyatt's problem in Tombstone was that he was very naive and unaware of the evil around him] was so close to his that it gave him the shudders. That became a focal point in Kevin's script.... Kevin had a deal to do the *Dracula* film and when that fell through, they were still committed to do a film with him. So it was really up to him to find the property. His real dream was to do the [Wild Bill] Hickok story. Earp was a prelude to doing that. He would invite me over to his place, cook me a steak and I'd just rattle on. He never took notes. I don't know how many times we did that.

We went out to Tombstone in October 1991 for less than a week. He'd ask me questions.... Kevin was really amazing. He never took notes. He never worked in a linear or chronological fashion. He studied enough and read enough of the Old West and Earp literature. He was interested in questions of motivation. He called me up one night out of the clear blue, and said, "Why do you think Wyatt liked Doc?" I said, "I think he made him laugh." ... He was very well read on the Old West. Kevin was wholly deceiving in his approach. You never got a sense of ego or arrogance about him. I think his original script was a masterpiece. Any fan who reads the original script and compares it to what they ended up with will feel the same way.

The differences between the released movie and Jarre's script are as disparate as silent films and sound films. While much of Jarre's January 22, 1992 script remains in the final film, numerous scenes were eventually cut or rearranged during production. Some of the more interesting sequences that were deleted include the following.

• In draft January 22, 1992, there is no opening narration or old film clips. Instead, the film begins with a small group of Mexican Federales trailing men through a canyon. They are ambushed by Old Man Clanton and several Cowboys, including Ringo and Curly Bill. One of the Mexican officers, before being shot, warns Old Man Clanton in Spanish that a rider on a pale horse will seek revenge. After killing the officers, the Cowboys ride up to the McLaury ranch, where Curly Bill asks Ringo what the Mexican officer meant about the pale horse and rider. Ringo relates that he was quoting from the Revelations chapter of the Bible.[3]

• In subsequent script drafts, the opening narration sequence has been included. Unlike that included in the final film, Jarre had a lengthy narration, setting up the period by first introducing Wild Bill Hickok, firing his guns as the narration tells us he was a lawman in several Kansas cowtowns and that he ultimately was killed in Deadwood.[4] The narration then switched to Dodge City, showing Wyatt and Bat Masterson buffaloing a few drunken Cowboys. During this scene, an armed Cowboy tries to ambush Wyatt and Bat, only to be killed by Doc Holliday, who is introduced via the narration as Wyatt's guardian angel. Josephine Marcus is introduced. The narration continues with the Texas Rangers running the criminal element out of Texas, Ed Schieffelin discovering silver, and the rise of Tombstone as a boomtown. It concludes, as does the narration in the final film, with the description of the lawless element from Texas coming into Arizona Territory and forming a gang that wears red sashes. The narrator intones, "They called themselves the Cowboys," as the screen goes to black.

• When the brothers and their wives leave the Tucson train station, there was a scene at an evening campsite that offered a strong feeling of family unity among the Earps. The script included some playful banter among the brothers and their wives while indicating that Mattie has a problem with drug dependency. It is here that Morgan makes his speech about the stars and a light leading one to Heaven. (These lines would be used in the final version of the film when the Earps walk outside the Bird Cage Theatre after seeing the show.)

• When the Earps attend the show at the Bird Cage, Marshal White sits next to Wyatt in the upper balcony and points out the various members of the Cowboy faction, giving him a brief description of them.

• After leaving Wyatt's faro table, Curly Bill and Ringo exit the saloon, with Curly Bill heading to an opium tent. The scene then shifts back to the Oriental Saloon where the high roller, who lost the deeds to his mines at Wyatt's faro table, is now drunk and insults Doc, who is playing the piano. From there we see a heavily drugged Curly Bill come out of the opium tent to begin shooting up the street. Marshal White goes out to arrest Curly Bill, as Wyatt makes the decision to back up White, asking Milt Joyce to lend him a gun. Wyatt exits the saloon as Curly Bill shoots the marshal. Wyatt buffaloes the cowboy and a crowd begins to gather, demanding that Curly Bill be hanged. The drunken high roller makes an attempt to free Curly Bill, but Wyatt points the gun at his head and holds him and the growing crowd off until Virgil and Morgan arrive.[5]

• A hearing on Curly Bill's shooting of Fred White is held in Judge Spicer's courtroom. Because Wyatt did not observe the shooting, charges against Curly Bill are dropped. The script then goes to the billiard hall, where the three Earps decline Clum's plea to wear a badge.[6]

• When Virgil leaves the billiard hall, he walks by a cottage with a small fenced-in yard. Some children are playing in the yard and he asks why they aren't playing on the street. One child says that their mother says it isn't safe. The mother comes out and relates that they want to move, but don't have the money. Virgil abruptly walks away. The script then shows Virgil (wearing the city marshal's badge) in his home, where the conversation between Virgil, Wyatt and Morgan about not getting involved takes place.[7]

• Virgil tells Wyatt that Wyatt's horse was stolen from the O.K. Corral. Borrowing Virgil's horse and gun, Wyatt follows the tracks which lead him to Henry Hooker's ranch. There is a brief scene between Wyatt and Hooker, who refuses to identify the rider, adding that he has to live with these people and that he isn't a recent arrival who will leave when the silver dries up. From there, Wyatt meets up with Sherman McMasters, who tells him that the Cowboys are "brothers to the bone." Wyatt and McMasters ride into the Cowboy's camp (referred to as Rustler's Park in the script), where Wyatt confronts Billy Clanton about his stolen horse. Wyatt says that he doesn't want Billy to get into any trouble, adding that he once stole a horse as a kid. Curly Bill orders Billy to give Wyatt his horse. Wyatt asks Curly to stay out of Virgil's way and he will make sure they stay out of the Cowboys' way.

• The Mexican Federales ambush and kill Old Man Clanton and others in Guadeloupe Canyon. Frank Stilwell gallops into Rustler's Park and tells the Cowboys of the killings. Curly Bill assumes command of the group, despite Ike's demands that he be in charge. When he does not get his way, Ike storms off.

• When Wyatt and Josephine rest after their ride, the scene in the script has more physical contact between them. As they passionately kiss, Josephine coyly says they are committing adultery; Wyatt suggests they get their money's worth. A lapse of time is suggested in the script, after which the two adjust their rumpled clothes. Wyatt says he cannot continue cheating on Mattie, although it is clear he is not happy with her. After he rides off, Josephine is seen in Fly's photo gallery, posing for a picture wearing nothing but a long black veil, claiming she wants to remember how she looked this day.[8]

• Doc collapses in the Oriental Saloon after a poker game and is taken to his hotel room, where he's examined by Dr. Goodfellow. The scene then returns to the saloon, where some time has passed. Ike is still drinking and is now obviously very drunk. It is here that he comments that he was cheated and slaps Milt Joyce. He makes his speech that the next time he sees the Earps and Holliday, he will send them to Hell on a shutter and lurches out of the saloon. On the street, Virgil sees Clanton carrying his guns and buffaloes him, dragging him off to jail.[9]

• After Wyatt tells Virgil to swear him in, he goes to his home and takes out his fabled Buntline Special pistol. Mattie says she thought he swore he would never carry that gun again. Wyatt replies he swore to a lot of things and walks out.[10]

• As the funeral ends at Boot Hill, Wyatt approaches Curly Bill, telling him they had no choice. Curly Bill reassures him, saying not to worry about a thing. As Wyatt walks off, Curly smiles, indicating he has other plans. The script then had Wyatt seeing Morgan in his room,[11] before cutting to Rustler's Park where Curly Bill makes an eloquent speech to the memory of Billy Clanton and the McLaury brothers. He says they are going to bide their time until everyone thinks things have blown over.

• Behan confronts Josephine on the street, telling her that she is his woman. Josephine calls him a dirty little fixer and wants nothing to do with him. Yelling at her, Behan calls her a "filthy Jew whore." Morgan, his arm in a sling, spins Behan around and punches him. As Josephine and Morgan walk away, Curly Bill, who has seen the whole thing, tells Ringo that she is "Wyatt's slice" and that they can add a new name to their list.[12]

• Walking out of the saloon after Morgan dies, Wyatt stands out on the street in the rain as people watch. Josephine pulls away from Behan and runs to Wyatt. He yells at her to get away from him, calling her a Jew whore. Doc restrains Kate, who wants to go after Wyatt, telling her that Wyatt said that to save Josephine's life, giving the impression to the Cowboys that she is no longer Wyatt's lady.[13]

• After Wyatt kills Stilwell at the train station, the script shows Doc saddling his horse, as Kate begs him to stay with her. Asking what will become of her if he gets killed, Doc replies that she will lose her meal ticket. As he mounts his horse, he asks, "Have you no kind word for me before I ride away?" She says nothing and he rides off. The script then has Wyatt riding into a wagon train camp, where he has a lengthy talk with the wagonmaster about his desire for revenge against the Cowboys. Wyatt, the wagonmaster says, is not out for revenge but for a reckoning. "If the Lord is my friend," Wyatt replies.[14] Doc, McMasters, Turkey Creek Johnson, and Texas Jack meet Wyatt at the wagon camp the next morning and form his posse. As they leave the wagon camp, a young boy delivers a long-winded speech about Wyatt Earp while a young father holds up his infant son. He tells his wife that he wants his son to say he was able to see Wyatt Earp ride out to bring the law.

• Unlike the film, there is no montage of Earp's vendetta ride in the script. Instead, Earp's posse rides into Galeyville and burns down the town, warning the Cowboys to leave the area. They then ride into Pete Spence's wood camp, where Wyatt confronts Florentino Cruz and kills him after he admits he was a lookout for Morgan's murder. Wyatt drags his body back to the wood camp and warns the others that is what will happen to them if they do not leave.

• After Curly Bill is killed, a Cowboy rides back to Rustler's Park and tells Ringo and the others what happened. Ringo kills the Cowboy to prove he is now in charge. Both Zwing Hunt and Billy Grounds decide to leave the group. The script then goes to Behan's office where he tells Ringo that Earp's vendetta ride is front page news across the country and that if things don't settle down, the military will be sent out.

• Hunt and Grounds rob the stage that carries Josephine and members of the acting troupe. Mr. Fabin is killed by the two men during the robbery. When the coach stops at Hooker's ranch, Wyatt talks briefly with Josephine before she leaves, apologizing for what he said the night of Morgan's death. Afterwards, Wyatt is sitting in Doc's room at the Hooker ranch, where he says that he will love Josephine when he's dust. Deputy Breckinridge comes across Hunt and Grounds at a campsite and attempts to arrest them. They refuse and he kills both of them. With the bodies in tow, Breckinridge rides into Hooker's ranch, where he tells Earp what happened. Earp respects the man and calls him "Deputy" for the first time. After the Earp posse rides out, leaving Doc at Hooker's ranch, Ringo and the other Cowboys show up, but Hooker refuses to tell them anything about Earp's posse or to let them see Doc.

• With Ringo's death, the Earp posse rides into Ike's camp and scatters the Cowboys. As they gallop in, everyone scatters and runs, except Deputy Breckinridge, who remains. As they ride by, Wyatt points at him in a gesture of respect.

• After the scene in the Denver theatre dressing room, we see Wyatt and Josephine on a train. As he takes her out onto the platform, a passenger asks a news reporter who he is. "That's Wyatt Earp, the lion of Tombstone, and his lady fair," replies the reporter.[15] As Wyatt and Josephine stand on the platform, the train crests a mountain top; they are bathed in light as the frame whites out. We then see an old Wyatt and Josephine walking arm in arm in the Mojave Desert. The two figures slowly fade away, leaving only the desert and the mountains. The narration discusses Wyatt's death, and a split screen image of William S. Hart and Tom Mix fills the screen as the narrator says that Tom Mix wept at Earp's funeral.

Jeff Morey recalled his impression of Jarre's work after reading the script. "I read it in June of 1992 and was very impressed with it. He always said he wanted to do a period movie and this script had all the period vernacular. I thought it had the potential to be one of the great classic Westerns.... What surprised me was how long it took him to write it [the script]. He labored over it for ten or eleven months."[16] In order to distinguish the members of the Cowboy faction from the rest of the people in the film, Jarre chose a visual item—the red sash—for the audience to easily identify the men as part of the Cowboy faction. When Jarre and Morey visited Tombstone, the writer-director, after seeing a sign in the real Bird Cage Theatre about an act that featured a man catching bullets with his teeth, got the idea of having one of the Cowboys shoot at a juggler. Morey said that after Jarre saw the original Bird Cage, he changed the location of the theatre sequence (it was originally to take place in Schieffelin Hall) because it offered so much more ambiance.[17]

Morey was equally amazed at how Jarre could remember a conversation from months earlier and incorporate it into the script. Morey recalled being at the writer's house once when he was asked what he wanted out of life. "I said, 'I just want a normal life.' He said, 'There's no such thing as a normal life.' I replied, 'Kevin, you live in Hollywood. You wouldn't know a normal life if it bit you in the ass.'" This conversation was incorporated into the last scene between Wyatt and Doc."[18] Morey also recalled he told Jarre about a line of dialogue that was in Walter Noble Burns's book about Tombstone, where Doc says, "I'm your huckleberry." Morey suggested to Jarre that if he had a scene with a confrontation between Ringo and Doc, that the line was too good to ignore. Again, Jarre incorporated this line into the script.

While Jarre used many of these little details in the script, he had problems incorporating certain historical events, which he was forced to drop. A perfect example is the lack of any courtroom sequence after the gunfight. Jarre simply could not work that piece into the script without harming the narrative flow. Morey said that Jarre also wanted to include the Benson stage robbery, but couldn't really figure out a way to do it without depriving the vendetta ride of its dramatic structure and purpose. "The irony is that the vendetta ride is what gets butchered in the Cosmatos version." Morey said.[19] The two men disagreed on one action during the gunfight, when Doc Holliday fires his shotgun into the air to spook Tom McLaury's horse. Morey doubted Holliday would have wasted a round of ammunition like that in a gunfight, but Jarre remained steadfast on the matter and it stayed in the script and in the film. Jarre was also reluctant to incorporate the famous Buntline gun into the story, since its legend is debatable. Morey argued that it was an important piece of history and that the gun itself could be a ten-inch barrel, instead of the twelve-inch barrel that was featured in the Earp television series.[20]

Universal Studios, which still owed Jarre a picture after backing out of the *Dracula* project, agreed to make *Tombstone* in late 1992. James Jacks, who was a production executive at Universal at the time, came on as producer of the film, with Jarre making his directorial debut. Casting choices were discussed and location sites were considered when the project was blindsided by the December 16 announcement that Kevin Costner's pay-per-view miniseries on Earp's life was now gearing up as a major feature film.

This had to feel like déjà vu for Jarre, especially because he had offered the role of Earp to Costner, who declined it in favor of his then-planned miniseries. According to Jarre, Costner contacted him (before the actor's announcement of making a feature film version of Earp's life), saying he wasn't trying to squeeze Jarre's project out and that he felt there was room for both movies. Jarre was not so certain, telling *The Hollywood Reporter* he thought the sudden change in Costner's project was "very odd," especially after the actor had read Jarre's screenplay.[21] One industry insider speculated that the script for the Costner feature version wasn't fully developed and this announcement was simply a "bluff to kill off the Universal project."[22] At first Universal put on a brave face saying that Costner's announcement would have no impact on their project.[23] However, things in Hollywood are not always as they seem. Not only was the studio faced with a competing Earp project starring Costner, who was at this time a major box-office draw, but they also were preparing to produce a large-budget film, *Waterworld*, starring Costner.[24] There is an unwritten law in Hollywood that you don't upset a major star, one with big box office clout, if you ever hope to do business with him or her in the future. (A planned film biography on IRA leader Michael Collins was also quickly dropped when Costner announced his intention to do a similar film.[25]) On February 5, 1993, Universal announced it was shelving *Tombstone*. While the studio publicly claimed they dropped the project because the budget was too high, the unspoken reason was that Universal did not want to lose their deal with Costner for *Waterworld*.[26] At first the studio refused to put *Tombstone* into what the industry calls "turnaround," but later relented. ("Turnaround" means the project is no longer active at the studio that developed the project and has been abandoned, leaving the producers free to shop it to another studio.)

With Kevin Costner's declaration of making a big-budget feature film on Earp's life, Kevin Jarre and James Jacks found it tough going to get any major stars or studios to commit to their film. During a 2004 revival screening of *Tombstone*, Jacks recalled that Kevin Costner's shadow loomed large over the *Tombstone* project. Costner was represented by the then-powerful Creative Artists Agency (CAA), and no one wanted to run afoul of the potent agency and its client. One actor both Jacks and Jarre thought they had wrapped up as Wyatt was Brad Pitt. The actor had agreed to the role (with Johnny Depp playing Doc), only to drop out a few days later.[27] The story, according to Jacks, was that Pitt, also represented by CAA, was dissuaded by his agent. The script eventually found its way to actor Kurt Russell,

Kurt Russell as Wyatt Earp.

who was very impressed. Russell was also represented by CAA, but the potential conflict did not deter him and he readily agreed to the role. Of the script, Russell would later say, "This is one brilliantly conceived piece. The characters are well drawn, it's a great story, and it's not weighed down by what I consider a 1950s perception of what the West was like. This is a script that offers drama, comedy, action, romance, not only seen through the shots but told through the characters. There are some tough characterizations that have not been backed away from by anyone. Kevin Jarre's understanding of the time period is remarkable."[28] Agreeing to star in the project, Russell contacted the independent film company Cinergi, which signed on in February 1993 to produce the film.[29] Like the mining town itself, *Tombstone* was once again booming.

With funding and distribution problems now resolved, Jarre turned his attention to casting the rest of the film. Originally, he had Liam Neeson in mind for the role of Wyatt, with David Bowie as a possible choice as Doc Holliday.[30] Jarre toyed with another casting idea which was to populate the movie with well-known actors (such as Hugh O'Brian, Charlton Heston, and Glenn Ford) and cast unknown actors for the roles of Wyatt and Doc. With Kurt Russell in the lead, Jarre had an actor who brought an authority to the role as well as bearing a striking resemblance to the real Wyatt Earp. Russell was no stranger to Westerns or the film industry, having begun acting in films and television before he was ten years old.[31] He appeared in two television series set in the American West, *Travels of Jamie McPheeters* (1963–64) and *The Quest* (1976), as well as in numerous films for Walt Disney. In 1979, Russell won an Emmy nomination for his performance in a television movie about Elvis Presley. His other film credits include *Escape from New York* (1981), *Swing Shift* (1984), *The Mean Season* (1985), *Backdraft* (1991), and *Miracles* (2004). For the role of Doc Holliday,

Jarre eventually cast Val Kilmer, who had made a mark for himself on the New York stage before he gained attention as Tom Cruise's jet pilot rival in *Top Gun* (1986). His credits include his critically acclaimed performance as Jim Morrison in *The Doors* (1991), a one-picture stint as Batman in *Batman Forever* (1995), and well-regarded performances in *Heat* (1995) and *The Saint* (1997).

Jarre originally had set Glenn Ford to play Marshal White, but the actor soon dropped out because of health problems. The role was then given to veteran character actor Harry Carey, Jr., who had been set to play the wagonmaster.[32] Jarre then cast Hugh O'Brian, television's Wyatt Earp, as the wagonmaster and planned on using Tommy Lee Jones for the role of Curly Bill and Powers Boothe as Ringo.[33] (Jones would soon drop out and the role of Curly Bill went to Powers Boothe.) Sam Elliott, a veteran of many Westerns, was chosen to play Virgil Earp, while Bill Paxton was given the role of Morgan Earp. Jarre's girlfriend at the time, actress Lisa Zane, had been promised the role of Josephine, but the producers chose actress Dana Delaney instead.[34] Michael Biehn and Stephen Lang were cast respectively as Johnny Ringo and Ike Clanton, while Jason Priestly, Michael Rooker and Buck Taylor rounded out the cast. Charlton Heston and Robert Mitchum were given cameo roles as Henry Hooker and Old Man Clanton, respectively.

One unique group in the film is the Buckaroos. This group of men with a passion for Old West history was assembled by actor Peter Sherayko, who played Texas Jack Vermillion in *Tombstone*. Sherayko had met Kevin through their mutual friend, director John Milius, and they would often go horseback riding together. When Universal scrapped Jarre's version of *Dracula*, Jarre was very upset, and Sherayko didn't hear from him for six months. When Jarre did contact him, he told Sherayko that he had a new project but had to remain very tight-lipped about it. When he was finally able to read a completed script, "I got home and literally couldn't put it down. It was such a wonderful script," Sherayko said.[35] Jarre was very specific about the types of saddles and gun rigs he wanted the actors to have and relied on Sherayko to help him obtain them. Saddles were originally going to be chosen from a prop rental house, but they were not accurate to the period. "Kevin luckily knew his saddles and he wanted exact period stuff. He knew the look he wanted and that look is what helped make the film.... Kevin was very precise."[36]

Sherayko formed Caravans West in the late 1980s, offering to filmmakers performers and authentic equipment that are specific to any period of the American West. "What got me started with this company was when, in 1985, I visited the set of *Wildside*. A guy named Monte Laird was the technical advisor. The show took place in 1883 and I noticed all the guns, gun rigs and 1892 Winchester's [rifles] were wrong for the period. I was talking with Monte and mentioned that, saying he knew better. He replied, 'Oh, a western gun is a western gun. The audience is stupid. They don't know any better.' That's what planted the seed in my head. That's how Caravans West was born," Sherayko recalled.[37] Sherayko assembled a group of men who had their own authentic clothing, guns, and saddles, as well as horses that would provide *Tombstone* with the accurate feel that had been lacking in many Westerns of recent years.[38] In the movie, the Buckaroos worked as members of the Cowboy faction, townspeople and even Mexican Federales. It was estimated that Sherayko and his group saved the company close to $400,000 by using the Buckaroos and other materials.

Jarre's attention to detail extended to the look of the sets. Most Westerns have towns with buildings that are faded from the sun and wind. For Tombstone, Jarre wanted the sets to look fresh and vibrant, as they really were in 1879–81. The decision to film *Tombstone* in the Tucson area had a lot to do with existing sets, including the Western town set located

The Tombstone street at Mescal. This set is located about 40 minutes south of Tucson and was built in 1970 for the original *Monte Walsh*. Other movies and TV shows such as *Tom Horn*, *The Quick and the Dead*, *Gunsmoke*, and *The Sacketts* have used this location. Many film historians feel that the set never looked better than it did in *Tombstone*. In this picture, Sam Elliott, Harry Carey, Jr., and Kurt Russell (center, under awning of Andy's building) are filming the scene (courtesy of Larry Zeug).

in Mescal, a half-hour drive south of Tucson. The standing set in Mescal would serve as the main street of Tombstone, with portions also filmed at Old Tucson, as well as around Elgin. (The latter two locations were heavily used in the 1957 film, *Gunfight at the O.K. Corral*.) The Mescal set was originally built for the film *Monte Walsh* (1970) and has been featured in *The Sacketts* (1979), *Tom Horn* (1980), *The Quick and the Dead* (1995) and the television series *Gunsmoke*.

Production designer Catherine Hardwicke had the task of turning the sets of Mescal and Old Tucson into a colorful boomtown with a minimal amount of money. "We rebuilt much of Mescal, which became very colorful and elegant. Tombstone was a boom town and we wanted it very vibrant and full of life.... A full range of twenty-six colors were available [in 1881] and the people used them," she recalled.[39] Hardwicke's budget included an estimated $50,789 to recreate the interior of the Oriental Saloon, $24,388 for the interior set of the Bird Cage Theatre, $13,721 for the outside of the buildings on the Mescal set, plus another $20,220 for general street construction and enhancement. For the O.K. Corral and empty lot for the gunfight, $31,188 was set aside for design, while the Boot Hill set cost $1,629.[40] Jeff Morey remembers one conversation he had with Jarre in which he was asked what he thought was wrong with Western towns in Western movies. "I said, 'One of the biggest mistakes they constantly make is the town is old and weathered, when these are brand new towns. So, in *Tombstone* we have a brand new town and one critic writes that 'It looks like it was built yesterday' as a criticism!"[41]

Equally important to the look of the film were the costumes. For costume designer Joseph Porro, *Tombstone* was his first chance to do a period film and a Western, something he had not done previously. "I really didn't have much period [film] experience on my résumé or any Westerns, but I went to the interview dressed in vintage Western clothing and the director [Jarre] just loved it. That had a lot to do with me getting [the job], and I brought a lot of research and information with me," Porro recalled. But once he got the job, he had to be inventive in creating his costumes because of budget and production restraints.

> That movie was done on a real tight little budget.... Preparation was nasty. I think I had four weeks at the most, and we were building [costumes] right through the whole thing, as I recall. It was really tough. It was long 16-, 18-hour days, six days a week. It was a nightmare. There was *Geronimo*, *Wyatt Earp*, and another movie going. There were four Westerns going at the same time and I was the last [costume designer] hired. So it made it really, really tough. There wasn't even like a cowboy hat left [to rent] anywhere at any of the studios.[42] I was totally freaked. Mine was the tightest budget and the least amount of money to work with. I had to come up with all of this stuff, so we had to make it all. We made everything from boots to gloves to everything.... Budget for the wardrobe was $250,000 to $300,000.[43] I had to get very, very creative. I even used some of the Buckaroos' wives. Whoever could make clothing, I used. The women's costumes were by the Tucson Opera Company. They made all the dresses for Dana Delany.
>
> Since this was a non-union film and a low budget, I had most of the stuff manufactured in downtown LA [in the garment district]. I had a Filipino shirtmaker who worked out of her house, and she made all the shirts. Everything was being manufactured at all these different places. Nothing was made in a costume house. It kept the cost down, and we couldn't afford a costume house. We made a couple of thousand pieces of individual wardrobe. All the shirts, hats and boots.... we even made several hundred cowboy boots. We couldn't find a pair of cowboy boots. Even in England they didn't have anything that looked right, either. I even had to make the damn gloves. I think I might have rented, all together, a rack of clothing. I did rent for the ladies' background, I did some rentals in England and some derbies and suits. But for the Earps and the Cowboys, everything was made.... I went to the director and asked him if he wanted me to do it [the wardrobe] in tan like everyone else. We talked a lot about it, and he wanted color. Kevin kinda really dug the idea of using colors. You got to give him credit for all of that. Kevin was very influential with me and the production designer, Catherine Hardwicke, in our looks. The director [George Cosmatos] we switched with would have done it all in beige. He was not really into it.... Kevin made the choice of keeping the Cowboys in the same clothes because there was so many of them that it was confusing. We figured the easiest way to deal with it was keeping them in the same clothes. It all becomes a full imprint, not just the face, but the body, and it imprints that it is the same person.
>
> Kurt's long coat was based on actual clothing. That coat exists, absolutely. No one ever used it in a movie before. It was probably a little more full and I might have thinned it out for him. The thing I did that you hadn't seen before was using all that color [in the wardrobe]. I used a lot of color. If you read the historical pieces of the period, and I did, analine dyes had just come out. Anyone with any money at all wanted to show off their wealth by wearing garments in these new rich colors that existed and were available. The Buckaroos that we had were wonderful people. They were the one joy in making the film a pleasant experience for me. They were influential in some ways and gave it a lot of character. I would let the Buckaroos suggest things to give themselves an individual look.[44]

Filming for *Tombstone*, which had its start date pushed back twice, began on May 17.[45] The first day of filming involved Wyatt and his posse driving off some of the Cowboy faction. The shooting schedule also called for part of the scene of Wyatt and Josephine racing their horses. Larry Zeug, who was one of the Buckaroos and the gunsmith on the film, remembers the first day of filming at the Babocomari Ranch. "It was the last scene in the film where the Earp posse is supposed to be riding towards the Cowboys. Jon Tenney, who plays Behan, and Stephen Lang, playing Ike Clanton, see the posse coming, and the rest of the Cowboys are in this bowl area and as they come riding in, one of the actors hollers out, 'Now it's time to get a working job.' Everybody turns and scatters out of the bowl. It was like bees out of a bees' nest. It was kind of a neat scene, 'cause they shot it above us and it looked like everybody was scattering," he recalled.[46] Another sequence shot that first day was some of the dialogue scenes between Wyatt and Josephine as they ride. The following day, May 18, was spent filming sections of Wyatt's posse attacking the Cowboys, including Wyatt riding and firing by hanging alongside the horse and shooting from under the horse's neck. In this scene, Kurt Russell actually did his own riding, eschewing a stunt double.

The wagon camp scene was shot over a three-day period, beginning on May 20. Peter Sherayko remembers this sequence as "a wonderful scene.... The scene calls for Wyatt coming in and talking to Hugh O'Brian. Doc goes and gets Turkey Creek and my character [Texas Jack], and we ride in. Wyatt wants us to come be his deputies. Then Mike Rooker rides in [as Sherman McMasters], and that's when he throws down the sash and says he'll join them.[47] The five of us go riding out from the wagon train.... They had a whole wagon train set up. Hugh O'Brian literally handed Kurt Russell something. The feeling of it [the scene] was the old Wyatt Earp from TV that we all grew up with was now giving his blessing to the new Wyatt Earp.... As we ride out, we did this wonderful scene. The wagon train is behind us,

Filming of scenes at the Henry Hooker ranch set took place during the last week of May 1993 (courtesy of Larry Zeug).

Hugh O'Brian watching us ride off. This little kid gives this speech, 'Go get 'em Wyatt,' and things like that, waving his fist in the air. The five of us simultaneously make a jump over a fallen tree. It was just a great shot."[48] From May 24 through May 27, scenes featuring the Henry Hooker ranch set were filmed. Charlton Heston, who played Hooker, was in many of these scenes. Larry Zeug recalled Heston as "very nice, very polite. He was walking kinda stooped over. Soon as they said 'roll 'em' he'd straighten that back up and you'd swear he never had any problems."[49]

Filming was not without its hazards. On June 2, stunt woman Terri Garland was doubling Dana Delany in shots in which Josephine rides at a full gallop with Russell's double. Garland, who was riding side-saddle, fell when the saddle broke. She was examined by the set medic before filming resumed, using a new saddle.[50] Three days later, the production report noted that "one cow died of natural causes and another cow gave birth to a calf" while filming at the Hooker ranch set. While this was not a terribly dramatic event, it was a harbinger of things to come.

By June 7, Jarre was two days behind schedule and the executive producers were getting nervous about falling further behind, thus stretching the already tight budget. As Jarre was filming scenes of Rustler's Park at the Babocomari Ranch, production executives were discussing how to eliminate certain scenes in order for Jarre to stay on schedule. The director was told "suggested changes" would be coming. James Jacks voiced concern that this was not a prudent way to handle things and that it would destroy Jarre's confidence, as well as upset the cast who loved the script.[51] Jarre was notified that since he was two days behind schedule as of June 12, the executive producers were making cuts to the script and changing the shooting schedule in order to finish the picture within the 62-day schedule. They allowed Jarre the option of making his own cuts in the script in order to come up with the same results. The storm clouds from Arizona's monsoon season foreshadowed things to come.

"Somebody called me in my hotel room around one in the morning on Saturday. Somebody called on Kevin's behalf—I didn't speak to Kevin—and said, 'Kevin said you are doing a wonderful job on this, but he's leaving.' I went, 'What?'" Peter Sherayko said.[52] Makeup artist David Atherton said Kevin's firing came as "a big, big surprise," while Larry Zeug remembers when Sherayko came down to tell the Buckaroos about Kevin's dismissal. "No one believed it. We were concerned that we'd get fired because Kevin was the one who brought us on board," he said.[53] Jeff Morey, who came down to visit the set on Wednesday, June 9, recalled that a party was held every Saturday night at the Holiday Inn where the cast and crew were staying, which was often a fun and lively event. However, on Saturday, June 12, it was "like a morgue. The word was that Kevin had been let go. The atmosphere was quite different," Morey said.[54] Bob Palmquist came with Jeff Morey to the hotel that night and said, "It was kind of like a funeral atmosphere [in the bar]. Everybody was kind of walking around in shock. Buck Taylor was shaking his head and admitted that in all his years in the business, nothing really surprised him anymore, but this one [Jarre's firing] did."[55] By Monday morning, June 14, *Daily Variety* stated that Kevin Jarre had been replaced with director George Cosmatos. The official spin was that Jarre's release had to do with his falling behind schedule.[56] As many in Hollywood know, falling two days behind schedule is hardly grounds for being fired. Numerous directors run behind schedule, yet that generally is no cause for dismissal. Many have wondered what led to Jarre's firing.

While few will give a definitive answer, there were signs that not everything was running evenly on the set. In an interview before the film's release, Sam Elliott flatly stated, "I

Jeff Morey (left) and director-writer Kevin Jarre on location for *Tombstone*. Three days after this picture was taken, Jarre was replaced as the director (courtesy of Jeff Morey).

knew from the third day Kevin couldn't direct. He wasn't getting the shots he needed."[57] Jeff Morey recalled an incident a few days before Jarre was fired:

> I was on the set when they filmed the killing of the Florentino [Cruz] character. The Earp posse rides into the Cowboy camp. It was pretty large—with 25 people. Russell's problem with the scene was he didn't understand why the Cowboys just didn't let loose as the Earp posse approached. He was very bothered by this. I remember him talking to Jacks or one of the other producers off to the side while Kevin was directing the scene, how he thought this was foolish.... I do very clearly remember Kurt being unhappy. That was a bad omen. I just didn't know it would go that far [Jarre's firing]. I don't think Kevin could have been surprised. I mean, he's directing a scene here and Kurt is there and I could hear him from several feet away [complaining about Jarre's direction]. Perhaps Kevin was too ambitious for his first film. Perhaps he should have made a smaller film first. It breaks my heart, and I think the world of Kevin Jarre. Jim Jacks told me that he fought to have Kevin retained. He thought the movie was salvageable with Kevin.[58]

Bob Palmquist recalled hearing Kurt Russell complaining about Jarre's work, as he was sitting in a camp chair behind Russell and Val Kilmer who were talking to James Jacks. "Kurt Russell, in particular, was keeping up a pretty heavy stream of criticism of the way things were going; it was going too slow, he didn't like the direction.... Jacks was just listening and said something like, 'I know, we're trying to take care of it.'"[59] David Atherton felt that Jarre became too obsessive on the minute details. "I think that he might have hit his stride if he had the chance. He might have really nailed it. But be that as it may, he really obsessed about the details. And that's a great thing, but he may have missed the big picture.... I do know that Bill Fraker [the cinematographer] really had a problem with how Kevin was having him shoot it. When you are not using your camera department the way you really can be using it, it is pretty easy to get frustrated."[60]

Another problem was Jarre's direction of the actors. Peter Sherayko recalled that they used to hold meetings for the actors on Monday nights in which Jarre and the producers would lay out what they would be doing during the week.

> I did this scene with Kurt Russell where I had a speech and as we were shooting it, Kevin would come up to me and would give me exactly how to read the line. He wasn't happy and made me say the line the way he wanted it. I was getting absolutely paranoid now. We had this one actors' meeting one night, and Michael Biehn and Powers Booth both said to Kevin, "Kevin, I can't act with you telling me how to deliver a line. You have to just trust me and let me do the line." Dana Delany was sitting next to me.... I had this surprised look on my face and I said, "My God, I thought it was just me." Dana said, "No, Peter, it's all of us." And that is what ultimately led to Kevin's downfall. As the writer, he knew what everybody should do.... Kevin wouldn't like it when an actor did it a different way.[61]

Jeff Morey remembered one actors' meeting he attended shortly before Jarre's departure. "They had this big meeting with Kevin and the actors that night. They were complaining about his directing, and I was very taken aback by that. I remember someone saying they didn't want to be in a movie that was being directed like a TV-movie or television. I didn't really appreciate what was going on at all.... Kevin looked extremely thin and nervous to my eye [compared to the last time Morey saw him]. I didn't know he was having any problems. But I thought the meeting with the actors was very troubling.... Kevin was trying to reassure them."[62]

This author has had the opportunity to view "dailies" from several days of filming under Jarre's direction.[63] It is quite obvious that Jarre was not obtaining adequate "coverage shots" in many scenes, not to mention that many of the performances are simply flat, lacking any energy, with only Charlton Heston managing to give any sense of color to his brief role. In all fairness, there were some Jarre scenes that have workmanlike staging and energy, such as when Wyatt and his posse leaves Doc behind at Hooker's ranch, and when Wyatt, tracking his stolen horse, first meets Hooker. Some of the dialogue, which may have read terrific on paper, comes off stilted and dull. Based on conversations with actors and crew members, the criticism for this comes from Jarre's direction.

This is painfully obvious in the scene in which McMasters rides into the Cowboy camp to refuse Ringo's offer to return to the fold. A comparison of Jarre's version with what George Cosmatos shot is literally night and day. In Jarre's version, McMasters rides into an area that is open with hills in the distance. Ringo and Ike Clanton, cleaning his shotgun, are sitting with several Cowboys around them and McMasters. The actors speak in low voices, with little inflection, reminding one of a scene from Jack Webb's *Dragnet* series. Although Michael Biehn tries to inject some life into his lines, the whole scene lacks energy and tension. Ringo finally stands to face McMasters and wishes him well. Ike then stands and comes up with the shotgun, asking how McMasters will get back to Hooker's ranch. Pushing the shotgun barrel down, McMasters tells Ike he's not the kind of man who would shoot a man in the back. He walks away as the camera pans to Ringo, who pulls his gun and says, "I am." From there the scene cuts to a rider dragging McMasters' body back to Hooker's ranch, saying that Ringo wants a stand-up fight against Wyatt. In the version shot by Cosmatos, McMasters rides into a hilly area that is surrounded by saguaro cactus. He is escorted by a few Cowboys, while others stand around Ringo and Ike, who are standing. Biehn's performance has more depth, energy, and danger to it in this version, and when Stephen Lang, as Ike, comes up, he smiles as he places the shotgun against McMasters' cheek and asks how he will get back. There is an immediate cut to the Hooker ranch with the man dragging the body. Cosmatos has given the actors a chance to inject some energy into their lines, and the staging is simple yet effective in creating tension in the scene. In fairness, watching Jarre's version, one sees the scene in numerous takes from several angles and not as a finished product. However, even in such an uneven form, the lack of energy in the scene is very obvious, and some of the dialogue comes off as too verbose. When Ringo pulls his gun to say he isn't above shooting a man in the back, it is done in such a fashion that it borders on cliché: pulling his gun out, holding it up in the air as he pulls the hammer back, and uttering his line. In this scene shot by Jarre, Ringo, who is perceived by the audience as a dangerous, unstable man, resorts to the hackneyed theatrics of a typical bad man, thus robbing the scene of any true sense of danger.

In another scene that shows how Jarre failed to extract any sense of emotion, Wyatt is in Doc's room at Hooker's ranch talking about his feelings for Josephine. (This scene, which was dropped from the film, would have taken place after the stagecoach carrying Josephine stops at Hooker's ranch for water.) Doc is lying in bed shaving himself; Wyatt sits alongside the bed, holding a mirror for his friend. Wyatt is looking out the window, recalling Josephine, when Doc notes that Wyatt is really in love with her. He agrees, admitting that he will love her when he's dust. Jarre shoots this scene in a typical two-shot, with Doc on the left side of frame as Wyatt takes the center. Most of his dialogue is delivered looking out the window, so the viewer only gets the actor's profile. Jarre does not shoot any type of reaction shot of Doc, nor does he bother to get a full close-up of Wyatt as he says he will love her when he's dust, which is the emotional key to this scene. Again, some of the dialogue sounds overblown for the scene, although this might have been mitigated had there been a close-up to show Earp's facial emotions. (During the fourth take, however, there was some levity as Russell looks at Val Kilmer after uttering his last lines and says, "You look like shit, Doc.") As it stands, even in an unedited version, the scene, which is an emotional key to the relationship of Wyatt and Josephine, is completely lost, and was scrapped from the final print.

A decade after the film was made, many of the actors are hesitant to discuss exactly what happened during filming. In a recent interview, Kurt Russell said, "There's a lot about *Tombstone* that I'm going to be taking with me to my grave."[64] What is certain is that the executive producers had been discussing the possibility of replacing Jarre with another director for at least a week prior to his release. One candidate they talked to was John McTiernan, who directed *Die Hard* (1988) and *The Hunt for Red October* (1990). He was very excited about the project but requested shutting down production for two weeks in order to view footage already shot and properly prepare. The executives refused to take any downtime because they had set a release date for December 17, 1993, in order to beat the Costner film, which was scheduled to be released in July 1994. George Cosmatos was chosen primarily because he agreed to step in right away, with only two days of downtime. "I read the script on a Wednesday, we made the deal on Thursday, and I was on a plane on Friday. Saturday, I changed some locations, some of the sets, some of the costumes. I changed some of the actors on Sunday, and on Monday we had a production meeting. By Tuesday we were shooting," Cosmatos recalled.[65]

Shooting the sequence where the Cowboys stop the stagecoach carrying the body of Fabian, the actor. The long pole near the team of horses is actually a crane arm that holds a camera and is remotely controlled. The tent in the upper left of the photograph is where the cameraman operates the camera and the director views the action on a monitor. In the film industry vernacular, this area is called "video village" (courtesy of Larry Zeug).

Cosmatos, who died in April 2005 of lung cancer, began his career working as an assistant director on such films as *Exodus* (1960) and *Zorba the Greek* (1964). He directed such films as *The Cassandra Crossing* (1977), *Escape to Athena* (1979), and *Rambo: First Blood II* (1985).[66]

Whenever an original director is replaced, it creates a feeling of uneasiness among the cast and crew of a production. For days and even weeks, people walk around the set as if they are on eggshells, not knowing whether something they might say or if even a facial expression might lead to being fired. The feeling was no different on the set of *Tombstone*. "Because of my personal relationship with Kevin, I probably would have been fired had I not put all the guns, Buckaroos and everything else together.... There was a lot of guesswork going on. My Buckaroos were wondering if they still had a job or not," Peter Sherayko stated. Buckaroo Larry Zeug remembered, "There was a lot of tension on the set to get the movie done.... After Kevin got fired, if you moved your head wrong or interpreted a scene wrong, you're outta there.... It was that kind of pressure on the set."[67]

Something else that is commonplace when directors are changed midway through a picture is alterations to the shooting schedule. Scenes originally planned are suddenly dropped or heavily edited, actors are replaced, and other changes occur. All of this happened in the few weeks after Cosmatos arrived. Makeup artist David Atherton recalled how these meetings with Cosmatos affected the makeup department.

The way Kevin originally had Curly Bill getting killed was [with] a shotgun which almost split him in half ... it was just somewhere out on the ground, it wasn't in the river. And so in pre-production I had built a whole apparatus for Powers to wear. It was a body and you buried Powers into the ground halfway and you've got a body that's just shredded by a shotgun. So in the meetings he [Cosmatos] would be telling me the things he had planned to do differently so we could be prepared for things. And that was one of them. He changed that whole scene into a river scene and Powers was just going to get shot in a river and that was that. There was nothing prosthetic-wise or anything fancy. It really would have looked good.... Things like that you miss, from a makeup point of view, things you've got ready to go and you know works good, looks good, and then they just cut it.[68]

Actors were also replaced or simply dropped. Lisa Zane was replaced by Joanna Pacula in the role of Kate. Veteran character actor Don Collier, who was originally signed to play C.S. Fly, saw his role dropped after Jarre's departure but was given a small part as the high roller at Wyatt's faro table. Even Robert Mitchum's role was eliminated. The publicity spin was that Mitchum hurt his back and chose to drop out, but it appears that his role was simply the victim of cost-cutting efforts. David Atherton remembers, "I was very disappointed when they cut the Old Man Clanton stuff out of the film, because I was so anxious to meet with him and work with him."[69]

The biggest victim of change was Jarre's script. James Jacks recalled that there was tremendous pressure from the executives to shave pages out of the script because the production was behind schedule. ("They forgot we had fired the director," Jacks noted.[70]) The executives hired writer John Fasano to rewrite Jarre's script, cutting many scenes out and rewriting things to meet the proposed schedule of 62 days. According to many people, Fasano cut a lot of heart out of the script and Jacks and Kurt Russell would literally burn the midnight oil on location rewriting the script, using every important character and plot point, putting them elsewhere in a scene in order not to lose any of the important material. Among the eliminated scenes that had already been shot was the wagon train scene with Hugh O'Brian. David Atherton recalled that the sequence didn't really help the film and he felt its removal was justified. "I don't think that it would have worked in this movie anyway. My feeling was it was too poetic.... I think if we did keep that scene in, people would have just rolled their eyes.... It was, to me, a little over the top ... you had this little kid making this speech just coming out of left field, and as Wyatt Earp is riding away, he's standing on top of a wagon waving at him saying this real flowery passage.... It was better they cut those scenes out."[71]

With Cosmatos aboard, the film's budget was revised. In addition to Cosmatos' salary, the producers elected to have a second unit, to be directed by stunt coordinator Terry Leonard, filming full-time in an attempt to make up for lost days.[72] The second unit budget for eight weeks of work totaled $212,000, while 12 days of re-shooting scenes was estimated at $120,000 a day.[73] This pushed the budget for the film to $25,332,851. The wrap date for the film, which was originally July 29, was now pushed back to August 10.

The second unit was responsible for staging stunt sequences in which few, if any, of the principal players were involved. Generally, stunt doubles work in second unit scenes. Much of the stunt work involved in *Tombstone* required horse falls, with either the stunt performer falling from the horse, or both rider and horse falling.[74] In the early days of Western movies, stunt performers invented the "running W" gag. (Any type of stunt is commonly referred to as a "gag.") A great deal of myth and misinformation has surrounded this stunt. A wire is attached to one of the horse's front legs, which then runs up to a band around the horse's belly and then to a three-ring compartment that resembles a W. The wire is then attached to the other front leg and when the cable becomes taut, it pulls the horse's legs up to its belly, which causes the horse to do a somersault into soft, prepared ground. All the strain, pull, and jerk is on the saddle, *not* on the horse's legs. Veteran stuntman Yakima Canutt said that he found that a flexible plane cable of ½-inch worked best and would actually break during a fall, which allowed the horse to get up and move immediately after the fall. Canutt said he did three hundred running W stunts and never hurt a horse. But there was always someone who would do it cheaper and quicker, which, of course, ended up getting a horse killed. These deadly gags garnered enough negative publicity that the stunt was outlawed in the 1940s. Cliff Lyons, another famous stuntman who served as John Ford's stunt coordinator for fifteen years, is credited with developing a safer way for horses to execute a stunt fall. He trained them to take a cue from the rider, who would start the horse into a gallop and then slow down to a canter, whereupon the stuntman would yank the reins to the left or right (depending on how the horse was trained), turning the horse's head slightly. This was how the horse knew what the rider wanted, and the animal would fall, using its shoulder area to land on soft dirt as the rider dropped from the saddle. To make the stunt look as if the horse were galloping, the camera speed would be altered. Unfortunately, this action always appeared artificial on the screen. Chuck Roberson, John Wayne's longtime stunt double, felt that a properly trained horse could do the stunt at a full gallop. Roberson found that horse in 1951—and trained it; they made numerous horse falls at a full gallop in many Westerns, as did other stuntmen who learned the process from Roberson.[75]

When it comes to riders falling from horses, a great deal of planning is required. Once the camera angle is chosen, the stunt coordinator sets up the area for the stunt person's fall. The ground is carefully dug up and softened; any debris, such as rocks, branches, and even twigs is removed. The stunt person protects himself (or herself) with a certain amount of padding (provided that the wardrobe will allow it) to help cushion the fall and offer protection from any injury. The rider generally falls from a horse at a gallop, usually riding without his feet in the stirrups, or using an open L stirrup that allows him to launch himself off the horse. Generally, the rider falls from the side of the horse and, according to plan, hits the target of soft ground. Sometimes the stunt might be a bit more elaborate and the rider rolls out of the saddle, doing a somersault off the back of the horse onto the soft ground. In both cases, there are more than enough chances for something to go wrong. The horse might be going too fast, or the director calls for the stunt rider to fall too late, so that the rider misses the soft spot of ground and instead lands on Mother Earth and all her shrubbery. "Even when all goes correctly, after doing horse falls you feel like a sacked quarterback the next morning," Harvey Parry noted.[76]

Filming resumed under Cosmatos' direction on June 15 at Sabino National Park, shooting the Iron Springs sequence in which Wyatt kills Curly Bill. Larry Zeug remembers that the three days of filming at that location kept him very busy. "We first shot the scene with Curly Bill's gang ambushing Wyatt's posse. At first we only shot from the angle of Wyatt's posse firing and you never saw the cowboys [in the brush]. You just see the gunfire and smoke come from out of the trees. I was running around loading guns, helping the armorer because he couldn't be on [both sides] of the river. Later, we [went] back to Sabino Canyon to work second unit, and the river had dried up! Because this was only to be scenes of the cowboys shooting, they could lay the [camera] track right down in the dry wash. They had to take buckets of water and put squibs in them to show bullets hitting in front of the camera [to give the effect of the bullets hitting the river water]."[77]

After Kevin Jarre's dismissal, filming resumed on June 15 at Sabino National Park, where a creek was created for the scene depicting the killing of Curly Bill. Kurt Russell (in white shirt and black vest) stands in the river to the right. Facing him is actor Buck Taylor (far right, wearing duster and hat) (courtesy of Larry Zeug).

As filming proceeded, not all was comfortable on the set. Many people chose to quit the film, some out of loyalty to Kevin Jarre, while others were forced out with his departure. Some left because they had other jobs waiting and couldn't stay longer than the original wrap date. Then there was an exodus of people who quit after working only a few days or weeks with George Cosmatos. Among them was cinematographer William Fraker, who quit three times, yet returned each time and did finish the picture. Actor Sal Cardile remembered the tension between the two men. "You could see the tension between Bill Fraker and Cosmatos. George wanted things done a certain way and Bill would tell him you can't do that, or it wouldn't look right or whatever the reasoning was, and George would press the issue. The incident I recall the most was when they got into it on the set and Fraker got really, really upset. He said some things back to George, I don't really remember exactly what it was about or what he said back to him, but I do remember at the end of the exchange he told George basically, 'When you figure out what the hell you are doing, I'll be in my trailer. You let me know and when I'm ready to come out, I'll come back.' He walked off the set. He was gone for quite a while."[78] One day Fraker was driving around the set in his golf cart, as was Cosmatos. The two men made a turn onto the same road and came face to face, each refusing to make way for the other. Both men advanced in their carts and crashed into each other. "George fell out of his cart. I didn't," Fraker said with a sly grin.[79]

"George Cosmatos' language on the set was horrible," recalled Larry Zeug. "Every other word was *fuck this* and *fuck that*. This memo came out from Cinergi, that I understand came out of Disney, about the language [on the set]. There was no language problem with anybody other than George. We had kids on the set, we shot scenes with kids ... it didn't matter. Every other word out of George's mouth was *fuck*. He used it like a general term and it was unnecessary. Maybe that was the way he was raised, that it was fine to use [that word]. But it was not fine for everybody else. I think that created most of the problems.... He was the only guy I ever saw who could piss off Sam Elliott. They were filming the scene where Sam's been shot. You could hear George from inside the building yelling 'Where the fuck is Sam? Where's my goddamn Sam?' Finally, Sam got pissed, stopped what he was reading [the script], walked over to the door and opened it and stuck his head in and yelled, 'George! I fucking hear you, George.' He backed up and slammed the door. Everything went quiet. A lot of tension on it [the set]. People told me if I could make that movie, I could work on any movie in my life."[80]

Evidently Cosmatos was also a bit liberal with his references to a certain female extra on the set. It seems most of the female extras hired to play saloon girls were not big-busted enough to please the director. "Finally they hired a gal who fit [George's] qualifications," Sal Cardile said. "She was a really nice gal and George kept referring to her as 'the girl with big tits.' He was told several times what her name was and to stop referring to her that way, but he ignored that. He'd just say, 'Okay! I'm ready for the girl with the big tits!' Finally the girl had enough, and she approached him and said, 'Look, this is my name. Would you please stop saying that? I take offense to that and it's very insulting.' He ignored that, too. Holly Hire, who did all the local casting for the film, pulled all her people [background extras] for two weeks. They tried to replace the people through another casting agency and they couldn't do it. I don't know what arrangements the production company made, but they resolved their differences and Holly brought her people back. George never referred to her as the 'girl with the big tits' again."[81] (The female extra eventually filed a sexual harassment lawsuit against Cosmatos and the company that was settled out of court.)

One person who endured Cosmatos' temper tantrums was first assistant director Adam Taylor.[82] Cosmatos would constantly yell at him. Yet, through it all, Taylor handled the pressure with grace. On June 25, Cosmatos fired Taylor, who simply went over to work with the second unit instead of going home. His banishment to second unit didn't last long; his replacement was soon relieved of duty and Taylor returned to the main unit on July 17.[83] Larry Zeug clearly remembers the event that brought Taylor back to the main unit.

> We had a scene in front of the hotel involving Val. The assistant director got into it with George and finally Val threw the script down and walked away. Everybody shut down that day, so we all stopped about noon time. After that, the A.D. [assistant director] was gone, and Adam came back from second unit.... He put up with more shit. Nobody would have put up with as much as he did; they would have quit and walked away. Adam hung in there.... When we finished the movie, on the last day of shooting, one of our guys had a pressure gauge made up with the needle bent beyond the red part and mounted on a plaque. We gave it to Adam. It read "Grace Under Pressure. Thanks from the Buckaroos. *Tombstone*, '93." He loved it.[84]

"I told Jim Jacks I didn't want my name on the credits when I found out how they were rewriting the script," Jeff Morey said. "I heard that for some reason they had Curly Bill being killed in the river and [they had] cut the wagon train scenes with Hugh O'Brian.... I just thought, I worked for Kevin and I was very upset with how things transpired. I can't say they were wrong in doing what they did because I never saw what his dailies were like. I do know he had problems with the actors. Maybe [Kevin] was too close to the script [and

Top: Adam Taylor proudly holds his plaque from the Buckaroos. Buckaroo Jerry Tarantino (right) looks on. *Bottom:* Assistant director Adam Taylor was given this plaque by the Buckaroos for his hard work under very trying circumstances (photographs courtesy of Larry Zeug).

couldn't] give the actors enough room to breathe. All I know is, he was the man who hired me. I never met Cosmatos, I heard enough about him that I didn't have any desire to meet him.... I wasn't happy with the way it was going."[85]

One night in the bar at the hotel, producer James Jacks was sitting with Powers Boothe when three separate people came up to say they were quitting. He calmly talked each one of them out of it, amazing Boothe with his ability to stay calm and focused. He told Jacks he was very good at [talking people out of quitting], to which Jacks replied that he was getting a lot of practice on this film.[86] In all, an estimated 120 people left during production.

Filming the confrontation scene between a drunken Johnny Ringo and the Earps and Holliday at Old Tucson. Center left, John Corbett, Powers Boothe and Wyatt Earp (the actor) restrain Michael Biehn, as Sam Elliott, Kurt Russell (in long frock coat) and Bill Paxton (between black flat and arc light) approach. Val Kilmer is hidden behind the black flat scrim (courtesy of Larry Zeug).

In late June, the company moved from the Elgin area to Old Tucson, where they would film scenes in the Bird Cage Theatre, Doc's street confrontation with Ringo, Wyatt's arrival in Tucson by train, Josephine's dressing room in Denver, and the final scene with Wyatt and Josephine dancing in the snow. To prepare for the last scene, set designer Catherine Hardwicke dressed a set to look like the exterior of an 1882 theatre in Denver in winter. Ground sheets were laid out around the building at Old Tucson and then covered with fake snow (made from shredded white plastic). Trees were flecked white and a snowman was added. Extras were dressed in winter clothing and huge fans (called "ritter fans") were placed on scaffolds high above the set to blow additional fake snow during the scene. This scene was shot at night in late June when the average evening temperature was about 90 degrees![87]

With the replacement of numerous crew members, the prop department saw the disappearance of a specific item—the deputy sheriff badges used by the men in Behan's Cowboy posse. By the time they were ready to shoot the scene in which the posse is seen with those badges, most of them had vanished, more than likely taken as souvenirs. Necessity being the mother of invention, the prop man and his crew quickly cut out cardboard badges and spray-painted them to resemble the missing ones.[88]

As filming progressed into July, the Arizona monsoon season started to play an unwanted role in the film. Every day like clockwork, a storm would show up and let loose

Members of the Cowboy faction of *Tombstone* strike a calm appearance between scenes. From left to right: Robert Burke (Frank McLaury), John Philbin (Tom McLaury), Stephen Lang (Ike Clanton), Powers Boothe (Curly Bill), and the actor Wyatt Earp (Billy Claiborne) (courtesy of Larry Zeug).

with rain and thunder (some of which was captured on film in the sequence leading up to Virgil's ambush), causing the company to stop any outdoor filming and head for cover.[89] When the company was filming out in the open or in the canyons, flash floods became a real danger. Larry Zeug remembers his last day reshooting the scene in which Wyatt rides into the Cowboy camp to retrieve his stolen horse. Down the canyon from the set, the Buckaroos had parked their trucks and horse trailers. As lunch was called for the cast and crew, Zeug noticed that it began clouding up very quickly and then it "started to rain harder and harder. Now we have a flash flood coming down the canyon through the Cowboy camp set. They're rushing around trying to save the cameras and stuff. Tents and props were being washed away. We're all walking hip high in water and it's getting higher and higher. Even our horse trailers were under two feet of water. And mud! What a way to finish a movie up!"[90]

If it wasn't the rain, it was the heat. "The heat was just, at times, oppressive," recalled makeup artist David Atherton. The interior set of the Bird Cage Theatre was built at Old Tucson and was filmed at night, with hopes of finding some relief from the heat, which averaged 110 degrees in the daytime. "When we shot the Bird Cage stuff," Atherton said, "it was night when we started filming and, you know, it really doesn't cool down very much in Arizona [at night] in the summer.... We shot with a lot of practical lights in there, which, for the Bird Cage Theatre [at that time] really means open flames. We packed so many people into [the set] and open flames, and there were two levels, so the heat was rising from the footlights on stage, and with all the people in there and then you had women [wearing] corsets—we had women passing out. I believe it was about 120 degrees up there [on the second level]. That was one of the hardest things about this picture, that scene, and keeping people from looking like they were absolutely melted."[91] The heat only got worse. On July 3, while filming the scene of the Prescott saloon where Doc stabs Ed Bailey (played by Frank Stallone), several trailers for the actors began warping. "Problems were also occurring with the electrical outlets—several meltdowns happened," the production report noted.[92]

Larry Zeug, along with many other Buckaroos, stayed with second unit when not needed on the main unit. After filming at Old Tucson, the second unit took a long drive out to Douglas Dry Lake bed outside Willcox, Arizona. The Buckaroos and stunt people were dressed as the Cowboys, complete with their red sashes, for the shot of them riding at a gallop across the lake bed for the opening credits. The group of riders was sent a mile out from the camera and, as Zeug recalls,

> They set up the camera so they could focus on us every [few] feet and we were beyond a mile out. Then we kicked up the pace to a gallop and we're holding our horses back, 'cause we have to stay behind the characters of McMasters, Curly Bill and others. They were using stunt guys, none of the actors were in that scene.... We started that gallop from a mile out and went all the way across.... We were just a spot and then they would focus in as we got closer.... While we were out there we could see lighting hitting the ground across the lake from us, and it was pretty scary, because you're the highest thing out there. While we were out there the Amtrak train stopped.... The tracks run right along the dry lake bed. One guy said, "Let's go rob the Amtrak train!" So we rode right up alongside the train.[93]

For many of the Buckaroos, working on this film, despite the setbacks and weather, was a lot of fun. The production company set up a series of chainlink fences for corrals for the Buckaroos' horses, plus they provided the feed. The men lived in tents, and a shower and bathroom were provided in a nearby trailer. For Zeug and the others, it was as close as you could get to being a real cowboy.

> After work we'd ride back to camp, clean up the corrals.... Then we usually got a shower at the trailer.... When I was out there with my two horses and myself, you lose track of everybody around you. It's like living like a cowboy. You have no worries in the world.... You spend a lot of time with your horse. They become part of you. They just were [more than] your pet, [they were] your transportation. We rode them from camp to the set every day. You had your horse with you all day long and you rode him back to camp. If you went to craft service, you got something for your horse. He was like your buddy, too. When we went back at night, you rode your horse back. You put him away and brushed him down, took his saddle off and you went and slept. Sometimes you'd sleep with your horse.... It changed my way of living. Not a care in the world. Just like a real cowboy in the West.[94]

By mid–July, the company moved to the Mescal set to film the scenes taking place in Tombstone. The gunfight sequence was filmed over a four-day period, beginning on July 25.[95] Kurt Russell recalled a moment as they started to film the actual gunfight. "We began the master and ran through it like clockwork. Just as George said 'action' there was a large crack of rolling thunder. We went perfectly through the scene, it worked just right. When it was over, everything went quiet, almost as though a train wreck had just happened, and once again, a long crack of ominous, rolling thunder punctuated the end."[96] One problem during the gunfight was the firing of black powder blanks, which would build up a residue of charcoal and could jam up the pistols. During the filming of the gunfight, a table was

The Earps and Holliday walking to the O.K. Corral. Note the burning building behind the actors. Director George Cosmatos chose to have the building aflame, with the Earps seemingly unfazed. In reality, a fire like this would have spelled danger and possible disaster, as it did in Tombstone in 1881 and 1882 (courtesy of Larry Zeug).

set up where the guns would be broken down, cleaned with Windex and then reassembled and reloaded before being put back into service for the completion of the scene.[97]

With the gunfight filmed, production was nearing completion, although the weather was still causing delays. On July 31, as Doc's death scene was being filmed in a building at Mescal, the main generator failed twice during the afternoon because of high temperatures, causing a half-hour delay. On August 2, the company had a late afternoon call. On this day, one of the scenes planned for filming was Wyatt walking out of the Oriental Saloon into the rain with Morgan's blood on his hands. The company experienced "severe thunderstorms and rain," which forced them to retreat to a covered set for several hours. Because of this delay, they were not able to pre-rig the street with lights and rain jets for the night sequence, which caused a ninety-minute delay.

But that was only the beginning. According to James Jacks, the unit manager had released two of the three rain jets needed in an effort to save some money. This meant that it would only appear to be raining on the part of the street where Russell was walking, while farther down the street, it would be dry. (Unfortunately, this is very apparent in the film.) The director wanted to do the scene in one big tracking shot with a camera crane. To achieve this kind of shot requires a considerable amount of set-up time, not to mention rehearsals, in order to get everything organized from the actors' movements to camera focus. Cosmatos was having a fit over the delay and constant rehearsals to get the shot just right. To make matters even worse, they were fighting against the rising sun to the east. (The saving grace for this shot was that they were filming the scene facing west, so they still had the darkness.

Filming a closer angle of the Earps and Holliday (front row: Kurt Russell, Sam Elliott; second row: Bill Paxton and Val Kilmer) walking to the O.K. Corral. Pat Brady (standing, with white apron) played Milt Joyce (courtesy of Larry Zeug).

Had the camera angle been reversed, they would have had to abandon it.) With literally less than five minutes left before the shot would have to be scrapped, Cosmatos called action and shot the scene. "The weird thing is, nobody was quite ready for the action, but we got the shot," Jacks said.[98]

Filming at night on the Mescal set had its own set of problems, primarily an abundance of tarantulas and bats. Larry Zeug remembers nights on location where "you'd see them [tarantulas] crossing the street set and they were big. Of course they don't hurt you, but they would scare the hell out of you." During the daytime hours, one had to be careful of coming across scorpions or rattlesnakes on the location. However, despite the fits of temper, weather delays, and creepy, crawling residents, the set was not without the occasional sense of fun. On August 9, the company was filming the sequence in which Wyatt holds off Ike and other Cowboys after Curly Bill has shot Marshal White. Part of the scene involves Virgil and Morgan running in to break up the crowd by Virgil's firing a shotgun. After a few rehearsals, the director called for one more. "During this rehearsal," Larry Zeug recalls, "Sam comes in and shoots the shotgun and everything went quiet. Nobody reacted to his shooting. Then we all started singing 'Happy Birthday' to him and brought out a cake."[99]

The final day of filming offered no relief from the weather or stress. The filmmakers were faced with an ultimatum from the financial backers that August 10 was absolutely the last day of filming—no matter what—but they still needed some aerial shots of Wyatt and his posse riding hard against the Cowboys. By now, many of the actors had overrun their contractual days scheduled and faced "overages," which meant they would be paid an additional portion of their salary for every day they ran over. Several of the leading actors gave up their overages as a show of loyalty to the film they so strongly believed in. With money getting really tight, favors were called in, including one star asking a pilot friend of his to fly the helicopter to get the needed shots on the last day. (No one would deny the story that this star reportedly paid his friend to come to the location out of his own pocket.) As the company assembled that morning, a heavy cloud cover hung over the location, preventing the helicopter from getting airborne. As the lunch hour approached, the cloud cover broke and the shot was quickly taken. *Tombstone* completed principal photography on August 10, eighteen days over the original schedule.

As the film entered the post-production phase, other decisions needed to be made, such as who would compose the musical score, who would be the narrator, and how to assemble the footage into a reasonable running time. The problems with *Tombstone* were far from over. The executive producers decided to give shared writing credit to John Fasano, which did not sit well with Kevin Jarre. Filing an arbitration grievance with the Writers Guild of America, Jarre ultimately won and was awarded sole writing credit. (In a conciliatory gesture, the executive producers gave Fasano an associate producer credit on the screen.[100])

As editing progressed, it was obvious to the producers that the film would run longer than the normal two-hour slot. Disney executives were not happy about the running time and urged massive cuts in the film. George Cosmatos requested that Robert Mitchum do the opening and closing narration, which was readily agreed to. In the opening of the film, clips from *The Great Train Robbery* (1903) and *The Bank Robbery* (1908) were used, along with some black-and-white footage shot of Kurt Russell and Val Kilmer as Wyatt and Doc to give the feel of archival footage.[101] Credit for this idea depends on whom one chooses to believe. Cosmatos claimed in his DVD audio commentary that it was *his* concept to use the old movie footage. However, Kevin Jarre's script (dated March 15, 1993) states that they would use "old photos and silent film clips" to cover the narration, as well as some recreated footage. Once Cosmatos delivered his final cut, which ran about 135 minutes, the producers began looking to shorten the running time. (James Jacks was reportedly shut out of the editing process.[102]) After viewing Cosmatos' cut, producer Sean Daniel made several suggestions to clarify certain scenes, as well as to suggest what could be cut without hurting the narrative flow. For example, the scene in which Wyatt and Josephine rest after their ride, and Wyatt says, "We could've been killed back there. Both of us"; Daniel recommended they change the line to "You could have been killed back there" and eliminate "Both of us" because the ride down the hill wasn't that difficult and someone like Earp would not fear it. Daniel also felt that Wyatt and Josephine should make love or at least kiss each other; otherwise scenes following this wouldn't make as much sense. Daniel asks, "Why is Wyatt so guilty when his wife accuses him? Why does he call Josephine 'whore' in the street? Why does Josephine forgive him? Kurt and Dana played the parts as if they made love and it shows." He noted that women who read romance novels would be drawn to the plot of Wyatt torn between two women.[103] (George Cosmatos chose to drop the rest of this scene, in which the two do passionately kiss, and there is a hint of lovemaking, feeling that it was best left to the audience's imagination. His choice remained in the final print.[104])

Daniel also felt that they needed to explain the plot of *Faust*, which was accomplished by a voice-over in which Billy Breckinridge (Jason Priestley) explains to Curly Bill that Faust sells his soul to the Devil. Daniel also recommended that they put back a shot in which Josephine looks up at Wyatt in his balcony box, indicating her interest in him. Daniel

A deleted scene directed by Kevin Jarre. In this sequence, Sherman McMasters (Michael Rooker), who has been invited to talk to Ringo and Clanton, tells Wyatt (Kurt Russell) to finish the vendetta ride no matter what happens to him. Texas Jack (Peter Sherayko) and Henry Hooker (Charlton Heston) look on (courtesy of the Academy of Motion Pictures Arts and Sciences).

lamented the missing exchange between Wyatt and Mattie when he retrieves his gun prior to the gunfight, feeling it showed that Mattie's and Wyatt's problems were longstanding and revolved around his being a lawman. (In the film, the dialogue exchange between Wyatt and Mattie is not included. It only shows Wyatt changing coats with his badge on his vest and taking out his Buntline pistol.) Daniel felt that if they had to shave 15 minutes from the film, they could remove scenes involving the stagecoach robbery, Breckinridge hunting down Fabian's killers, Doc bidding Kate goodbye, Behan warning Josephine at the hotel, and the attack on the Earp wives. (The latter two scenes remain in the film.) Daniels also suggested that they could trim the vendetta montage sequences and some of the death scene with Doc, including the piece in which he mourns his lost love for his cousin and his reaction to the book, *My Friend, Doc Holliday by Wyatt Earp*.[105]

Composer Jerry Goldsmith was originally contacted to score the film but dropped out. Bruce Broughton, who received an Oscar nomination for composing the music for *Silverado* (1985), took over, providing a memorable score. Broughton's composition is not typical for a Western, yet it provides the movie with the necessary elements to heighten the drama. It is one of the best movie scores written for a Western in the last twenty years.

Broughton opens the film with the sounds of a tinny piano to accompany the early movie footage. We have the feeling of being in a nickelodeon as we see the flickering images on the screen. The music suddenly changes into a dramatic explosion of heavy chords as

Another deleted scene from Kevin Jarre's version. Here, Earp and his posse (Val Kilmer, Peter Sherayko, Kurt Russell and Michael Rooker) hold the Cowboys at bay and tell them to leave the area (courtesy of the Academy of Motion Pictures Arts and Sciences).

we see the large group of Cowboys ride across the screen. As we see shots of the Cowboys loading their guns, the score tells us in no uncertain terms that these men are deadly and that danger is approaching. Within a few moments, Broughton has taken the audience from passively watching clips of old silent films to being caught in the middle of the Cowboys exacting revenge, and by doing so helped to set the tone of the movie.

Broughton uses two major motifs throughout the movie. One is the main theme, which could also be called Wyatt's theme. We are first introduced to this theme as the Earps ride into the bustling town of Tombstone. In this sequence, the music is reflective of the events taking place on screen, with the score playing in a light, melodious tone. The main theme is punctuated with horns, violins, flutes, and a tambourine. As the Earps continue down the main street of Tombstone, the music adds to the action on screen of the brisk activity of the town. As the famous gunfight erupts, the main theme takes on a more action-oriented pace, capturing the confusion and danger inside the empty lot. Yet it is also heroic, reflecting the birth of the legend of Wyatt Earp. Standing alone in the lot after the gunfight, Wyatt looks at his friend, Doc Holliday. Wyatt simply nods to him and the two men walk away while the main theme plays slowly and solemnly. In this one sequence, Broughton has taken the same theme and used it in different modes to attain the proper emotional effect on the audience.

The second major motif is Josephine's theme. We are introduced to it when Josephine exits the stagecoach, as she and Wyatt first see each other. In this moment, the score takes on a delicate, light tone, relying on a flute and violins to suggest the hint of a budding romance between the two characters. The theme is used to greater effect when Wyatt and Josephine meet while riding their horses. At first the theme is soft and gentle, reprising what we heard when Josephine got off the stagecoach. But it quickly becomes more spirited as Josephine challenges Wyatt to a ride. The score drops from the soft, gentle notes to a full-bodied explosion of the theme as the two race their horses, with Broughton using violins, horns, bass drums, and an occasional triangle to capture the flirtation between the two characters. When the two come to a stop and rest, the score once again reverts to the soft and gentle tone, as Wyatt and Josephine grow more connected.

Broughton also uses Josephine's theme to capture the sense of Wyatt and Josephine's unfulfilled love when they are briefly reunited at Hooker's ranch. Here the score relies on violins, soft horns, and a harp to capture the aching sense of a love unclaimed. As Wyatt watches Josephine ride away on the stagecoach, Broughton reprises Wyatt's theme, thus connecting the two, even though they have yet to declare their love. When Wyatt finds Josephine in Denver, the theme is once again a replay of what we first heard when they met on horseback. Violins build up the theme as Wyatt promises to love her for the rest of her life. As they run outside the theatre, the theme reverts to a more playful tone and slowly builds as Wyatt asks Josephine to dance with him in the snow. As they go into their dance, the theme explodes into a bright, joyous waltz, signifying a happy ending for the couple.

Broughton returns to a complete rendition of Wyatt's theme as the end credits begin, using bass drums, horns, trombones, and snare drums as we see the Earp brothers and Holliday marching to their destiny. With this version of the main theme, Broughton is able to project the significance of the famous gunfight in history and mythology. In short, Bruce Broughton created a film score that provides the right emotional impact for the audience watching it.

Once the score was completed, a sneak preview was held in El Monte, California, where the film scored an 83 percent positive review by the audience.[106] No doubt pleased with the preview results, executives at Disney Studios ordered the film trimmed by 15 minutes. In doing so, the film's release date, which was scheduled for December 17, was pushed back to December 25, Christmas Day, because the film "needed a bit more time in post-production."[107]

When the film was released, reviews were generally mixed. Comparing the film to Clint Eastwood's recent *Unforgiven* (1992), *The Village Voice* called it "a postrevisionist kid-brother wannabe.... *Tombstone* starts terrifically, tiptoeing through innumerable film versions, borrowing here and there, and introducing quite a bit of actual historical fact in a cautious, intelligent way.... The picture picks up a lot of heady steam on its inevitable journey to the O.K. Corral, and all is well until about midpoint when the bottom drops out and we find ourselves watching a different movie with the same cast."[108] "*Tombstone* will not pan out much at the boxoffice for Buena Vista [Disney's distributing arm]. It's likely to lose most of its audience during its infrequent conversational rides down philosophical box canyons.... . While Kevin Jarre's full-swept screenplay captures the contradictory energy of such an edgy outpost, it shoots itself in the foot with endless big talk as our earnest Earps ponder such queries as 'What do you want out of life?.' ... Still, *Tombstone* has a lot going for it, including some solid performances," *The Hollywood Reporter* noted.[109]

"The actors in *Tombstone* playing bad guys and good guys and in-between guys spit very convincingly. They also slouch well and reach for their pistols with aplomb. So much for authenticity. Just about everything else in this aggressively overlong Western about trouble in Tombstone seems posed and facetious.... It's supposed to be a 'real' look at the gunfight at the O.K. Corral but mostly it looks like a bunch of overweening actors playing cowboys," the *Los Angeles Times* commented.[110] *Variety* called the film a "tough-talking, but soft-hearted tale that is entertaining in a sprawling, old-fashion manner.... this never-dull oater should do brisker B.O., particularly with younger viewers.... Ultimately, pic's chief virtue is that its handsome actors show a gleaming pleasure in being cast against type. Russell brings a measure of authority and sensitivity to Wyatt Earp.... But it's Kilmer who delivers the standout performance, giving fresh shadings to the lethal but humorous Doc Holliday.... Another in the grand Western tradition that has seen many ups and downs but is still the most unique American genre."[111]

Disney Studios, which was already smarting from all the harmful press relating to Jarre's firing and other problems on the set, chose not to make the film available in advance to film critics. Such a move usually signals that the studio has little faith in a film or that the picture is so flawed that the studio fears negative reviews will drive away any potential viewers. Generally, such actions on the part of a studio support this theory; however, in the case of *Tombstone*, Disney executives misjudged their audience.

By early January 1994, *Tombstone* was close to grossing $40 million at the domestic box office. One publicist said the film had "the best word of mouth I've heard in years." One theatre manager in New York City said the audience was "really responding to it. You hear people laughing, cheering. They come out of the theatre repeating Doc Holliday's lines. When people react like that to a movie, they tell their friends."[112] Yet by the time Disney realized what it had, it had missed the boat for Oscar nominations. The studio, which appears to have had little faith in the film, hardly did anything to help publicize it at the time of its release. After seeing the numbers at the box office, however, the studio quickly reversed its course and tried everything to promote the film. Noted film critics Roger Ebert and Gene Siskel used their syndicated television show not only to praise the film but also to push Val Kilmer's performance as worthy to be considered for an Oscar. Once again, Disney dropped the ball. The studio failed to send out video cassettes of the movie to members of the Academy of Motion Picture Arts and Sciences, thus ensuring that *Tombstone* would be ignored for any Oscar nomination.[113] Costume designer Joseph Porro was one of the craftspeople who lost out on a much-deserved nomination. "I missed the Oscar nomination [for best costume design] by two votes on that movie. It depends on what you're up against. I lost to *Schindler's List*, which was completely rented [costumes]," Porro said.[114]

Despite the mistakes by Disney Studios, *Tombstone* went on to earn over $60 million at the box office. When it was originally released on video tape the following summer (in time for the release of Costner's film), *Tombstone* sold more than 600,000 units. It has become a popular cult classic. In 1994, President Bill Clinton showed a print of the film during his three-day visit to Russia, calling it "a classic Americana movie."[115]

Tombstone opens with black-and-white clips from early silent films, with the narrator quickly setting the tone of the film.[116] As we see a large close-up of a cowboy (George Barnes in *The Great Train Robbery*, 1903) firing his gun into the camera, the screen fills with a wide panorama shot of a bunch of Cowboys, galloping across a lake bed. The sky behind them is gray and overcast, a harbinger of things to come. We then see a quiet Mexican village; Spanish music is being played, and a large party table is being prepared with food and drink. This serene village is contrasted with shots of the Cowboys loading their guns and Curly Bill's unique boots with four aces carved into the tops. A wedding party emerges from the church, with a young bride and the groom, a Mexican Rurale. Curly, with the Cowboys, stands in front of the young couple and tosses two red sashes into the air. "Y'all killed two

Cowboys," he says, before opening fire on the officer's men. Villagers run in panic; gunfire and shouts fill the air. Only the priest, the bride, and groom are unhurt. One of the Cowboys shoots the groom in the leg as Curly warns that they should make way for him and his men. (Looking directly into camera, Curly warns, "I ain't kiddin,' neither!") The wounded but defiant groom tells Curly to go to Hell and is promptly shot. His bride is dragged off by other Cowboys and is also killed. As the priest comes up to the group he warns them, in Spanish, that a rider on a pale horse will come to avenge them. Ringo calmly draws and fires his gun, killing the priest with one shot. While the other Cowboys are seen as dangerous, by having Ringo kill the priest (he refrains from the initial shooting, looking half-dazed), we immediately know that this man is the most deadly. Sitting at the banquet table, Curly asks Ringo what the priest meant. Ringo tells him he was quoting from the bible: "Behold a pale horse. The man that sat on him was death, and hell followed with him."

A steaming locomotive pulls into the Tucson station and we see a man dressed in a black suit step off the train. The camera pans up to his face and we are introduced to Wyatt Earp. His attention is called to a man pulling his horse off the train and hitting the animal with a rope. Wyatt grabs the rope and hits the man with it. In a hushed tone he asks if it hurts, then takes the horse from the man. This is our protagonist. He will step in and defend a helpless horse from being abused. In almost the same breath, he refuses an offer made by U.S. Marshal Crawley Dake to take a law enforcement position, stating that he's retired. He is through with the law and makes a point to say he doesn't even carry a gun, as if doing so would oblige him to take up the law. He says that he's going into business for himself in Tombstone. The marshal reminds him that a rich man will have a guilty conscience. "I already have a guilty conscience, might as well have the money, too," Earp flatly replies. This sets the stage for the tragedy that will befall Wyatt, forcing him to become the reluctant hero, much as in Ford's *My Darling Clementine*.

At the train station, the Earp brothers and their wives are reunited as a family. This is obvious in the way Wyatt greets Virgil and Morgan. There is a strong sense of familial bond between the brothers and a loving acceptance of the women in their lives. Seeing their reflection in a window, Wyatt gathers the family for a look at themselves. It is as close as they ever will get to a family portrait. "Thank you for this, Wyatt. This is all your doing," Virgil tells him. Again, this comment presages Wyatt's guilt when tragedy later strikes and forces him to take action. This is a happy moment for the family, full of hope and dreams. It also builds sympathy with the audience. This scene gives a sense of the strong family ties between the brothers, and the audience quickly accepts them.

We are prepared for the introduction of Doc Holliday when Wyatt asks Virgil if he had seen his friend. Wyatt says he misses "that old rip," adding that he makes him laugh. A large stash of money on a gaming table lies before us as we hear a player say he has bet $500 and demands the other player either play or fold. The camera pans up to Doc Holliday, dressed in black and manipulating a silver dollar between his fingers. "$500? Must be a peach of a hand," he says, with puckish humor. His opponent in the card game, Ed Bailey, is angry at Holliday's continued winning streak, and at one point he jumps from his chair and calls Doc a "skinny lunger." Doc drolly says such language is ugly and he abhors ugliness, as a finger taps the grip of his pistol. He is taunting Bailey, like a spider luring its prey into the web. Before Bailey can make a move, Doc draws his two guns with lightning speed, an obvious nod to the overblown image Holliday has had in other films and books of being a deadly killer. Laying the guns down on the table, Holliday tells Bailey, "There, now we can be friends again." As Bailey lunges for one of the guns, he is grabbed by Doc, who plunges a knife into him. Clearly, Holliday is not a man whom any foe should take lightly, despite his illness. This also sets up for the audience, in a short amount of time, what can be expected from this character throughout the film. As he and Kate clear the winnings off the table, Holliday slowly strolls out of the saloon, pausing long enough to take money off another gaming table before calmly bidding the patrons a good evening. Holliday is a man who is cool in a tense situation and whose demeanor can change from puckish to deadly in the blink of an eye.

Arriving in Tombstone, Wyatt tells his brothers that "you can smell the silver in this town!" The streets are a beehive of activity, with people going about their business. This is the first time any film has given Tombstone a sense of being a bustling boomtown, and with a variety of ethnic types. Pulling up to the Grand Hotel, the Earps are greeted by Sheriff John Behan, who introduces himself to Wyatt as a "man of many parts," who also appears to be very impressed with himself. When Behan recognizes Earp's name from his days in Dodge City, Wyatt tells him that he's retired and doesn't even carry a gun. Once again, this reinforces the fact that Wyatt wants no part of the law and that it would take a major event to force him back into that position. Later, Morgan and Virgil introduce Wyatt to the city marshal, Fred White, who proceeds to explain to the Earps (and the audience) that the real law in town is the Cowboys, who wear red sashes. Wyatt comments on all the saloons, and White tells him they are the real bonanza in town, excepting the Oriental, which White calls a "slaughter house."[117] Looking at the building, Wyatt goes inside the lushly furnished, yet sparsely populated saloon, and strikes up a conversation with the owner, Milt Joyce, who says the lack of business is due to the abusive faro dealer, Johnny Tyler, who continues to harass the few remaining patrons. Telling Joyce that he is Wyatt Earp, the man cynically chuckles, "Yeah, right." Smiling, Wyatt cannot help but find humor in the man's response. This moment takes a poke at the so-called legendary status of Earp, showing that the protagonist even finds the comment ironically funny. Earp walks over to the faro table and stares at Tyler, who challenges his gaze. In a calm, conversational tone, Wyatt tells Tyler that he's sitting in his chair. Noting that he doesn't carry a gun, Tyler says Earp runs off at the mouth. "Don't need to go heeled to get the bulge on a dub like you," he replies. Wyatt moves in on Tyler, who is now stammering; his bluff is being called. Earp dares him to draw his gun and slaps Tyler on the face three times, causing his lip to bleed. "You gonna do something? Or just stand there and bleed?" he asks. Disarming Tyler, he tosses the pistol to Joyce, then throws Tyler out by the ear. Turning to Joyce, he asks if twenty-five percent of the house would be a fair amount. In this brief scene, we see that Wyatt Earp can be deadly and that he has an utter lack of fear in a tense situation. This shows us that he is indeed capable of handling himself and why he was an effective lawman in the past—and will be a dangerous foe in the future.

Out on the street, Wyatt meets his brothers—and Doc Holliday, newly arrived—and explains that he now owns a quarter interest in the gaming at the saloon. As they speak, Tyler reappears with a shotgun, obviously out for revenge. It is Doc Holliday, calling Tyler's name, who saves Wyatt's life. When he learns that his opponent is Wyatt Earp, Tyler all but caves in, standing there bewildered until Holliday casually dismisses him. "Thank you," Tyler says meekly, as he drops the shotgun in the street and scurries away. Spotting Sheriff Behan, Wyatt calls him over and asks if he knows Doc Holliday. "Piss on you, Wyatt," Doc mutters. Behan, quick to glad hand anyone, struts over and asks Earp how he likes the town. Wyatt suggests building a race track and Behan agrees, adding it will show how grown up they are. Holliday reminds them that this is just another mining town and they are getting way ahead of themselves. Behan, the typical booster of what will benefit him, says the town is quite sophisticated—just as gunfire erupts. Stumbling out of another saloon is a wounded man, followed by Turkey Creek Jack Johnson and Texas Jack Vermillion. Johnson warns the man not to raise his gun, and when he does, Johnson quickly dispatches him. "Very cosmopolitan," Doc wryly says. Despite what others may hope, this brief gunfight illustrates the lawlessness of Tombstone, which will frame the events to come. Standing in the street, as Marshal White takes the guns from Johnson and Vermillion, Virgil asks Behan, "What kind of a town is this?"[118] As a stagecoach arrives and Josephine Marcus exits, Morgan, looking at the new arrival, comments that the scenery is nice. Wyatt and Josephine look at each other, and it is obvious that she is attracted to him and that she has also caught his eye.

During the evening performance at the Bird Cage Theatre, the Cowboys dominate the seats on the floor, even evicting others to make room for themselves. Wyatt and his family sit in the balcony, with Holliday and Kate, when Mayor Clum approaches and tries to discuss the subject of Wyatt's taking a law enforcement position. Earp abruptly cuts him off with, "Not a prayer. Nice meeting you." As the tabloid performance of *Faust* ends, Wyatt asks Doc who played the Devil, only to see it is Josephine, who makes sure their eyes meet. When Wyatt says he'll be damned, Doc adds, "You may indeed, if you get lucky." The comment obviously infuriates Mattie and embarrasses Wyatt, which makes clear that their marriage is having problems. After the performance, the Earps stand outside the theatre, where Morgan comments on the stars and how little they make him feel. He tells his brothers that he read a book about spiritualism and that people who are dying see a light that supposedly leads them to Heaven. ("Oh, God. Here he goes again," Virgil grumbles.) Wyatt teases him, asking if they have a sign for Hell, and then tells Mattie he has to go to work. She pleads with him to stay with her, but Wyatt persists. Seeing her expression, however, he relents, only to be rebuffed by Mattie, who pulls out a laudanum bottle. When he suggests she see a doctor, Mattie becomes defensive. She tells him to go to work and walks off, coldly thanking him for his compliment about her looking beautiful. The relationship between Wyatt and Mattie is unraveling, and the pain on Wyatt's face is obvious.

At the saloon, Wyatt takes a break, and Doc asks him if he has forsaken all other women for Mattie. Wyatt admits that both he and Mattie had made mistakes in the past, but he is now loyal to Mattie. When he says he would ignore Josephine if she appeared in the saloon, Doc smiles as if he's the cat who swallowed the canary. Wyatt turns to see that Josephine has entered the Oriental and has begun to dance with several men. She turns around and holds out her hands to Wyatt, who shyly turns away. Behan quickly steps in, asking her to share a drink of champagne with him. Doc says he has been corrected, calling Wyatt "an oak."

At Wyatt's faro table, Curly Bill, Ringo, and a drunken Ike Clanton confront Earp. Wyatt calmly tells the men that he has retired from law enforcement. As Curly puts a bet on the faro table, Wyatt casually moves his bet to another number, draws a winning card and pays Curly $500. Ringo looks at Doc and taunts him, asking if he's retired as well. "Not me, I'm in my prime," Doc says. He tells Kate that Ringo is the "deadliest pistolero since Wild Bill." Doc returns Ringo's taunts by asking Kate if he should hate the Cowboy, saying it is something around the eyes that reminds him of himself. "I'm sure of it, I hate him," Doc unconcernedly says. Sensing a potential problem, Wyatt reaches underneath his table, where he has attached a sawed-off shotgun, pulling back the hammers. Doc speaks Latin, and Ringo surprises him by replying in kind, starting a verbal duel of Latin.[119] Doc tells Kate that Ringo is an educated man and now he really hates him, which causes Ringo to draw his pistol. He proceeds to spin and twirl his weapon in Doc's face, but Doc remains unfazed by the spectacle. As Ringo finishes his show with a theatrical twirl, landing his gun in its holster, the saloon crowd applauds. Doc, using his silver drinking cup, imitates Ringo's actions, which elicits laughter from others, but not from Ringo. The two men have baited each other in a verbal confrontation, and Ringo has displayed his ability at handling a gun, with Doc openly mocking him. This sequence sets the stage for a future deadly confrontation between the two men.

Wyatt meets Josephine one day while riding his horse. Not only is there a mutual attraction between them, but their horses also echo their feelings—Josephine's mare is in season. Wyatt suggests they split the horses up, but she says they should run it out of them as she takes off at a gallop. "Yeah, I'm an oak, all right," Wyatt sarcastically says as he follows her lead. Their racing the horses can be seen as an allegory to their physical attraction to each other. After the ride, Wyatt and Josephine stop to rest in a field with wild flowers as their two horses nuzzle each other. Again, the horses duplicate the emotions Wyatt and Josephine feel. Laying a blanket down, Wyatt chuckles at Josephine's comment that she would die for fun. She peppers him with questions, asking if he's happy and what he wants out of life. When he tells her he wants children, she says it doesn't suit him. Josephine gets Wyatt to laugh when she says that what she wants out of life is room service, seeing the world, and never looking back. He asks her why she is with Behan if she isn't completely in love with him, and Josephine replies that she likes men and wants to live. Her opinions fascinate Wyatt, and the physical and emotional attraction between them is palpable. When he arrives home, he finds Mattie heavily drugged from the laudanum. When he asks how she is, Mattie laughs nervously and her condition wears on Wyatt. He tries to ask her if she'd like to pull out of town and see the world, living on room service. It is obvious that Josephine has sparked something inside Wyatt that isn't there with Mattie. When she laughs at his offer, Wyatt realizes that his relationship with Mattie has reached an impasse, that he's trapped with a woman who is helplessly addicted to a drug and will never get better. Telling her to forget his idea, he lies back on the bed, lost in thought at what he has and what he wants.

When Marshal Fred White is killed by Curly Bill, Wyatt (despite his insistence that he has no interest in enforcing the law) steps in and buffaloes Curly. As an angry mob calls for Curly to be lynched, Wyatt, with a pistol in hand, holds them at bay. We see that Wyatt is all business and is determined to do what is necessary to preserve order. When Ike Clanton and other Cowboys slowly circle around Wyatt, much like a pack of lions waiting to attack their prey, Wyatt doesn't hesitate to aim a loaded gun at Ike's head, promising to kill him first. Wyatt is cold and calculating in his actions, and no one doubts him.

After the incident, as the brothers play billiards, Wyatt reflects on Judge Spicer's ruling that set Curly free for White's death. He is dismayed by the ruling, adding, "Who cares? None of my business anyway." Although Wyatt has given up seeing law and order enforced, it begins to weigh heavily on his brother, Virgil. He is torn between agreeing with his brother and his moral call to duty, even when they rebuff Mayor Clum's pleas to take over the city marshal's position. It is only after he leaves the billiard hall that Virgil makes his decision. As a mother escorts her several children along the sidewalk, her young son drops his ball and chases after it into the street just as a group of Cowboys gallop by, shooting their guns. It is only Virgil's quick reaction of grabbing the boy that saves his life. Returning the boy to his frightened mother, who bears a disfiguring facial scar (possibly an action by some of the Cowboys), he tips his hat to her and watches her and her children as they continue down the street. Virgil has made his decision, for better or worse.

The posting of a notice that no one is allowed to carry a gun on the streets of Tombstone enrages the citizens, but it is Virgil's accepting the job as city marshal that causes problems within the Earp family. Wyatt is incensed that Virgil has taken the job after he told his brothers not to get involved. Virgil tells Wyatt that he got them involved when he brought them to Tombstone. He reminds Wyatt that people are afraid to walk the street "and I'm trying to make money off that like some goddamn vulture! If we're going to have a future in this town, it's got to have some law and order." Learning that his younger brother, Morgan, has also pinned on a badge, Wyatt says that in all his years as a peace officer he was only involved in one shooting—and that shooting took a man's life. "You don't know how that feels, Morg. Believe me, boy, you don't ever want to know," he advises his brother. Virgil and Morgan are undaunted by his comments. Enforcement of the law overrides any personal concerns. Unlike their brother, Virgil and Morgan are not reluctant heroes, and their decision will bring tragic results.

Releasing Ike Clanton from jail, after he has been arrested for making death threats against the Earps and Holliday and for carrying guns in town, does little to ease the growing tension between the Clantons and McLaurys and the Earps. It is further exacerbated when Tom McLaury has words with Wyatt outside the jail and displays a revolver, saying that he is ready to fight. Despite Wyatt's reluctance to become involved, he is quick to disarm the man by buffaloing him on the head. His action only adds to an already volatile situation. A few hours later, the Earps see the men ride into town, carrying weapons. Virgil expresses concern while Wyatt remains calm, although he suggests that he be sworn in as a deputy. Sensing a storm on the horizon, the reluctant hero takes up the badge once more. Returning to his cottage, he trades his frock coat for his longer jacket and his Buntline gun. Like a mythical hero, Wyatt Earp is now dressed in his battle clothes and claims his weapon. The gun, like Earp's previous reputation in Dodge City, is impressive. Myth and reality have merged.

As they walk toward the empty lot to confront the Clantons and McLaurys, Wyatt asks himself how the hell they got involved in this mess. Walking down Fifth Street, the Earps and Holliday are framed by a burning building in the background. The Mexican priest's prophecy that a pale rider would come to revenge them and bring hell with him has come to pass. Advancing into the empty lot, the four men confront their adversaries. As Frank McLaury and Billy Clanton reach for their guns, Virgil shouts that this is not what he wants. There is a momentary pause as the opponents eye one another, until Doc roguishly winks at Billy Clanton, whose face goes dead. "Oh, my God!" Wyatt utters under his breath, knowing they have passed the point of no return as gunfire erupts. Throughout the gunfight Wyatt stands tall in his black coat and firing his weapon, becoming the symbol of the hero who remains cool in battle. As the gunfire subsides, he quietly tells the wounded Morgan to remain still, becoming the protective brother. When Behan attempts to make a scene by announcing he will arrest the Earps and Holliday, Wyatt firmly says that they will not be arrested. As Virgil and Morgan are escorted away by their wives to have their wounds treated, Wyatt coldly comments to Mayor Clum, "I guess we did our good deed for today."

Wyatt's fear that trouble will follow the family comes to pass. The situation accelerates when, in one night, Virgil is ambushed (as are the Earp wives at Virgil's cottage) and Morgan is killed. Wyatt is not the leader when these tragedies happen to his family. As Virgil is having his arm worked on by the doctor, Wyatt appears lost, unsure of what he should do next. He wants to get out of town, but Morgan questions his decision, asking him what kind of action is that? Morgan wants revenge and, in a fit of anger, bolts out the door. Turning to his older brother, Wyatt asks Virgil what he should do now. Virgil begs to be left alone as he fights for his life. The family that was so happy together is now fractured, and Wyatt cannot help but feel the guilt because he is the one who brought them to Tombstone. Outside Virgil's cottage, Wyatt meets McMasters, as well as Texas Jack and Turkey Creek Johnson. McMasters tells Earp he had nothing to do with either ambush and throws down his red sash, abdicating his association with the Cowboys. He, along with the other two men, will stand by to help Earp if he needs assistance. Morgan goes to the Oriental Saloon where he is killed playing billiards. As Morgan lies dying on the pool table, Wyatt tries to comfort his brother in his final moments. Morgan tells Wyatt that all the talk of seeing a light leading to Heaven isn't true, and he slips away. Outside the billiard hall, as the rain pelts down, a crowd has gathered, including Morgan's wife. Wyatt leaves his brother's body with his hands covered in Morgan's blood. Walking past Mattie, Wyatt holds up his hands as he stumbles out, as though he cannot believe his brother is dead. Going out into the rain, Wyatt's emotion over losing his younger brother, whom he tried to protect, overcomes him. Standing in the middle of the street while the rain pours down on him, Wyatt cries out, asking why it had to be Morgan. Josephine comes running to him, but he yells at her to get away from him. He realizes that if he embraces her, she will become a target of the Cowboys. Again, even in his moment of grief, Wyatt attempts what he could not do for Morgan or Virgil— to protect Josephine's life. Turning from her, Wyatt sees Mattie standing in the street looking at him with contempt. She walks away from Wyatt, leaving him alone in the street. Standing in the rain with his brother's blood on his hands, Wyatt is silently denounced for his earlier apathy that they should not get involved or try to stop the criminality that now rages unchecked. One can make the argument that by standing in the rain, Wyatt is being baptized into action. He will now take up the cause, however belated, and wipe clean those who drew blood. The pale horse with its rider of death has awakened, and he will extract a terrible revenge.

Preparing to leave Tombstone, Wyatt is not the eager man we saw arriving in the town. He is withdrawn, as if he is merely going through his paces without a purpose. It is only with Doc Holliday's help that he gets his family out of town. Wyatt silently watches Josephine cross the street; she barely looks at him. Doc, as if speaking for Wyatt's conscience, softly says as he watches her, "And so she walked out of our lives forever." The entire town watches from a distance, with no one standing close to the Earps. They wanted law and order, but when the ultimate price had to be paid, they don't want it to touch them. Stopping his wagon in front of Curly Bill, Ringo, Ike, and the other Cowboys, Wyatt says he wants them to know "it is over." Curly breezily bids goodbye, as Ringo asks if he smells something. "Smells like someone died," he says. Curly chuckles, as Wyatt's inner rage boils; yet he will not do or say anything. As the Earp party leaves, Curly tells Ike to "finish it."

Doc saddles his horse as Kate begs him to stay. She cannot understand "why is it always Wyatt?" He tries to explain, saying that if he calls himself Wyatt's friend—but he stops. Doc finds it absurd to explain something to this woman who does not understand anything about loyalty. She is concerned only about herself and her own welfare. Asking Doc what will become of her if he is killed, Doc cynically says that she will be left without a meal ticket. His comment cuts her, as she realizes he sees through her. Stepping into the saddle, he calmly asks if she has "no kind word to say to me before I ride away?" When she doesn't answer, he goes, leaving her to call after him.[120]

At the Tucson train station, Ike Clanton and Frank Stilwell try to attack Virgil and the others on the train. Standing on the train platform, Stilwell calls out to Mattie, asking where

Wyatt is. "Right behind you," Wyatt says, as he unloads both barrels of his shotgun on Stilwell. Ike immediately drops his shotgun and lies prone on the ground, begging for mercy. Looking at Virgil in the train car, Wyatt raises one finger, letting him know those responsible for his ambush and Morgan's death will pay the price. Wyatt places his boot over Ike's throat, warning him to take a good look at the dead man. He promises to exact the same from every Cowboy he sees wearing a red sash. Backed up by Doc, Texas Jack, Turkey Creek Johnson and McMasters, Wyatt displays his marshal's badge to the cowering Clanton and says, "Tell them I'm coming and Hell's coming with me!" Behind a red fire ball of the sun, the silhouettes of Earp and his posse come galloping up, reminiscent of the Four Horsemen of the Apocalypse. Earp's vendetta ride will now exact revenge, partly for his brothers and partly for his own sin of indifference. The vendetta ride is Wyatt's way of seeking absolution for his previous inaction.

Knowing they are now being pursued by a posse headed by Behan, Ringo and Ike, Earp's group takes refuge at Henry Hooker's ranch. At the ranch, Wyatt is briefly reunited with Josephine, whose stagecoach has stopped for water. Attempting to apologize for his actions on the night of Morgan's death, Josephine tells him she forgave him the moment he said it, realizing his intent. There are so many things both want to say to each other, but time and circumstances will not allow it. Their parting looks speak volumes.

When McMasters' body is dumped at Hooker's ranch (after he went to talk to Ringo's posse), Wyatt is told that Ringo wants a "straight up fight" between the two of them. Talking to Doc, whose health is failing, he asks his old friend what makes Ringo do the things he does. Doc says that Ringo wants revenge for being born. Wyatt relates that during the shootout at Iron Springs with Curly Bill, he didn't think about what was happening, but he realizes he cannot beat Ringo. When Doc confirms this, Wyatt slowly nods, accepting his fate. He will do what is necessary, even if it means his death. Doc tries to get out of bed, but collapses, apologizing for not being able to help. He asks Wyatt what it is like to wear a badge, and his friend gives him his own.

Ringo, seeing who he believes is Wyatt approaching, brashly says he didn't think he "had it in him" for a showdown. "I'm your huckleberry," Doc calmly says, lifting his head to see Ringo's surprised expression. The two men, whose previous showdown was interrupted, now square off, slowly circling each other like dancers as they wait for the right moment. Doc quickly dispatches Ringo and lays the badge Wyatt had given him on the dead man's chest. Wyatt finds Doc, who admits he wasn't as sick as he made out. Once again, Doc was prepared to make the ultimate sacrifice for his friend. Wyatt says it is time to finish things. "Indeed, sir. The last charge of Wyatt Earp and his immortals," Doc replies. Again, Earp's posse goes after the Cowboys, ending with Ike fleeing and throwing away his red sash. The four of them—Wyatt, Doc, Vermillion and Johnson—ride as one, as we look down from above and watch them pass into the history books.

Doc has come to a Glenwood Springs, Colorado, sanitarium to die. Wyatt visits Doc and brings him a small book. Doc won't look at it, nor does he want to play poker with his old friend. He told Wyatt not to come back, but despite his protests, Wyatt deals the cards as Doc tells him that he was the only man in his life who ever gave him hope. Moved by Doc's statement, Wyatt can say nothing. The man who means so much to him is dying. He cannot bring himself to say anything; his emotions are spent. Responding to Doc's question of what he wants out of life, Wyatt says he just wants to live a normal life. "There is no normal life, Wyatt. There's just life," Doc tells him. He urges Wyatt to say goodbye and go find Josephine and to live for him. Knowing the end is at hand, Doc begs Wyatt to leave him. He wants to save his friend from one last witnessing of death. Wyatt stands but is hesitant to leave. Doc manages a weak smile and nods, as if giving Wyatt the final permission to leave his bedside. Holding back tears, Wyatt manages to thank his friend for always being there before he walks out. Looking at the booklet Wyatt left him, Doc sees that it is entitled, *My Friend Doc Holliday by Wyatt Earp*. Before passing away, Doc sees that he is without his boots, and comments, "I'll be damned. This is funny."

Finding Josephine performing in Denver, Wyatt enters to her dressing room. He tells her he has no money, no pride, and that he doesn't know how he will make a living. But he promises to love her for the rest of her life. The two embrace, and Josephine tells him not to worry, that her parents are rich. Outside the theatre, a light snowfall greets them. Wyatt asks her to do what she wanted the first time they met. Taking his hat off, he bows and asks her to dance, adding, "Then we'll have room service!" The two, lost in each other, dance together in the snow.

Tombstone has come to be regarded as a modern classic despite the many obstacles its production endured, as James Jacks recalled:

It's one of those things.... CAA felt ours was going to be a pale imitation of what the Costner movie was going to be. I never really thought that. They never had a script and we had a really good script.... By the way, making a Western wasn't the easiest decision in the world anyway in those days, and still isn't.... I think it was the deal end that attracted Cinergi [to make the film].... We used to say on the set that we didn't really think they quite understood the movie. But they knew they were getting a really good cast for not that much money, and that as long as the movie didn't go over budget, they would probably do very well.

We actually contacted both Glenn Ford and Kirk Douglas, but it was all for the same part—Old Man Clanton.... Gregory Peck at one time was asked, but Robert Mitchum was the one who said he wanted to do it. We always wanted Charlton Heston for the rancher. Glenn Ford we actually talked about as the town sheriff, the one Harry Carey, Jr. ended up playing.... By the time we had Mitchum, we had already decided that we couldn't afford to do that extra scene. He never came and got fitted [for wardrobe], or anything like that. He wasn't in very good health, anyway.

The one scene I really felt that could have been cut was the montage after the death of Ringo.... I mean, the whole point of killing Ringo was that was the end of the leadership of the Cowboys. What was supposed to be the last ride of Wyatt Earp and his immortals is they ride right into thirty cowboys, and you kinda see it there [in the final print], and they all start breaking and running. It's thirty guys against four but because they [the Cowboys] don't have any leadership, they all run.... In fact, there is a funny line, that is no longer in the movie, one guy saying, "I think it's time to start working for a living," and turns and rides away. Another guy rides away and they all start scattering. Ike Clanton is sitting there, yelling, "No, it's just four men. We can beat them!" One guy just stops and says, "You beat them." Then he [Ike] turns and runs and drops his red sash.

The scene [cut from the final print] I really miss is with Charlton Heston and Ringo, when he comes to the ranch.... The Cowboys ride down and they say "We saw three guys leave, who got left behind?" Heston says "It's Holliday. I think he's dying." Ringo says, "Well, bring the boy out. Let's take a look." Heston kinda looks at Ringo and says, "Ya know, Ringo, I watched you do a lot of terrible things and never lifted a finger. But I won't let you take a dying man from my house, that's where I draw the line." Ringo says, "All right, I'm gonna go kill Wyatt Earp now. Then I'm gonna come back and we're gonna have this conversation again." And Heston goes, "I'll be here." I really did miss that scene.

I don't know if Kevin [Jarre] could have finished the movie. It's not just Kevin's fault. He wasn't getting a lot of support from [executive producer and head of Cinergi Productions] Andy Vanja. Andy had no real confidence in Kevin. At one point the actors began to have less confidence in him. When that happened, the flame was burning out at that point. I don't know, I don't think Kevin, in the end, could have finished it. It's too bad.

We had to shoot this film the way you shoot an independent film. We didn't have a lot of money.... It was a huge epic, but we had to shoot it for $25 million.... I think if we had shut down production [after Jarre's firing] it would have helped the film.... We would have had more time to work things out, instead of making things up as we went.... At night, Kurt Russell and I would figure out (of the scenes they have cut) what information we needed for the movie. We knew the script better than anybody else. We would put lines back into other scenes so that there was a certain coherent state to the story. Now in the end, some of the scenes wound up being cut. There is some stuff at the end of the movie that bothers me to hell all over the place. I think it bothered me, it bothered the critics. That's why one of the reasons why the movie didn't review as well as it should have.... But when it came out on video, it just did some ridiculous amount. It has the record of VHS copies ratioed to gross [box office earnings] to ultimate [video] sale. It was the only movie ever to do something like 750,000 video sales for a movie that didn't gross $100 million [at the box office].

We really did try to make it [the movie] as accurate as we could. Kevin came from a point of view, that Wyatt and his men, were good guys (flawed good guys. Whereas, there are historians who think Wyatt Earp was no better, or worse than the Cowboys. We certainly didn't take that position. But we tried to show the flaws of him. For instance, his whole adulterous affair (a lot of that got cut. And the relationship with his wife. There was another moment in the movie I really miss, too. He comes in to get his Buntline Special, and his wife is sitting there stoned out of her mind. He reaches in to get the gun and she says to him, "I thought you promised me to never use that again." He says, "Yeah, I guess I promised a lot of things." And he walks out.

Kurt was great. And Val, of course, was great. There were a lot of little scenes texture scenes (that I do miss in the movie. I felt badly for the actors, because some of them did this movie because of one or two scenes and sometimes those scenes got cut. Like Heston, for instance. I felt terrible about it, but on the other hand I didn't have final cut [approval]. There wasn't really a lot of time to argue because when we finished shooting, we literally had three months before it came out.... I actually think it was my best job as a producer, talking people down and keeping things together.... We worked real hard. It's just too bad the studio didn't get behind it more. I know it had its champions inside at Disney, but I wish that some people would have liked it a little bit more, because I have a feeling it would have been a significant hit. I think it could have grossed twice as much as it did, and that would have been very good for Westerns in general.

In the end it's a good movie. As Kurt says, and we often talk about it, "We don't take a lot of pride in the movie, because it's a really good movie, but was probably the best script I ever read." That's the problem. We don't feel we quite delivered on the script.... It should have been a great movie. After one of the previews, George Cosmatos came up to me and said, "You see, we were right! They love the movie." I said, "George, you had a great script and a great cast and you made a good movie. It's not something we should be doing cartwheels over." But on the other hand, it's better than it being a bad movie. (James Jacks to the author, November 28, 2005.)

For all of its problems during production, *Tombstone* emerges as a vibrant, exciting, and involving movie. Despite his on-set persona, credit must be given to George Cosmatos, who imbues the film with the energy level it needs, and that was lacking under Jarre's guidance. He moves the camera with a purpose, allowing it to carrying the audience along, and lets the actors give life to their characters. This is one of several factors in the film's success and popularity.

Kurt Russell delivers one of his best and strongest performances as Wyatt Earp, allowing the lawman to be caring and vulnerable, yet cold-blooded when seeking revenge. His Wyatt has a sense of humor; when he laughs, his enjoyment has a warmth that appeals to the audience. Some Earp historians disagree with Russell's crying in the street after Morgan's death, feeling that it is not an accurate portrayal of the real man. It would have been more effective if Russell's Earp had walked out of the saloon into the rain, grim-faced, and kept on walking, instead of crying in the street. This is by no means meant as a criticism of Russell's acting in this scene; to the contrary, his is a gut-wrenching performance. But had the scene been done the other way, it might have offered a better explanation, from a storytelling point of view, of how Earp became so ruthless when he was hunting down Morgan's killers. Russell adds little bits of business to his character that give his performance life, such as when he and Josephine are talking after their ride. He stands with his hands behind him, bringing to mind the image of a shy schoolboy talking to his first love. As she starts to get up, Wyatt moves forward and offers his hand, only to quickly place his hands behind his back again when she rises on her own. This little bit of business gives a boyish quality to his character and makes the scene between them more meaningful. When Doc tells him he cannot beat Ringo in a gunfight, Wyatt gives a simple nod, understanding what his friend is telling him and accepting the fact he will likely die in the face-off. By making only this small gesture, Russell has allowed his character to convey his emotions without resorting to unnecessary dialogue. The final scene between Russell's Wyatt and Val Kilmer's Doc is moving and touching, remindful of the final parting between James Garner and Jason Robards in *Hour of the Gun.*

Val Kilmer gives a standout performance as Doc Holliday, showing Holliday as a scamp, yet capable of killing at a moment's notice. Doc's friendship and devotion displayed toward Wyatt, which is returned in kind by Wyatt, is essential to the audience's ability to identify

During a break in filming the train station sequence, director George Cosmatos (far left) talks with actors Sam Elliott, Bill Paxton and Kurt Russell. This scene was filmed at Old Tucson (courtesy of Larry Zeug).

with the main protagonists, and also to establish sympathy with them when tragedy strikes. When Holliday is asked why he is along on this posse ride instead of taking care of his fragile health, Doc replies with conviction, "Wyatt Earp is my friend." "Hell, I got lots of friends," Turkey Creek Johnson says. "I don't," Doc states flatly, which causes the audience to respond immediately with sympathy and admiration for this character. (Interestingly, this is the first time in any film that Holliday is portrayed with a Southern accent.) Kilmer's Holliday often displays a deadpan yet innocent look in sequences of confrontation. When he draws his guns on Ed Bailey, this expression comes across his face, which makes Bailey (and the audience) wonder if he is jesting or deadly serious. By doing this, Kilmer gives his Holliday a sense of danger, which is quickly counterbalanced when he lays the guns down on the gaming table with a droll delivery, "There, now we can be friends again." Kilmer's Holliday taunts his adversaries with humor, be it mocking Ringo's gun-twirling ability with a silver drinking cup, challenging Ike Clanton to a spelling contest, or quietly offering "I'm your huckleberry" when Ringo goads the Earps into a gunfight.

Powers Boothe's Curly Bill is a *tour de force* portrayal, giving the character a larger-than-life appeal, infusing humor that masks his deadly intentions. His character is a villain, thanks to Boothe's performance, but the audience actually likes Curly Bill, despite his corrupt ways. In contrast, Michael Biehn's Ringo is actually feared by the audience, as we realize that this Johnny Ringo is very dangerous and would kill a person without reason, as he does with the priest. In having him commit that act, the filmmakers quickly establish that Ringo is indeed a very bad man and will kill anyone if it suits his purpose. Biehn's Ringo is a tortured soul whose drinking exacerbates his violent outbursts. In a drunken state, he will challenge anyone, even Doc Holliday. Yet, while expecting Wyatt for the final confrontation, he is taken aback, albeit briefly, when he sees it is Holliday come to confront him. After being taunted by Doc into a showdown, his reaction quickly becomes unbalanced, as he ominously whispers, "All right, lunger. Let's do it!" Stephen Lang delivers a definitive rendering of Ike Clanton, bearing an uncanny resemblance to the real man. Lang shows Clanton to be a boisterous braggart when under the influence of liquor, yet a man who quickly cowers and runs away when confronted with violence. Of all the actors to portray these three characters, Boothe, Biehn and Lang have managed to deliver the most impressive performances in any film about the gunfight.

The film also is strongly supported by many other actors, such as Dana Delany in the role of Josephine, Dana Wheeler-Nicholson as Mattie, Thomas Haden Church as Billy Clanton and John Philbin and Robert John Burke as Tom and Frank McLaury. Audiences look forward to actors who can bring a sense of weight and authority to their roles, especially in a Western. This film is well-served in that capacity with such fine supporting actors as Sam Elliott, Harry Carey, Jr. and Buck Taylor. Elliott offers a solid performance as Virgil Earp, a man who is torn between duty and avoidance. Once he makes his decision, he does not waver, even when Wyatt tries to downplay the crime by reminding him that it is only a misdemeanor offense for the Cowboys to be carrying guns. "They're breaking the law!" he growls. He will not back down on this point, and his authority is not to be questioned. Both Harry Carey, Jr. and Buck Taylor give depth to their roles even without much dialogue. Their mere presence on the screen is enough, as they are able to etch out a personality for each of their characters.

If one has to explain what makes this film so outstanding, it must be its visuality, especially with regard to sets and costuming. We are treated to images of the town of Tombstone that are vibrant and spirited, giving the film a lively appeal. The sets are not windblown, faded brown buildings, but are new and alive, active and full of life. The same can be said for the costumes. No one looks the same, nor are the characters dressed in dull blacks or browns. Instead, the wealth of a mining town is shown by the well-dressed men and women and by the dashing Cowboys with their red sashes and colorful shirts and scarves. It is as if the audience has been transported back in time, and we are seeing these colorful visions for the first time. Like the sets, the wardrobe also gives life to the film, adding to the story and drawing the audience in. Both set designer Catherine Hardwicke and costume designer Joseph Porro did excellent work, but, ultimately, it is Kevin Jarre who must be given credit for establishing the look and feel of the film. It was his vision, and his alone, that gives this film its life. Despite any shortcomings in his direction, he had a solid vision for the film that was carried on and not discarded. As many crew members have stated, Jarre cannot be given enough credit for his visual taste and his extremely well-crafted, witty, and involving screenplay.

The gunfight in this film is well executed, although a few factual elements are discarded for filmmaking purposes. While the empty lot is twice the size of the original one, it does give the actors and camera the ability to move around and create a sense of chaos during the gunfight. Discarding the history of the Earps and Holliday standing on the edge of the lot in the street, this gunfight takes place entirely inside the empty lot, giving it a theatrical feel, with the lot serving as the stage and the audience watching from close-up. In this version,

Although *Tombstone* took some liberties with the famous gunfight, it remains one of the more accurate depictions. Here, Frank McLaury (Robert Burke, foreground) lies wounded as both Virgil Earp (Sam Elliott, on ground) and Morgan Earp (Bill Paxton, far right) have just been shot. Doc (Val Kilmer, left) is about to draw his pistol as Wyatt (Kurt Russell) looks at Morgan (courtesy of the Academy of Motion Pictures Arts and Sciences).

both Tom and Frank McLaury die in the empty lot instead of out on Fremont Street. The production also add Ike Clanton grabbing a gun from Behan inside Fly's Photo Gallery and shooting out the window at the Earps, before fleeing the building and running down the street.[121] (The gunfight runs two minutes and eleven seconds.) This is the first movie to show the accurate ways Tom and Frank McLaury were shot, although Frank McLaury was shot in the forehead.[122]

In filming action scenes such as this, continuity is extremely important. One has to be careful to make certain the actors fire the right amount of bullets without expending their rounds and that the actions of the performers match in each shot. On the set, much of this responsibility belongs to the script supervisor. When the film is in the process of cutting, it is up to the film editor to make sure shots properly match. However, mistakes do occur, and *Tombstone* is no exception. Two glaring mistakes occur in the gunfight with Doc Holliday. The first one, which should have been caught during the editing process, is when Doc fires one barrel of his shotgun in the air to get Tom McLaury's horse to bolt, exposing him to Doc, who fires the second barrel into Tom's body. We see Doc fire the second round at Tom and then cut to the reverse shot, showing McLaury's body being hit by the shotgun round and the blood squib exploding as he begins to fall. The next immediate shot is a reverse angle, with McLaury's back to us, favoring Holliday as he fires the shotgun and McLaury falls. By cutting the film in this manner, it appears that Holliday has fired three rounds from a two-round shotgun. The film editors could have used the reverse shot favoring Doc Holliday if they had simply cut out his firing the gun, picking up the shot as McLaury falls.

The second mistake is when Holliday is firing at Billy Clanton (who is to his right) with one gun, fanning the gun hammer back in rapid action, expending five rounds within a few seconds. Moments later, he turns his attention to Ike Clanton (on his left) and uses *both guns*, firing rapidly, easily expending twelve rounds from both guns. Again, these mistakes should have been caught during production, although to be fair, a script supervisor— or any crew member, for that matter—has only so much say in what is correct in continuity. The final word is always the director's. If during filming he is unconcerned with how many shots Doc Holliday fires from one gun, no amount of protesting by anyone (except possibly the star) can change the matter. It is possible to fix the mistake in the editing process, but again, that becomes a discussion of aesthetics between the director and producers. Generally when such transgressions occur, most filmmakers are of the opinion that if the audience notices something like that, the film is in trouble. While this remark is usually accurate, in such cases as this (a gunfight), audiences today are much more discerning and knowledgeable about such things, no doubt having seen too many inaccurate gunfights in previous films![123]

Despite mismatched shots, *Tombstone* is a well-crafted and well-performed film. It captures most of the Earp legend and is careful to show the man as a human being, not entirely as the knight in shining armor of past motion pictures. This Earp has personal conflicts, he carries the guilt of taking a person's life, and he yearns to have a normal life. He is the reluctant hero who, when pressed into action, answers the call (harking back to the old myth) and quickly dispatches the criminal element. However, in doing so, Wyatt must suffer for his actions. He loses one brother, another is crippled, his marriage dissolves, the woman he truly loves is gone, and he had to kill to see justice served. He tells Doc that he doesn't know how to have a normal life. He is lost. It takes Doc's last moments on earth to turn him around and urge him to live life for his best friend. Finding Josephine and reclaiming his love allows our hero to survive and move on with his life. The audience can understand this Wyatt Earp. They understand his feeling of guilt, which he carries because he has killed a man, and that he wants nothing more to do with the law. They share his frustration with Mattie who slips farther and farther away from him into her drug dependency, and his inability to leave her for Josephine. By doing this, the filmmakers have given Wyatt an acceptable way out at the end of the film; if Mattie were not addicted to laudanum, the audience would not readily accept his leaving Mattie for Josephine. With Mattie being helplessly addicted and falling further into the abyss, the audience grants Wyatt their approval to court Josephine, and this ends the film on a positive note. However, the most essential love affair in this film is between Wyatt and Doc. Their strong bond of friendship is what draws the audience, which can readily identify with this powerful bond between two friends. Everyone wishes he or she had a friend like Wyatt or Doc—someone who is there at a moment's notice, willing to stand by your side in times of trouble, and even willing to sacrifice himself for your well-being. This type of friendship is one of the main points in telling a story that draws in an audience and, in *Tombstone*, it succeeds completely.

Tombstone has clearly become classic Western during the past decade of the genre's existence. The film has also sparked a renewed interest in Wyatt Earp and the history of the gunfight. Since the release of the film, numerous historians have uncovered information about Earp and others involved in Tombstone. One important example is the tremendous amount of facts learned regarding many of the members of Earp's vendetta posse. Prior to the release of this film, little, if anything, was known about Dan Tipton, Texas Jack Vermillion, Turkey Creek Jack Johnson and Sherman McMaster. Thanks to this film, new light has been shed on these people, and on others, giving us a better understanding of our past. The film has also spurred growing activity among reenactors of the Old West that not only encompasses all fifty states in America—but also countries such as England, Canada, and Australia, as well as many parts of Europe.

Tombstone gave new life to the Wyatt Earp legend by inspiring a whole new generation. Despite the many problems involved in getting this film completed, it still ranks as one of the top Westerns among many historians and fans, and it created a paradigm that Kevin Costner's film would fail to match.

Tombstone

From Hollywood Pictures. Andrew G. Vajna Presents a Sean Daniel, James Jacks, Cinergi Production. *Released:* December 25, 1993. *In Production:* May 17–August 10, 1993.

Executive Producers: Andrew G. Vajna, Buzz Feitshans. *Producers:* James Jacks, Sean Daniel, Bob Misiorowski. *Associate Producers:* Michael R. Sloan, John Fasano. *Director:* George P. Cosmatos. *Screenplay:* Kevin Jarre. *Cinematographer:* William A. Fraker. *Musical Score:* Bruce Broughton. *Film Editors:* Harvey Rosenstock, Roberto Silvi and Frank J. Aeriest. *Production Design:* Catherine Hardwicke. *Art Direction:* Chris Golan, Kim Dix and Mark Worthington. *Set Decoration:* Gene Serdena. *Costume Designer:* Joseph A. Porro. *Makeup Artists:* David Atherton, Marilyn Carbone, Karen Dahl, Kathleen Hagan, Cheryl Nick, Dennis Liddiard. *Hair Stylists:* Patty Androff, Roberta Gruden, Cheryl Markowitz, Tina Simms, Candy Walken. *Unit Production Manager:* Terry Collis. *Assistant Directors:* Adam C. Taylor, Conte Matal, Vince McEveety. *Second Unit Director:* Terry J. Leonard. *Props:* Michael Courville, Steve Melton, Greg Poulos. *Sound:* Walter B. Martin, Brent Brewington, Paul Coogan. *Special Effects:* Garry Elmendorf, Matt Kutcher, Dale Martin, Kevin C. Parker, Lambert Powell. *Second Unit Special Effects:* Joe Quinlivan, Philip A. Schwartz, Paul Stewart, Blumes Tracy. *Costume Supervisors:* Mary Hobin, Christi K. Work. *Set Costumers:* Layne Brightwell, Gina G. Aller, Maria Cittadini, Rani Cunningham, Lee Foy, Sanja Milkovic Hays, Nisa Kellner, Linda Ketchmark, Raquel Stewart. *Script Super-*

visor: Mary Wright. *Steadicam Operator:* Elizabeth Ziegler. *Steadicam Assistant:* Annie McEveety. *Camera Operators:* David Diano, Kristin Glover. *Best Boy:* Lynn Dodson. *Dolly Grip:* Jerry Madore. *Armorer:* Thell Reed. *Location Manager:* Lauren Ross. *Still Photographer:* John Bramley. *Technical Advisor:* Jeff Morey. *Filming Locations:* Filmed at Old Tucson Studios, Elgin and Mescal, Arizona. *Running Time:* 128 minutes. *Stunt Coordinator:* Terry J. Leonard. *Stunts:* Perry Barndt, Michael Barnett, Tony Lee Boggs, Chris Branham, Hal Burton, Danny Costa, Richard Duran, Kip Farnsworth, Teri Garland, J.B. Getzwiller, John Hock, Cody Lee, Malosi Leonard, Matt Leonard, Clint Lilley, Bobby McLaughlin, Cliff McLaughlin, Ben Miller, Jimmy Ortega, Ben Scott, Russell Solberg, Chris Swinney, Matthew Taylor, R.L. Tolbert, Mark Warrick, Jerry Wills, John Casino. *Buckaroo Coordinator:* Peter Sherayko. *Assistant Buckaroo Coordinator:* Frank J. Trigani. *Buckaroos:* Jemison Beshears, Hunter Brown, Jerry Brown, Reggie Byron, Jerry Crandall, Jeff Dolan, Heath Hammond, John Jackinson, John Peel, Terry Rick, Garrett W. Roberts, Chris Ramirez, Curt Stokes, Jerry Tarantino, Bob Vincent, Charlie Ward, Paul Ward, Tom Ward, Larry Zeug. *Head Wrangler:* Kim Burke. *Wranglers:* George Abos, Robin Baldwin, Joseph Brown, Brad Wm. Clark, Holly Edwards, John Fearn Jr., Gary Gang, Joseph Getzweiler, William Getzweiler, Ron Grayes, J.T. Hall, Clint James, J. Chris Knagge, Robin C. Larson, Ron Mitchell, Harold Clay Scott, Brenda Sue Washington, Byron Wilkerson, Ivan Red Wolverton, Kip Wolverton, Wendy Wolverton. *Narrator:* Robert Mitchum. *Cut from final print:* Forrie J. Smith (*Pony Deal*), Hugh O'Brian (*Wagonmaster*).

Cast: Kurt Russell (*Wyatt Earp*), Val Kilmer (*Doc Holliday*), Sam Elliott (*Virgil Earp*), Dana Delany (*Josie Marcus*), Bill Paxton (*Morgan Earp*), Powers Boothe (*Curly Bill*), Stephen Lang (*Ike Clanton*), Michael Biehn (*Johnny Ringo*), Charlton Heston (*Henry Hooker*), Jason Priestley (*Deputy Billy Breckinridge*), Joanna Pacula (*Big Nose Kate Elder*), Harry Carey, Jr. (*Marshal Fred White*), Buck Taylor (*Turkey Creek Jack Johnson*), Peter Sherayko (*Texas Jack Vermillion*), Michael Rooker (*Sherman McMasters*), Billy Bob Thornton (*Johnny Tyler*), Jon Tenney (*Johnny Behan*), Terry O'Quinn (*John Clum*), Robert Burke (*Frank McLaury*), John Philbin (*Tom McLaury*), Thomas Haden Church (*Billy Clanton*), Pedro Armendáriz Jr. (*Priest*), Gary Clarke (*U.S. Marshal Crawley Dake*), Frank Stallone (*Ed Bailey*), Don Collier (*High roller in Oriental Saloon*), Tomas Arana (*Frank Stillwell*), Pat Brady (*Milt Joyce*), Paul Ben-Victor (*Florentino*), John Philbin (*Tom McLaury*), Robert John Burke (*Frank McLaury*), Billy Zane (*Mr. Fabian*), Sal Cardile (*Man at Wyatt's Faro table*), Christopher Mitchum (*One of Hooker's Ranch hands*), Dana Wheeler-Nicholson (*Mattie Earp*), Paula Malcomson (*Allie Earp*), Lisa Collins (*Louisa Earp*), Wyatt Earp (*Billy Claiborne*), John Corbett (*Barnes*), W.R. Bo Gray (*Wes Fuller*), Charles Schneider (*Prof. Gillman*), Billy Joe Patton (*Deputy*), Bobby Joe McFadden (*Gambler #1*), Michael N. Garcia (*Rurale Captain/Groom*), Michelle Beauchamp (*Mexican bride*), Stephen C. Foster (*Hank Swilling*), Grant James (*Dr. Goodfellow*), Cecil Hoffmann (*Town resident*), Charlie Ward (*Cowboy #1*), Clark A. Ray (*Cowboy #2*), Sandy Gibbons (*Father Feeney*), Evan Osborne (*Piano player*), Shane McCabe (*Bird Cage Theatre audience member*), Grant Wheeler (*Drunk*), Jim Dunham (*Miner*), Jim Flowers (*Blackjack dealer*), J. Nathan Simmons, Sam Dolan (*Townsmen*), Michael Wise (*Emigrant*).

10

Wyatt Earp (1994)

"Do you believe in friendship, Wyatt Earp?"

In the motion picture industry, studios are always looking for ways to top their rivals in box office profits. Given this predilection, it is not surprising when two competing studios announce projects based on the same material. This has happened often. In the mid-1960s, two different studios released films about actress Jean Harlow. One production company even resorted to using live cameras and filming in black-and-white, then transferring everything to a film print, in order to be the first released.[1] When Irwin Allen learned that Warner Bros. was planning to make a film about a fire in a high-rise building at the same time that he was planning one for 20th Century-Fox, the producer, in his typical showmanship style, did the unthinkable: he was able to get the studios to combine their two films into one, *The Towering Inferno* (1974). The studios shared in the costs and profits, thereby avoiding any competition.[2] Two years later, both Universal and Paramount Studios announced they would release their own versions of *King Kong*. Universal ultimately backed out, leaving the large ape to Paramount.[3] In the late 1990s, both Universal and 20th Century-Fox released films centering on erupting volcanoes, one in Los Angeles and the other in Washington.

As these examples illustrate, studios will occasionally go toe-to-toe on competing projects, typically with mixed results. "The Dueling Earps" is what industry insiders called *Tombstone* and Kevin Costner's project. At the time, most people were betting on Costner's production to be the winner in the race, given his box office clout. But, as a magician once said, nothing is as it seems.

Screenwriter Dan Gordon had pitched the idea of a feature film about Wyatt Earp to Kevin Costner. Gordon recalled that Costner said, "God, there is so much story here. It's much more than just a feature."

> He suggested we take it in to CBS and pitch it as a mini[series]. And we did. I wound up doing a six-hour version of it [the script], a three-part miniseries.... When we worked together, Kevin was great. He kept saying, "Give me more, give me more." Kevin was wonderful to work with. I was hoping Kevin would direct it. I think part of the time he had his director's hat on, and it was really interesting to watch him begin to visualize the movie that never got shot. We worked together for a period of, I think, three years [on the script].... We would do a certain amount, and then he'd go off and do a movie.... When he was doing *Robin Hood*, he didn't want to think about the Earps. He didn't want to mix that at all. So we had to wait until he was finished shooting and then we'd work.... When he was in between pictures, we'd work well together.[4]

Although the plan with CBS eventually fell through, Costner seized upon the idea of making it as a miniseries for pay-per-view cable television. Producing a miniseries of this scale for pay television was a massive undertaking, and a huge financial gamble. Costner was used to gambling, though; many people did not expect his *Dances With Wolves* (1990) to be as successful as it was, both critically and financially. Plans for the miniseries idea were progressing when Universal announced it would produce Kevin Jarre's version of *Tombstone*.

Exactly when the idea of switching from a miniseries to a feature film actually happened is vague, and much depends on what version one chooses to believe. Jarre claimed that he felt Costner made the decision to switch to a feature film after he read his (Jarre's) script, which Costner denies.[5] Costner claimed in a *Premiere* magazine interview in July 1994 that he personally went to Universal and asked them to release the Jarre version into turnaround and let another studio pick up the project, which is what happened. (*Tombstone* producer James Jacks said that Universal canceled the project when Costner announced he would make a feature film version of Earp's life, but they would not release the project to be shopped around.) Dan Gordon recalled that he was very concerned about two films being made on Wyatt Earp, but Costner wasn't. "I thought that, quite frankly, whoever got out first had a huge advantage. But Kevin had faith that he had an audience and the audience would come to see both pictures and make a judgment," Gordon noted.[6] Costner later said that allowing both films to proceed was "the right thing to do—but I knew that it would certainly muddy the waters."[7]

The movie opens inside the Oriental Saloon, where Wyatt sits at a table drinking a cup of coffee. Morgan and Virgil Earp walk in, saying that the Clantons and the McLaurys, carrying guns, are in the empty lot near the O.K. Corral. Wyatt stands, holsters his gun, and calmly says, "Let's go." The three men walk outside. The scene dissolves to a vast cornfield in 1865, where a young Wyatt bids goodbye to his younger brothers. Making his way out of the cornfield, he is confronted by his father, Nicholas; the boy admits that he was running off to join the Union army. When Wyatt's two older brothers, Virgil and James, come home from the war, Nicholas announces that the family will head to California to start a new life.

On the cross-country wagon trip, Wyatt quickly grows fond of the vast openness of the plains. Seven years later, Wyatt works in Wyoming, driving freight wagons, before moving to Lamar, Missouri, where he courts Urilla Sutherland. The two marry and begin a life together, which ends tragically with her death from typhoid fever. Grief-stricken, Wyatt leaves Lamar and goes on a drunken binge, eventually robbing a man of his money and horse. He is arrested and his father bails him out, telling him to ride away. After a stint as a buffalo hunter, Wyatt drifts to Wichita, working in a saloon dealing faro games. After he subdues a drunken cowboy, the town offers him a job as deputy marshal. Marshal Larry Deger of Dodge City asks Wyatt to help him in the new cowtown, where both Virgil and Morgan Earp join up as deputy marshals. Wyatt's tactic of buffaloing drunken cowboys soon draws complaints from various city officials and he is fired. Tracking a train robber to Fort Griffin, Texas, Wyatt meets Doc Holliday.

Tired of working for others, Wyatt, his brothers, and their wives travel to Tombstone with the intention of opening a business. Instead, they serve as law officers. Wyatt's relationship with Mattie begins to deteriorate soon after he meets Josephine Marcus, the former lover of Sheriff John Behan. The Earps and Doc Holliday develop conflicts with the Clantons, McLaurys, and others, which eventually lead to a deadly gunfight. The Earps and Holliday are acquitted of murder charges, but shortly after that, Morgan is murdered and Virgil severely wounded. In Tucson, Wyatt kills Frank Stilwell, then goes on to track down the other men responsible for killing his brother. Eight years later, Wyatt and Josephine are on a ship heading to the Alaskan gold rush when a boy meets them and relates a story about his uncle, whom Wyatt once saved from a lynch mob in Tombstone. After the boy leaves, Wyatt tells Josephine that some people said it didn't happen that way. "Never mind, Wyatt," Josephine says. "It happened that way."

Director-writer Lawrence Kasdan, who had directed Costner in *Silverado*, discussed the Earp project with the actor when the two men made a brief trip to Deadwood, South Dakota, where Costner owns land and a restaurant-casino. Reportedly, Kasdan approached Costner a few days after returning from their trip and told the actor he wanted to rewrite the script and direct the Wyatt Earp project, but only as a feature film. Kasdan, who claimed he did not like Gordon's script, would later state, "I used some elements from that other script, but only the things I really loved, and there weren't that many."[8] This comment is very disingenuous, especially when one compares the two scripts. It is readily apparent that Kasdan has taken a good deal of material from Gordon's miniseries volume (including exact dialogue) and placed it into his own draft. No one can explain why Kasdan would make such comments, although one could theorize that Kasdan, known for taking sole writing credit for such screenplays as *Raiders of the Lost Ark*, *Body Heat*, *The Bodyguard*, and *Continental Divide*, may have wanted to maintain that image.

With Kasdan coming on board, Dan Gordon quickly found himself locked out of the project. "[Costner] certainly had a relationship with him, but I think Kasdan betrayed him. This was Kevin's project, he had developed it, he should have respected what Kevin did and respected the work that was there. But he didn't. He just let his ego get out of hand and [he] had to put his fingerprints on it and [he] dicked up a good movie," Gordon recalled. When the film was released, Gordon was honest with the press about distancing himself from Kasdan's version, with which he was hardly enamored; yet tried to be somewhat diplomatic. In an interview with this author, Gordon was more blunt about the deficiencies in Kasdan's script:

Kevin Costner as Wyatt.

> It is a piece of shit. They just ruined it [Gordon's original script]. It was boring. He cut out the bad guys. How do you have a Western without villains? Mike Gray is not in the piece. That was my biggest piece of contribution to the whole Earp lore, was sticking in the character of Mike Gray, which hasn't been in any of the other movies. How do you do the story of the Earps

and not have Old Man Clanton in the movie? You never knew what the hell was going on or why there was a rift between these guys or why there was this enmity between them. They were just a bunch of grubby guys going, "Arrugh, kill the Earps!"

In that movie you have that dumb-ass coda in Alaska.... standing on the bridge, reminiscing about some story that has no connection to anything. Then his wife says that's sort of the way it was, even if it wasn't. I didn't understand the ending. I didn't know what the movie was about. I thought it sucked.... The thing that was upsetting to me, outside of the usual writer's lament of [his script] being rewritten, was no one's ever done the real story of what was going on there [in Tombstone]. This was as close as anybody had ever gotten, as far as I know [to the real story], as opposed to the usual portrait of the Clantons and McLaurys as sort of grubby rustlers, or sort of a cow conflict or something like that. [In reality], this was a very sophisticated crime family. This was a land grab worth $20 million in 1882 dollars.... Kevin's thrust through this whole thing, his whole deal, was, "Let's do the Western as *The Godfather*." That's what we did, and that's what Kasdan dicked up.[9]

With Gordon no longer associated with the project ("I was banned from the set," he stated), Costner and Kasdan went to work on fine-tuning the script, often arguing over scenes Costner wanted to include from the miniseries version and that Kasdan did not. One specific scene involved Johnny Behan showing a picture of a naked Josephine to some men in the Oriental Saloon. In Gordon's script, Wyatt is drinking a beer while sitting next to a faro dealer watching a game in progress. Wyatt can easily overhear Behan say how he got Josephine to pose in the nude. Wyatt is both jealous and curious to see the picture the men are ogling. He finally gets up and goes over to Behan, who turns to him and taunts him, asking if he wants to see a picture of a "Jew girl naked.... They're somethin,' I'll tell ya." Earp, looking at the picture, calls Behan a fool, and the sheriff further taunts Wyatt with the picture, adding, "Take a good look. I can see you're droolin' for it." Wyatt asks what she sees in him, to which Behan quickly replies, "You want me to describe it for ya? Or shall I tell ya what she does with it...." As the men laugh, Wyatt walks out of the saloon.[10] Kasdan felt the scene "gave me the creeps. It was crass." However, Costner wanted this sequence included, so he rewrote it.[11] In Kasdan's script, Behan is showing the photo to several men as he talks about how he got Josephine to pose for the picture. He says she was afraid that others would see the photograph, but he assured her that would never happen (this is also stated in Gordon's script). Wyatt walks in, looking for his brother James, when one of the men tells Wyatt he has to see this picture. Behan taunts Earp, saying that he is much too upstanding, righteous and married to see a picture of a naked Josephine. Wyatt calls him a fool, and Behan says maybe he is, but he is the one climbing into bed every night with her. As Wyatt leaves, one man asks Behan what she is doing with him. The sheriff replies, "Anything I can think of. How much detail do you want?" Ultimately there is little difference between the scenes, with only minor changes to the dialogue.

With the script problems finally worked out, pre-production work began, including casting. Dennis Quiad was cast as Doc Holliday, and he brought a strong touch of realism to his role. The actor asked Kasdan if he wanted him to lose weight and the director thought that would be a great idea. He went on a strict diet, losing more than forty pounds. In doing so, Quaid, who says he works on a character "from the outside in," gives his Holliday the emaciated look of someone suffering from tuberculosis. Gene Hackman was cast as Wyatt's father, Nicholas Earp. Mary Steenburgen was signed to play Doc Holliday's paramour, but she was replaced by Isabella Rossellini. Joanna Going and Mare Winningham would play Josephine and Mattie Earp, respectively. Jeff Fahey and Lewis Smith were set for the roles of Ike Clanton and Curly Bill, while Mark Harmon would play John Behan. David

Andrews, Michael Madsen and Linden Ashby respectively would play James, Virgil, and Morgan Earp.

In choosing locations for a film of this scope, the filmmakers looked at a variety of areas. The producers were concerned that they would have to travel to many states to capture the regions featured in the script. Ultimately, Kasdan chose to return to New Mexico, where he had filmed *Silverado*. He felt the terrain offered a variety of choices and could easily portray the Earp family farm in Illinois as well as Dodge City, Wichita, and Tombstone. The film had a 113-day shooting schedule, starting in July 1993, with a budget in the vicinity of $55.9 million. One of the biggest challenges for the filmmakers was building the towns of Dodge City and Tombstone, which are featured heavily in the film. Using fourteen acres outside Santa Fe, production designer Ida Random chose to use the same location and set for both Tombstone and Dodge City with aesthetic alterations. Building the sets for the Tombstone sequences first, Random kept many of the buildings as single stories with high porches. She also used burnish colors for the buildings of Tombstone, while the sets for Dodge City were painted in cooler colors such as blue and green because much of the set was shot at night. Once the Tombstone sequences were completed, construction workers changed the set into one for Dodge City by eliminating the high porches, adding second stories, and even reshaping the streets to give the impression of a different town. Using the same sets for two different towns, consideration had to be given to camera placement and angles when filming each one. Random noted that in the Dodge City sequences, we never see the horizon, as we do during the Tombstone scenes.[12]

As the sets were being readied, the wardrobe department went to work assembling costumes not only for the 120 speaking parts but also for as many as 1,500 extras. More than 20,000 pieces of wardrobe were used for the actors and extras. By the time the Dodge City sequences were ready to be shot, much of the clothing for the extras were in desperate need of repair because they had been used so much in other scenes. Part of the costume wear problem was that most of the wardrobe was rented from various costume houses, and it was quite old. The constant use over the years had begun to take its toll on the material. The prop department found themselves with similar problems. Many of the props for the saloons were simply worn out, and new bottles, glasses, and even poker chips and playing cards had to be completely recreated.

Another department that had to contend with the historical sweep of the film was makeup. Oscar-nominated Michael Mills landed the job, partially, he felt, because his college minor was in U.S. History, with an emphasis on the Western Expansion. "I knew the material, historically, inside and out. I think I have read virtually everything that has been written journal-wise, and things that were written in the period and also the histories that have been written about the subject. So I think that impressed them. Not only was I a character makeup artist and lab technician, but [I was] also well versed in the material without even reading the script," Mills recalled.[13] After interviewing with Kasdan, he was offered the job of running the makeup department and proceeded to prepare for the long shoot.

Part of the makeup artist's job for this picture was to carry several characters over a period of years, often aging them from young adult to middle age. Most of this was done by using "facial lifts." These lifts were an adhesive tab that pulls back the skin, giving a taut, younger look to the face, and covered over with either facial hair or a wig. Another job was preparing numerous moustaches, sideburns, and beards for the extras as well as the actors. Given the limited budget, many facial hair pieces were hand laid on the performer's face instead of using what are called "lace pieces."[14] Other lace pieces, such as the moustaches

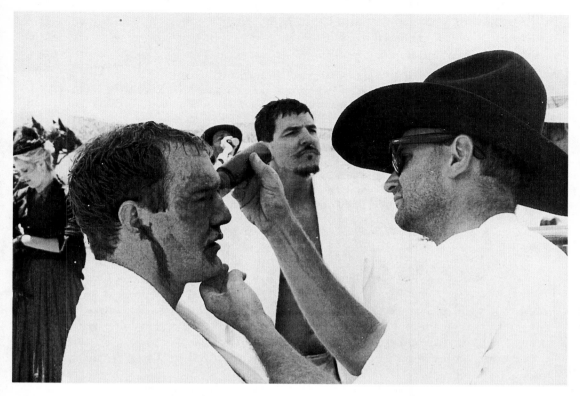

Makeup artist Michael Mills (right) applies "blood" to the face of Michael McGrady (playing John Shanssey) during the boxing match sequence (courtesy of Gerald Quist).

for the Earp brothers, had been designed a specific way, as large handlebars, based on historical photographs. However, once on location, Mills learned from Costner's makeup artist, Frank Perez, that Kevin did not want to wear a large mustache. "The reason they [handlebar mustaches] are not in the movie was that Kevin didn't like the look of them. He felt that it didn't matter that much to be historically accurate with the hair pieces. So he had his makeup artist cut his mustache back.... Morgan and Virgil Earp's mustaches had to be cut back to match Kevin's. So my hand was forced. Larry [Kasdan] wasn't going to fight that fight. It wasn't that important to him. I'm sure he had bigger things on his mind," Mills said.[15]

Another thing that changed from the initial discussions was the look of the McLaurys and Clantons. Originally they were going to be well-dressed, and their facial hair would always be coiffed and clean, but things changed once on location. "Originally, Mike and I had envisioned the McLaurys and Clantons as more polished and groomed. They had money to spend, so they would spiff themselves up. They [the producers] took, in my opinion, totally the wrong approach. I think it really hurt the film visually. All the bad guys looked the same and you couldn't tell who was or wasn't a bad guy. They were saying they wanted the guys dirtier than we had made them up," remembered makeup artist Gerald Quist.[16]

The producers were also going for a realistic look when it came to gunshots on the body. "In the original script, there was quite a lot of violence that they were going to show. It was sort of a *Saving Private Ryan* approach to the Old West. It was going to be quite bloody and very graphic, and it was going to need a lot of special makeup work on top of the day-to-day stuff with facial hair," recalled Quist. Ultimately, as production plodded along, the need for graphic effects began to fall by the wayside. Quist remembers one incident that was a harbinger of the elimination of the violent aspects:

> When we were preparing the squib gag for the Indian Charlie effect [being shot in the forehead], we had shown Larry a test of it on a plaster cast of the actor's face and glued a foam rubber piece on the forehead, colored it, wired it up and put a wig around it, and set off the squib. Larry thought it was way too bloody, and scrapped the effect.
>   We had a sequence where a guy was literally cut in two by a shotgun blast. We had gone so far as to budget it and really reason out how we'd achieve this. Then we started getting the word that they really weren't going to need this, and [we] started toning it [the violence] down. Originally, we had talks that the gunfight sequence was going to be really bloody. The reason they toned it down was aesthetics. I think Larry was afraid of alienating people. He was going for a general, broad audience, and he didn't want to creep them out with all the bloodshed.[17]

As production began, it became readily apparent that the company was split into two camps: those who had worked previously with Kasdan or were hired by him, and those who had worked with Kevin Costner. An unspoken caste line began to emerge within the first few weeks of filming. One crew member noted that the quickest way to get fired from the picture was to say something negative about the film and have word get back to Costner. Most crew members learned to say little that might place their jobs in jeopardy, which gave the production an atmosphere of walking on eggshells. "We were treated fine, but you just didn't feel like part of either camp," Quist said.

Production began on July 19, filming the sequence in which Wyatt, driving a freight wagon, fights off robbers. The locations for this sequence, as well as many others in the film,

First day of filming *Wyatt Earp* at the Cook Ranch. The stuntmen, who will ride after the freight wagon driven by Costner's double, prepare for a shot (courtesy of Gerald Quist).

The freight wagon in this sequence had to be heavily weighted to keep it from tipping over. Final adjustments are being made before filming begins (courtesy of Gerald Quist).

were various ranches outside the Santa Fe area. These ranches provided the filmmakers the vast open space needed for numerous scenes as well as ample land to build the various sets. The freight wagon sequence was one of the most dangerous scenes in the film, offering plenty of things that could go wrong—driving a weighted wagon with six horses at a full run along a narrow road. Both the stunt coordinator, Norman Howell, and head wrangler, Rusty Hendrickson, spent three weeks preparing for this scene. The wagon was properly weighted down to avoid flipping over, and the road was graded to provide traction. There were two sets of horse teams; one was dubbed "runners," and the other was called "quiet." The runners would be used for the shots in which the wagon was moving along at a full gallop, while the quiet team would be used for any dialogue sequences with the actors.[18] It took three days to film the sequence before moving on to the scene in which Wyatt referees a prize fight. The next two days, July 23 and 24, involved scenes inside the Lucky Saloon, where Wyatt is first exposed to the game of faro and has a run-in with a gambler, Ross, over the prize fight. The company spent July 26 and 27 filming Wyatt driving the wagon into the railroad tent town, a scene that runs less than five minutes on screen. The last few days of the month of July were spent shooting all of the scenes that took place inside Wyatt and Urilla's house (including the scenes of the doctor examining her and of her death). These were shot at Garston Studios in Santa Fe.

The company moved to the town of Las Vegas, New Mexico, for two days (August 3 and 4) to film the exteriors of Urilla's parents' house. The following day, the company moved

Kevin Costner's makeup artist, Frank Perez, puts final touches on Norman Howell, Cost-ner's stunt double and the film's stunt coordinator (courtesy of Gerald Quist).

to Eaves Ranch, where they would film a variety of sequences, including Wyatt selling his stolen horse, his arrival in Fort Griffin, Texas, and his receipt of the telegram regarding Ed Masterson's death. The company spent the next two evenings at the ranch filming Wyatt stealing a man's horse and having his father bail him out of jail. The wagon train sequence, which takes place in the early part of the film, was filmed at various locations on the Ghost Ranch from August 9 through 13, while scenes of Wyatt and Urilla's wedding, as well as her funeral, were filmed at Las Golondrinas on August 17. The corn field for the opening sequence, in which Wyatt attempts to run off and join the Union Army, was filmed the following day at the ranch of New Mexico Governor Bruce King.

On August 22, the company left Santa Fe for Antonio, Colorado, where they would use the Cumbres and Toltec Scenic Railroad for railroad sequences.[19] The following day, they filmed the scene in which Wyatt has Morgan's body placed on the train and goes to Tucson with Virgil, Doc, and other posse members. On August 24, the company moved to Chama, New Mexico. The railroad's train station would stand-in for Tucson and provide the setting for the killing of Frank Stilwell. The filming of this sequence would take three nights, and they were hardly what one could call balmy summer evenings. "The Chama sequence was tough, as it was raining cats and dogs. It was all night shots and it was *cold*! I remember our first night shooting in Chama became a big issue because we didn't get our first shot until after dinner, like two in the morning. It was such an elaborate lighting set-up because [cinematographer] Owen Roizman lit everything so you wouldn't see the sheets of rain coming down," recalled Gerald Quist.[20]

Stunt coordinator Norman Howell, doubling for Costner, has wrapped his arms for added safety; they are being sprayed brown to resemble the brown gloves Costner wears in the scene (courtesy of Gerald Quist).

The company completed filming in Chama on August 27, whereupon they returned to Santa Fe. The following day, they began filming the shootout in which Wyatt kills Curly Bill at a location called Plaza Blanco. The company would be at this location for the next five days, shooting various stunts, including a high fall off a cliff by stunt coordinator Norman Howell.

Upon completing these sequences, they filmed the scenes of Wyatt and the Masterson brothers hunting buffalo. Although a large herd of real buffalo was photographed for certain scenes, when it came time to show Wyatt and the Masterson brothers killing them, Hollywood magic took over—sort of. "The buffaloes were mechanical. They were fake, and they were supposed to fall over after being shot.... It reminded me of the shark in *Jaws* that didn't quite work. They wouldn't fall over the way they wanted them to. [They] would fall half-way and stop. One got shot and did a back flip! We also had a fake buffalo that the actors would skin and we put all the blood over the fake body," said Gerald Quist.[21]

On September 11, the first scenes on the Tombstone set were shot at the Cook Ranch, involving the Earp brothers discussing their finances. From September 12 through 17, the company filmed a variety of scenes, including Josephine's arrival in Tombstone, her meeting Wyatt on the street, and Curly Bill being thrown out of the jail, with Ike Clanton making threats against the Earps.

On September 18 filming began on scenes leading up to the gunfight, including Virgil leaving his house and the brothers walking out of the Oriental Saloon. The following two days were spent shooting the Earps and Holliday walking to the empty lot, as well as Behan warning them off. September 21 through 25 were devoted to filming the gunfight, which ran a mere forty-seven seconds on film. Prior to filming this sequence, the actors, as well as members of the prop and special effects departments, would go to the set of the empty lot and practice firing the guns with blank rounds. Three cameras were used to film the "master shot" (a wide shot of the entire scene) of the gunfight.

Makeup artist Michael Mills recalled a special moment as he watched the gunfight being filmed.

> I've had a couple of instances where you're watching a scene, and the scene plays out so perfectly that it takes you there. It's a really odd feeling, but it's happened to me a couple of times in my career. And when that happens, to me as a screen technician, you know you're working on something special. I watched the master [shot] from behind the [second] camera that particular day when they shot the master, and it was unbelievable how well choreographed [it was] and everything had come off. It worked.... And it took me there. I thought I had just seen the O.K. Corral. It was that dramatic. It was that dynamic of an experience. And I have read about it, I've seen the maps that have been drawn out about it that eyewitnesses have seen. I've seen all the recreations on TV and heard all the talk about the details and the articles that were written, and this was it. It couldn't have been done any better, I didn't think. And if I were a filmmaker, that's what I would have put in the movie. I would have taken the B [second] camera footage and just blown off everything else and that's what you would have seen. Because it was like you were across the street looking in that alley watching this gunfight unfold. It was unbelievably real. It gave me goosebumps to see it.[22]

Gerald Quist recalled that when they prepared the blood squib to go off on the forehead of actor Rex Linn (playing Frank McLaury), they advised the director that in order for it to work, it should be treated like a magic act. "Like any magic trick, it is going to be very effective, but it has to be staged right. You have very little leeway [to photograph it right]. It has to be shot straight on.... So we go off and put the forehead piece on, which included fake eyebrows, running the wire charge for the squib behind his head. Lots of work. We take him out to the set and now they're fighting the light [losing the sunlight]. They [were] rushing to get it done before they lost the light. Unfortunately, Rex moved around and it [the forehead piece] looked like a goose egg! Luckily, when you see it on film, it happens so fast [the blood squib going off] that you can't see it."[23]

The first six nights of October were spent filming Morgan's death scene and Virgil's ambush. The following week found the company filming the scenes in which Wyatt and Doc are arrested after the gunfight (this was cut from the final print), Wyatt's posse stands off Behan and rides out of Tombstone, and Behan shows off Josephine's picture in the saloon. The third week of October involved scenes inside the Oriental Saloon, including Wyatt and Behan's face-off and Doc challenging a drunken Ike Clanton. The last week of October was devoted to shooting courtroom sequences at Garson Studios, before moving back to Eaves Ranch to film scenes that take place in Wichita and Fort Griffin, Texas, where Wyatt first meets Doc Holliday.

On November 13 the company finished filming scenes at Eaves Ranch and returned to Cook Ranch, with the town set now dressed as Dodge City. The sequence featuring the Gilbert and Sullivan number (performed by members of the Albuquerque Civic Light Opera Association) in the Comique Theatre set began filming on November 16. (This is where Wyatt—and the audience—sees Josephine for the first time.) By now, finding enough extras for the production was becoming harder as the company had switched to night filming, which meant working from 6 P.M. to at least 6 A.M. Since most of the extras working on this film had day jobs and could only take a few days off to be in the picture, it became increasingly difficult to fill the sets with the necessary people. Many crew members were pressed into service, including the cinematographer, Costner's hair stylist, and even makeup artist Gerald Quist.

> I got the job as the bartender in the film because the locals were tired of working for us. That last half of the film was shot almost exclusively at night and the local people didn't want to come out and work at night. Colleen Atwood, the costume designer on the show, said, "Why don't you be the bartender?" It didn't occur to me that I would be working five nights in a row, plus doing makeup for the actors. She said, "Come over to the wardrobe department and we'll get you hooked up." They didn't have any pants in my size and they built me a pair of pants in twenty minutes. Suspenders, buttons, and everything![24]

The shooting schedule for the film was nothing short of grueling for the cast and especially the crew members. They worked six days a week, often averaging 110 hours a week, with one day off, in all sorts of weather conditions—heat, rain, and snow. Many crew members were away from their families even over Thanksgiving. The company was filming the evening before Thanksgiving and went well into the early morning hours of Thursday, November 25. On Friday, November 26, everyone was back to work at 11 A.M.

The making of the movie progressed slowly over the months, the main holdup being numerous discussions between Kasdan and Costner about the script or how to shoot a specific scene. It was becoming obvious to those on the set (as well as industry insiders) that there was an ongoing clash of wills, with two men trying to guide the film in two very different directions. Wags began referring to the production as "Kevingate," a reference to the disastrous Heaven's Gate (1980).[25] Having two people who insist on putting their own unique creative stamp on a production can do more to damage to a film than anything. "I think that divisiveness affected the outcome of the film. Larry Kasdan had his opinions and Kevin had his and they didn't always see eye-to-eye," said Gerald Quist.[26] Ultimately, there must be only one director on a movie set, just as there is only one captain on a ship. It is that one person who must guide the film and have final say on things. Anything less not only hurts the outcome of the film but can also destroy the morale of the cast and crew.

Although most people kept their opinions to themselves or confided only in a small group of friends, actor Michael Masden, who played Virgil, bluntly states on his website that the film was "a tremendous waste of my time." There were many days that the cast and crew would come in at 7 A.M., get into makeup and wardrobe, and just sit around, sometimes until after lunch, before even rehearsing a scene. Michael Mills agrees: "There was a lot of people's time wasted, which was really unfortunate and, ultimately, it hurt the film. Anybody that was on the crew could see it. You know, you're on a crew and you're on a show for six or seven months out in the middle of nowhere, separated from your family; you have nothing else to focus on except for what's going on in front of you. It's so easy to see what's happening. I think it was a huge disappointment to Larry Kasdan. On one particular day, there was some talk about the way the film was going, and Michael Madsen was pretty vocal about the situation he found himself in.... Kevin made a comment about the way careers go and being number one on the call sheet [a position usually reserved for the star of the film], being a producer, being a director—Kevin had won a couple of Oscars— basically he was telling Madsen to shut up. In full character, Dennis Quaid walked by as Doc Holliday and said, 'Well, it's really interesting to see the grandiose ego get in the way of making a good movie.' Kevin didn't say anything, not a word. Of course, Dennis walked off as Doc Holliday, with his cane."[27]

CONGRATULATIONS!

Today is "<u>half-way day!</u>"

*So far, you made it through
rain and hail,
heat and cold,
mosquitos and flys,
early days and late nights,
<u>and</u>
corny greetings at the gate...*

In honor of half-way day, your pals in the Location Department invite you to come down to Tommy's (a.k.a. "Paul's Place") tonight for a half-priced celebration toast. Just present this coupon to the barkeep for half-off your favorite adult beverage. Don't be half-way about it! Stop bye, and raise your glass to a great crew, a great cast and <u>truly great picture</u>.

For updates, keep tuned to KERP, 87.9 on your FM dial

WYATT EARP CELEBRATES "HALF-WAY DAY"

Tommy's, 208 Galisteo Street, Santa Fe, New Mexico   505/989-4407

"rain, wind, heat, bugs, dust and port-a-johns..."

To break up the monotony of sitting around, the crew started a baseball league they called the Dust Bowl. Mills remembers that there was enough downtime that "we had time to get full games in.... That was something to blow off steam during the working day."[28]

The show did have its lighter moments, such as when Michael Madsen had a birthday party, complete with a band, and invited the entire cast and crew. "It was catered, it was wonderful. It was one of those great things where an actor will spend $30,000, $40,000 just [to] say it's my birthday, everybody come over to my house, and just show up and [have] as much as you want, whatever you want all night long. That was fun. It didn't happen a lot but that was fun," remembered Mills. Another cast member who helped to make things tolerable for the crew was Dennis Quaid. Michael Mills recalled Quaid's generosity toward him in late October.

> Dennis, I thought, really went out of his way to try to help the average working man. Halloween is a big thing for my kids, it's about the biggest holiday. My little boy loves makeup, and he loves being made up, and I try to be home every Halloween. You know Dennis knew that and he flew me back [in his plane] so I could wake up in my house on Halloween and be there to make my son up and go out trick-or-treating.[29]

The company finished filming at Cook Ranch on December 1 and moved on to Garson Studios to complete interior scenes for the next seven days. Filming in Santa Fe wrapped on December 10, and the company left the next day for Port Angeles, Washington. Many of the crew left the film after finishing in Santa Fe, while a smaller scale crew traveled to Washington, where they would film the scenes aboard a steamer heading for the Alaskan gold fields. They began filming on Sunday, December 12, and finished three days later. *Wyatt Earp* completed production eight days over schedule.

Just after production was completed, *Tombstone* was released. During the filming of *Wyatt Earp*, there were discussions (mainly by the producers) about *Tombstone*. The conversations focused on how the film was being made cheaply, how it also had numerous problems and had been rushed into production once they had learned of Kasdan's project.[30] When *Tombstone* proved to be a hit at the box office, it certainly must have caused the producers of *Wyatt Earp* some concern about their project. Meanwhile, Warner Bros. was preparing to make the film one of its major summer releases of 1994.

Released on June 24, 1994, *Wyatt Earp* received uniformly negative reviews. *Time*, which headlined its review "Shoot-Out at the ZZ Corral," called the film a "solemn biopic, grinding relentlessly, without selectivity or point of view.... the exact nature of the quarrel between the Earps and Ike Clanton's crowd is never satisfactorily explained. Like almost everything else in this fragmented and ambiguous movie, it just sort of happens.... Since Earp's life uninstructively limped along after that event, so must the movie, further abusing our overtaxed patience and undertaxed intelligence."[31] The *Los Angeles Times* noted, "Impressive but uninviting, *Wyatt Earp* is easier to admire from a distance than pull up a chair and enjoy close-up. A self-conscious attempt at epic filmmaking that feels orchestrated as much as directed, it has noticeable virtues but chooses not to wear them lightly.... Not exactly a failure, *Wyatt Earp* is more accurately described as simply not the picture it wants so hard to be."[32]

Newsweek noted, "[G]orgeously shot by Owen Roizman, designed with all the detail a $60 million budget can buy and pumped up with an overbearing James Newton Howard

Opposite: **The production company, as a way of thanking the cast and crew for their hard work, threw a "half-way" celebration at the hotel's bar (courtesy of Gerald Quist).**

score, *Wyatt Earp* is big, solemn—and barely alive.... For a movie so sure of its importance, it seems oddly uncertain of what it wants to say.... We feel nothing but impatience, because in three hours, Kasdan hasn't found the time to individualize the villains. What kind of a Western has anonymous bad guys? This is neither classic nor revisionist. It's just bad story-telling."[33] *Variety* commented, "If you're going to ask an audience to sit through a three-hour, nine-minute rendition of a story that has been told many times before, it would help to have a strong point of view on your material and an urgent reason to relate it. Such is not sufficiently the case with *Wyatt Earp*, a stately, handsome, grandiose gentleman's Western that evenhandedly but too doggedly tries to tell more about the famous Tombstone lawman than has ever been put onscreen.... [U]ndue length poses a drawback, as do subject's familiarity and lack of sustained excitement, resulting in brawny but less than brilliant B.O. [box office] prospects.... [C]ontemporary viewers will draw primary comparison to the messy but brassily entertaining *Tombstone*, which came out, and performed surprisingly well, just six months ago."[34]

The studio's hope for a major summer hit began to fade quickly. In its first week of release, *Wyatt Earp* grossed a mere $7.4 million, coming in fourth behind *The Lion King*, *Speed*, and *Wolf*. With its lengthy running time and negative reviews, the film was fighting an uphill battle. It didn't help matters when the movie was compared to the problem-plagued, but successful, *Tombstone*. In fact, Disney Studios made sure viewers would compare their film to the Costner epic, by releasing *Tombstone* on video the same week *Wyatt Earp* premiered. "When you have a $65-million picture starring Kevin Costner that doesn't open to $10 million in the summertime, you have problems," stated a studio marketing executive.[35] Warner Bros. executives tried to put a positive spin on things, but the writing was on the wall: the film was quickly sinking at the box office. By mid-September, the movie had grossed $15 million—the amount the studio reportedly spent to promote the film.[36] "I remember hearing a lot of people on the set saying, 'We're making a classic. It's going to last forever.' They forgot to make a good movie," commented Gerald Quist.[37]

Wyatt Earp opens with the three Earp brothers inside a saloon just moments before the famous confrontation near the O.K. Corral. As the men walk out, the scene dissolves to a vast cornfield and a young Wyatt Earp running away to join the Union Army in the waning days of the Civil War. The contrast between the two scenes illustrates the dichotomy between the man, who is about to become a legend, and the young boy and his dreams. When his father, Nicholas, catches him running away, he reminds young Wyatt that he is expected to handle the farm chores while his older brothers are off fighting the war. Nicholas tells his son that when a man takes on a job, he finishes it no matter what. In the early morning hours, Wyatt sneaks out of the house with an unloaded rifle and, as young boys have always done, he plays war. Firing the rifle at objects that don't return fire is a fine game, but it also is an eerie harbinger of the reality Wyatt will witness throughout his life.

The family travels to California, and Wyatt is sent to a town for supplies, where he witnesses a violent act in a town without law enforcement. Two drunken men stumble out of a saloon and shoot at each other, killing not only themselves but also a horse. Seeing two men die so violently causes Wyatt to become sick to his stomach. Later, his father warns him about evil in the world where law is nonexistent. He tells his son that, when he finds himself in a fight, to strike back hard and first. Those words serve Wyatt well several years later when, after he has refereed a prize fight in Wyoming, he is confronted in a saloon by a gambler who disagrees with his decision about the fight. A drunken friend of Wyatt's brags that Earp will shoot the gambler. The gambler then challenges Wyatt; although the young man tries to talk his way out of the situation, the gambler will not back down. Before anything can happen, Wyatt throws a billiard ball at the man's throat, disabling him. Earp has now managed to avoid bloodshed, and still he has followed his father's advice.

In Missouri, he finds his first love, Urilla. The love between the two is evident, and despite his talk about the vast West, he is willing to give it all up to be with her. When she dies, Wyatt is devastated. His world and his future are now lost. In a fit of drunken rage, he sets fire to their house and rides away, beginning his personal and moral downward spiral. He reaches the bottom after stealing money and a horse. Arrested for his crime, he cares nothing about his punishment. To Wyatt, life without Urilla has no meaning. It takes his father, who bails him out of jail, to awaken him. Nicholas tells Wyatt that life is about loss and that he is not the only man to lose a wife. Giving his son a horse and a gun, he tells him to start anew.

In Wichita, after hunting buffalo, Wyatt becomes a faro dealer in a saloon. His brother James works as a bartender, while his wife, Bessie, entertains men upstairs. Wyatt is bothered by this arrangement, partly because, since Urilla's death, he refuses to rely on any woman, fearing abandonment. When a drunken cowboy shoots up a saloon, and the deputy marshal quits, Wyatt quickly steps in and disarms the man. His actions earn him a job offer as a deputy marshal.

Morgan arrives in Wichita, where Wyatt meets Morgan's wife, Louisa. Her beauty haunts Wyatt, reminding him of his lost love. Moving to Dodge City, Wyatt works as a deputy marshal along with Morgan and Virgil. Bat Masterson and his brother, Ed, soon join Wyatt as deputies, but Ed's style of handling drunken cowboys is alien to Wyatt, who warns the affable Ed that he could get killed in this business. Ed lacks the instinct that Wyatt has acquired in dealing with cowboys. Ed is more inclined to talk a man out of his gun, while Wyatt is reserved and brutal when the need arises. He will not waste time trying to be nice to a drunken cowboy. A bruised skull and complaints from a hungover drunk are of little concern to Wyatt compared to an errant bullet striking an innocent victim. As civilization moves into Dodge City, Wyatt's style of law enforcement is viewed as brutal and harsh compared with the cordial ways of Ed Masterson. Under this scrutiny, Wyatt is forced to leave Dodge City.

Since Urilla's death, Wyatt has had only distant and wary relationships with women. Although he once chastised his brother James about his wife being a prostitute, Wyatt has taken up with Mattie, a prostitute, who is in love with him and believes that he will eventually marry her. Mattie's delusional beliefs will lead to her demise because Wyatt will not commit after losing Urilla. It is a wound that causes him too much pain, and he carefully guards his feelings. By doing so, Wyatt appears cold to others, including his brothers' wives.

The friendship between Wyatt and Doc Holliday begins in Fort Griffin, Texas. Wyatt explains that he is tracking a robber whom Holliday once considered killing. "Self-control got the better of me," Holliday dryly adds. The two men take a liking to each other, with an ineffable bond that immediately takes root between them. In Dodge City, after a drunken fight with his lover, Kate, Doc is dragged out by Wyatt and dunked into a horse trough. Doc tells Wyatt that he knows being his friend is not easy. "But I'll be there when you need me," he adds. Much like his brothers, Wyatt accepts Doc as part of his family, a man he trusts implicitly.

Ed Masterson's urbane style fails him one night, as Wyatt had predicted. He berates a drunken cowboy into handing over his gun, and the cowboy later kills Masterson. Dodge City runs wild without any strong law enforcement. Wyatt returns to Dodge and, with his brothers, restores law and order to the cowtown. Working as a lawman wears on Wyatt; he knows he will never get rich in this line of work. Virgil wonders whether being lawmen is all they are good at, as a bunch of drunken cowboys begin shooting up the town. Wyatt is forced to kill one of them, dashing his hopes of never having to kill a man. Once again, a death forces him to emotionally withdraw. It will not be the last one.

Talk of moving to Tombstone causes a rift in the Earp family, which escalates when the Earp wives ask Wyatt to meet with them. They want Wyatt to stop talking to their husbands about going to Tombstone; they like Dodge City. Wyatt, angry that they excluded his brothers, stalks out. This further distances Wyatt from women, especially Mattie, because he views their actions as being disloyal. For the Earps, Tombstone is no different from Dodge City. Their investments are not as fruitful as hoped, forcing Wyatt, Morgan and Virgil back into law enforcement. Enforcing the law brings the Earps into conflict with the Clantons and McLaurys, who are running stolen cattle. Instead of looking the other way or, as Sheriff John Behan says, "Live and let live," the Earps stand by the law. In doing so, they set in motion the catalyst for their confrontation.

The arrival of Josephine Marcus heightens the tension between Wyatt and Behan. Angry that Behan has shown a nude photo of her to others, Josephine walks out on him. Wyatt is strongly attracted to this independent woman, the first to strike a chord in his heart since Urilla. Although Wyatt feels obligated to Mattie, there is little love in their relationship. Nor is he terribly discreet about sleeping with Josephine, which drives Mattie to attempt suicide. Mattie, who tells Wyatt to go "back to your Jew whore," is spiraling deeper into a drug-induced state. She will slowly die over the loss of her only love. Unlike Wyatt, who shrouds his emotions to protect himself, Mattie is openly emotional and unstable. With Mattie's first suicide attempt, Wyatt is conflicted both by her words and in his actions. He attempts to ease his pain, as he did once before, in alcohol. Sensing his friend's turmoil, Doc joins Wyatt at the bar. He quickly drinks the whiskey before Wyatt has a chance to, and then coughs into the glass. Doc's actions tell us he will do whatever is needed to stop his friend from making a mistake. As in other movie depictions, Doc becomes Wyatt's conscience, supplying a clear head in his moment of need. Placing a drink before Wyatt, Doc asks him why they are still alive after being around so many incidents of death. He tells Wyatt that maybe death, which Doc faces every day, is the better option for some people, possibly even Mattie. Doc reminds Wyatt that for some, "the world isn't ever gonna be right." After taking a drink, Wyatt asks if that lets him off the hook. "There is no hook, my friend ... there's only what we do," Doc says.

The conflict with the Clantons and McLaurys grows and quickly spins out of control, leading to a gunfight. Afterward, not only are opinions split on the Earps' actions but the Earps also now face murder charges. The Earps and Holliday are soon vindicated, but the price of enforcing the law grows heavier when Morgan is killed. Again, Wyatt is faced with the loss of a loved one. Backing away from his brother's body on the pool table, Wyatt further withdraws into himself. His decision to bring the family to Tombstone has resulted in Morgan's death and Virgil's being maimed. Standing at a window in the hotel hallway, with rain pouring down and lighting flashing (an ominous sign of things to come) Doc asks Wyatt what they should do. "Kill 'em all," he flatly answers. He will now strike back harder than he ever has in his life. There will be no mercy. He will use his badge to dispense his own brand of justice.

Years later, Wyatt and Josephine are on a ship off the Alaskan coast. The Klondike gold rush draws them, and others, in search of riches. On the ship a young man recognizes

Wyatt and relates to him the story he was told about Earp saving his uncle's life in Tombstone. His uncle, Tommy, had killed a gambler, and Earp stood off a lynch mob singlehandedly. After the young man leaves, Wyatt confides to his wife that some people said the story never happened that way. Josephine tells him to never mind, that the story did happen that way. The man is now a legend, for better or worse.

Wyatt Earp is an epic in search of a story. It longs to join the echelon of David Lean's classics. It did not. The attempts to include a large amount of Earp's life drag down the narrative flow and, in the end, leave the audience uninvolved. This is the movie's fatal flaw. There is no dramatic story arc to include us. Instead, we are left on the sidelines with no emotional investment. Scenes are lumped together with no true narrative flow. Some have a wonderful feel or visual appeal, but this is not enough to carry a film, especially one that runs three-plus hours.

The story that is presented provides no one the audience can care about. With the possible exception of Doc Holliday, none of the characters—including Wyatt Earp—is interesting or evokes any sympathy from us. When the audience lacks an emotional bond to the protagonist, a movie is doomed. Viewers *want* to become involved with the story and the main characters. They want a hero—especially a legendary one like Earp—to root and cheer for. They want to believe in the hero, even if he has faults in his character. They are not interested in whether Wyatt Earp was ambiguous in his morals. Audiences can accept that

Some locations on *Wyatt Earp* were so remote that it was easier for crew members to walk there rather than endure a bumpy van ride. Here, makeup artists Michael Mills (left) and Gerry Quist (right) carry their equipment to location (courtesy of Gerald Quist).

if there is something about the character they can respond to emotionally. Unfortunately, *Wyatt Earp* offers us nothing in this regard.

The screenplay wanders, with no cohesive plot other than displaying events in Wyatt Earp's life. Nothing really tells us why Earp became the person he did or why he is such an important figure in history. Too many facts are presented, most of them uninteresting except to hardcore Earp buffs, and they do little to give us an idea of the man or legend. A main reason for this problem appears to be that Kevin Costner fell in love with the material in the miniseries script and attempted to include as much of it as he could in the feature film script. Sometimes a filmmaker can be too in love with the material to see any potential flaws or problems and lacks the artistic distance to make wise judgments. This seems to have been the case with *Wyatt Earp*. Despite Lawrence Kasdan's serving as producer-director-writer, apparently no one was in complete control of the project. (Costner and his company, Tig Productions, were co-producers of the movie.) Although filmmaking is a collaborative effort, there must be a strong hand guiding a production through its paces. Too many people offering their ideas or making demands hurts a film; ultimately, the results show up in the finished project. Such actions can be disastrous for a movie, particularly one with such a large budget.

Most filmmakers readily agree that a script needs to be tightly constructed and complete before a single frame of film is exposed. To do otherwise invites delays and problems. With Costner so enamored of much of the material, and with no one willing to stand up to him to say enough is enough, the story suffered. Some scenes drag on, while others are too short for any satisfying resolution. Characters are not well developed, and some of the dialogue borders on the ridiculous. The buffalo hunting sequence offered interesting possibilities, but unfortunately it goes nowhere. This sequence does not advance the story other than to show us how Wyatt meets Bat and Ed Masterson. Some shots are visually stunning, but that is not sufficient to warrant so much screen time. The same can be said for the Wyoming sequence, in which the railroad is being built. Other than to show how Earp became interested in faro and how he handles the incident with the gambler, it does not justify the audience's time. One serious flaw, as pointed out in the *Newsweek* review, is that the villains in this film are not well delineated. The audience is not given a clear reason why the Clantons and McLaurys hate the Earps. Nor are the reasons for the gunfight well established. One of the basic rules of dramatic structure is that a protagonist must have an antagonist. In the case of *Wyatt Earp*, the Clantons and the McLaurys are the villains, yet they are not defined and their actions are not established. Like others in this film, they are characters who come and go like the tide.

The gunfight is the main drawing card for the movie audience. In every film discussed in this book, the filmmakers use the gunfight as a buildup to the final act or as the main component of the film that drives the ensuing action. Audiences come to movies about Wyatt Earp to see the gunfight. Whether the shootout happens at the beginning (as in *Hour of the Gun*) or at the conclusion (as in *My Darling Clementine* and *Gunfight at the O.K. Corral*), the viewer expects the filmmaker to set up the gunfight as a major plot point. In *Wyatt Earp*, the O.K. Corral gunfight comes off as just another incident in the film, with little dramatic impact. Nor is it staged with sufficient drama or emotional impact. As edited, the entire sequence is filled with close shots of the actors and few wide shots. Because of the many close angles, the gunfight fails to draw in the audience in and create the willing suspension of

Opposite: **Storyboard art for the gunfight sequence of the movie (courtesy of Gerald Quist).**

156 EXT. FOURTH STREET DAY

DOC - WYATT - VIRGIL AND MORGAN DIALOGUE -.

THE FOUR MEN CONTINUE DOWN FOURTH S

ALGLE FROM FREEMONT ST.

disbelief. Instead, the closer shots remind us that we are watching a film, and the emotional impact is squandered. In addition, although the gunfight shown is a reasonable facsimile of the actual event, it contains some important mistakes. Virgil does not tell the Cowboys, "Hold! I don't mean that!" They have Morgan firing first, using a two-gun rig, and Doc is shown being shot by Frank McLaury, but exactly where remains unclear. (In reality, Doc was grazed by his hip holster by one of Frank McLaury's bullets.) Wyatt does not tell Ike get to fighting or run, and it is Wyatt, *not* Doc and Morgan, who kills Frank McLaury. One could forgive these historical transgressions if the gunfight was well staged and had suspenseful pacing. Unfortunately, it has neither and leaves the audience disappointed.

As Wyatt Earp, Kevin Costner does nothing to make the character interesting, and he lacks any warmth. Although in the scenes taking place in Wyoming and with Urilla, Costner's Earp comes off an earnest, likable fellow, these are not enough to carry the film. Other than reacting to the loss of his wife, Costner does not offer sufficient dramatic change in Wyatt to gain the audience's sympathy and interest. Neither does he give Wyatt any type of personality, reading many of his lines in a flat tone. By doing so, he fails to bring any life or appeal to Wyatt Earp. Some historians lauded Costner for his restrained portrayal, saying that he captured Wyatt's emotional coolness. However, his performance fails to offer the audience anything to root for or care about, unlike those of other actors who have played Earp. In short, Costner's portrayal falls flat and drags the movie down.

Dennis Quaid's portrayal of Doc Holliday is a different story. His Doc Holliday is a brilliantly realized performance. The movie sparks to life when Quaid appears in any scene, as his Holliday takes center stage. Quaid invests a dry wit in his Holliday, tinged with a jeopardous edge. He is like a beautiful lion that can turn deadly in the blink of an eye. Quaid's physical appearance only adds to the performance; we really believe that the man is dying of tuberculosis. Unfortunately, try as Quaid does to breathe life into the chemistry between his Holliday and Costner's Wyatt, he is hampered by the latter's deadpan performance. The audience never gets a

During a break on the *Tombstone* set, Dennis Quaid eerily makes one think they are looking at the real Doc Holliday (courtesy of Gerald Quist).

sense of the loyalty and friendship between the two men. Additionally, there is no closing act between Wyatt and Doc in the film. They have a conversation at the campfire about leaving and coming back later to get those responsible for Morgan's death. A coughing fit causes Wyatt to urge Doc to go to a sanitarium in Colorado. Doc will go if Wyatt takes him. Wyatt tells Doc that he has been a good friend to him. "Shut up!" Holliday replies. That is the last spoken scene between the two main characters. (Holliday is present at the Iron Springs shootout, where Wyatt kills Curly Bill.) We are left hanging with a supposedly important friendship that has no sense of closure. Because the film was so negatively panned, Quaid's rich portrayal was sadly overlooked when it came time to give Academy Award nominations.

Gene Hackman, as Nicholas Earp, is given little to do but pontificate to his family. While some of the things his character says have meaning, ultimately they come off as boring orations. This is no fault of Hackman's, who tries his best to instill a patriarchal tone to his Nicholas. He is hampered by poorly scripted dialogue and lackluster direction. Isabella Rossellini's talent is also wasted in the movie. Her brief appearances as Big Nose Kate give a slight indication of what depth she could have brought to the film. Sadly, many of her scenes landed on the editing room floor. Tom Sizemore is completely miscast as Bat Masterson. He downplays his role to the point that it undermines the importance of the character in Earp's life. Both Michael Madsen, as Virgil, and Joanna Going, as Josephine, are equally miscast. Madsen, who does well in roles set in urban stories, simply does not come across believably as a man who has spent his entire adult life in the West. Going, who is hampered by a poorly written role, comes across as cold and indifferent as Josephine. There is nothing warm or inviting about her that would lead Wyatt to become romantically interested. The scene in which Costner and Going finally kiss each other lacks any sense of chemistry or attraction between the two actors. This, along with the poorly written dialogue, renders the moment false, and the audience does not believe what these two characters are saying. Jeff Fahey, who normally delivers strong performances, is left with little to do as Ike Clanton. Although the actor tries to bring something to his role, he, like the others, is stymied by a poor script and aimless direction. To *Wyatt Earp*'s credit, Mark Harmon comes closer to the real John Behan than ever presented in previous films. While not the ready glad-hander Jon Tenny played in *Tombstone*, Harmon shows Behan as a politically savvy man who will do whatever he can to benefit himself. The performances of JoBeth Williams, Catherine O'Hara, and Alison Elliott as the wives of the Earp brothers are nothing but shrill and bitchy portrayals. Here again, these actresses, who are accomplished talents, are at the mercy of the script and direction.

It is inevitable that the sets and wardrobe of *Wyatt Earp* would be compared to those of *Tombstone*. The latter movie literally dares the audience to draw the similarities, and those in *Wyatt Earp* wind up suffering. The town sets of Dodge City and Tombstone look too much the same, despite the tricks of the trade by the production designer to vary the look. The Tombstone set lacks any sense of openness or indication of wealth that came with a mining strike. Nor is there anything to suggest to the audience that this is a major mining boom town. There are no mine shafts, ore cars, or anything else that would readily tell the audience they are in a location where mining takes place. The entire outdoor set of Tombstone looks and feels like a studio back-lot set, as does the Dodge City location. The wardrobe for the movie appears to have been limited to three colors: black, brown, and gray. The men all look the same, which makes more work for the audience in attempting to distinguish the Cowboy element from the townspeople. From a historical perspective, many of the hats, especially Wyatt's, are not accurate for the time period.[38] By clothing the characters in similar colors and not varying the visual palette, the overall look of the film is harmed.

With the movie failing at the box office, Warner Bros. issued a new poster. Using a picture of Costner kissing Joanna Going, the studio hoped to sell the movie as a romance as well. Nothing helped (author's collection).

James Newton Howard's score gives the movie the epic scope it desperately is looking for. He captures the right emotions for the moments in the film, such as Urilla's theme. It is a soft, haunting theme that expresses what is not on the screen; he reprises it when Wyatt loses her and when he tell Josephine about his time in Missouri. The main theme for the film has the feel of an epic score that vainly tries to bring life to the movie. Although some critics disliked Howard's score, calling it bombastic, it really is not. It is a fully and well developed score, deserving of a much better film.

Ultimately, the movie fails because of the ponderous script and lackluster direction by Lawrence Kasdan. Wyatt Earp lacks a general rhythm, and many scenes are woefully in need of tighter pacing. The movie moves in a series of false starts that build a touch of momentum, only to fall apart over and over throughout. Not only does the movie lack the sweeping style of an epic, it also does little to hold the audience's interest. One of the biggest showpieces in the film is the Earps' arrival in Tombstone. It is a major event in the story, yet Kasdan treats it as just another scene. The way the scene is filmed, Tombstone looks just like Dodge City. In his original miniseries script, Dan Gordon opens the Tombstone sequence with a stagecoach coming to town carrying French prostitutes. As the stagecoach makes its way through the surrounding area, we get a glimpse of the town. By doing so, the sequence tells the audience that the story has moved to Tombstone and the town, which plays a major role in the film, is properly introduced. Instead, in the completed movie, the camera pans from a sign prohibiting the carrying of firearms to a young boy carrying two pails of beer down the street. In filming the scene this way, Kasdan has cheated the audience, and the film loses any sense of an epic touch.

Wyatt Earp falls victim of its own elephantine desires. A perfect example is the sequence that takes place in the Tucson train station. The audience, as well as the main characters, knows that Frank Stilwell and others are lying in wait to ambush the Earps. Kasdan draws out the cat-and-mouse game of finding the killers. Yet because the scene of people moving between trains goes on too long, any tension that has built is lost, and when Wyatt finally kills Stilwell, the dramatic payoff loses any impact. Equally disturbing is the ending of the film. Aboard a steamer taking Wyatt and Josephine to the Alaskan gold rush, the young boy relates how Wyatt single-handily held off a lynch mob.[39] When Wyatt, looking off into the distance, says that some people said it never happened that way, Josephine reassures him that it did. The scene is open-ended and ambiguous, leaving us confused. If the director's attempt was to reflect the oft-stated line from John Ford's The Man Who Shot Liberty Valance (1962)—when the legend becomes fact, print the legend—then the scene fails. It also appears to have been dragged in and tacked on at the end with no real justification, other than that perhaps the audience was to be left to make its own decision as to whether the story and Earp's heroics are really true. Whatever the reason, the scene leaves the audience, and the movie's narrative, befuddled.

In the end, Wyatt Earp is a victim of its own ambitions. It is not the sweeping epic it aches to be, and the intimate moments, which could draw the audience closer, are sorely lacking. Wyatt Earp, sad to say, is a perfect example of how not to make a film. Despite a large budget, huge ambitions, and an impressive cast of actors, the film is defeated by clashing egos, a misshaped script, and different visions that ran amok with no control. Perhaps the film could have used the real Wyatt Earp to bring order to it.

Wyatt Earp

Warner Bros. Presents a Tig Productions/Kasdan Pictures Production. *Released:* June 24, 1994. *Executive Producers:* Dan Gordon, Michael Grillo, Charles Okun, Jon Slan. *Producers:* Kevin Costner, Lawrence Kasdan, Jim Wilson. *Director:* Lawrence Kasdan. *Screenplay:* Dan Gordon and Lawrence Kasdan. *Cinematographer:* Owen Roizman. *Musical Score:* James Newton Howard. *Film Editor:* Carol Littleton. *Production Design:* Ida Random. *Art Direction:* Gary Wissner. *Set Decoration:* Cheryl Carasik. *Costume Designer:* Colleen Atwood. *Makeup Artists:* Michael Mills, Gerald Quist. *Additional Makeup:* Bonita De Haven. *Kevin Costner's Makeup:* F. X. Perez. *Hair Stylists:* Marlene Williams, Dorothy Fox, Elle Elliott, Sharon McVey. *Unit Production Managers:* Michael Grillo, Charles Okun. *Assistant Directors:* Stephen Dunn, Peter Hirsch, Jeff Rafner, L. David Silva, Christina Stauffer. *Props:* Bill Petrotta, Victor Petrotta Jr., Mike Gannon, Kevin M. Gannon. *Sound:* John Pritchett, John Glaeser, Joel Shryack. *Special Effects:* Rod Byrd, Burt Dalton, Dale Ettema, Joe Heffernan, Dick Hogle, Don Myers, Sol Rivera. *Costume Supervisors:* Le Dawson, Cha Blevins. *Set Costumers:* Barry Delaney, James M. George, Ruby Manis, Adrienne Wait, Jennifer Alexander, Cynthia Black-Montoya, Marci R. Johnson, Adrienne Manhan. *Script Supervisor:* Anne Rapp. *Camera Operators:* Ian Fox, Bill Roe. *Camera Assistants:* Jeffrey Gershman, Michael Raspa, Anthony Rivetti, Eric Roizman. *Still Photographer:* Ben Glass. *Gun Expert:* Branko Wohlfahrt. *Steadicam Operator:* Rusty Geller. *Steadicam Assistant:* Richard Mosier. *Location Manager:* Paul Hargrave. *Dolly Grip:* David Merrill. *Best Boy:* Mitch Lookabaugh. *Stunt Coordinator:* Norman Howell. *Stunts:* William H. Burton Jr., Will Cascio, Stacy Courtney, David Efron, H.P. Evetts, Gregory Goossen, Beau Holden, Kanin J. Howell, Shawn Howell, Tricia Howell, Gary McLarty, William Ray, L. David Silva. *Head Wrangler:* Rusty Hendrickson. *Wranglers:* John Campbell, Justin Lundin, Benny Manning, Darwin Mitchell, Larry Motes, Noel Phillips, Jimmy Sherwood, Monty Stewart, Rick Wyant. *Filming Locations:* Filmed on location at Santa Fe, Tesuque, Chama, Las Vegas, Cook Ranch and Ghost Ranch and Garson Studios, New Mexico and Port Angeles, Washington. *Running Time:* 189 minutes.

Cast: Kevin Costner (*Wyatt Earp*), Dennis Quaid (*Doc Holliday*), Gene Hackman (*Nicholas Earp*), Mark Harmon (*Johnny Behan*), Jeff Fahey (*Ike Clanton*), Isabella Rossellini (*Big Nose Kate Elder*), Tom Sizemore (*Bat Masterson*), Michael Masden (*Virgil Earp*), David Andrews (*James Earp*), Joanna Going (*Josie Marcus*), Linden Ashby (*Morgan Earp*), Bill Pullman (*Ed Masterson*), Mare Winningham (*Mattie Earp*), Randle Mell (*John Clum*), Rex Linn (*Frank McLaury*), Adam Baldwin (*Tom McLaury*), Catherine O'Hara (*Allie Earp*), JoBeth Williams (*Bessie Earp*), James Gammon (*Mr. Sutherland*), Annabeth Gish (*Urilla Sutherland*), Lewis Smith (*Curly Bill Brocius*), Ian Bohen (*Young Wyatt*), Betty Buckley (*Virginia Earp*), Alison Elliott (*Louisa Earp*), Todd Allen (*Sherm McMasters*), Mackenzie Astin (*Young Man on Boat*), James Caviezel (*Warren Earp*), Karen Grassle (*Mrs. Sutherland*), John Dennis Johnston (*Frank Stillwell*), Téa Leoni (*Sally*), Martin Kove (*Ed Ross*), Jack Kehler (*Bob Hatch*), Kirk Fox (*Pete Spence*), Norman Howell (*Johnny Ringo*), Boots Southerland (*Marshal Fred White*), Scotty Augare (*Indian Charlie*), Gabriel Folse (*Billy Clanton*), Kris Kamm (*Billy Claiborne*), John Lawlor (*Judge Spicer*), Monty Stuart (*Dutch Wiley*), Hugh Ross (*Erwin Sutherland*), Gregory Avellone (*Traveler*), Michael McGrady (*John Shanssey*), Mary Jo Niedzielski (*Martha Earp*), Scott Paul (*Young Morgan*), Oliver Hendrickson (*Young Warren*), Darwin Mitchell (*Tom Chapman*), Gerald Quist (*Dodge City Bartender*), Steve Kniesel (*Bullwacker*), Larry Sims (*Dirty Sodbuster*), Greg Goossen (*Friend of Bullwacker*), Heath Kizzier (*Red*), Clark Sanchez (*Mike Donovan*), Ed Beimfohr (*Faro Dealer*), Giorgio E. Tripoli (*Judge Earp*), Ben Zeller (*Dr. Seger*), Rockne Tarkington (*Stable Hand*), Scott Rasmussen (*Minister*), Ellen Blake (*Paris*), Steph Benseman (*Pine Bluff Sheriff*), Bob "Dutch" Holland (*Tubercular Inmate*), Steve Cormier (*Tent Saloon Bartender*), Matt Langseth (*Link Borland*), David Doty (*Mayor Wilson*), Steven G. Tyler (*Deputy Ford*), Billy Streater (*Marshal Meagher*), David L. Stone (*Larry Deger*), Jake Walker (*Mannen Clements*), Matt O'Toole (*Gyp Clements*), George Cook (*Big Cowboy*), Dillinger Steele, Steve Lindsay (*Drunk Cowboys*), Marlene Williams (*Saloon Dealer*), Dick Beach (*Wagner*), Benny Manning (*Walker*), Kathleen O'Hara (*Hotel Resident*), Nicholas Benseman (*Delivery Boy*), Sarge McGraw (*Deputy Black*), Steven Hartley (*Spangenberg*), Brett Cullen (*Saddle Tramp*), Paul Ukena (*Bar Regular*), Owen Roizman (*Danny*), Karen Schwartz (*Marshal White's Wife*), Glen Burns (*Bar Patron*), John Furlong (*Clem Hafford*), Zack McGillis (*Rancher*), Adam Taylor (*Texas Jack Vermillion*), Rusty Hendrickson (*Turkey Creek Jack Johnson*), Hanley Smith (*Billiard Parlor Patron*), Jon Kasdan (*Bar Boy*), Dale West (*Station Master*), Michael Huddleston (*Albert*), Al Trujillo (*Camp Foreman*), John Doe (*Tommy Behind-the-Deuce*), Matt Beck (*McGee*), Gary Dueer (*Dirk Gird*), Joe Bernier (*Fast Draw Cowboy*), Shannon Denton (*Man with whores*), James "JR" Pollard (*Carpetbagger in Saloon*), John Pritchett (*The Drummer*), Mark Thomason (*Cowboy at Table*).

Epilogue

"Suppose. Suppose."

—*Wyatt Earp on his deathbed*

As you drive today through Tombstone, Wyatt Earp's image is seen literally everywhere. A local computer company uses his image as part of their logo. His face is plastered on a display advertising a local antique store. As you drive into town, a large poster of Earp and Holliday look-alikes, pointing their guns, stare at you to advertise the O.K. Corral site. Literally every store on Allen Street has photographs or artwork of the most famous Earp brother, as well as numerous posters from *Tombstone*. (Oddly, one finds very few posters of *Wyatt Earp* in the souvenir stores.) The sidewalks on Allen Street are made of wood, so today's cowboy can hear the echoes of their boot heels as they walk the same path as the Earps and Holliday tread a hundred and twenty-five years ago. The Bird Cage Theatre still has the bullet holes in the walls and ceiling that were put there in the 1880s. Sixth Street, where the red light district once stood, is now home to the city's high school. The various mines that crisscross underneath the town remain silent, silver still waiting to be mined.

In Spangenberg's gunshop (now located across from its original location on Fourth Street), a video of *Tombstone* plays constantly, while young and old alike look at the real guns for sale in the display cases. Looking outside their store window on Fourth Street, one can almost see the Earps and Holliday heading toward their destiny. Hafford's saloon is now an art gallery, while the site of the old Oriental Saloon now sells clothing. Cowboys standing at the corners of Fourth and Allen Streets urge tourists to visit a nearby place where they recreate gunfights, while Wyatt and Doc look-alikes head toward the site where they reenact the shootout at the O.K. Corral. They all are tied to those thirty seconds of October 26, 1881.

Unlike its old days, the streets of Tombstone quickly empty after 5 P.M. Only a few saloons remain open, with one occasionally playing music from the 1880s on a piano. Allen Street, which in the daytime is thriving with tourists and would-be cowboys from all over the world, is empty as darkness envelopes the area. By early evening, only the occasional late tourist, who must walk the wood-plank sidewalks of Allen Street, and the locals who frequent the saloons are left. The piano music from a saloon fills the evening air, drawing one back over 125 years ago when the town was operating on a 24-hour basis. Unlike its boom days, Tombstone has become a bedroom community. By midnight, a few die-hards remain in the saloons, while Allen Street is barren. Only the ghosts are left to wander.

The real O.K. Corral still draws the curious from around the world. Behind the vacant lot where the shootout took place, a small walled-in arena, complete with bleachers and false fronts of buildings, houses a small group that reenacts the famous events of October 26,

1881. After the show, children, who grew up long after the TV Western craze had ridden into the sunset, look at the less-than-accurate figures of the Earps, Holliday, Clantons and McLaurys. The figures are now enclosed by a wrought iron fence to duplicate the actual size of the small lot. The entire area is sealed off from Fremont Street, and visitors must pay an admission to see the most famous (and visited) site in town. When the tourists finally leave, only the immobile figures remain. The occasional sound of trucks and cars passing down Highway 80 (Fremont Street) breaks the silence. The figures, frozen in time, remain as they have for over forty years.

As the sun slowly sets behind the hills facing the town that was too tough to die, standing in the silence of the empty lot, one cannot help but wonder what it was like to be in that same location on that chilly afternoon of October 26, 1881. Standing in that lot, none of the Earps, Holliday, Clantons or McLaurys knew they were about to be forever immortalized in the pages of American Western lore, as well as cinematic history. Standing there, in those brief seconds before all hell would break lose, Wyatt Earp, the man, was to become forever lost to Wyatt Earp, the myth and legend. In a thirty-second period, he would become a hero to some, a villain to others, and an icon to a declining mining town that became an international tourist attraction.

However, Wyatt Earp doesn't only belong to Tombstone. It needs a Wyatt Earp." Later that year, Dodge City unveiled a statue of Earp, complete with the Buntline Special gun at his side. In 2004, Dodge City unveiled a statue of Earp and Doc Holliday, near the exact location where Earp killed Frank Stilwell. Hollywood, with its proclivity to return to familiar stories, will no doubt return to the story of Earp and the famous gunfight. After all, a good story is hard to ignore.

Notes

Chapter 1

1. The Dragoon Mountains were also referred to as "Cachise's [Cochise] Stronghold" because of his ability to elude the military. Cachise is the proper spelling, yet when the area that includes Tombstone was delineated as a new county, it was recorded as Cochise. That spelling has remained ever since. It is said that when Cachise died in 1874, his people buried him within this area. The exact location of his grave remains unknown to this day.

2. After the 1887 earthquake, the water table of the San Pedro River changed dramatically. The river today is merely a trickle except during the monsoon season, when it can quickly fill up and just as quickly recede.

3. Born in Pennsylvania in 1847, Schieffelin migrated with his family to California, where he was introduced to mining in Jackson County. Schieffelin roamed the West from Utah, Idaho, Nevada, and various areas of Arizona Territory.

4. The boomtowns of the American West had a social system unto themselves. Morals were loose compared with those of "civilized" cities, or outright nonexistent. Gamblers, saloon owners, prostitutes, con men, mercantilers, and thieves were part and parcel of the population. Miners, with money in their pockets, were easy pickings for those who knew how to take advantage of the gullible rubes, and there was money to be made off the hard work of miners. A gambler might win a deed to a mine and sell it at a handsome profit without ever getting dirt under his fingernails. Prostitutes (often called "soiled doves") followed the circuit, working for a madam or even independently. Many prostitutes married gamblers or saloon owners while continuing to ply their trade. James Earp, Wyatt's older brother, worked as a saloon owner, while his wife, Bessie, worked a brothel in many towns, including Wichita, Kansas. Wyatt was serving as a deputy city marshal of the town at the same time.

5. No railroads delivered passengers or freight to Tombstone, but in 1880 train service from the new town of Benson, twenty-two miles north, would make round trips to Tucson. Once train service was established in Benson, stagecoaches could make the trip between Benson to Tombstone in six hours.

6. Driving a stagecoach was a hazardous job. The driver, often called a "ribbon man" because of the series of reins he held, drove a team of four or six horses (called "four ups" or "six ups") at a fast pace, depending on the terrain.

7. When a stage carried any kind of bullion shipment or money from Wells Fargo, a shotgun messenger rode alongside the driver on the box.

8. While in Tombstone, Mrs. Brown sent several letters to the *San Diego Daily Union*. These became a recurring column about life in the mining camp from a woman's perspective. Like George Parsons's diary, Clara Spaulding Brown's columns offer a unique insight into the daily life of Tombstone. *San Diego Daily Union*, July 14, 1880.

9. Wyatt's full name, Wyatt Berry Stamp Earp, was in honor of the officer under whom Nicholas served during the Mexican-American War. Nicholas Earp married Abigail Storm in 1836 and son Newton was born the following year. Abigail died in 1839 and Nicholas married Virginia Cooksey in 1840. James, their first child, was born in 1841 and Virgil in 1843. A daughter, Martha, was born in 1845. Morgan was born in 1851, Warren in 1855 and Virginia in 1858.

10. There are no death certificates and town newspaper are missing editions about the time Urilla died. Even Earp did not help in this matter in later years, remaining tight-lipped about his past. Many speculate that she died either from typhoid fever or while giving birth to a stillborn child.

11. Abilene, Kansas was one of the first cowtowns in the state, and the primary one from 1867 to 1872. Ellsworth took over in 1872, but its heyday lasted only a year before Wichita became the major cowtown. Like most cowtowns, Abilene was near a river, which provided enough grazing land and water for the cattle before they were sent to market back east.

12. James was working as a bartender, while his wife, Bessie, was busy in the brothel trade. The 1875 census lists Bessie's profession as "sporting," a colorful term for prostitution.

13. By buffaloing an opponent, Wyatt left them dazed and bewildered, allowing him to take control of the matter before there was any bloodshed. Usually the cowhand would be hit with the barrel of the pistol, just above the ear.

14. Discharging firearms while racing through town on horseback was known as "hurrahing."

15. As the Union forces marched into Georgia in 1864, John's cousins came to live with them at their new estate in hopes of remaining safe from the war's onslaught. During their stay, John formed a close friendship with his cousin, Mattie. There are rumors that Mattie joined a convent over an affair she had with John.

16. Known as "Big Nose" Kate, she was born in Hungary in 1850, before coming to the United States with her family. They settled in Iowa in 1863, and after the death of her parents in 1865, Kate struck out on her own. In Wichita in 1874, she was working in a "sporting house" run by James and Bessie Earp. How she got to Fort Griffin and met Holliday is unknown. After Holliday's death in 1887, she lived in Globe, Arizona, operating a hotel. She married George Cummings in 1888 and divorced him in 1899. She died in 1940 at the age of 90.

17. Ed Masterson was shot at point-blank range in the abdomen as he tried to disarm a drunken cowboy. The bullet went completely through and set Ed's clothing on fire. He staggered to a saloon and collapsed, dying 40 minutes later. It was widely believed that Ed Masterson shot both drunken cowboys, Jack Wagner and Alf Walker, although new evidence shows it was Bat Masterson who fired the shots. My thanks to Bob Palmquist for sharing this information.

18. Wyatt had become romantically involved with Celia Blaylock while in Dodge City. Called "Mattie," little is known of her background or life other than that she was born in Iowa, where she reportedly ran away from home at 16 and eventually headed to Dodge City. She may have worked as a prostitute, although there is no documentation to support that theory. There is no known marriage license between Wyatt and Mattie, and most historians believe they maintained a common-law marriage.

The Earps stopped in Las Vegas, New Mexico, where Doc Holliday was gambling. Doc, along with Kate, quickly joined the Earps on the trip from Las Vegas to Prescott. In that city, Doc hit a streak of luck at the gaming tables and decided to stay. Before the Earps left Prescott for Tombstone, U.S. Marshal Crawley Dake secured an appointment for Virgil as deputy U.S. Marshal. Virgil took his oath of office on November 27, 1879. His primary job was to help the other law enforcement agencies of the Tombstone area, as well as enforce federal laws.

19. Tombstone's population in 1880 was 2,173. The town had descendants of Irish, German, and Mexican heritage as well as a large Jewish population. There were also a few opium dens in the Chinese section.

20. The *Tombstone Nugget* began publishing on October 2, 1879, while the *Tombstone Epitaph*, run by John Clum, began in May 1880.

21. Although this group used smaller towns like Charleston, Galeyville, or Contention City as their base, they came into Tombstone to spend freely. Estimations of the Cowboy element ranged from 40 to 400. Some were believed to have been involved in the Lincoln County War in New Mexico before coming to Arizona.

22. Little is known about Curly Bill Brocius other than his attempt to rob a U.S. Army ambulance with another criminal in May 1878 in Texas. They were arrested in Mexico and brought back for trial in Texas, where they were found guilty and sentenced to five years. While an appeal was pending, Curly Bill escaped on November 2, 1878, most likely heading for Mexico, and by late 1879, he surfaced in Tombstone. Brocius was a friendly type (except when drinking), and even Virgil and Wyatt had a cordial relationship with him—for a while. As with man of the people associated with the story of Wyatt Earp, there would be little consensus among screenwriters about how to spell his name, a fact reflected in the chapters that follow. John Ringo hailed from Indiana and made the westward trek to California with his parents. He worked as a farm laborer as a teenager, and it is believed he started to drink heavily during this time. His drinking and subsequent behavior caused his family to expel him, and he drifted to Texas before coming to Tombstone in 1879. Ringo may have had some formal education; he at least was well read. Many historians believed he may have suffered from bouts of depression which, coupled with his drinking, exacerbated his mood swings and temper.

23. Although she called herself Mrs. Behan, it is doubtful that Behan and Sadie were ever married. It is believed that Sadie first met Behan in Prescott while she was performing with the troupe. Bob Palmquist says that the

"Pinafore on Wheels," the troupe Sadie was appearing with, was playing in Tombstone on December 1, 1879, the time the Earp family arrived.

24. Contrary to portrayals in some films, Earp researchers have found no evidence to prove that during this time Mattie was hopelessly hooked on laudanum.

25. The empty lot is now where the Bird Cage Theatre stands on the corner of Allen and Sixth streets.

26. Virgil Earp was appointed to take over the post of marshal until a new election was held on November 12. Fred White's funeral was held on October 31, drawing more than 1,000 people. He's buried in Boothill Cemetery, which is next to Highway 80, the main road into Tombstone. Also buried at this site are Tom and Frank McLaury, Billy Clanton, and Florentino Cruz. One of the more unusual stories surrounding those buried in the cemetery concerns Lester Moore. Moore was a Wells Fargo agent in the border town of Naco. Hank Dunstan came to the office to pick up a package, which had been damaged in shipment. An argument erupted, with both men drawing their guns. Moore was killed with four shots to the chest, and Dunstan died from one shot by Moore. The marker on Moore's grave bears one of Western history's famous epitaphs: "Here lies Lester Moore. Four slugs from a .44. No Les. No More."

27. The deal never materialized because the three men were killed before Clanton could arrange a set-up meeting.

28. The term "heeled" meant to have armed oneself with a weapon.

29. Butcher Appolinar Bauer witnessed the altercation between Wyatt and Tom McLaury. He said that Tom was carrying a pistol in his waistband at the time. He described Wyatt's gun as being fairly large, 14 to 16 inches in length. That would be the overall length, with a ten-inch barrel. Jeff Morey to the author, October 30, 2003.

30. During his preliminary hearing testimony, Wyatt claimed that as they walked past Behan, Behan called to them, "For God's sake, don't go down there or you will get murdered."

31. Behan, according to the *Nugget*, stated to the Earps, "Don't go down there, there'll be trouble." He also reportedly said that he told the Earps, "I've just been down there to disarm them," denying that he ever said "I have disarmed them all."

32. While he certainly didn't plan it, Ike's running up to and struggling with Wyatt inadvertently saved Earp from becoming a target.

33. McLaury's great grand-niece Pam Potter points out that there has never been any proof that Tom McLaury was armed with a pistol and shot Morgan. It is *possible* that Morgan's wound may have been caused by a bullet fired by one of his brothers. Pam Potter to the author, January 27, 2004.

34. Despite the claim by witness P. H. Felley that Frank McLaury was trying to say something to him when he went over to his body, Jeff Morey says it was more of an "electrical storm" within the brain after being shot. He contends that McLaury was dead by the time he fell to the ground. Jeff Morey to the author, October 30, 2003.

35. Alford Turner, ed., *The O.K. Corral Inquest*. College Station, TX: Creative Publishing Company, 1981, p. 30.

36. In the coroner's report, only the wounds that were mortal were mentioned. Any type of gunshot wound that did not prove to be fatal was ignored.

37. *Tombstone Nugget*, October 27, 1881.

38. Lyttleton Price, the Cochise County district attorney, served as lead prosecutor, while Tom Fitch, a former member of the Arizona territorial legislature, was the

defense attorney. The other lawyers at the prosecuting table included Ike's lawyer, Benjamin Goodrich, as well as J. S. Robinson and Alexander Campbell. Thomas J. Drum handled Holliday's defense and John Howard also was on the defense team. My thanks to Clay Parker for providing me with the names of the lawyers.

Will McLaury, who arrived in Tombstone on November 3, was a practicing attorney in Texas. He helped fund the prosecution's case and was allowed to be part of the prosecution table. A Civil War veteran, Will worked as a farmer, then a stagecoach driver, before being admitted to the bar. In 1876 he and his wife, Lona, moved to Fort Worth, Texas, where he opened a law office. His wife died in the summer of 1881. Will left his three children in the care of friends and placed his law practice on hold while he went to Tombstone. My thanks to Clay Parker and Pam Potter for providing me with Will's background.

The hearings were held in the Mining Exchange instead of Spicer's small courtroom because of the number of attorneys on both sides. The Mining Exchange was on the north side of Fremont Street, next door to the offices of the *Epitaph*, just down from the gunfight site.

39. Ike was excused from testifying for a day because of suffering from "neuralgia of the head" (oppressive pain in the front of the head). The usual treatment in those days was administering a solution of cocaine and water, although there is no proof Ike used such a treatment. Resuming his testimony, Ike explained his secret deal with Wyatt, claiming Earp confided that he wasn't interested in capturing the robbers but killing them. He also stated that Wyatt claimed he and his brother, Morgan, tipped off Doc Holliday and William Leonard about the stage carrying money and sought to split the stolen cash. Wyatt, Ike claimed, was worried that if the robbers were caught, Wyatt would be implicated. To make matters worse for the prosecution's case, Ike, under redirect questioning, claimed that Doc Holliday had told him that he was at the site of the stage robbery site and killed Bud Philpott himself. The defense knew they had an opening and mockingly asked Ike if Wells Fargo agent Marshall Williams had confided in him about his involvement in the stage robbery. The objection to question was quickly sustained, but they had made their point to the judge.

40. Sills was the railroad man who overheard the Clantons and McLaurys say they would kill Virgil Earp on sight. Sills was a stranger to Tombstone, so his testimony was quite effective. Winfield Scott Williams contradicted Behan's testimony and basically said he was lying. This was damaging testimony coming from an officer of the court.

41. It wasn't until the stage arrived in Contention City that anyone noticed he was missing. Arriving in Benson, Clum wired Tombstone of his safe arrival before continuing his trip east.

42. Some pellets lodged in his back near the spinal column but missed any vital organs. The doctors removed 5½ inches of shattered bone from Virgil's upper arm.

43. Lynn R. Bailey, ed., *A Tenderfoot in Tombstone: The Private Journal of George Whitewell Parsons: The Turbulent Years: 1880–82*. Tucson, AZ: Westernlore Press, 1996, p.199.

44. Until recently, background information on Dan Tipton, Sherman McMaster, and Jack Johnson was either nonexistent or filled with inaccuracies. (Most writers have erroneously spelled Sherman McMaster as McMasters.) It was not until recently that historian Peter Brand's revealing articles shed light on these men, giving a fuller, detailed picture. I am indebted to Peter Brand for graciously sharing his information with me.

Dan Tipton was born in New York state and served as a sailor for the Union army on the USS *Malvern*. During his service, he saw considerable action, including the battle of Fort Fisher in January 1865. Not much else is known about him until he appeared in Tombstone in late 1881, seeking work as a miner. Peter Brand, "Daniel G. Tipton and the Earp Vendetta Posse." *National Association for Outlaw and Lawman History*, October-December 2000, p. 17.

Sherman McMaster had an equally varied background that would serve Earp well. Fluent in Spanish and an excellent tracker, McMaster was known as a confederate of the Cowboy faction. Wyatt maintained that McMaster was actually an informant during his years in Tombstone. Born in Illinois, McMaster struck out on his own by the 1870s. He joined the Texas Rangers on September 1, 1878, based out of Ysleta, Texas. Interestingly, McMaster was likely a guard when Curly Bill was arrested for attempting to rob an army ambulance. McMaster left the Rangers the following April, and historian Peter Brand notes that there is a great probability that McMaster was associated with Pony Deal, Curly Bill, and Johnny Ringo before heading to Tombstone. Peter Brand, "Sherman W. McMaster(s): The El Paso Salt War, Texas Rangers and Tombstone." *Western Outlaw-Lawman History Association*, Winter 1999, pp. 2, 5.

Jack Johnson, who was labeled "Turkey Creek" Jack Johnson by Stuart Lake, was really Jack Blount. Born in Missouri in 1847, he worked as a lead miner before turning to more exciting ventures with his brother, Bud, such as running off stock and hurrahing towns. They proceeded to cause trouble, even attempting to break a friend out of jail in nearby Webb City, Missouri. Eventually both John Blount and his brother moved to Arizona, where Bud was involved in a murder and sent to prison in Yuma. In Tombstone, John Blount, now going by the name Jack Johnson, became friendly with the Cowboy faction and even helped rustle cows from Mexico. Johnson reportedly offered to work for Wyatt as an undercover informant. Wyatt wrote a letter to Acting Governor John Gosper on behalf of John's brother, urging that Bud be paroled, and also had U.S. Marshal Crawley Dake write a letter on Blount's behalf. Bud was released from Yuma prison on March 11, 1882. Peter Brand, "Wyatt Earp, Jack Johnson and the Notorious Blount Brothers." *National Association for Outlaw and Lawman History*, October-December 2003, pp. 37, 39, 43–44.

"Texas Jack" Vermillion was working as a carpenter in Tombstone and had the reputation of being a crack shot. Little else is known about his background, other than that he served in the Confederacy during the Civil War.

45. At Morgan's coroner's inquest, Dr. Goodfellow noted that the bullet had entered his back, just left of the spinal column, gone through Morgan's left kidney, and emerged on the right side near the gall bladder, severely injuring many arteries, which caused massive hemorrhaging.

46. March 26, 1882.

47. Dan Tipton stayed behind in Tombstone. Some speculate that he did so to keep an eye on certain people in town and to wire the Earps of any suspicious activity.

48. Allen Barra, *Inventing Wyatt Earp: His Life and Many Legends*. New York: Carroll & Graf Publishers, Inc., 1998, p. 249.

49. Clara Spaulding Brown disputed Behan's claims. In her column, Brown noted, "Behan claims they tried to resist an arrest, but the bystanders claim that this was all that passed [the verbal exchange], and nothing was said about an arrest. He [Behan] also asserts that every one of the party drew their guns on him, which is denied by the

spectators. All were heavily armed, but no motion was made." *San Diego Daily Union*, March 31, 1882.

50. How Cruz was actually killed is in question. Stuart Lake says that Cruz told Earp he was paid $25 simply to be a lookout and that after giving the information, he was challenged by Wyatt to draw his gun. What is most likely is Earp caught Cruz, obtained information about who else was involved in Morgan's murder, and killed him. Years later, Earp said that he was convinced, based on information from Cruz, that Pete Spence had nothing to do with Morgan's murder, even though he had been against them. Allen Barra, *Inventing Wyatt Earp: His Life and Many Legends*. New York: Carroll & Graf Publishers, Inc., 1998, p. 260.

51. Warren Earp was left to wait for the rider with the money at an area near Iron Springs and was not involved in this gunfight.

52. *San Francisco Examiner*, August 2, 1896.

53. Barnes later died from his wound.

54. Perry Mallen was quickly discovered to be a fraud and was never a deputy sheriff in Los Angeles or elsewhere.

55. There were claims that Curly Bill was never killed by Wyatt. Years after the incident, people swore to Curly Bill sightings just like they would years later for Elvis Presley. The *Epitaph* offered to donate $2,000 to any charity if Curly Bill would come into their office to prove his existence. The money offer was never accepted. Johnny Barnes told Fred Dodge that Curly Bill was indeed killed by Wyatt and his body was buried in an unmarked grave on Frank Patterson's ranch. Jeff Morey to the author, February 15, 2004.

56. This was the second fire to strike the town within one year. On June 22, 1881, a large section of Allen Street caught fire. The Golden Eagle Brewery would be rebuilt and renamed The Crystal Palace. It still stands at Fifth and Allen streets today.

57. A miner's strike, which shut down mining operations for four months, allowed the water levels in many mines to rise. Several smaller mines closed their lower-level areas because of the rising water. By 1911, all efforts to pump water out of the mines had ceased.

58. By 1890, the remaining Tombstone mines produced less than $300,000 gross per year. Wm. B. Shillingberg, *Tombstone, A.T.: A History of Early Mining, Milling and Mayhem*. Spokane, WA: Arthur H. Clark Company, 1999, p. 340.

59. No one knows who really killed Ringo, although some suspected it was Wyatt Earp. Many historians find this hard to believe, given that Wyatt was in Colorado and would have had to make a long trip as well as know exactly where to find and kill Ringo. Others believe that "Buckskin Frank" Leslie killed him.

60. Peter Brand, "Daniel G. Tipton and the Earp Vendetta Posse." *National Association for Outlaw and Lawman History*, October-December 2000, p. 25.

61. Peter Brand, "Wyatt Earp, Jack Johnson and the Notorious Blount Brothers." *National Association for Outlaw and Lawman History*, October-December 2003, p. 45.

62. Peter Brand, "Sherman W. McMaster(s): The El Paso Salt War, Texas Rangers and Tombstone." *Western Outlaw-Lawman History Association*, Winter 1999, pp. 15–16.

63. Casey Tefertiller, *Wyatt Earp: The Life Behind the Legend*. New York: John Wiley & Sons, Inc., 1997, p. 279.

64. Bob Boze Bell, *The Illustrated Life and Times of Wyatt Earp*. Phoenix, AZ: Tri Star-Boze Publications, 1993, p. 97.

Chapter 2

1. The films focusing on Davy Crockett were *The Martyrs of the Alamo* (1915), *Davy Crockett* (1916), and *Davy Crockett at the Fall of the Alamo* (1926). Wild Bill Hickok was a featured character in two films, John Ford's *The Iron Horse* (1924) and *The Last Frontier* (1926). William S. Hart played a highly fictionalized Hickok in *Wild Bill Hickok* (1923). General George A. Custer had four films made about his exploits: *Britton of the Seventh* (1916), *The Scarlet West* (1925), *General Custer at the Little Big Horn*, and *The Last Frontier* (both 1926). He was a featured character in *Wild Bill Hickok* (1923) and *Spoilers of the West* (1927).

2. Letter from Wyatt Earp to longtime friend John Hays Hammond, dated May 21, 1925. Casey Tefertiller, *Wyatt Earp: The Life Behind the Legend*. New York: John Wiley & Sons, Inc., 1997, p. 319.

3. Poverty Row was an industry term for studios or production companies that made movies with extremely low budgets, often forsaking interior sets to save money.

4. William S. Hart collection, Box 112, Seaver Center for Western History Research, Natural History Museum of Los Angeles County. (Hereinafter referred to as William S. Hart Collection.)

5. January 15, 1924. William S. Hart Collection.

6. Anne Johnston to William S. Hart, February 21, 1927. Ibid.

7. Walter Noble Burns had contacted Earp to see if he could write a book about him with his assistance. Earp declined as Flood was already doing that. Burns then spoke to Earp about Holliday, which was another book he had in mind. Burns turned down Earp's later offer, as he was already at work on his own book about the events in Tombstone. Burns' 1927 book, *Tombstone: An Iliad of the Southwest*, dubbed Earp as the "Lion of Tombstone."

8. John Flood to William S. Hart, March 24, 1927. William S. Hart Collection.

9. January 3, 1929. *Ibid.*

10. Sadie went so far as to travel east to talk to Lake's book editor, insisting on her point of view that it be "a nice, clean story."

11. *New York Times*, January 10, 1932.

12. Donald Chaput's *Virgil Earp: Western Peace Officer* has attempted to correct that mistake, giving Virgil the credit he was sorely lacking as a law officer.

13. Allen Barra, *Inventing Wyatt Earp: His Life and Many Legends*. New York: Carroll & Graf Publishers, Inc., 1998, p. 345.

14. Both *Law and Order* and *Frontier Marshal* were fairly low budget films for their time, giving Universal and Fox a modest profit but hardly setting the box office afire. Other films over the years would loosely base their story on the Earp saga in Tombstone, using fictional characters to avoid any legal conflict with Stuart Lake or Sadie.

15. Double bills were an indirect result of the ongoing Depression. By 1935, almost every theater chain in the United States was showing double bills, except for the movie palaces in larger urban cities like New York, Chicago, and Los Angeles.

16. Bogart made only two Westerns in his career, *The Oklahoma Kid* (1939) with James Cagney and *Virginia City* (1940). Cagney would make two more oaters in the 1950s: *Run for Cover* (1955) and *Tribute to a Bad Man* (1956). Errol Flynn made only one Western in the 1930s, *Dodge City* (1939), but would go one to make several more in the 1940s, including *Virginia City* (1940), *Santa Fe Trail* (1940), *They Died With Their Boots On* (1941), and *San Antonio* (1945).

17. Sadie died on December 20, 1944. It was said that

she died of senility; it's possible that her death was due to Alzheimer's disease. She was cremated and her ashes, along with Wyatt's, are buried in a Jewish cemetery in Colma, California.

18. Lake never published another book, although he did consider other subjects, including Doc Holliday, Pat Garrett, a history of the J. B. Stetson Company, and Wells Fargo. He did work in the film industry, supplying story ideas for many films, including *The Westerner* (1940), *Wells Fargo Days* (1944), *Winchester '73* (1950), and *Powder River* (1953). He also suggested to Walt Disney stories about Francis Marion, the legendary Swamp Fox of the Revolutionary War, and Texas John Slaughter as potential subjects for film or television projects. Disney did produce for his weekly TV show limited run series based on both characters. My thanks to Allen Barra, Tim Fattig, and Jeff Morey for sharing this information with me.

19. For the truly trivia-minded, the sixteen films featuring Earp from 1939 to 1994 are: *Frontier Marshal* (1939), *Tombstone: The Town Too Tough to Die* (1942), *My Darling Clementine* (1946), *Winchester '73* (1950), *Gun Belt* (1953), *Masterson of Kansas* (1954), *Wichita* (1955), *Gunfight at the O.K. Corral* (1957), *Badman's Country* (1958), *Cheyenne Autumn* (1964), *The Outlaws Is Coming* (1965; a Three Stooges movie!), *Hour of the Gun* (1967), *Doc* (1971), *Sunset* (1988), *Tombstone* (1993), and *Wyatt Earp* (1994). The four television movies: *I Married Wyatt Earp* (1983), *The Gambler Returns: The Luck of the Draw* (1991), *Four Eyes and Six Guns* (1992) and *Young Indiana Jones and the Hollywood Follies* (1994). Hugh O'Brian reprised his role as Earp in a television movie called *Wyatt Earp: Return to Tombstone* (1993), which featured clips from his TV series (now colorized!) that recounted his exploits in Tombstone, including the gunfight. One interesting aspect of this highly fictionalized show was it was the *only* television movie to be filmed in the real Tombstone.

20. The episode, which aired on October 25, 1968, was called *Specter of the Gun*.

Chapter 3

1. Zanuck left Fox in 1956 to work as an independent producer. His most famous film during this time was *The Longest Day* (1962). That same year, 1962, he returned to help salvage the studio after the financial disaster of *Cleopatra*. In May 1971, Zanuck resigned as chief executive; he died eight years later at the age of 77.

2. Sol Wurtzel began at Fox as a stenographer. In 1917, he became William Fox's personal secretary and was soon overseeing many Fox productions. By the mid–1930s, Wurtzel had graduated to a producer of mostly B-pictures, such as the Mr. *Moto* series. He died in 1958.

3. Dwan began his career in motion pictures in 1911 as a director for the American Film Company, after he was sent to California from the main office in New York City to see why a production was being held up. The director had gone off on a drinking binge, leaving the actors and crew stranded. Dwan stepped in and took over. He worked at Universal in the teens, directing an unknown Lon Chaney in some films, and went on to direct many movies with Douglas Fairbanks and Gloria Swanson. Dwan made the transition to sound films with ease. He left Fox in 1945 to work at Republic. He made his last film, *Most Dangerous Man Alive*, in 1958 (released in 1961). His filmography boasts over 400 films, including *Robin Hood* (1922), *Manhandled* (1924), *Stage Struck* (1925), *The Iron Mask* (1929), *Brewster's Millions* (1945), and *Sands of Iwo Jima* (1949).

4. Kevin Brownlow, *The War, The West, and The Wilderness*. New York: Alfred A. Knopf, Inc., 1978, p. 280.

5. It is not known why Doc Holliday's last name was changed to Halliday.

6. *American Film Institute Catalogue, Feature Films 1931–1940*. Berkeley, CA: University of California Press, 1993, p. 711.

7. Bogdanovich, Peter, *Who the Devil Made It*. New York: Alfred A. Knopf, Inc., 1997, p. 109.

8. *Frontier Marshal* script. June 1, 1939. Margaret Herrick Library, Academy of Motion Picture Arts and Sciences. Beverly Hills, California.

9. *Ibid.*

10. June 28, 1939. *Ibid.*

11. The threats of federal intervention grew from a series of scandals that rocked the film industry during 1922–23. First there was the Roscoe Arbuckle trial, in which the comedian was falsely accused of rape. Three juries later (the first two were hung), Arbuckle was found innocent, but the damage was done. He was banned from appearing in films, although he did return in the early 1930s in a series of comedy shorts before his death in 1933. There was also the mysterious death of director William Desmond Taylor, which romantically linked actresses Mabel Normand and Mary Miles Minter with him. Their careers were damaged by the press reports. It is still believed that Minter's mother shot the director. Then actor Wallace Reid died of a drug overdose. Reid was a popular star of the period and during the making of one film was hurt on the job. Paramount, his studio, gave him shots of morphine to ease his pain so he could finish the film. By completion of the picture, Reid was hooked on the drug, and the studio found it easier to supply him with the narcotic rather than risk the publicity if Reed went through a course of detoxification.

12. The PCA began to see its authority fade in the 1950s. Some theaters began showing films that did not have a PCA seal of approval, including *The Moon Is Blue* (1953) and *The Man With the Golden Arm* (1955). More and more films simply ignored the PCA approval and, following liberal rulings by the Supreme Court on obscenity and civil liberties, the code was vastly rewritten in 1966. Two years later, a ratings system was introduced that put an end to the PCA.

13. Talk about strange bedfellows! Jason Joy had been an executive in the MPPDA under Will Hays where, before taking his position at Fox, he had the authority to suggest changes in the scripts and films that were submitted. Breen himself later left the PCA for a short tenure as head of production at RKO in the early 1940s.

14. *Frontier Marshal* PCA notes. Margaret Herrick Library, Academy of Motion Picture Arts and Sciences. Beverly Hills, California.

15. *Ibid.*

16. *Ibid.*

17. One could also count actor Russell Simpson, who appeared as a judge in *Law and Order* (1932), a fictional version of the famous gunfight. He is also the newspaper editor in the 1934 version of *Frontier Marshal* and *My Darling Clementine* (1946).

18. Eddie Foy, Jr.'s, film appearances as his father include *Frontier Marshal* (1939), *Lillian Russell* (1940), *Yankee Doodle Dandy* (1942), and *Wilson* (1944). He would play his father in a *Bob Hope Chrysler Theatre* episode called "The Seven Little Foys" in 1964, with Mickey Rooney playing George M. Cohan. Eddie Foy, Jr., also provided his father's voice in a scene in *Gunfight at the O.K. Corral* (1957).

19. Armond Fields, *Eddie Foy: A Biography*. Jefferson, NC: McFarland and Company, Inc., 1999, p. 42.

20. *Hollywood Reporter*, June 3, 1939, p. 2.

21. Bogdanovich, Peter, *Who the Devil Made It*. New York: Alfred A. Knopf, Inc., 1997, p. 108.

22. *Ibid*.

23. *Hollywood Reporter*, July 7, 1939, p. 7.

24. In one scene at the bar, Doc is showing Wyatt his gun, saying it is a Buntline Special but that he cut the barrel down and smoothed the trigger work. This line will cause an Earp historian to laugh loudly. Reportedly, Ned Buntline, a writer of Western pulps in the 1870s and 1880s, gave Wyatt and Bat Masterson special Colt .45 pistols with a twelve-inch barrel. There is some doubt whether this gun ever existed at all, but many Earp historians believe that Wyatt may have used a ten-inch-barrel pistol, possibly in the famous gunfight.

25. John Ford would do a similar shot, although more effectively in *My Darling Clementine*, with Doc alone in his hotel room, looking at his medical degrees. "Doctor John Holliday," he says with great sarcasm, before hurling a shot glass at the framed papers.

Chapter 4

1. Sherman also obtained the western distribution rights of the film, which made him a large sum of money. *Daily Variety*, September 26, 1952, pp. 1, 9.

2. August 25, 1941, first script draft. Paramount Collection. Margaret Herrick Library, Academy of Motion Picture Arts and Sciences. Beverly Hills, California.

3. *Ibid*.

4. September 8, 1941, final script draft. Paramount Collection. Margaret Herrick Library, Academy of Motion Picture Arts and Sciences. Beverly Hills, California.

5. *Tombstone: The Town Too Tough to Die* PCA notes. Margaret Herrick Library, Academy of Motion Picture Arts and Sciences. Beverly Hills, California.

6. Another concern of the PCA was the way the dancing girls in the saloon were presented. The script described a poster out in front of the Bird Cage Theatre that promoted the girls as "exquisite, charming, adorable beauties—*at your service*." The PCA stressed that none of these girls should suggest they were prostitutes. When Ruth is made up by Queenie in the Bird Cage, she exclaims, "Oh! I look just like a *hussy!*" Queenie laughingly replies, "That's what we want you to look like, honey—*just like me*." The PCA stated that this exchange was unacceptable as it classified them as prostitutes. "If Ruth's line is changed to read, 'Oh! I look just like a barmaid,' it will be acceptable," they told Sherman. *Ibid*.

7. *Ibid*.

8. *Ibid*.

9. Selander directed 137 films in his career, from *Ride 'em Cowboy* (1936; his first movie with Buck Jones) to his last in 1968, *Arizona Bushwhackers*. He also directed numerous television series before his death in 1979.

10. *Hollywood Reporter*, November 1, 1940, p. 2.

11. *The Whistler* spawned six sequels: *The Mark of the Whistler* (1944), *The Voice of the Whistler*, *The Power of the Whistler* (both 1945), *Mysterious Intruder*, *The Secret of the Whistler* (both 1946), and *The Thirteenth Hour* (1947).

12. Frances Gifford's career is an unusual story. She was visiting a movie set where a casting director offered her a screen test. Signed by Samuel Goldwyn, she was loaned out to other studios and, after a small part in *Mr. Smith Goes to Washington* (1939), she began getting better roles. She is probably best known for her lead role in the *Jungle Girl* serial for Republic Pictures. In 1948 she was involved in a serious car accident that left her with severe head injuries. Although she appeared to recover, in 1958 she was admitted into a California state mental hospital for treatment. It was later reported that she was released in 1978 and was working at the Pasadena library for many years. She died in 1994 at the age of 74.

Edgar Buchanan entered films in 1939. Prior to that, he was a respected oral surgeon in Eugene, Oregon. Moving his practice to Altadena, California, he began performing in plays at the Pasadena Playhouse. At the age of 36, he gave up his dental practice and worked steadily for 38 years as a character actor. He is probably best known for his role of Uncle Joe in the television series *Petticoat Junction*. He died in 1979 at the age of 76.

13. All of the major studios, except Universal, had ranch facilities where they built their outdoor sets. Most of the studios bought their ranches in the early 1930s, when the San Fernando Valley, when the area was still mainly farmland. By the mid–1960s, most of these properties were sold off when studios were downsizing in favor of using actual locations. Both the Fox and Paramount ranches are now part of the California State Parks Department and are still used for filmmaking. The only studio to retain its ranch facilities today is the Walt Disney Studio, which rents the property to many filmmakers.

14. *Hollywood Reporter*, August 7, 1941, p. 7.

15. *Hollywood Reporter*, September 3, 1941, pp. 1, 4.

16. *Tombstone: The Town Too Tough to Die* shooting schedule. Margaret Herrick Library, Academy of Motion Picture Arts and Sciences. Beverly Hills, California.

17. *Hollywood Reporter*, January 22, 1941.

18. The score, although originally composed for the film, is awful. It sounds like the typical accompaniment for other low-budget B Westerns of the time, with nothing to enhance the scenes. The music during the scene where Johnny washes Ruth's face is terribly overplayed with comical tones, as if to tell the audience the scene is funny. There is nothing to the score that enhances the film other than the music leading up to the famous gunfight.

Chapter 5

1. Bogdanovich, Peter, *John Ford*. Berkeley, CA: University of California Press, 1978, pp. 84–5.

2. *The American West of John Ford*, TV documentary, Group One–Timex–CBS Productions, 1971.

3. Larry Blake to the author, April, 1981.

4. Ford had very poor eyesight all his life. After surgery for cataracts in 1953, he wore an eye patch over his left eye—partially for comfort to his eye, but also to create an image.

5. Ford went on to earn two Oscars for Best Documentary, *Battle of Midway* (1942) and *December 7th* (1943).

6. Fox studios loaned Ford to MGM to make the film, and his entire salary of $30,000 went to fund the Ford Photo Field Farm in the San Fernando Valley. It was built as a gathering place for members of the Photo Field Unit.

7. *My Darling Clementine* was also the first film for Henry Fonda and Victor Mature since the end of World War II.

8. This would be the first of thirteen Western films Ford would direct over the next eighteen years.

9. Rudy Behlmer, ed., *Memo from Darryl F. Zanuck: The Golden Years at 20th Century-Fox*. New York: Grove Press, 1993, p. 101.

10. Miller's other writing credits included *Tripoli* (1950), *The Far Horizons* (1955), and *Run For Cover* (1955),

as well as episodes of *Gunsmoke* and *Rawhide*. He also served as producer at various times on such television series as *The Virginian*, *It Takes a Thief*, *Ironside*, *Cannon*, and *Little House on the Prairie*.

11. Lyons, Robert, ed., *My Darling Clementine*. New Brunswick, NJ: Rutgers University Press, 1984, p. 141.

12. *My Darling Clementine* story conference notes, March 5, 1946. John Ford Collection, Lilly Library, Indiana University, Bloomington, Indiana.

13. *Ibid.*

14. *Ibid.*

15. In the first draft of the script, James bought a brooch for his fiancée. In the film the brooch became a cross. *Ibid.*

16. *Ibid.*

17. *Ibid.*

18. Lyons, Robert, ed., *My Darling Clementine*. New Brunswick, NJ: Rutgers University Press, 1984, p. 144.

19. *My Darling Clementine* PCA notes. Margaret Herrick Library, Academy of Motion Picture Arts and Sciences. Beverly Hills, California.

20. *Ibid.*

21. March 5, 1946. *Ibid.*

22. There would be two additional script revisions dated March 25 and 30, 1946.

23. *My Darling Clementine*, March 11, 1946 draft. 20th Century-Fox Script Collection. UCLA Special Collections.

24. *My Darling Clementine* PCA notes. Margaret Herrick Library, Academy of Motion Picture Arts and Sciences. Beverly Hills, California.

25. In a studio memo to Ford from Samuel G. Engel, dated March 30, 1946, he stated, "I do think that it would be useless to shoot Old Man Clanton's exit from the story two ways. I had forgotten that he kills Virgil in cold blood and hence—as an out and out murderer—he must pay the penalty of the law. I think you will agree with this." *Ibid.*

26. April 16, 1946. *Ibid.*

27. Fonda was under contract to Fox, as were Darnell and Crain. Rudy Behlmer, ed., *Memo from Darryl F. Zanuck: The Golden Years at 20th Century-Fox*. New York: Grove Press, 1993, p. 101.

28. Fonda's films with Ford, in chronological order, were *Young Mr. Lincoln*, *Drums Along the Mohawk* (both 1939), *The Grapes of Wrath* (1940), *Battle of Midway* (1942, narrator), *My Darling Clementine* (1946), *The Fugitive* (1947), *Fort Apache* (1948), and *Mister Roberts* (1955).

29. Ford began drinking on the set after his fight with Fonda, something he very rarely did prior to this incident. Some believe the gall bladder surgery was a story concocted by the studio publicity department to cover up the fact that Ford was actually fired.

30. Fonda and Stewart would have made an interesting pair because the two men were lifelong friends, beginning when they were struggling stage actors and roommates in the early 1930s. Later they again shared an apartment when they were starting out in Hollywood.

31. Eyman, Scott, *Print the Legend: The Life and Times of John Ford*. New York: Simon and Schuster, 1999, p. 311.

32. Memo dated January 8, 1946. Behlmer, Rudy, ed., *Memo from Darryl F. Zanuck: The Golden Years at 20th Century-Fox*. New York: Grove Press, 1993, p. 102.

33. *Ibid.*, p. 103.

34. Cathy Downs had modest experience, having been signed by Fox to a contract in 1944. She previously appeared in five films. The rest of her career was limited to B Westerns and science fiction films, including *The She-Creature* (1956) and *The Amazing Colossal Man* (1957). She died in 1976 at the age of 52.

35. John Ireland is one of several actors who have something of an incestuous relationship in the Earp-gunfight filmographies. Playing Billy Clanton in Ford's film, he was also cast as Johnny Ringo in *Gunfight at the O.K. Corral* (1957).

36. For the truly trivia-minded, both Jane Darwell and Fred Libby were in seven Ford films, Russell Simpson made ten, William Steele appeared in eleven, Mae Marsh did sixteen, Ward Bond and Russell Simpson are tied at twenty-six films, brother Francis Ford appeared in thirty-two films, while Jack Pennick holds the record of forty-one film appearances. He began with Ford in 1926 on *The Blue Eagle* and was the director's unofficial aide-de-camp during World War II. Although Danny Borzage appeared in only thirteen films, he worked steadily for Ford since 1924, providing accordion music on the set and between scenes.

37. McBride, Joseph, *Searching for John Ford: A Life*. New York: St. Martin's Press, 1999, p. 433–34.

38. Behlmer, Rudy, ed., *Memo from Darryl F. Zanuck: The Golden Years at 20th Century-Fox*. New York: Grove Press, 1993, p. 101–02.

39. The building was used as the fort headquarters in *She Wore a Yellow Ribbon*. It is also seen in *My Darling Clementine* when Billy Clanton rides up and collapses on what is supposed to be the porch of his family ranch.

40. *Hollywood Reporter*, February 27, 1946.

41. "Clementine on Horseback." *Cue*, November 16, 1946.

42. *My Darling Clementine* production file. Margaret Herrick Library, Academy of Motion Picture Arts and Sciences. Beverly Hills, California.

43. The shot of Holt's horse falling can be seen in the preview version of the film on the DVD release.

44. *Directed by John Ford*, American Film Institute, 1971.

45. *The American West of John Ford*, Group One-Timex-CBS Productions, 1971.

46. *Directed by John Ford*, American Film Institute, 1971.

47. Lyons, Robert, ed., *My Darling Clementine*. New Brunswick, NJ: Rutgers University Press, 1984, p. 142.

48. Bogdanovich, Peter, *Who The Hell's In It*. New York: Alfred A. Knopf, Inc., 2004, p. 307.

49. Eyman, Scott, *Print the Legend: The Life and Times of John Ford*. New York: Simon and Schuster, 1999, p. 313.

50. Lyons, Robert, ed., *My Darling Clementine*. New Brunswick, NJ: Rutgers University Press, 1984, p. 148.

51. Behlmer, Rudy, ed., *Memo from Darryl F. Zanuck: The Golden Years at 20th Century-Fox*. New York: Grove Press, 1993, p. 103–05.

52. *My Darling Clementine*, DVD special features.

53. *Ibid.*

54. Eyman, Scott, *Print the Legend: The Life and Times of John Ford*. New York: Simon and Schuster, 1999, p. 313.

55. *Time*, November 11, 1946.

56. *The Hollywood Reporter*, October 9, 1946.

57. *Variety*, October 9, 1946.

58. *Motion Picture Herald*, October 2, 1946.

59. The recently released DVD contains both the preview and final release prints of the film.

60. John Sturges would use a similar idea in his *Gunfight at the O.K. Corral* (1957), and Ford would revisit the reflection of one's face in a framed picture in *Cheyenne Autumn* (1964). In that scene, the Secretary of the Interior (Edward G. Robinson) agrees to meet with the Cheyenne Indians and walks to a framed picture of Abraham Lincoln. With his reflection in the framed picture, he asks, "Old friend, what would you do?"

61. The film does not mention such people as Ringo, Curly Bill, Johnny Behan, and the McLaurys. Neither is

there any mention of Wyatt nor any of the brothers, for that matter, having a wife.

Chapter 6

1. In 1959, there were 27 Western series on the three major television networks (ABC, CBS, and NBC).

2. The first season of the show dealt with Wyatt Earp in Ellsworth and Wichita, Kansas. The next three seasons saw him in Dodge City.

3. Hugh O'Brian, the star of the series, wanted to branch out and had tired of playing the same part. While the show's ratings for the last season (1960–61) had dropped from the top 20, it was still popular enough with the critics and audiences to have run one more season. Yoggy, Gary A., *Riding the Video Range: The Rise and Fall of the Western on Television*. Jefferson, NC: McFarland and Company, Inc., 1995, p. 140.

4. Letter dated July 10, 1954. Hal B. Wallis Collection, Margaret Herrick Library, Academy of Motion Picture Arts and Sciences. Beverly Hills, California.

5. Memo dated August 4, 1954. Paul Nathan correspondence. *Ibid.*

6. Wallis moved his company to Universal in 1969, where he made his last seven films. He died in 1986 at the age of 87.

7. Winston Miller wrote the screenplay for *My Darling Clementine*. David Dortort would go on to create and produce two popular Western TV series, *Bonanza* and *The High Chaparral*. James Warner Bellah wrote the screenplays for Ford's *Sergeant Rutledge* (1960; based on his novel) and *The Man Who Shot Liberty Valance* (1962). Oscar Brodney wrote the screenplays for *Harvey* (1950), *The Glenn Miller Story* (1954), and *Tammy and the Bachelor* (1957). Dudley Nichols wrote many scripts for John Ford, including *Judge Priest*, *The Lost Patrol* (both 1934), *The Informer* (1935), *Mary of Scotland* (1936), and *Stagecoach* (1939). He also wrote *For Whom the Bell Tolls* (1943), *Bells of St. Mary's* (1945), *The Big Sky* (1952), and *The Tin Star* (1957). They also considered Western novel writers A. B. Guthrie, Borden Chase, and Jack Schaefer. Paul Nathan correspondence, Hal B. Wallis Collection, Margaret Herrick Library, Academy of Motion Picture Arts and Sciences. Beverly Hills, California.

8. Memo dated February 7, 1955. *Ibid.*

9. *Ibid.*

10. Memo dated May 11, 1955. *Ibid.*

11. Lake's outline focused more on Holliday than Earp. He created the Laura Denbow character during this time. Lake to Nathan, May 26, 1955. *Ibid.*

12. In the July 23, 1955 memo, Wallis called Earp "the outstanding law enforcement officer in Western history," while noting that Holliday was "perhaps the most ruthless killer." Hal B. Wallis correspondence, Hal B. Wallis Collection, Margaret Herrick Library, Academy of Motion Picture Arts and Sciences. Beverly Hills, California.

13. *Ibid.*

14. There is no mention of why Curtiz read the script, either by Wallis's invitation or through the Hollywood grapevine. Nor was there any discussion at this point of Curtiz as a possible director. Memo dated September 30, 1955. *Ibid.*

15. Memo dated December 5, 1955. *Ibid.*

16. In a letter to Wallis, Curtiz described the 148-page script as too long. "It is difficult to suggest definitely what to cut, because each scene is interesting. . . . I know I can make an exciting and very successful picture. . . . I'm very anxious to hear your decision," he wrote. Letter dated December 5, 1955. *Ibid.*

17. Sturges was paid a salary of $60,000. *Gunfight at the O.K. Corral* budget file, Hal B. Wallis Collection, Margaret Herrick Library, Academy of Motion Picture Arts and Sciences. Beverly Hills, California.

18. Certainly the constant cough that Bogart had developed would have been ideal for the role, but it was too close to reality: The actor was suffering from throat cancer and would die in January 1957.

19. Memo dated January 19, 1956. Paul Nathan correspondence, Hal B. Wallis Collection, Margaret Herrick Library, Academy of Motion Picture Arts and Sciences. Beverly Hills, California.

20. Kirk Douglas, *Climbing the Mountain: My Search For Meaning*. New York: Simon and Schuster, 1997, p. 103.

21. *Gunfight at the O.K. Corral* production budget file. Hal B. Wallis Collection, Margaret Herrick Library, Academy of Motion Picture Arts and Sciences. Beverly Hills, California.

22. Kirk Douglas, *The Ragman's Son*. New York: Simon and Schuster, 1988, p. 270.

23. Other actresses they considered for Laura Denbow were Eleanor Parker, Ruth Roman, Donna Reed, Vera Miles, and Susan Hayward. Actresses moderately under consideration included Barbara Rush, Gene Tierney, Olivia de Havilland, and Janet Leigh. Memo dated March 5, 1956. Paul Nathan correspondence, Hal B. Wallis Collection, Margaret Herrick Library, Academy of Motion Picture Arts and Sciences. Beverly Hills, California.

24. There is an interesting side note to the Kate Fisher character. Paul Nathan received a memo on October 4, 1955, from another Paramount production executive, John Mock, about a screenplay the studio bought that May entitled *The Sons of Katie Elder*. Producer Sam Briskin had planned to start production on the film in April 1956 and was concerned that the Kate Elder (her name in the original script draft) in the *Gunfight at the O.K. Corral* screenplay would "hurt the value of the title of our subsequent picture. From what I know of your script, it does not seem to me that you would lose any value to call your villainess 'Ellis,' 'Edwards' or a similar name." *The Sons of Katie Elder* was not made in 1956. It would have to wait until 1965, when Hal B. Wallis produced it starring John Wayne, his first film after his lung cancer surgery.

25. Sheb Wooley is best known as one of the killers in *High Noon*. Frank de Kova, James Westerfield, and Robert Middleton were well-known character actors. Lee Marvin was making a name for himself as a villain in films and would go on to win a Best Actor Oscar for *Cat Ballou* (1965). Raymond Burr played numerous villains in films, before finding stardom on television in *Perry Mason* (1957–66) and *Ironside* (1967–75). Richard Boone was another actor who played numerous bad guy roles before finding television success with TV series *Medic* (1954–56), *Have Gun–Will Travel* (1957–63) and *Hec Ramsey* (1972–74). Casting notes, Hal B. Wallis Collection, Margaret Herrick Library, Academy of Motion Picture Arts and Sciences. Beverly Hills, California.

26. Kelley, who played Morgan Earp, appeared as Ike Clanton in an episode about the gunfight on the television series, *You Are There*. Wallis and Nathan also considered him for the role of Ed Bailey.

27. The role of the corrupt sheriff, Cotton Wilson, went to character actor Frank Faylen, although Walter Matthau, Karl Malden, Kent Taylor, Charles McGraw, William Bendix, Lloyd Nolan, Dean Jagger, Broderick Crawford, and John McIntire were under consideration for the part. Ken Tobey, Chuck Connors, Myron Healey,

Bruce Bennett, Don Castle, and James Whitmore were casting choices for Bat Masterson (Tobey won the role). DeForest Kelley, Lee Van Cleef, and Charles Bronson were in the running to play Ed Bailey (Van Cleef got the job). Dean Stockwell and John Lupton were listed as possibilities for Jimmy Earp, but Martin Milner got the role. Leo Gordon, Ray Teal, and Ted de Corsia were up for John Shaughnessy. The role went to George Mathews, but Ted de Corsia was cast as Shanghai Pierce. John Hudson was chosen for Virgil Earp, although Harry Carey, Jr., and Lloyd Bridges were considered. Beulah Bondi and Olive Carey (the mother of Harry Carey, Jr.) were in contention for the part of Mrs. Clanton, with the role going to the latter actress. Robert Wilke, Jack Elam, Henry Brandon, Leo Gordon, Lee Van Cleef, and James Westerfield were considered for roles as various Clanton brothers. The role of Dodge City mayor was open to E. G. Marshall, John McIntire, Walter Brennan, and Jesse White; it eventually went to actor Frank Carter. Character actor Whit Bissell won the role of John Clum from a list that included Bruce Bennett, Ray Teal, Walter Brennan, and Kent Taylor. *Ibid.*

28. There is a large group of actors and actresses who had an incestuous relationship with several films about Wyatt Earp and the famous gunfight. Aside from Don Castle in this film is Bing Russell, playing a bartender. His son, Kurt, would later play Wyatt in *Tombstone* (1993). Olive Carey played Mrs. Clanton and her son, Harry Carey, Jr. (who was up for Virgil Earp in this film), would later play Marshal Fred White in *Tombstone*. As noted earlier, Ken Tobey played Bat Masterson in this film and played Wyatt in an episode of *Cavalcade of America* in 1954. Lee Van Cleef, who played Ed Bailey in this film, also appeared in that television episode of *Cavalcade of America*. Mickey Simpson, who played Frank McLowery in this film, played Sam Clanton in Ford's *My Darling Clementine*. Danny Borzage, who was the accordionist in *My Darling Clementine*, plays a similar role in the Social Hall Dance that is interrupted by Shanghai Pierce and his men.

29. *Gunfight at the O.K. Corral* first draft script. John Sturges Collection, Margaret Herrick Library, Academy of Motion Picture Arts and Sciences. Beverly Hills, California.

30. *Ibid.*

31. In the film, this scene is played entirely in front of Wyatt's office, with Bat and Wyatt sitting on a bench watching the stage arrive and seeing Laura get off and take a buggy. All the dialogue of Virgil's letter is dropped at this point in the story.

32. In England, and other countries, the word "bum" was a colorful expression for ass. The line was changed to "scum."

33. In reality, White was killed where the Bird Cage Theatre now stands.

34. The scene would be revised as of April 10, 1956. *Gunfight at the O.K. Corral* first draft script. John Sturges Collection, Margaret Herrick Library, Academy of Motion Picture Arts and Sciences. Beverly Hills, California.

35. In this version of the script, Wyatt does not pick up James's body and walk away. Nor does he light the lantern on the wagon as he walks by the O.K. Corral. These actions, however, would be in the film. *Ibid.*

36. *Ibid.*

37. In this draft, Tom MacLowery (a misspelling of the McLaury name) gets burned, but Sturges changed it to Frank MacLowery after Mickey Simpson, who was a stuntman, was cast in the role. *Ibid.*

38. In the script, the area of the gunfight was described as being much closer to the original location. The final shootout was altered based on locations available.

39. *Gunfight at the O.K. Corral* first draft script. John Sturges Collection, Margaret Herrick Library, Academy of Motion Picture Arts and Sciences. Beverly Hills, California.

40. *Gunfight at the O.K. Corral* PCA notes. Margaret Herrick Library, Academy of Motion Picture Arts and Sciences. Beverly Hills, California.

41. *Ibid.*

42. *Ibid.*

43. *Ibid.*

44. *Ibid.*

45. Hal B. Wallis correspondence. Hal B. Wallis Collection, Margaret Herrick Library, Academy of Motion Picture Arts and Sciences. Beverly Hills, California.

46. Old Tucson has a long association with Hollywood. Built for the Columbia Pictures 1939 production *Arizona*, the location had a few buildings. By the 1950s, additional sets had been built as well as a small rail line with an authentic 1872 steam engine and cars. The train, dubbed *The Reno*, served the rail lines of the Comstock Lode in northern Nevada before MGM studios bought it in the mid-1940s. It was used in such films as *The Harvey Girls* (1946) and it was moved to Old Tucson in 1970. (The train and the depot set can be seen in *Tombstone* (1993), when Wyatt arrives in Tucson.) *Winchester '73, The Lone Ranger and the Lost City of Gold, Rio Bravo, El Dorado, McLintock!, Hombre, Rio Lobo, Joe Kidd, The Outlaw Josey Wales, The Last Hard Men,* and *Tombstone* are some of the films that used this location. Television series such as *Gunsmoke, Little House on the Prairie, Bonanza,* and *Have Gun–Will Travel* used the street sets for some episodes, as did *The High Chaparral,* which had permanent sets on the location.

47. Budget dated March 9, 1956. *Gunfight at the O.K. Corral* budget file. Hal B. Wallis Collection, Margaret Herrick Library, Academy of Motion Picture Arts and Sciences. Beverly Hills, California.

48. *Ibid.*

49. The budget for Lancaster's wardrobe was $2,015, while Douglas's ran $1,920. This included three sets of the same wardrobe (often called "doubles") for stunt work. In comparison to the male leads, the wardrobe budget for Rhonda Fleming was $4,100 and for Jo Van Fleet's clothing, $4,130. *Ibid.*

50. In the film, we see a banner across Schieffelin Hall announcing Foy's name and hear him singing in the background. Memo dated November 15, 1955. Paul Nathan Correspondence. Hal B. Wallis Collection, Margaret Herrick Library, Academy of Motion Picture Arts and Sciences. Beverly Hills, California.

51. In comparison, Roseman was asking $10,000 to score the picture and North had a salary of $12,500. Memo dated November 17, 1955. *Ibid.*

52. Tiomkin and Washington had a string of successes writing music and lyrics for many films, notably "Do Not Forsake Me, Oh My Darlin'" for *High Noon* (1952), which won them Oscars for Best Song.

53. Lake's letter to Nathan dated March 11, 1956. Uris's telegram to Nathan dated March 10, 1956. Paul Nathan Correspondence. Hal B. Wallis Collection, Margaret Herrick Library, Academy of Motion Picture Arts and Sciences. Beverly Hills, California.

54. *Ibid.*

55. *Ibid.*

56. Lake's letter of complaint was sent the same day he sent his letter to Wallis. Stuart Lake to Mary Dorfman at Screen Writers Guild. Letter dated March 18, 1956. *Ibid.*

57. *Gunfight at the O.K. Corral* daily production report. Hal B. Wallis Collection, Margaret Herrick Library, Academy of Motion Picture Arts and Sciences. Beverly Hills, California.

58. *Ibid.*

59. Douglas, Kirk. *The Ragman's Son.* New York: Simon and Schuster, 1988, p. 270.

60. Godbout, Oscar. "Echoes from *Gunfight at the O.K. Corral.*" *New York Times,* May 20, 1956.

61. Wallis, Hal B., and Charles Higham. *Starmaker: The Autobiography of Hal Wallis.* New York: MacMillan Publishing Co. Inc., 1980, p. 156.

62. *Gunfight at the O.K. Corral* daily production report. Hal B. Wallis Collection, Margaret Herrick Library, Academy of Motion Picture Arts and Sciences. Beverly Hills, California.

63. Lancaster would be brought back for one quick pick-up shot on July 24. Filming on Stage 15, they started at 5 p.m. and finished at 6:13 p.m. *Ibid.*

64. Laine was paid $7,500. Memo dated April 19, 1956. Paul Nathan Correspondence. Hal B. Wallis Collection, Margaret Herrick Library, Academy of Motion Picture Arts and Sciences. Beverly Hills, California.

65. *Gunfight at the O.K. Corral* PCA notes. Margaret Herrick Library, Academy of Motion Picture Arts and Sciences. Beverly Hills, California.

66. Lancaster was nominated for *From Here to Eternity* (1953), *Birdman of Alcatraz* (1962), and *Atlantic City* (1981).

67. Buford, Kate. *Burt Lancaster: An American Life.* New York: Alfred A. Knopf, 2000, p. 166.

68. *Ibid.*

69. On the set of *Tough Guys* (1986), Lancaster's departure on the last day was a quiet affair. He went to several members of the crew, shook hands, and in a soft voice bid them farewell. Douglas, on the other hand, posed for pictures during production with each crew member and on the last day gave the pictures, signed by him. He also sent out a letter to each crew member thanking them.

70. Lancaster and Douglas would co-star in five films: *I Walk Alone* (1948), *Gunfight at the O.K. Corral* (1957), *The Devil's Disciple* (1959, *Seven Days in May* (1964), and *Tough Guys* (1986). Burt Lancaster to the author, March 3, 1986.

71. Douglas, Kirk. *The Ragman's Son.* New York: Simon and Schuster, 1988, p. 271.

72. Buford, Kate. *Burt Lancaster: An American Life.* New York: Alfred A. Knopf, 2000, p. 165.

73. Part of the reason Earp's entrance is filmed this way is for dramatic purposes and partly to use cheating camera angles so that other areas of Old Tucson could be used for the Tombstone sequence.

74. This is the first film to show a confrontation between Doc and Ringo over Kate, something other films chose to ignore.

75. Jason Robards' Doc would utter similar lines to James Garner's Wyatt in *Hour of the Gun* (1967), also directed by Sturges.

76. Tiomkin used the theme song in various areas of the film for certain dramatic moments, although the entire gunfight is void of any music, relying only on sound effects and minimal dialogue, which makes it more effective.

Chapter 7

1. Two of the television Western series in the 1967 line-up didn't survive past the 13-week engagement. *Legend of Custer* lasted three months before being canceled, in part because of complaints by Native American groups. *Dundee and the Culhane* was the other canceled television series. *The Life and Legend of Wyatt Earp* went off the air in 1961.

2. The term "spaghetti Western" is very misleading. While many of these Westerns were made by Italian directors and featured Italian actors (as well as German and Spanish performers), many were also made by German film production companies, mainly shot in various areas of Spain. The choice of Spain, with many places serving as American Western states, was basically a budgetary decision. It was cheaper to film a Western in Spain than in America, and the same was true for Mexico. A cottage industry town in Durango, Mexico grew from several Westerns being filmed south of the border, including many starring John Wayne. Cheaper labor was the main incentive for producers to go to Mexico or Spain, with different locations as an additional motive.

3. By this point in his career, Sturges had directed such major hits as *Last Train from Gun Hill* (1959), *The Magnificent Seven* (1960), *Sergeants 3* (1962, featuring the fabled "Rat Pack" in a Western version of *Gunga Din*), and *The Great Escape* (1963).

4. Anhalt had written the screenplays for two other Sturges films, *A Girl Named Tamiko* (1963), and *The Satan Bug* (1965). Anhalt won his first Oscar (along with his wife, Edna) for *Panic in the Streets* (1950). His second Oscar was for the screenplay of *Becket* (1964). Anhalt's other credits include *Member of the Wedding* (1952), *The Young Lions* (1958), *The Boston Strangler* (1968), *Jeremiah Johnson* (1972), and the TV miniseries, *QBVII* (1974). Anhalt died in 2000.

5. Again, this film misspelled the McLaury name, no doubt taken from newspaper articles of the time.

6. 1964 script draft courtesy of the Don Cannon collection.

7. *Ibid.*

8. Wyatt and Doc were initially held on $10,000 bail each, but money was quickly raised, including Wyatt's putting up $7,000 of his own money for Holliday. Their bail was revoked on November 7 during the hearing, and the two men were not freed until November 24.

9. 1964 script draft courtesy of the Don Cannon collection.

10. *Ibid.*

11. During production, Sturges did film the election parade, with the Pete Spence character (played by Michael Tolan) taking part. The entire scene was cut from the film.

12. By the final draft, the Florentino Cruz character would be renamed Andy Warshaw. 1964 script draft courtesy of the Don Cannon collection.

13. This scene is in both the 1964 and 1966 script draft. Both script drafts courtesy of the Don Cannon collection.

14. *Ibid.*

15. Anhalt had an odd sequence right after this that really did not make much sense. Wyatt, riding alone, comes up alongside a high hacienda wall. From his horse, he can see over the wall, and he throws himself over the wall as a shot rings out. He kills the man who shot at him and then gets back on his horse. A little later, Wyatt stops at an adobe hut as he sees a stagecoach approach. As it rides by, the shotgun rider fires at Wyatt, hitting his horse. Wyatt, pinned beneath the animal, fires back, kills the shotgun rider and wounds the driver as the stage goes on. Getting out from under his horse, Wyatt starts walking toward Nogales. There was no story point to this scene and it was quickly removed.

16. There is a bit of irony with this scene. Jason Robards, who would play Doc, dies in a similar way in *Once Upon a Time in the West* (1968). In that film, he's following Charles Bronson out of town when he falls off his horse and dies.

17. 1964 script draft courtesy of the Don Cannon collection.

18. The original titles would read: "The most famous gunfight in the history of the American west was the gunfight at O.K. Corral. It took place on October 26, 1881 in the city of Tombstone, territory of Arizona." All this would take place as Clanton rides into town. August 15, 1966 script draft, John Sturges Collection, Margaret Herrick Library, Academy of Motion Picture Arts and Sciences. Beverly Hills, California.

19. *Ibid.*

20. *Ibid.*

21. *Ibid.*

22. *Ibid.*

23. *Ibid.*

24. This scene is somewhat identical to the one in *Frontier Marshal* (1939), when Doc, looking out his hotel room window, sees that Wyatt is about to be ambushed by two men and kills them.

25. Second 1966 script draft courtesy of the Don Cannon collection.

26. *The Hollywood Reporter*, July 19, 1966.

27. James Garner to the author, July 20, 2004.

28. Garner returned to the role of Maverick in 1981, when he starred in a new TV series for NBC titled *Bret Maverick*. The show lasted less than one season (1981–82). He also had another hugely popular television series, *The Rockford Files*, which ran from 1974–80.

29. The latter film involved an aging Wyatt Earp coming to Hollywood to serve as a technical consultant in a story about his life as a marshal, to be played by silent movie star Tom Mix (played by an unconvincing and completely miscast Bruce Willis). In the film, as Wyatt watches the filming of a movie version of the O.K. Corral gunfight, he has a brief flashback of the real event. The two men get involved in a murder mystery in Hollywood. The *only* thing worth watching about this film is Garner's effortless performance. When this author reminded him he was the only actor to play Earp twice, he referred to *Sunset* as, "Oh, *that* thing." James Garner to the author, July 20, 2004.

30. Robards would get a third nomination for his role as Howard Hughes in *Melvin and Howard* (1980). He also won a Tony award for his performance in *The Disenchanted* in 1959, and an Emmy award for *Inherit the Wind* in 1988.

31. *Hour of the Gun* production file. Margaret Herrick Library, Academy of Motion Picture Arts and Sciences. Beverly Hills, California.

32. *The Hollywood Reporter*, November 17, 1966.

33. *Hour of the Gun* production file. John Sturges Collection, Margaret Herrick Library, Academy of Motion Picture Arts and Sciences. Beverly Hills, California.

34. *Hour of the Gun* shooting schedule. John Sturges Collection, Margaret Herrick Library, Academy of Motion Picture Arts and Sciences. Beverly Hills, California.

35. The dates spent filming the opening credits and the gunfight were November 22 through 26 and December 3 and 5 through 8. *Ibid.*

36. Sturges had filmed 67 days, including various holidays. *Hour of the Gun* production file. Margaret Herrick Library, Academy of Motion Picture Arts and Sciences. Beverly Hills, California.

37. Ferris Webster and Sturges worked together as editor and director on a total of fifteen films, among them *The Magnificent Yankee* (1950), *The Law and Jake Wade* (1958), *The Magnificent Seven* (1960), *The Great Escape* (1963), *Sergeants 3* (1963), *The Hallelujah Trail* (1965), *Ice Station Zebra* (1968), and *Joe Kidd* (1972), their last collaboration. In 1972, Webster began a seven-year association with Clint Eastwood. He retired in 1979.

38. James Garner to the author, July 20, 2004.

39. October 4, 1967.

40. The term multiples meant the film was released into several movie theaters at the same time. October 4, 1967.

41. October 11, 1967.

42. Interestingly, none of the films had Doc dying in the correct location. Holliday died in Glenwood Springs, Colorado, but in the Glenwood Hotel, not a sanatorium.

43. James Garner to the author, July 20, 2004.

44. *Ibid.*

45. *Ibid.*

Chapter 8

1. In 1971, the TV Westerns consisted of *Gunsmoke, Bonanza, Alias Smith & Jones*, and *Nichols*. In 1961, the lineup included *Gunsmoke, Bonanza, Have Gun Will Travel, Laramie, Maverick, The Lawman, Cheyenne, Marshal Dillon* (reruns of the half-hour versions of the *Gunsmoke* series), *Wagon Train, Frontier Circus, Rawhide, The Outlaws, Tales of Wells Fargo*, and *The Tall Man*.

2. The studios counted in this tally include Universal, MGM, Warner Bros., Paramount, 20th Century-Fox, Columbia and United Artists.

3. Hamill, Pete. "The New American Western: On Writing *Doc*." *Harper's Bazaar*, 1971, p. 98.

4. *Ibid.*

5. Hamill, Pete. *Doc: The Original Screenplay*. New York: Paperback Library, 1971, pp.113, 115–16.

6. *Ibid.*, pp. 28–30.

7. In the film, all of this is dropped, as Doc is a willing participant. The film also dropped the campsite scene that suggested a homosexual bond between the two men. *Ibid.*, pp. 107, 109.

8. *Ibid.*, pp. 135, 138–39.

9. *Ibid.*, pp.198–99, 202.

10. *Daily Variety*, November 24, 1969.

11. All of the "spaghetti Westerns" that were popular in the late 1960s and early 1970s were filmed in various areas of Spain.

12. Greenburg, Dan. "Diary of a Frustrated Cowboy." *New York Times*, November 1, 1970.

13. December 3, 1969.

14. A carbon arc light is equivalent to a 50,000-watt light bulb. Greenburg, Dan. "Diary of a Frustrated Cowboy." *New York Times*, November 1, 1970.

15. *Ibid.*

16. Hugh O'Brian had a similar gun rig for the television series, *The Life and Legend of Wyatt Earp*.

17. Nine years later, this same company allowed another filmmaker, Michael Cimino, to make *Heaven's Gate* (1980), an epic Western that nearly forced United Artists into bankruptcy. The company was saved from the grosses of the next James Bond film. While Cimino had won an Oscar for his direction of *The Deer Hunter* (1978), his work on the Western was met with negative reviews.

Chapter 9

1. There have been only three Western films to win the coveted Best Picture award: *Cimarron* (1931), *Dances with Wolves* (1990) and Eastwood's *Unforgiven* (1992). Other Westerns to be nominated for Best Picture include *Stagecoach* (1939), *The Ox-Bow Incident* (1943), *High Noon* (1952), *Shane* (1953), *How the West Was Won* (1963) and *Butch Cassidy and the Sundance Kid* (1969).

2. Jeff Morey to the author, June 20, 2004.

3. In Kevin Jarre's January 22, 1992 script, much of the dialogue that Old Man Clanton speaks to the Mexican officer and his men was eventually changed after Jarre's departure from the set. In the film, it is Curly Bill who utters these lines when he and his men ride into the Mexican village and interrupt the wedding ceremony. Script from author's collection.

4. According to Jeff Morey, Kevin Jarre was going to play Hickok in the opening sequence. His ultimate goal was to write and direct a film based on the life of Hickok and was he using *Tombstone* as a springboard.

5. In the film, the above-mentioned sequence was broken up, and it appears to happen on a different night. The lines of dialogue for the drunken high roller were given to the Billy Clanton character, and it is Ike Clanton and Billy who attempt to free Curly Bill as the crowd gathers.

6. In the film, the entire sequence happens in the billiard hall, with Wyatt relating what occurred in Spicer's courtroom.

7. In the film, as Virgil comes out of the billiard hall, a woman with several children is going up the street when a group of Cowboys hurrahs the town. A small boy drops his ball in the street and runs to get it. Virgil grabs him and pulls him out of the way of the oncoming Cowboys. He tips his hat to the frightened woman and watches them as they move down the street. There is then a direct cut to Virgil posting the no-guns ordinance. Wyatt rides up and the conversation between the brothers takes place in the marshal's office.

8. For years there has been a rumor that a picture of a woman wearing nothing but a long black veil was Josephine Marcus. Many historians dispute the fact, citing that the picture was taken in the early 1900s and is not Josephine. It is one of the many myths that surround the Earp legend to this day.

9. In the film, Wyatt and Morgan drag Doc out of the saloon to take him to his hotel room. The scene continues in the saloon, where Ike demands his pistol and rifle and makes the threat that he will kill Holliday and the Earps on sight. Virgil is standing at the saloon door and buffaloes Ike, dragging him to jail. The scene then cuts to Doc's room with Dr. Goodfellow.

10. There is no dialogue in this sequence in the final film. Instead, Wyatt enters the house, takes off his coat, and, as he dons his long duster, we see a badge on his vest. He opens a drawer where the gun sits in a case and the camera, in a close-up, pans across to the engraved shield on the pistol's handle.

11. In the film, the scene was shot between Wyatt and Curly Bill, and happens in front of Earp's cottage, which is across from the Boothill set. It was cut from the film. Instead, we see the funeral pass by as Wyatt watches. He then sits on the front porch with Morgan, who admits a gunfight is nothing like he thought it would be.

12. This would have taken place after the scene in which Wyatt confronts Mattie about the empty laudanum bottles in their home.

13. While this scene is still in the film, there were some changes made. Wyatt now just yells at Josephine, telling her to get away from him. The scene was shot with him calling her a Jew whore, but it was later changed in a post-production dubbing session. The scene between Doc and Kate was dropped.

14. The script had Wyatt killing Stilwell by himself, without the posse, as it is in the film, at the train station. There are two homages to the Burt Lancaster-Kirk Douglas film, with Doc's line about Kate losing a meal ticket.

In the 1957 film, Kate asks Holliday the same thing in the Fort Griffin hotel room, and Doc says that exact line. Doc's line of Kate's not having a kind word to say as he rides away, and Wyatt's "if the Lord is my friend," are taken from the film's ballad.

15. The line "his lady fair" is a homage to John Ford's *My Darling Clementine*, when Russell Simpson says this at the church dance. Jarre also named the priest at Doc's deathbed Father Feeney, in tribute to John Ford, whose last name was originally Feeney.

16. Jeff Morey to the author, June 20, 2004.

17. *Ibid.*

18. *Ibid.*

19. *Ibid.*

20. In the film, the gun has a small shield embedded in the handle. Jarre himself drafted the inscription, which read: "To Wyatt Earp, Peacemaker. From the grateful people of Dodge City. 1876." *Ibid.*

21. Honeycutt, Kirk. "Dueling Earps at Uni, Warners." *The Hollywood Reporter*, December 17, 1992, pp. 1, 33.

22. *Ibid.*

23. *Ibid.*

24. *Waterworld* was plagued by production problems since most of the film takes place on the ocean. The budget for the film increased during production. Also there were rumors that Costner and director Kevin Reynolds had disagreements over the direction. The film was one of the highest budgeted films in recent years and was not received well by critics or the public.

25. The film was eventually made and starred Liam Neeson as Collins. "Costner the Movie Killer." *Newsweek*, February 22, 1993.

26. *Tombstone*'s budget at the time was estimated to be $20 million. Costner would also receive producing credit on *Waterworld*.

27. James Jacks and William Fraker discussion of *Tombstone*, Arc Light Cinemas, Hollywood, CA, May 4, 2004.

28. *Tombstone* publicity kit. Author's collection.

29. Cinergi had a distribution deal with Hollywood Pictures, which was a division of the Walt Disney Company. That division was folded by the studio in 1998. Two other companies, Interscope Communications and Carolco Pictures, had been in negotiations to produce the film as well. Busch, Anita M. "Cinergi Carves *Tombstone*." *The Hollywood Reporter*, February 12, 1993.

Thompson, Anne. "Shoot First (Ask Questions Later)." *Entertainment Weekly*, December 24, 1993, pp. 30–32.

The film's budget estimate, as of May 8, 1993, was $23,915,012. This was for a 62-day shooting schedule. *Tombstone* budget file. Buzz Feitshans Collection. Margaret Herrick Library, Academy of Motion Picture Arts and Sciences. Beverly Hills, California.

30. Jeremy Irons and even Michael Douglas were other possible casting choices for the role of Holliday. Jeff Morey to the author, June 20, 2004.

31. His father, Bing Russell, was a well-known character actor for many years. He played a bartender in the early part of *Gunfight at the O.K. Corral* (1957).

32. The casting idea of Harry Carey, Jr. as the wagonmaster was a homage to the actor's starring in John Ford's 1950 classic, *Wagonmaster*.

33. Jeff Morey to the author, June 20, 2004.

34. According to Jeff Morey, Jarre did not want Delany for the role but she was forced on him by executive producer Andrew Vajna. Jarre cast Zane as Big Nose Kate. *Ibid.*

35. Peter Sherayko to the author, May 21, 2004.

36. *Ibid.*

37. *Ibid.*

38. The Buckaroos were each paid $700 a week and provided their own horses. Larry Zeug to the author, May 14, 2004.

39. *Tombstone* press book. Author's collection.

40. *Tombstone* budget file. Buzz Feitshans Collection. Margaret Herrick Library, Academy of Motion Picture Arts and Sciences. Beverly Hills, California.

41. Jeff Morey to the author, June 20, 2004.

42. The *Wyatt Earp* production rented a huge amount of period clothing from Western Costume and other studio wardrobe departments, which made it virtually impossible for Joseph Porro to rent anything.

43. According to the budget estimate, dated May 8, 1993, wardrobe for the film was allocated $402,692. *Tombstone* budget file. Buzz Feitshans Collection. Margaret Herrick Library, Academy of Motion Picture Arts and Sciences. Beverly Hills, California.

44. Joseph Porro to the author, July 22, 2004.

45. Larry Zeug to the author, May 14, 2004.

46. The original start date was March 29. The production was then pushed back to April 26 and finally to May 17. They had hoped to be finished by July 29 and complete all exteriors before the monsoon season hit in late June.

47. This scene exists in the film, but was moved to where Wyatt comes out of Virgil's cottage after being ambushed. McMasters, who rides up with Texas Jack and Turkey Creek Johnson, tells Wyatt he is finished with the Cowboys and throws his sash down.

48. Peter Sherayko to the author, May 21, 2004.

49. Larry Zeug to the author, May 14, 2004.

50. *Tombstone* shooting schedule. Buzz Feitshans Collection. Margaret Herrick Library, Academy of Motion Picture Arts and Sciences. Beverly Hills, California.

51. Memo dated June 7, 1993, *Tombstone* correspondence file. *Ibid*.

52. Peter Sherayko to the author, May 21, 2004.

53. David Atherton to the author, July 21, 2004. Larry Zeug to the author, May 14, 2004.

54. Jeff Morey to the author, December 22, 2003.

55. Bob Palmquist to the author, May 20, 2004.

56. Klady, Leonard. "Jarre off *Tombstone*." *Daily Variety*, June 14, 1993.

57. Thompson, Anne. "Shoot First (Ask Questions Later)." *Entertainment Weekly*, December 24, 1993, pp. 30–32.

58. Jeff Morey to the author, December 22, 2003.

59. Bob Palmquist to the author, May 20, 2004.

60. David Atherton to the author, July 21, 2004.

61. Peter Sherayko to the author, May 21, 2004.

62. Jeff Morey to the author, December 22, 2003.

63. James Jacks and William Fraker discussion of *Tombstone*, Arc Light Cinemas, Hollywood, California, May 4, 2004.

64. "Kurt Russell." *Cowboys and Indians*, October 2005, p. 92.

65. Stiman, Elias. "Hollywood Pictures Welcomes Audiences Back to the Old West in 'Tombstone.'" *Drama-Logue*, January 13–19, 1994.

66. Interestingly, Kevin Jarre wrote the story on which the script of *Rambo: First Blood II* was based. Cosmatos would make only one more film after *Tombstone*, *The Shadow Conspiracy* (1997).

67. Larry Zeug to the author, May 14, 2004.

68. David Atherton to the author, July 21, 2004.

69. *Ibid*.

70. James Jacks and William Fraker discussion of *Tombstone*, Arc Light Cinemas, Hollywood, California, May 4, 2004.

71. David Atherton to the author, July 21, 2004.

72. Cosmatos was paid $775,000. Kevin Jarre was contracted for $200,000 for his script and an additional $150,000 for directing. *Tombstone* budget file. Buzz Feitshans Collection. Margaret Herrick Library, Academy of Motion Picture Arts and Sciences. Beverly Hills, California.

73. Some of the reshot scenes included Wyatt, Texas Jack and Turkey Creek Johnson discovering McMasters' body, McMasters' meeting with Ringo and Ike, Wyatt seeing Josephine at Hooker's ranch, and Wyatt and Josephine's first meeting.

The only footage remaining in the film that Jarre directed are the scenes featuring Charlton Heston and the one which Wyatt's posse stops as Doc collapses. Since Heston had already completed his scenes weeks prior to Jarre's dismissal, it would have been too costly to have the actor return for reshoots.

74. Another notable stunt was when Kurt Russell rides his horse into a barbershop, shooting at several Cowboys. In this stunt, the rider and horse rode right through a breakaway glass window, called "candy glass." This stunt had not been done since Chuck Roberson did it in John Wayne's *Chisum* (1970).

75. *The Fall Guy: 30 Years as the Duke's Double*. North Vancouver, British Columbia: Hancock House Publishers Ltd., 1980, pp. 70–71.

76. Harvey Parry to the author, July 1974.

77. Larry Zeug to the author, May 14, 2004.

78. Sal Cardile to the author, July 8, 2004.

79. James Jacks and William Fraker discussion of *Tombstone*, Arc Light Cinemas, Hollywood, California, May 4, 2004.

80. Larry Zeug to the author, May 14, 2004.

81. Sal Cardile to the author, July 8, 2004.

82. Adam Taylor was the son of actor Buck Taylor, who played Turkey Creek Jack Johnson in the film.

83. *Tombstone* shooting schedule. Buzz Feitshans Collection. Margaret Herrick Library, Academy of Motion Picture Arts and Sciences. Beverly Hills, California.

84. Larry Zeug to the author, May 14, 2004.

85. Jeff Morey to the author, June 20, 2004.

86. James Jacks and William Fraker discussion of *Tombstone*, Arc Light Cinemas, Hollywood, CA, May 4, 2004.

87. Watching this scene, one can see that, when Kurt Russell throws his hat into the air, it gets caught in the blast from one of the fans and flies backward at a great distance. The budget to dress the set for the snow scene was $3,207. *Tombstone* budget file. Buzz Feitshans Collection. Margaret Herrick Library, Academy of Motion Picture Arts and Sciences. Beverly Hills, California.

88. David Atherton to the author, July 21, 2004.

89. A cover set is a term used in the industry when filming exterior scenes are halted because of weather conditions. The cover sets are interior scenes that can be filmed during inclement weather. However, on *Tombstone*, even interior cover sets had problems because the thunder would often interrupt dialogue during a take.

90. Larry Zeug to the author, May 14, 2004.

91. David Atherton to the author, July 21, 2004.

92. *Tombstone* shooting schedule. Buzz Feitshans Collection. Margaret Herrick Library, Academy of Motion Picture Arts and Sciences. Beverly Hills, California.

93. Larry Zeug to the author, May 14, 2004.

94. *Ibid*.

95. Kevin Jarre had planned, prior to filming the gunfight sequence, to have Jeff Morey accompany the director and actors to Tombstone one Sunday. Morey would have given a lecture about the gunfight in the actual

locations for the actors. Once Cosmatos came aboard, the idea was quickly dropped. Jeff Morey to the author, December 22, 2003.

96. *Tombstone* publicity kit. Author's collection.

97. Larry Zeug to the author, May 14, 2004.

98. James Jacks and William Fraker discussion of *Tombstone*, Arc Light Cinemas, Hollywood, CA, May 4, 2004.

99. Larry Zeug to the author, May 14, 2004.

100. Cinematographer William Fraker was given an associate producer credit as well.

101. *Tombstone* script from the author's collection.

102. Thompson, Anne. "Shoot First (Ask Questions Later)." *Entertainment Weekly*, December 24, 1993, p.32.

Jacks stated that, at one point, executive producer Andrew Vajna tried to fire him. Jacks was unaware of this until the film was completed, but several of the actors told Vajna that if Jacks was removed, he would have a really difficult time getting them out of their trailers. James Jacks and William Fraker discussion of *Tombstone*, Arc Light Cinemas, Hollywood, California, May 4, 2004.

103. Sean Daniel cutting suggestions. *Tombstone* correspondence file. Buzz Feitshans Collection. Margaret Herrick Library, Academy of Motion Picture Arts and Sciences. Beverly Hills, California.

104. George Cosmatos DVD audio commentary, *Tombstone* special edition DVD.

105. While Earp never wrote such a book, many people who saw the film believed he did. In Tombstone, after the release of the film, tourists asked about this book in several of the town's bookstores and gift shops. One enterprising person actually put together a fictitious book and sold numerous copies.

Sean Daniel cutting suggestions. *Tombstone* correspondence file. Buzz Feitshans Collection. Margaret Herrick Library, Academy of Motion Picture Arts and Sciences. Beverly Hills, California.

106. *Daily Variety*, November 23, 1993.

107. *The Hollywood Reporter*, November 24, 1993.

108. January 4, 1994.

109. December 23, 1993.

110. December 25, 1993.

111. January 3, 1994.

112. Barra, Allen. "*Tombstone* Full of Box-Office Life." *Los Angeles Times*, January 18, 1994, pp. F1, F3.

113. Barra, Allen. "And the Winner Isn't." *Village Voice*, March 29, 1994.

114. Joseph Porro to the author, July 22, 2004.

115. *Los Angeles Times*, January 11, 1994.

116. The film uses clips from *The Great Train Robbery* (1903) and *The Bank Robbery* (1908). The latter film was produced by legendary lawman Bill Tilghman and also featured Al Jennings, a well-known outlaw in the Oklahoma Territory. Jennings later made several films based on his exploits.

117. The quote of describing the Oriental Saloon as a "slaughter house" is from the diary of George Parsons.

118. This was another of Jarre's tributes to John Ford, borrowing Henry Fonda's line from *My Darling Clementine*.

119. The complete text and translation of this duel of Latin is:

DOC: In vino veritas ("In wine there is truth").

RINGO: Age quod agis ("Do what you do").

DOC: Credat Judaeus Apella, non ego ("Let Apella the Jew believe, not I").

RINGO: Iuventus stultorum magister ("Youth is the teacher of fools").

DOC: In pace requiescat ("May he rest in peace").

Doc's line of letting Apella the Jew believe comes from

Horace's Satires. Horace is traveling through Italy and sees a religiously related divine flame at a shrine. He does not believe in the miracle, so he says those words. Doc's "may he rest in peace" comes from Edgar Allan Poe's "The Cask of Amontillado" and commonly appeared on tombstones.

120. This scene was cut before the film was released. It was subsequently put back in, with other excised scenes, when the movie was released as "director's cut" DVD.

121. This may be an allusion to the comments by Wyatt in which he claimed he thought someone was shooting behind them, when it may have actually been a ricocheted bullet.

122. This was primarily done because the director wanted a shot showing the bullet hitting the actor in the head. It is much easier, not to mention safer, to apply a blood squib to the forehead and cover it with a foam rubber appliance than to rig a squib to the side of the head, dangerously close to the ear, where the real Frank McLaury was hit. Blood squibs are set off with a small powder charge, which could easily damage one's hearing. This also negated the use of one on the side of the actor's head.

123. The film has a similar problem when Curly Bill hurrahs the town after his visit to an opium tent. Using two guns, he fires off more than twelve rounds before being confronted by Marshal White. Another glaring mistake is the blood on the hands of Wyatt after Morgan's death. In one shot, his hands have a minimal amount of blood, while the next camera angle has them covered in blood. Again, the makeup artist is at the mercy of the director, who may suddenly decide he wants more blood, despite what was in the previous shot.

Chapter 10

1. Being the first out did not help the movie; it fared poorly at the box office.

2. By producing one film, both studios came out winners. *The Towering Inferno* was an enormous box office hit and was nominated for Best Picture.

3. The movie was not successful. Ironically, Universal released a third version of the ape story in 2005 under the direction of Peter Jackson.

4. Dan Gordon to the author, July 20, 2004.

5. Honeycutt, Kirk. "Dueling Earps at Uni, Warners." *The Hollywood Reporter*, December 17, 1992, pp. 1, 33.

6. Dan Gordon to the author, July 20, 2004.

7. *Premiere*, July 1994, p. 54.

8. McCloskey, Jason. "*Wyatt Earp* Shoots 'Em Up in Style." *Drama-Logue*, June 23–29, 1994, p. 4.

9. Dan Gordon to the author, July 20, 2004.

10. *Wyatt Earp* miniseries script. Author's collection.

11. *Premiere*, July 1994, p. 52.

12. Kasdan, Lawrence, and Jake Kasdan. *Wyatt Earp: The Film and the Filmmakers*. New York: Newmarket Press, 1994, p. 92.

13. Michael Mills to the author, June 10, 2004.

14. Lace pieces are made of human hair that is individually sewn onto lace that is later cut and styled with a heated curling iron to the desired effect. Lace pieces are often preferred by makeup artists because they can be quickly applied and require minimum maintenance throughout a day's filming.

15. Michael Mills to the author, June 10, 2004.

16. Gerald Quist to the author, June 4, 2004.

17. *Ibid.*

18. Kasdan, Lawrence, and Jake Kasdan. *Wyatt Earp: The Film and the Filmmakers.* New York: Newmarket Press, 1994, p. 13.

19. The rail line was originally built in 1880 by the Denver and Rio Grande Railway to ship silver from the various mining camps in southern Colorado. In 1970, the states of Colorado and New Mexico bought the rail line that runs from Antonio, Colorado, to Chama, New Mexico, as well as the engines and cars. That same year, the trains began taking tourists along the 64-mile route. It has been used in numerous films including *The Good Guys and the Bad Guys* (1968), *Shootout* (1970), *Bite the Bullet* (1974), and *Indiana Jones and the Last Crusade* (1989).

20. Gerald Quist to the author, June 4, 2004.

21. *Ibid.*

22. Michael Mills to the author, June 10, 2004.

23. Gerald Quist to the author, June 4, 2004.

24. *Ibid.*

25. United Artists' *Heaven's Gate*, which ran over budget and running time (almost four hours), was savagely panned by the critics. The film was such a disaster at the box office that it almost bankrupted United Artists.

26. Gerald Quist to the author, June 4, 2004.

27. Michael Mills to the author, June 10, 2004.

28. *Ibid.*

29. *Ibid.*

30. *Ibid.*

31. July 4, 1994.

32. June 24, 1994.

33. July 4, 1994.

34. June 20, 1994.

35. Dutka, Elaine. "Leave *Wyatt Earp* Off His Tombstone." *Los Angeles Times*, August 5, 1994, pp. F1, F8.

36. Hamilton, Kendall, and Charles Fleming. "Universal's Costner Overruns." *Newsweek*, September 19, 1994.

37. Gerald Quist to the author, June 4, 2004.

38. Originally, the film was to have correct period gun belts for the actors, but these were dropped for the more common buscadero-style gun belts commonly found in Western movies of the 1950s and 1960s.

39. This scene is full of mistakes, beginning with calling the jailed character "Tommy-Behind-the-Deuce." His real moniker was "Johnny-Behind-the-Deuce." The young actor relating the story says Wyatt's brothers were gone chasing renegade Indians. In reality, it was Virgil who brought the criminal into town, ahead of the lynch mob, and Morgan, as well as Doc and Wyatt, lent a hand in protecting the man and getting him out of town. The young man in the scene states that his uncle was later killed, but in reality, Mike Roake escaped from the Tucson jail and was never heard of again.

Bibliography

Books

American Film Institute Catalogue, Feature Films 1931–1940. Berkeley: University of California Press, 1993.

American Film Institute Catalogue, Feature Films 1941–1950. Berkeley: University of California Press, 1999.

Bailey, Lynn R., ed. A Tenderfoot in Tombstone: The Private Journal of George Whitewell Parsons: The Turbulent Years: 1880–82. Tucson, AZ: Westernlore Press, 1996.

_____. Too Tough to Die: The Rise, Fall and Resurrection of a Silver Camp; 1878 to 1990. Tucson, AZ: Westernlore Press, 2004.

Barra, Allen. Inventing Wyatt Earp: His Life and Many Legends. New York: Carroll & Graf Publishers, 1998.

Behlmer, Rudy, ed. Memo from Darryl F. Zanuck: The Golden Years at 20th Century-Fox. New York: Grove Press, 1993.

Bell, Bob Boze. The Illustrated Life and Times of Doc Holliday. Phoenix, AZ: Tri Star-Boze Publications, 1994.

_____. The Illustrated Life and Times of Wyatt Earp. Phoenix, AZ: Tri Star-Boze Publications, 1993.

Bogdanovich, Peter. John Ford. Berkeley: University of California Press, 1978.

_____. Who the Devil Made It. New York: Alfred A. Knopf, 1997.

_____. Who the Hell's in It. New York: Alfred A. Knopf, 2004.

Brooks, Tim, and Earle Marsh. The Complete Directory to Prime Time Network and Cable TV Shows. New York: Ballantine Books, 1995.

Brownlow, Kevin. The War, the West, and the Wilderness. New York: Alfred A. Knopf, 1978.

Buford, Kate. Burt Lancaster: An American Life. New York: Alfred A. Knopf, 2000.

Burns, Walter Noble. Tombstone: An Iliad of the Southwest. New York: Doubleday, 1927.

Burrows, Jack. John Ringo: The Gunfighter Who Never Was. Tucson: University of Arizona Press, 1996.

Chaput, Donald. Virgil Earp: Western Peace Officer. Norman: University of Oklahoma Press, 1994.

Custen, George F. Twentieth Century's Fox: Darryl F. Zanuck and the Culture of Hollywood. New York: Basic Books, 1997.

Davis, Ronald. John Ford: Hollywood's Old Master. Norman: University of Oklahoma Press, 1995.

_____. William S. Hart: Project the American West. Norman: University of Oklahoma Press, 2003.

DeArment, Robert K. Bat Masterson: The Man and the Legend. Norman: University of Oklahoma Press, 1979.

Dick, Bernard F. Hal Wallis: Producer to the Stars. Lexington: University of Kentucky Press, 2004.

Douglas, Kirk. Climbing the Mountain: My Search for Meaning. New York: Simon and Schuster, 1997.

_____. The Ragman's Son. New York: Simon and Schuster, 1988.

Eames, John Douglas. The Paramount Story. New York: Crown Publishers, 1985.

Everson, William K., and George N. Fenin. The Western: From Silents to the Seventies. New York: Grossman Publishers, 1973.

Eyman, Scott. Print the Legend: The Life and Times of John Ford. New York: Simon and Schuster, 1999.

Fields, Armond. Eddie Foy: A Biography. Jefferson, NC: McFarland, 1999.

Ford, Dan. Pappy: The Life of John Ford. Engelwood Cliffs, NJ: Prentice-Hall, 1979.

Gallagher, Tag. John Ford: The Man and His Films. Berkeley: University of California Press, 1986.

Garfield, Brian. Western Films: A Complete Guide. New York: Rawson Associates, 1982.

Hamill, Pete. Doc: The Original Screenplay. New York: Paperback Library, 1971.

Hardy, Phil, ed. The Encyclopedia of Western Movies. London: Octopus Books, 1985.

Kasdan, Lawrence, and Jake Kasdan. Wyatt Earp: The Film and the Filmmakers. New York: Newmarket Press, 1994.

Lake, Stuart. Wyatt Earp: Frontier Marshal. New York: Houghton Mifflin Company, 1931.

Lamar, Howard R., ed. The American West: The Reader's Encyclopedia. New York: Thomas Y. Crowell Company, 1977.

Lenihan, John H. Showdown: Confronting Modern America in the Western Film. Chicago: University of Illinois Press, 1985.

Lyons, Robert, ed. *My Darling Clementine.* New Brunswick, NJ: Rutgers University Press, 1984.

Martin, Douglas D. *Tombstone's Epitaph.* Norman: University of Oklahoma Press, 1997.

McBride, Joseph. *Searching for John Ford: A Life.* New York: St. Martin's Press, 1999.

Roberson, Chuck, with Bodie Thoene. *The Fall Guy: 30 Years as The Duke's Double.* North Vancouver, British Columbia: Hancock House Publishers Ltd., 1980.

Schatz, Thomas. *Hollywood Genres.* New York: McGraw-Hill, 1981.

Schiefflin, Edward. *Destination Tombstone: Adventures of a Prospector.* Mesa, AZ: Royal Spectrum Publishing, 1996.

Shillingberg, Wm. B. *Tombstone, A.T.: A History of Early Mining, Milling and Mayhem.* Spokane, WA: Arthur H. Clark Company, 1999.

Tefertiller, Casey. *Wyatt Earp: The Life Behind the Legend.* New York: John Wiley & Sons, 1997.

Tractman, Paul. *The Old West: The Gunfighters.* Alexander, VA: Time-Life Books, 1974.

Traywick, Ben T. *The Chronicles of Tombstone.* Tombstone, AZ: Red Marie's Bookstore, 1994.

_____, ed. *Tombstone Clippings.* Tombstone, AZ: Red Marie's Bookstore, 1994.

Turner, Alford, ed. *The O.K. Corral Inquest.* College Station, TX: Creative Publishing Company, 1981.

Wallis, Hal B., and Charles Higham. *Starmaker: The Autobiography of Hal Wallis.* New York: Macmillan, 1980.

Wright, Mike. *What They Didn't Teach You About the Wild West.* Novato, CA: Presidio Press, 2000.

Yoggy, Gary A. *Riding the Video Range: The Rise and Fall of the Western on Television.* Jefferson, NC: McFarland, 1995.

Newspapers and Magazines

Anez, Nicholas. "Wyatt Earp (Part 1)." *Films in Review,* June-July 1990, pp. 323–33.

_____. "Wyatt Earp (Part 2)." *Films in Review,* August-September 1990, pp. 395–406.

Barra, Allen. "And the Winner Isn't." *Village Voice,* March 29, 1994.

_____. "No He Wasn't." *True West,* July 2003, p. 39.

_____. "*Tombstone* Full of Box-Office Life." *Los Angeles Times,* January 18, 1994, pp. F1, F3.

Bell, Bob Boze, and Jeff Morey. "A Question of Character." *True West,* July 2003, p. 37.

_____. "Wyatt Earp: Without a Scratch." *True West,* February-March 2001, pp. 13–47.

Brand, Peter. "Daniel G. Tipton and the Earp Vendetta Posse." *National Association for Outlaw and Lawman History,* October-December 2000, pp. 17–27.

_____. "Sherman W. McMaster(s): The El Paso Salt War, Texas Rangers and Tombstone." *Western Outlaw-Lawman History Association,* Winter 1999, pp. 2–19.

_____. "Wyatt Earp, Jack Johnson and the Notorious Blount Brothers." *National Association for Outlaw and Lawman History,* October-December 2003, pp. 36–47.

Busch, Anita M. "Cinergi Carves *Tombstone.*" *The Hollywood Reporter,* February 12, 1993.

"Clementine on Horseback." *Cue,* November 16, 1946.

Cogshell, Tim. "No Complaints." *Entertainment Today,* December 24–30, 1993.

"Costner the Movie Killer." *Newsweek,* February 22, 1993.

Dutka, Elaine. "Leave *Wyatt Earp* Off His Tombstone." *Los Angeles Times,* August 5, 1994, pp. F1, F8.

French, Philip. "The Town That Refused to Die." *The Observer* (London), January 16, 1994.

Gatto, Steve. "Wyatt Earp Was a Pimp." *True West,* July 2003, p. 36.

Godbout, Oscar. "Echoes from *Gunfight at the O.K. Corral.*" *New York Times,* May 20, 1956.

Greenburg, Dan. "Diary of a Frustrated Cowboy." *New York Times,* November 1, 1970.

"Hal Wallis Will Make *Gunfight.*" *The Hollywood Reporter,* December 2, 1955.

Hamill, Pete. "The New American Western: On Writing *Doc.*" *Harper's Bazaar,* 1971.

Hamilton, Kendall, and Charles Fleming. "Universal's Costner Overruns." *Newsweek,* September 19, 1994.

Honeycutt, Kirk. "Dueling Earps at Uni, Warners." *The Hollywood Reporter,* December 17, 1992, pp. 1, 33.

Klady, Leonard. "Jarre off *Tombstone.*" *Daily Variety,* June 14, 1993.

Levine, Stuart. "Turf Warriors." *Daily Variety,* December 19, 2003.

Leydon, Joe. "Kurt Russell." *Cowboys and Indians,* October 2005, pp. 86–93.

Lowery, Steve. "The Man from Tombstone." *Long Beach Press-Telegram,* February 27, 1994.

Lubet, Steven. "Should Wyatt Earp Have Been Hanged?" *True West,* February-March 2001, pp. 50–56.

McCloskey, Jason. "*Wyatt Earp* Shoots 'Em Up in Style." *Drama-Logue,* June 23–29, 1994, p. 4.

Osbourne, Robert. "Rambling Reporter." *The Hollywood Reporter,* April 13, 1993.

Rowe, Jeremy. "Is This Mrs. Earp?" *True West,* May-June 2002, pp. 18–20.

Ryan, James. "Dana Delany Trades Fatigues for Hoops, Corset." *Long Beach Press-Telegram,* January 3, 1994.

"Shootout." *Variety,* February, 8, 1993.

Stiman, Elias. "Hollywood Pictures Welcomes Audiences Back to the Old West in *Tombstone.*" *Drama-Logue,* January 13–19, 1994.

Thompson, Anne. "Shoot First (Ask Questions

Later)." *Entertainment Weekly*, December 24, 1993, pp.30–32.

"Universal's Costner Overruns." *Newsweek*, September 9, 1994.

Watson, Dorothy. "Harry Sherman Warns Against Cheap Films." *Hollywood Citizen-News*, June 20, 1944, p. 6.

Wood, Thomas. "Classic 'Gunfight' Immortalized." *New York Herald Tribune*, May 13, 1956.

Documentaries and Videos

The American West of John Ford, Group One-Timex-CBS Productions, 1971.

Directed by John Ford, American Film Institute, 1971.

Hollywood: Out West, video documentary, Thames Television/HBO Video, 1980.

John Ford's America, American Movie Classics, 1989.

Special Collections

Buzz Feitshans Collection, Margaret Herrick Library, Academy of Motion Picture Arts and Sciences. Beverly Hills, California.

John Ford Collection, Lilly Library, Indiana University, Bloomington, Indiana.

William S. Hart Collection, Sever Center for Western History Research, Natural History Museum of Los Angeles County.

John Sturges Collection, Margaret Herrick Library, Academy of Motion Picture Arts and Sciences. Beverly Hills, California.

Hal B. Wallis Collection, Margaret Herrick Library, Academy of Motion Picture Arts and Sciences. Beverly Hills, California.

Interviews

David Atherton to the author, July 21, 2004.
Sal Cardile to the author, July 8, 2004.
James Garner to the author, July 20, 2004.
Dan Gordon to the author, July 20, 2004.
Burt Lancaster to the author, March 3, 1986.
Michael Mills to the author, June 10, 2004.
Jeff Morey to the author, October 30, 2003; December 22, 2003; June 20, 2004.
Bob Palmquist to the author, May 20, 2004.
Harvey Parry to the author, July 1974.
Joseph Porro to the author, July 22, 2004.
Pam Potter to the author, January 27, 2004.
Gerald Quist to the author, June 4, 2004.
Peter Sherayko to the author, May 21, 2004.
Larry Zeug to the author, May 14, 2004.

Index

Numbers in **bold italics** indicate pages with photographs.